DATE DUE

MAR 17 1994	
MAR 30 1994	
OCT 12 2001	

BRODART   Cat. No. 23-221

EVERYMAN,
I WILL GO WITH THEE,
AND BE THY GUIDE,
IN THY MOST NEED
TO GO BY THY SIDE

WILLIAM BLAKE

Poems and Prophecies

E V E R Y M A N ' S   L I B R A R Y

Alfred A. Knopf New York

34

THIS IS A BORZOI BOOK

PUBLISHED BY ALFRED A. KNOPF, INC.

First included in Everyman's Library, 1927
Introduction, Bibliography, and Chronology Copyright © 1991 by
David Campbell Publishers Ltd.

ISBN 0-679-40552-6
LC 91-52990

Printed and bound in Germany

CONTENTS

POEMS AND PROPHECIES

CONTENTS

II
FRAGMENTS FROM BLAKE'S MSS.

viii

CONTENTS

III
POETICAL SKETCHES

POEMS AND PROPHECIES

INTRODUCTION

Although the years of William Blake's natural life (1757–1827) were at the turn of the eighteenth century it can be said, both literally and in respect of his thought, that he was a century in advance of his time. He lived the life of a hard-working engraver, respected by his colleagues in the world of art, but falling into obscurity and poverty as with advancing years his compelling genius carried him into regions ever more remote from the preoccupations of his contemporaries. At the end of his life he re-emerged as the honoured Master of that glorious group of English Romantic artists who described themselves as 'the Shoreham Ancients', Palmer and Calvert, Richmond and Finch, who frequented the valley of Shoreham, where Samuel Palmer's father lived in his retirement. There Blake, that lifelong Londoner, used to visit them, walking from London to enjoy the pastoral beauty of the English countryside which throughout his life had delighted him. To these young men Blake was 'the Interpreter' – so named from Bunyan's *Pilgrim's Progress* – and Samuel Palmer, in his beautiful memoir (included in Gilchrist's *Life*), recalled that Blake's humble door in Fountain Court (off the Strand – now long vanished) was 'more attractive than the threshold of princes'. Blake was – by his own declaration – 'a mental prince', and those who knew him best, from his fellow artist Flaxman the sculptor to the young men of Shoreham – recognized in him a spiritual stature from which his worldly obscurity detracted nothing. Samuel Palmer thus describes him in a letter to his biographer Alexander Gilchrist:

His knowledge was various and extensive, and his conversation so nervous and brilliant, that, if recorded at the time, it would now have thrown much light upon his character, and in no way lessened him in the estimation of those who know him only by his works.

In him you saw at once the Maker, the Inventor; one of the few in any age: a fitting companion for Dante. He was energy itself, and shed around him a kindling influence; an atmosphere of life, full of the ideal. To walk with him in the country was to perceive the soul of beauty through the forms of matter; and the high, gloomy buildings between which, from his study window, a glimpse was caught of the Thames and the Surrey shore, assumed a kind of grandeur from the man dwelling near them. Those may laugh at this who never knew such an one as Blake; but of him it is the simple truth.

He was a man without a mask; his aim single, his path straight-forwards and his wants few; so he was free, noble and happy.

But beyond that small circle Blake's works remained virtually unknown, until this century. Only one collection of his poems, the early *Poetical Sketches* (1783), was published in the ordinary way, through the patronage of Mrs Harriet Matthews, wife of a London clergyman and friend of Flaxman. But Blake's misfortune – if such it was – has proved our gain, and his 'illuminated books', written, illustrated, printed and coloured by himself, are among the treasures of the nation. The text of his 'Prophetic Books' (so he described them) was first published only at the end of the nineteenth century (Quaritch, 1893), edited by Edwin J. Ellis and the young W. B. Yeats, Blake's greatest disciple, and the first to situate Blake within the Western esoteric tradition. Later the *Complete Writings*, edited by Geoffrey Keynes, were published by the Nonesuch Press in 1925, in one volume in 1927, and a revised edition in 1957. The Keynes edition has since been the standard text through which Blake has become known. There have been superb facsimile reproductions of all the illuminated books, issued by the Blake Trust (Trianon Press), and others less perfect and less costly before and since. It is necessary to remember that the text of Blake's poems gives only the words of great visual compositions whose uniqueness lies in the harmonizing of text and visual designs, which do not so much illustrate, as expand the meaning of the text. But Blake is more than a poet, more than a painter, more than one of the world's supreme masters in the art of engraving, whose twenty-two engravings on the Book of Job are as familiar as those of Dürer. Blake called himself 'a prophet': for him poetry, painting and the other arts were not ends but means to express a vision. With a simplicity more baffling to a materialist age than his obscurities, he declared, 'The Nature of my Work is Visionary or Imaginative; it is an Endeavour to Restore what the

INTRODUCTION

Ancients call'd the Golden Age' (*Notebook*, pp. 71–2). Blake's Golden Age is neither a lost world of the remote past, nor a Utopia of the future: it is a state of consciousness accessible at all times to whoever will 'awake' into that imaginative reality it was Blake's 'great task' to communicate to his nation. Blake was not, like Yeats, an esotericist, possessing knowledge accessible only to a few: on the contrary, he appealed 'to the public' against the professional critics of his day who were blind to that vision. The 'knowledge' to which Blake addressed himself is innate in all:

> Knowledge is not by deduction, but Immediate by Perception or Sense at once. Christ addresses himself to the Man, not to his Reason.

and

> Jesus supposes every Thing to be Evident to the Child & to the Poor & Unlearned. Such is the Gospel.

> (*Annotations to Berkeley*)

So believing, Blake summons 'the Giant Albion' – the English nation – to the joyful spiritual liberation of self-discovery,

> ... melting apparent surfaces away, and displaying the infinite which was hid.

> If the doors of perception were cleansed everything would appear to man as it is, infinite.

> For man has closed himself up, till he sees all things thro' narrow chinks of his cavern.

> (*The Marriage of Heaven and Hell*, pl. 14)

A 'prophet', by definition, is 'one who speaks for God', and Blake claimed that his inspiration was of the same order as the prophets of the Old Testament, of Isaiah and Ezekiel, whose works he knew and admired so deeply. But the God for whom Blake spoke is 'the God within', the 'Divine Humanity' whom he calls Jesus. In *The Marriage of Heaven and Hell* he called the older prophets to witness:

> The Prophets Isaiah and Ezekiel dined with me, and I asked them how they dared so roundly to assert that God spoke to them; and whether they did not think at the time that they would be misunderstood, & so be the cause of imposition.

xiii

Isaiah answer'd, 'I saw no God, nor heard any, in a finite organical perception; but my senses discover'd the infinite in everything, and as I was then perswaded, & remain confirm'd, that the voice of honest indignation is the voice of God, I cared not for the consequences, but wrote'.

(*The Marriage of Heaven and Hell*, pls. 12–13)

Blake did likewise.

The radiant power of Blake's words is indeed the mark of what former ages have known as 'inspiration'; he spoke to England with the voice of prophecy as authentic as that of his Hebrew predecessors, and with no less immediacy on national events, passing on what the Irish mystic AE called 'the politics of time', the judgement of 'the politics of eternity'. If Blake was a mystic and a visionary his was no private world – on the contrary his judgements are on public events, on institutions both civil and religious, on false ideologies, on the exploitation of women and children, on the Industrial Revolution, on the atrocity of war. If in his youth he was a supporter of the American and the French Revolutions and opposed England's military intervention in Europe, his motives were not in the ordinary sense political. He saw in these events evidence of a 'New Age', an overturning of old systems and the advent of a new liberation of the human spirit, and of the reign of the Divine Humanity, the God within, which his early Master Swedenborg had proclaimed in the year 1757 – the year of Blake's birth.

*

Blake was the son of a hosier in Golden Square, in the parish of Westminster, not far from Oxford Street. He was baptized in the beautiful Grinling Gibbon font of the church of St James's, Piccadilly. His father seems to have been tolerant of his son's determination not to go to school. Blake's early poem *Tiriel* is a dramatic and horrendous indictment of the education which 'forms' the child according to a system superimposed rather than allowing the innate gifts to develop according to Nature – a view he shared with Jean-Jacques Rousseau. He continued to hold education to be wrong, as may be seen from more than one of the 'Proverbs of Hell' (*The Marriage of Heaven and Hell*):

INTRODUCTION

'The eagle never lost so much time as when he submitted to learn of the crow', or 'Improvement makes strait roads; but the crooked roads without Improvement are roads of Genius.' However, Blake's father sent his son to Pars' Drawing School, where he received the best education in art available in London at that time. With a tradesman's caution he advised his son to become an engraver rather than risk the precarious profession of a painter, and apprenticed him to James Basire, where Blake handled a number of books appearing at that time on antiquities and mythologies, a kind of education most congenial to him. One such book was Jacob Bryant's *New System of Mythology*, a work abounding in examples of comparative mythology of the ancient world; Blake himself engraved some of the plates, including illustrations of Zoroastrian cave-temples, whose visual themes appear in his later work. His conclusion that 'All religions are one' owes something to his familiarity with Bryant, besides other works on ancient mythology, such as Bishop Percy's *Northern Antiquities* (on the Eddas), Macpherson's *Ossian* and works on British antiquities. Blake was also interested in the beliefs of the North American aboriginal people. Blake's 'crooked road' of genius led him into many learned fields outside the mainstream of his time and place.

*

It is possible that Blake's family were Swedenborgians, followers of the Swedish visionary (1688–1772), who spent much time in London. Blake, who was fifteen at the time of Swedenborg's death, might well have seen him. Be that as it may, Blake and his wife, together with Flaxman and his wife, attended the inaugural meeting of the New Jerusalem Church, and were signatories of its foundation manifesto. The importance of Swedenborg as an influence in Blake's life has generally been underestimated: Blake's much-discussed 'system' is, from first to last, Swedenborgian, with one important difference. Before discussing this difference we will enumerate those teachings which Blake derived from Swedenborg and never abandoned. Swedenborg, a distinguished scientist and Assessor of Minerals to the Swedish government, experienced,

in middle life, a visionary 'opening', after which he claimed to
see and communicate with discarnate spirits. But, beyond
that, he perceived that the Divine Humanity (a term Blake
adopted and developed in his writings with such power and
depth of understanding) is not an historical Person but the
universal Being of the one-in-many and many-in-one of all
humankind, Christian and non-Christian alike. Blake has
embodied throughout his work this Swedenborgian realiza-
tion of 'the Grand Man of the Heavens' embracing all
humankind. The 'heavens', as Swedenborg uses the word, are
the inner worlds; thus his vision is essentially an interiorization
of the teachings of the Apostolic Church, for whom the sacred
events of Christianity had become increasingly historicized, at
the expense of other dimensions of understanding. Blake's
poem 'The Divine Image' 'To Mercy, Pity, Peace and Love' is
a simple summary of the Swedenborgian teaching that the
Divine Humanity is in every heart;

> Then every man, of every clime,
> That prays in his distress,
> Prays to the human form divine,
> Love, Mercy, Pity, Peace.
>
> And all must love the human form,
> In heathen, turk, or jew;
> Where Mercy, Love, & Pity dwell
> There God is dwelling too.
> *(Songs of Innocence)*

One might say that Blake has made the Swedenborgian
teachings, expressed in volumes of pedantic Latin, widely
known and accepted unawares in the English-speaking world,
which for the most part knows nothing of Swedenborg.

In his early prophetic poem, *Vala* or *The Four Zoas*, Blake
summarizes this Swedenborgian vision:

> Then those in Great Eternity met in the Council of God
> As one Man...
> As One Man all the Universal family and that One Man
> They call Jesus the Christ, & they in him & he in them
> Live in Perfect Harmony, in Eden the land of life.
> *(The Four Zoas, 1.468–74)*

INTRODUCTION

The late poem *The Everlasting Gospel* summarizes the 'leading doctrines' of the New Church. Interviewed in his late years by the diarist Crabb Robinson, Blake, asked what were his beliefs concerning Jesus Christ, replied, that he was the Son of God; but then he added 'and so am I, and so are you'. ('We are all co-existent with God – members of the Divine Body. We are all partakers of the divine nature': for Blake 'God is Jesus' and 'there is no other God than the God who is the intellectual fountain of Humanity'.) The vision of this universal Person is in Christian terms revolutionary, but would cause no surprise to a Vedantist, and one can equate Blake's 'Divine Humanity' with the universal Self of the Upanishads. 'I rest not from my great task' Blake wrote,

> To open the Eternal Worlds, to open the immortal Eyes
> Of Man inwards into the Worlds of Thought, into Eternity
> Ever expanding in the Bosom of God, the Human Imagination.
> *(Jerusalem*, 5 17-20)

It need hardly be said that Blake was at the opposite extreme from being a 'humanist' in the modern sense of the word; for to exalt the natural man as lord of creation is far indeed from the affirmation that 'God is man and exists in us and we in him.' Natural man Blake calls 'the garment, not the man', the 'worm of sixty winters', whereas the 'true man' is Imagination, boundless and immortal:

> This world of Imagination is the world of Eternity, it is the divine bosom into which we shall all go after the death of the Vegetated body. This World of Imagination is Infinite and Eternal, whereas the World of Generation is Finite & Temporal.
> *(Vision of the Last Judgment: Notebook*, pp. 69-70)

(The equating of Swedenborg's Divine Humanity with the Imagination Blake seems to have taken from the German Theosophist Jacob Boehme, who equates the second Person of the Christian Trinity, the Son, with the 'Imagination of God'.)

Blake also took from Swedenborg the hierarchic view, common to all spiritual traditions, of a threefold order, of celestial, 'spiritual' (in the sense of belonging to the world of spirits) and natural.

Now I a fourfold vision see,
And a fourfold vision is given to me
'Tis fourfold in my supreme delight
and threefold in soft Beulah's night
And Twofold Always. May God us keep
From single vision and Newton's sleep
(Letter to Thomas Butts,
22 November 1802)

Blake's fourth order – 'single vision' – is outside the world of life altogether, for the natural world is a living world, whereas Newton had postulated a universe which is a mechanism, lifeless and dead, in 'a void outside existence', which Blake calls the 'Ulro'. Each of these orders is related to the other symbolically, by what Swedenborg calls 'correspondence'. Thus, it is the living nature of every creature that determines its outer form, and Blake is expressing the Swedenborgian theme of 'correspondence' when in *Visions of the Daughters of Albion* he rejects the notion that it is the sense-organs that determine the behaviour of living creatures:

With what sense is it that the chicken shuns the ravenous hawk?
With what sense does the tame pigeon measure out the expanse?
With what sense does the bee form cells? Have not the mouse & frog
Eyes and ears and sense of touch? yet are their habitations
And their pursuits as different as their forms and as their joys.
Ask the wild ass why he refuses burdens, and the meek camel
Why he loves man: is it because of eye, ear, mouth, or skin,
Or breathing nostrils? No, for these the wolf and tyger have.
(pl. 3)

It is the living nature of each creature that determines its form and directs its behaviour, not its material structure; and Blake draws the conclusion that the freedom to be each according to its nature is the true law of life:

And trees & birds & beasts & men behold their eternal joy.
Arise, you little glancing wings, and sing your infant joy:
Arise, and drink your bliss, for every thing that lives is holy!

Blake's is a world of joyous uncurbed life; in the first plate of *Europe: A Prophecy* a fairy – a spirit of vegetation – promises to

xviii

...shew you all alive
The world where every particle of dust breathes forth its joy.

Immeasurable life is not confined within the dimensions of the material order. We find throughout Blake's works weightless figures which inhabit the world of life, not the solid physical bodies depicted 'warts and all' as the materialist mentality assumed supremacy in the post-Renaissance world. So with his landscapes, as these are depicted and described, in the pastoral beauty of *The Book of Thel*, or the barren desolation scattered with tombs and altars of sacrifice in the illustrations to the Book of Job, all these existing as in Swedenborg's world of spirits, in 'correspondence' with some mood or state.

The other great Swedenborgian theme which occupied Blake throughout his life is the Last Judgment. In both his Prophetic Books and in the great pictorial composition on which he was occupied at the end of his life, the Last Judgment is paramount – not as the 'day of wrath and day of mourning' of the Church, with the consigning of sinners to Hell and the righteous to Heaven, but as a judgment of this world by the Divine Humanity, the God within, 'Jesus the Imagination'. When we see the world and its laws, both legal and religious, in the light of the divine nature innate in all men, we will reject, not human souls (who in the course of a life-time pass through many 'states') but the laws both religious and civil which condemn and punish. Blake believed that all humankind must experience, individually and collectively, a 'Last Judgment' in this sense. 'Whenever any Individual Rejects Error & Embraces Truth, a Last Judgment passes upon that Individual' (*Vision of the Last Judgment*, pp. 81-4). Blake himself claimed to have undergone this all-transforming experience in which the temporal world is judged in the light of eternal values. This experience is to be feared only by those who cling to illusion; for the divine humanity innate in all it is a joyous liberation. Blake's prophetic works are from first to last a proclamation of the coming of the reign of 'Jesus, the Imagination', the realization of which will bring to an end all externally imposed codes and laws, all legal and religious systems. In *The Marriage of Heaven and Hell* he shows Jesus as a breaker of all the Laws of Moses, because 'Jesus was all virtue, and acted from impulse, not from rules.' Such prophecies are self-realizing; throughout his life Blake presents the contrast between the cruel laws of Church and State and the reign of the God within, the Divine Humanity.

Here we come to Blake's one, but fundamental, criticism of Swedenborg: his moral dualism, taken over uncritically from the existing Apostolic Church and the Mosaic Law, imposed not from within but by the rulers of this world. In *The Marriage of Heaven and Hell* Blake wrote:

Now hear a plain fact: Swedenborg has not written one new truth. Now hear another: he has written all the old falsehoods.

And now hear the reason. He conversed with Angels who are all religious, & conversed not with Devils who all hate religion...

(pls. 21-2)

Blake's 'devils' are spirits of energy, angels, of reason: the two contraries without which, he says, there is 'no progression'. The title of Blake's work itself presents his criticism of the 'old falsehoods' implicit in Swedenborg's *Heaven and Hell*, of which it is so brilliant a satire. For Blake understood that in the Kingdom of Jesus the Imagination 'Good and Evil are no more': Imagination frees but it does not condemn. Blake criticized Milton for his moralistic condemnation of Satan and the rebel angels by a rational Messiah, and his objection to Swedenborg was the same:

O Swedenborg! Strongest of men, a Samson shorn by the Churches Shewing the Transgressors in Hell, the proud Warriors in Heaven, Heaven as a Punisher, & Hell as One under Punishment

(pl.22)

So with Dante, the fellow-visionary whose work he so superbly illustrated at the end of his life: 'Dante saw devils where I saw none.' 'Not all is sin that Satan calls so,' Blake declared, 'All the loves and graces of Eternity.' Of all evils Blake most condemned self-righteousness, 'the selfish virtues of the natural heart'. His illustrations of the Book of Job represent a 'Last Judgment' undergone by self-righteous Job. The story of Job is indeed open to many interpretations, but such was

Blake's reading of it, and so he wished it to be understood by his own nation, 'the Giant Albion', enslaved, as Blake saw it, to the external law and not the inner freedom of the Divine Humanity.

All the same, in later life Blake introduced a note of caution:

Many Persons, such as Paine and Voltaire, with some of the Ancient Greeks, say: 'we will not converse concerning Good & Evil; we will live in Paradise & Liberty.' You may do so in Spirit, but not in the Mortal Body, till after the Last Judgment; for in Paradise they have no Corporeal & Mortal Body ... while we are in the World of Mortality we Must Suffer.

(Vision of the Last Judgment, 92–5)

*

Between the year 1790 (when Blake was writing *The Marriage of Heaven and Hell*) and 1810 when he wrote, in his account of the *Vision of the Last Judgment*, the passage quoted, lay twenty troubled years of revolution and wars in Europe, and in the lives of Blake and his circle, caught in these events. Blake had known Thomas Paine, the freethinker and revolutionary, who was a fellow member of the radical circle who used to meet at Johnson's bookshop in St Paul's Churchyard. Paine had spent many years in America (1774–87) where he was an active supporter of the American Revolution. Back in England he published (in 1791) *The Rights of Man*, considered a seditious book, for which he was outlawed from England. The story is that it was Blake who warned him of danger of arrest, and enabled him to escape to France, where in 1793 he was elected a member of the French Convention, only to be put in prison the following year. Paine's revolutionary enthusiasm surely influenced Blake's early 'Lambeth Books', (Blake and his wife were living in those years in Lambeth). Blake wore at the time a *bonnet rouge* to display his support for the French Revolution, until disillusioned by the Terror in Paris. But in 1798, in his marginalia to Bishop Watson's *Apology for the Bible*, a series of letters addressed to Thomas Paine, he hotly supported his former friend.

Another member of Johnson's circle was the feminist Mary Wollstonecraft, an admirer of Rousseau and advocate of 'free love'. Blake illustrated Mary's book for children, *Original Stories from Real Life*, and his impassioned plea for 'free love' in *Visions of the Daughters of Albion* suggests a very warm affection for Mary, whose own tragic life must have been in Blake's thoughts when he wrote that we cannot 'live in Paradise and liberty' in this world. Mary was deserted by her American lover Gilbert Imlay, and then married William Godwin, the political theorist (whom Blake disliked). She died in 1797, in childbirth. Her daughter by Godwin was to become the second wife of Shelley, whose attempts to live in Paradise and liberty also ended in tears. Had a copy of Blake's *Visions of the Daughters of Albion* been among Mary Wollstonecraft's possessions? Perhaps, even, the author of *Prometheus Unbound* had read Blake's poem? But that is speculation.

Blake's own life meanwhile had not been without involvement with the powers of this world. In 1800 Blake left London for the village of Felpham, at the invitation of Flaxman's friend Hayley, country squire, minor poet, and biographer of the poet Cowper. Blake was in financial straits, but it is also possible that Flaxman and other friends felt that the late wearer of the *bonnet rouge* was safer on the Sussex coast than in London. Blake and his wife Catharine loved their cottage and at first all seemed to go well. But soon Blake was to find Hayley's uncomprehending patronage – setting him to trifling tasks and fussing over the results – increasingly unbearable. 'Natural friends are spiritual enemies' is an observation that no doubt reflects Blake's feelings. Yet Hayley was truly well intentioned and perhaps saved Blake's life after an episode that would be comic if it had not come so near to disaster. Blake, republican and revolutionary, hated the war in Europe and England's involvement in it and was no doubt outspoken on this theme. The climax came when he found a soldier in his cottage garden, sent to work there by his gardener. Infuriated, Blake turned him out, with (so the soldier reported) decidedly pro-Bonapartist words. (Blake was later disillusioned also with Bonaparte, who had at first seemed the champion of a New Age in Europe.) A trial for sedition followed in which Squire

Hayley loyally defended Blake, who denied the charge, and whose evident innocence of involvement in 'the politics of time' carried the day.

Samuel Palmer, who knew Blake in his later years, records (in his memoir written for Gilchrist, op. cit.) a very different picture:

He was fond of the works of St. Theresa, and often quoted them with other writers on the interior life. Among his eccentricities will, no doubt, be numbered his preference for ecclesiastical governments. He used to ask how it was that we hear so much of priestcraft and so little of soldier-craft and lawyer-craft. The Bible, he said, was the book of liberty, and Christianity the sole regenerator of nations. In politics a Platonist, he put no trust in demagogues. His ideal home was with Fra Angelico: a little later he might have been a reformer, but after the fashion of Savonarola.

*

Whereas the spiritual masters of India and the Far East teach some form of meditation as the supreme means of spiritual enlightenment Blake taught what might be called a *yoga* of the arts – 'Poetry, Painting & Music, the three Powers in Man of conversing with Paradise that the Flood did not sweep away' (*Vision of the Last Judgment, Notebook*, 81-2) – the 'flood' of the five senses, in Blake's symbolic language. Jesus and his disciples are 'all artists', Blake affirms, not because they practised one or another of the arts but because they lived by the Imagination. Conversely, the arts are a 'way' of spiritual enlightenment:

I know of no other Christianity and of no other Gospel than the liberty both of body & mind to exercise the Divine Arts of the Imagination ... Imagination, the real & eternal World of which this Vegetable Universe is but a Faint shadow, & in which we shall live in our Eternal or Imaginative Bodies when these Vegetable Mortal Bodies are no more. The Apostles knew of no other Gospel. What were all their spiritual gifts? What is the Divine Spirit? Is the Holy Ghost any other than an Intellectual Fountain?

(*Jerusalem*, 77)

Some would question whether Blake's 'way' of the arts is in reality the same, or an equivalent, of the royal road of meditation; or one may see, in contrast with oriental religions, an expression of the Christian doctrine of the Incarnation – the building 'in earth as it is in heaven' of the Holy City of Jerusalem:

> A Poet, a Painter, a Musician, an Architect: the Man Or
> Woman who is not one of these is not a Christian.
> You must leave Fathers & Mothers & Houses & Lands
> if they stand in the way of Art.
> Prayer is the study of Art.
> Praise is the Practise of Art.
> Fasting &c., all relate to Art.
> The outward Ceremony is Antichrist.
> The Eternal Body of Man is The Imagination, that is
>   God himself | יֵשׁוּעַ
>   The Divine Body | Jesus: we are his Members.
> It manifests itself in his works of Art (In Eternity
>   All is Vision.)
>   (*Laocoön*)

Conversely we are to remember that not all that passes for 'art' is held sacred by Blake: commenting on Wordsworth's *Poems*, and Wordsworth's statement that 'The powers requisite for the production of poetry are, first, those of observation and description ... 2ndly, Sensibility...' Blake wrote in the margin, 'One Power alone makes a Poet: Imagination, The Divine Vision.' Without that vision is that 'Bad Art' Blake castigated when in his account of the *Vision of the Last Judgment* he writes, in his last paragraph:

> Some People flatter themselves that there will be No Last Judgment & that Bad Art will be adopted & mixed with Good Art, That Error or Experiment will make a Part of Truth, & they Boast that it is its Foundation. These People flatter themselves: I will not Flatter them. Error is Created. Truth is Eternal.
>   (*Notebook*, pp. 92–5)

The lesson is clear in Blake's illustrations to the Book of Job. On the first plate Job and his family are seated under the Tree of Life reading the scriptures, and under the plate is written 'The letter killeth.' On the tree hang musical instruments, unused. In the last plate, Job, who after his many ordeals, has 'seen' God, is playing the harp, while all his family are playing their instruments, or singing. One can almost hear Vaughan Williams' music sounding! Blake's spiritual intent was not 'other-worldly', had no concern with a heaven elsewhere, 'an allegoric abode where existence has never come', but to discover 'the infinite in all things'. Perhaps his whole prophetic message is contained in the four lines:

> To see a World in a Grain of Sand
> And a Heaven in a Wild Flower,
> Hold Infinity in the palm of your hand
> And Eternity in an hour.
>   ('Auguries of Innocence')

But what can be said in four lines can be expanded into many hundreds, and Blake's prophetic message touches all levels and circumstances of life. Blake was concerned to bring about nothing less than a reversal of the premises of Western materialism, the very foundation of the civilization we now inherit. At a moment when scientific materialism – or a materialist science – was rising to assume the authority once possessed by religion Blake challenged those culture-heroes of materialist thought: Bacon, Founder of the Royal Society; Newton, measurer of the 'astronomical telescopic heavens' which Blake contrasts with the immeasurable 'Heaven in a Wild Flower'; and Locke, who believed that man had no innate ideas but received knowledge only through the senses. In the Industrial Revolution, then in its infancy, Blake saw an embodiment of the 'dark Satanic Mills' of Newton's universe reflected in machines, which are soul-destroying. Albion's machines are 'woven with his life' by an ideology which turned the living world into a lifeless mechanism. For Blake the world of Imagination is this world, seen truly. To a patron who had criticized him for painting visions 'not to be found in this world' Blake wrote:

I feel that a Man may be happy In This World. And I know that This World Is a World of Imagination & Vision. I see Everything I paint In This World, but Every body does not see alike. To the Eyes of a Miser a Guinea is more beautiful than the Sun, & a bag worn with the use of Money has more beautiful proportions than a Vine filled with Grapes. The tree which moves some to tears of joy is in the Eyes of others only a Green thing that stands in the way. Some See Nature all Ridicule & Deformity, & by these I shall not regulate my proportions; & Some Scarce see Nature at all. But to the Eyes of the Man of Imagination, Nature is Imagination itself. As a man is, So he Sees. As the Eye is formed, such are its Powers. You certainly mistake when you say that the Visions of Fancy are not to be found in This World. To Me This World is all One continued Vision of Fancy or Imagination...

(to Dr Trusler, 23 August 1799)

The word 'Imagination', as Blake uses it, is not synonymous with 'imaginary' in the current sense of the word – something unreal. On the contrary, Imagination, as both Blake and Coleridge use the word, is reality itself, the living creative principle. It is not one of the four 'functions' of the soul, known alike to tradition and to modern psychology, Blake's 'Four Zoas', but the Person from whom the functions arise. Henry Corbin, the great French Ismaeli scholar, a co-founder with Jung of the Eranos circle, has coined the word 'Imaginal' to distinguish between this order of reality, and the word 'imaginary' in the sense of fictitious or unreal. Nothing is more real than the soul's universe of forms both of the outer and of the inner worlds, the living Person, as Blake understood, within whose being all forms – images – are perpetually generated.

*

When first I read Blake's voluminous Prophetic Books more than fifty years ago many things were then obscure that we are now in a better position to understand. To suggest that the earth is a living being rather than a lifeless mechanism is no longer seen, even among scientists, as a mere poetic fancy. Blake himself had seen the materialist premises with horror, whose representatives 'call the rocks Atomic Origins of Existence, denying Eternity' (*Jerusalem*, 67). 'They call the Rocks Parents of Men, & adore the frowning Chaos' (*Jerusalem*, 67).

Those who criticize this or that detail of a system are more likely to be heard than those who challenge its premises. It was, besides, generally held that Blake presented his challenge with no other authority than his 'visions'. In reality Blake was remarkably widely read in a great body of excluded knowledge, which formed no part of English culture during what Yeats has called 'the three provincial centuries' of the dominance of materialism. His visionary insights were indeed profound, but my own work on Blake's sources has confirmed a view first expressed by Ruthven Todd, that Blake was drawing on a rich inheritance of humankind's spiritual knowledge. His sources were not a few eccentric figures long ago forgotten but Plato and Plotinus, the *Hermetica* and the *Bhagavad Gita*, the mythologies of the world from Iceland to India, the Celtic antiquities of Britain and the mystical Cabbala, in other words the mainstream of the spiritual and metaphysical heritage of the world's recorded experience.

How came Blake to know these sources, so largely disregarded by his contemporaries? They were not in reality so far to seek as it seemed to his early students, who marvelled at his visionary genius which they believed was innate and autonomous. But where there is deep wisdom it is likely that there will also prove to be continuity with tradition. Blake was re-stating, at the end of the eighteenth century and beginning of the Industrial Revolution, the 'perennial philosophy', held by the consensus of all civilizations before our own, which may be seen as the norm and orthodoxy of humankind, rooted as it is both in the nature of man and of the cosmos It underlies all spiritual traditions and is confined to none. A. K. Coomaraswamy was the first to state the view that, far from being an eccentric in a normal society, Blake was following the human mainstream in a deviant society, and in this respect places him with Dante as one of the two supreme 'orthodox' and traditional poets of Europe. Blake himself, following the Millennist language he inherited from the Protestant mystical tradition which reached him in several forms, calls this unanimous and universal tradition 'the Everlasting Gospel'. 'All had originally one language, and one religion: this was the religion of Jesus, the everlasting Gospel. Antiquity preached the Gospel of Jesus' (*Descriptive Catalogue*, 'The Ancient Britains'). This was not, of course, the same thing as the version of Christianity taught by the Church or the Churches. Blake, that patriot of the 'England of the Imagination', held that 'Albion was the parent of the Druids' – priests of that ancient universal religion – and that 'All things Begin & End in Albion's Ancient Druid Rocky Shore.' Addressing the Jews, he writes that the Hebrew patriarchs were 'Druids':

> You have a tradition, that Man anciently contain'd in his mighty limbs all things in Heaven & Earth: this you received from the Druids. 'But now the Starry Heavens are fled from the mighty limbs of Albion'.

> (*Jerusalem*, 27)

The Newtonian system had, Blake held, externalized the 'outer' spaces of the universe from the living and universal Imagination.

We discover easily what we know we are looking for, and Blake's sources are not so far to seek as might have been anticipated. We are inclined to overlook the obvious, and to forget the centrality of the King James Bible within the mainstream of English culture, and Blake's illustrations to the Bible comprise the greater part of his work; and if he did 'Read black where you read white' he read with the understanding of the Imagination where the habit of the time was to read only the superficial sense. The landscape, and indeed the language, of Blake's Prophetic Books is Miltonic. Dr K. D. Sethna, the Indian Blake scholar, in his work on Blake's *The Tyger*, has well observed that Blake's Tyger roams in Milton's 'deeps and skies'; it is Milton's Rebel Angels who 'threw down their spears/ And water'd Heaven with their tears'. For Blake (as for Boehme) the flaming fires of the Abyss are the creative source from which a Messiah of reason 'formed a heaven of what he stole from the Abyss' (*The Marriage of Heaven and Hell*, pls. 5–6). Blake had read the Koran, and the *Bhagavad Gita* in the translation of Charles Wilkins, a member of Sir William Jones' learned circle who contributed to *Asiatick Researches*, issued by the Calcutta Society of Bengal. A painting shown by Blake in his one public exhibition (1809) (now lost) is entitled *The Bramins – A Drawing*, and 'The subject is, Mr. Wilkin translating the Geeta' (*Descriptive Catalogue*, no. X). Blake also knew Moore's *Hindoo Pantheon*, containing many illustrations of the

Indian god-forms. These gods on their lotus-thrones no doubt suggested Plate 53 of *Jerusalem* which shows Vala on a sunflower; and other similar compositions. He had read the Holy Koran and refers with approval to a parable in that work; and much besides. The 'serpent-temple' depicted on Plate 100 of *Jerusalem* is taken from Stukeley, whose works and theories of Avebury and Stonehenge Blake had attentively studied.

*

Another major influence on Blake in his exploration of the excluded tradition of 'the learning of the Imagination' is that of Neoplatonism. Blake's contemporary and one-time friend, Thomas Taylor, 'the English Pagan', was the first translator into English of Plato's complete works, together with the *Commentaries* of Proclus, the complete works of Aristotle, much of Plotinus, and of Plotinus' disciple and biographer Porphyry, and others of the 'Platonic succession', of whom Proclus (fifth century), was the last. This remarkable scholar was in his way as impassioned an advocate of a reversal of the premises of materialism as was Blake. In an essay 'On The Restoration of the Platonic Philosophy by the Late Platonists' Taylor sets out his claim that the Platonic theology is the mainstream of that universal theology Blake proclaimed as the 'Everlasting Gospel'. Taylor wrote of:

that sublime theology which was first obscurely promulgated by Orpheus, Pythagoras and Plato, and was afterwards perspicuously unfolded by their legitimate disciples; in oblivion in *barbarous*, and derided in *impious* ages, will flourish again for very extended periods, through all the revolutions of time.

(*Miscellanies In Prose & Verse*, 1805)

This important essay, included in a volume of Proclus' *Commentaries* on Euclid (1792), was probably the substance of a series of lectures on the Platonic philosophy which Taylor had given, in 1787, at Flaxman's house. Although Blake's still unknown name is not included among those more famous who attended, it is unlikely that Flaxman's friend and fellow Swedenborgian would not have been present. Blake certainly knew Taylor, and a record exists in the *Journals* of the architect William Meredith of a visit to Taylor's house where Meredith found Taylor expounding to Blake the *theorem Pythagoras*. Another link is Mary Wollstonecraft, who was at one time a lodger at Taylor's house, where she called his study 'the abode of peace'. Taylor however was scornful of Christianity; as indeed was Blake but for different reasons. This remarkable scholar was not loved by the academic establishment of the day, a disdain fully reciprocated by Taylor. The 'black-coated gentlemen' of Oxford were, of course, Anglican clergymen, whereas Taylor was an impassioned and profound Platonic philosopher. Taylor must be seen as a key figure in the Greek Revival; his writings were seminal in the American Transcendentalist movement, and some were reissued by the Theosophical Society at the end of the century, to play their part in forming the thought of the Irish mystic AE (George Russell) and of W. B. Yeats. The marbles from the Parthenon were brought to England between 1801 and 1803 by Lord Elgin, and Blake himself in the course of his profession as an engraver made engravings of some of these sculptures for the beautiful volumes of Stuart and Revett's *Antiquities of Athens*. He also made a series of engravings of the Barberini Vase brought to England by Sir William Hamilton (later known as 'the Portland Vase') of which the Wedgwood potteries made their famous replicas. Blake's engravings were made for *The Botanic Garden*, a poem by Erasmus Darwin (grandfather of Charles Darwin) who was a friend of the Wedgwoods, for whom Blake's friend Flaxman made many designs in the Greek style. Then as now the world of the arts was a small world, in which many strands of interconnection become apparent. If Blake does not at first sight appear in any way connected with the Greek Revival, closer examination finds many traces, both visual and poetic, of Greek – and specifically Neoplatonic – themes in his work. On 16 August 1799 Blake was writing to a patron, the Rev. Dr Trusler, of 'the purpose for which alone I live, which is, with such men as my friend Cumberland, to renew the lost art of the Greeks', and on 2 July the following year of 'the immense flood of Grecian light and glory which is coming to Europe'. Many tributaries flowed into Blake's

enthusiastically receptive mind of mythological and meta-
physical writings expressing 'each Nation's different reception
of the Poetic Genius' (*All Religions are One*, 1788).

*

Taylor's remarkable essay *On the Mysteries of Eleusis and
Dionysus* is doubtless the source of Blake's re-telling of that
ancient myth of the 'descent of the soul' into generation in the
two poems 'The Little Girl Lost' and 'Found' (*Songs of
Innocence*). Blake gives his own turn to the story of the Two
Goddesses and the Mother's search for her daughter, when he
makes the lion-king of the Underworld

> A Spirit arm'd in Gold

> On his head a crown,
> On his shoulders down
> Flow'd his golden hair.
> Gone was all their care.

> 'Follow me' he said;
> 'Weep not for the maid;
> 'In my palace deep
> 'Lyca lies asleep.'

Already Blake is expressing his belief that 'God is in the lowest
effects as well as in the highest causes' and affirming a
'marriage' of 'heaven' and 'hell'.

Blake's belief that the soul exists before birth as well as after
death is not Christian but Platonic, and may well derive from
Taylor's translations from Plotinus. One of Blake's leading
themes is the fall of the generated souls (and above all the
Giant Albion) into 'sleep' – the 'deadly sleep' of forgetfulness
of eternal things. Blake never speaks of 'sin' into which the soul
falls, but of the sleep of forgetfulness of her true nature. There
are many passages in which it is clear that Blake believed in
reincarnation. One of Blake's late works (the Arlington Court
tempera, 1821) is an illustration of Porphyry's renowned
treatise, *On the Cave of the Nymphs*, that rich treasury of
Neoplatonic symbolic thought. The treatise is a symbolic
narration of the soul's descent into generation, to be woven

into an earthly body on the 'stone looms' of the Nymphs, and the return after the stormy voyage over 'the sea of time and space' like Odysseus to his native country. His last work was a visiting card for his old friend the Greek enthusiast George Cumberland, an abbreviated drawing of the painting itself, which suggests that the painting was commissioned by Cumberland. Many images from Porphyry's treatise occur throughout Blake's Prophetic Books, the 'stone looms' of the Nymphs, and the weaving of the mortal garments, in detail that points unmistakably to this source.

In later years Blake rejected the Greeks with some violence, mainly on account of their glorification of war. In 1804 he wrote in his Preface to *Milton* of 'the silly Greek & Latin slaves of the sword' and in terms that seem to be a renunciation of a previous admiration (as is indeed the case) 'We do not want either Greek or Roman Models if we are but just and true to our own Imaginations, these worlds of Eternity in which we shall live for every in Jesus our Lord.' He also held the Greeks accountable for the cult of homosexuality:

> 'Twas the Greeks' love of war
> Turn'd love into a Boy
> And Woman into a Statue of Stone
> And away fled every joy.
> ('Why Was Cupid a Boy?')

'A Warlike State can never produce Art,' Blake held; and bitterly attacked Gibbon's exaltation of the military ideals of the Roman Empire and his condemnation of Christianity. 'The Classics! it is the Classics, & not Goths nor Monks, that Desolate Europe with Wars' (*On Homer's Poetry*). This however did not lessen his love for Greek mythology, whose language he assimilated into his own. Far from lessening Blake's stature, as a visionary genius of supposed 'originality', this situation of Blake within the mainstream of the world's spiritual knowledge – with Plato and Plotinus, the *Hermetica* and the *Bhagavad Gita*, the Jewish mystical tradiation of Cabbala and the mythologies of all cultures known to him, raises his stature from that of an English eccentric to that of a world-teacher.

Another important change of a different kind has also made it possible at this time to understand what for his contemporaries and for the nineteenth century remained impenetrably obscure – Blake's bewildering mythology of the Four Zoas, their feminine 'emanations', their many sons and daughters, in landscapes and circumstances as strange as dreams. These events are indeed comparable only to the irrational enactments of mythologies, but the understanding of mythology during the eighteenth and nineteenth centuries took no account of enactments of the inner worlds. Perhaps our most outstanding advance in knowledge in this century has been in the field of psychology, especially in the work of C. G. Jung and his successors. The inner worlds described in the 'visions' of Swedenborg, and of Blake also, would be seen now as events of the 'imaginal' world of psyche. The great early Blake scholar and collector Kerrison Preston was the first to point out the comparison between Blake's description of the structure of the inner worlds he describes and Jung's fourfold 'mandala' of the collective 'unconscious' which are in every way similar. There have since been works by Jungian scholars detailing these similarities. In part the similarities arise from the fact that both Blake and Jung were familiar with works of the Western esoteric tradition. Blake's theme is already defined at the beginning of *Vala* or *The Four Zoas* (1797)

Four Mighty Ones are in every Man; a Perfect Unity
Cannot Exist but from the Universal Brotherhood of Eden
The Universal Man, to whom be Glory Evermore. Amen.
What are the natures of those Living Creatures the Heav'nly Father only
Knoweth, No Individual Knoweth nor can know in all Eternity.
(*The Four Zoas*, I. 9-13)

Jung has familiarized our century with the fourfold archetypal structure of the soul, with the *anima* or soul-image Blake calls Jerusalem, the 'bride' of the Divine Humanity, of the continual presence of these, their conflicts and functions, both in our dreams and in our waking life.

Blake's Zoas (the word derives from *zoe* = life) are based on the 'Four Living Creatures' of the Book of Revelation and the four-faced man of the Book of Ezekiel. Jung knew also of other sources of the fourfold symbol, but the parallels are striking. Jung's four 'functions' are reason, feeling, sensation and intuition. The rational function is personified in Blake's Urizen, the aged reasoner, laborious and short-sighted, poring over his books or struggling to enforce the 'laws' he formulates. Feeling – Blake's Orc, fiery youth and spirit of energy, rejects Urizen's laws, which to him are mere bondage. Tharmas, Blake's 'mildest son of heaven', is the function of the senses, becoming formless and chaotic like an enraged sea when separated from the unity of the Divine Humanity. Los, the visionary (with whom Blake identified himself), is the time spirit, creator and destroyer of forms in his 'furnaces', blacksmith and potter, who labours incessantly to embody on earth the order of heaven; and who, in Blake's words, 'kept the divine vision in time of trouble'. The principal cause of the conflicts in the inner worlds of the English nation Blake saw as the usurpation by Urizen, the reasoner, of the supremacy of Imagination, which is not a function but 'the human existence itself'. Jerusalem, the soul, and bride of the 'god within' is driven into exile by Vala, the cruel 'goddess nature' who seduces 'the Giant Albion'. Each of these Persons has (like the gods of all pantheons) his attributes and surroundings – Urizen his heavy books and his 'iron pen'; Los his furnaces; Vala, like other nature goddesses, her 'veil' and her 'garden', Tharmas his watery world. Each, according to the Swedenborgian system of 'correspondences' lives in a world appropriate to his nature – Urizen in the starry voids of the Newtonian universe; fiery Orc chained Prometheus-like to his rock, and so on. As in dream or myth there is no consecutive time-sequence, for events take place in a world which is not subject to categories of time and space, only of being, and meaning.

As in Homer's epics of Troy and its warriors, as in the *Mahabharata* and the *Ramayana*, as in all epic poetry, the acts of gods and men, the timeless and the time-world, interact and are interwoven; the two worlds, in Blake also, are seen as one world. Milton becomes an actor in the drama, as type of 'the inspired man'; and other historical characters are woven into the myth, Pitt and Nelson, Newton and Wesley, Isaiah and Ezekiel. In the same way London becomes Blake's 'emblematic city' and the whole topography of England takes an inner dimension of symbolic correspondences. Battersea (where Blake had met his wife Catharine, daughter of a market gardener) and Chelsea ('the place of the wounded soldiers'); Lambeth ('lovely Lambeth' where Blake and his wife made in their marriage a shelter for Jerusalem); 'Tyburn's deathful shades' where public hangings took place; the 'healing leaves' of Oxford, 'Snowdon sublime' where 'the Divine Family' had its seat, as in Greece on Olympus, or in the Himalayas on Mount Kailasa. Once we have understood that for Blake the universe is, in its parts and in its whole, a living universe, this is seen to be natural and inevitable. The Zoas are not 'personifications' of archetypal moods and functions: it would be more true to see 'reason', 'feeling' and the rest as abstractions from persons than these 'personifications' of abstractions. Our own dreams, to go no further, are inhabited by soul images in the form of the 'wise old man' or the *anima*, the Tree of Life, serpents and heraldic animals, wells, trees and rivers, all conveying profound meaning we seldom encounter in an outer world long stripped bare of the significance our ancestors encountered in bird and beast, holy well, impenetrable mystery of caves, light of sun and moon and stars. Blake's universe is, in its parts and in its whole, a living universe, existing not (as for the materialist) in only a material dimension, but in all the four 'worlds'. Thus, Blake's city of Golgonooza, 'the spiritual fourfold London eternal' is a fourfold *mandala*, repeated in every individual:

And every part of the City is fourfold: & every inhabitant, fourfold
And every pot & vessel & garment & utensil of the house,
And every house, fourfold; but the third Gate in every one
Is clos'd as with a threefold curtain of ivory & fine linen & ermine.
(*Jerusalem*, 13)

Since 'all things exist in the Human Imagination' everything exists in its fourfold reality. The 'third gate' is the closed gate of Eden, Man's native country – the sensible world which has become external and separate from the soul. Properly understood outer and inner reality are alike living aspects of the one humanity. Nature is, in Vedantic parlance, a 'maya', a world of appearances. The 'curtain' which shuts off Eden in the 'third gate' is the physical garment that the Nymphs of the Cave of Generation weave on their stone looms.

But if Blake is and will always remain a 'difficult' writer, it is not because his poetry requires of the reader some special knowledge not accessible to everyone. He expected to be understood, in his own country, England, by whoever shared our history, legends and great poets, and the Bible. It is not for want of information that he has remained so long obscure, but because he challenged and reversed in all his work the accepted premises of Western materialist culture. These premises no longer remain unchallenged – have indeed, one might almost say, already taken their place in the 'history of ideas'. Blake knew that for those who are willing to follow the 'golden string' he offers, his promise will be kept:

> I give you the end of a golden string:
>   Only wind it into a ball,
> It will lead you in at Heaven's gate
>   Built in Jerusalem's wall.
>
> (*Jerusalem*, 77)

Kathleen Raine

SELECT BIBLIOGRAPHY

———

BENTLEY, G. E. JR, ed., *William Blake, The Critical Heritage*, Routledge, 1975. Brings together all the contemporary and Victorian views about Blake.

BINDMAN, DAVID, *William Blake, His Art and Times*, Thames & Hudson, 1982. Originally issued for the Yale Center Blake Exhibition, it relates his work to contemporary painting and the visual language of the age; well documented and illustrated.

BOTTRALL, MARGARET, ed., *William Blake: Songs of Innocence and Experience*, Casebook Series, Macmillan, 1986. Gathers together some key essays on the *Songs*, plus contemporary and Victorian comments.

BLUNT, ANTHONY, *The Art of William Blake*, Columbia University Press, 1959. A pioneering and scholarly book on Blake's visual sources.

DAMON, S. FOSTER, *A Blake Dictionary*, Thames & Hudson, 1979. A useful students' handbook, offering guidance through Blake's world via its ideas, symbols, names and motifs.

DAMROSCH, LEOPOLD JR, *Symbol and Truth in Blake's Myth*, Princeton, 1980. A sophisticated, stimulating exploration of 'the conceptual bases of Blake's myth'.

ERDMAN, DAVID V., annotated by, *The Illuminated Blake*, Oxford, 1975. A black-and-white facsimile of all the illuminated books, plus commentary, enabling students to see how Blake wanted to be read.

ERDMAN, DAVID V., *Blake: Prophet Against Empire, A Poet's Interpretation of the History of His Own Times*, Princeton, 1977. The standard work tracing the manifold connections between Blake's text and designs and the social-political realities of his age.

FRYE, NORTHROP, *Fearful Symmetry, A Study of William Blake*, Princeton, 1947. One of the first post-war books influential for Blake studies; reprinted several times.

GALLANT, CHRISTINE, *Blake and the Assimilation of Chaos*, Princeton, 1978. A recent and more rigorous Jungian approach.

GILCHRIST, ALEXANDER, *Life of William Blake*, ed. Ruthven Todd, Everyman, 1945. The classic Victorian biography; unreliable, but vivid with anecdotes and primary sources.

HONOUR, HUGH, *Neo-classicism*, Penguin, 1968. A first-rate art-historical study of the Greek Revival in the arts, to which Blake is related.

KEYNES, GEOFFREY, introduction and commentary, *Blake: Songs of Innocence and of Experience*, Oxford, 1985. Full colour facsimile of the 1955 Trianon Press edition; several others now available.

SELECT BIBLIOGRAPHY

LISTER, RAYMOND, *Infernal Methods, A Study of William Blake's Art Techniques*, Bell, 1975. A lucid account of the engraving, printing and design techniques related to Blake's way of seeing.

MITCHELL, W.J.T., *Blake's Composite Art, A Study of the Illuminated Poetry*, Princeton, 1978. Examines the visual-verbal dialectics of the illuminated books and their place in 'the sister arts' tradition.

RAINE, KATHLEEN, *Blake and Antiquity*, Routledge, 1979. A shortened version of the author's monumental 2-vol. *Blake and Tradition*, Princeton, 1968, which pioneered Blake's indebtedness to a 'philosophia perennis'.

RAINE, KATHLEEN, *Blake and the New Age*, Allen & Unwin, 1979. Argues trenchantly for Blake as the great forerunner of a New Age of spiritual realities opposed to the materialist culture and ideologies of our own time.

RAINE, KATHLEEN, and HARPER, GEORGE MILLS, eds., *Thomas Taylor the Platonist, Selected Writings*, Routledge, 1969. An excellent selection of essays and translations by Taylor, with two long introductions on his key role in English Romanticism and American Transcendentalism.

WARNER, JANET A., *Blake and the Language of Art*, McGill-Queen's University Press, 1984. Researches 'archetypes of gesture and stance ... as a kind of visual vocabulary' inherited and developed by Blake.

WILSON, MONA, *The Life of William Blake*, ed. Geoffrey Keynes, Oxford, 1971. The standard life, which also relates Blake's inner development to stages of the mystic way.

YEATS, W. B., *Essays and Introductions*, Macmillan, 1961. See the fine essays 'William Blake and the Imagination' and 'William Blake and His Illustrations to the "Divine Comedy"'.

CHRONOLOGY

___

DATE	AUTHOR'S LIFE	LITERARY CONTEXT
1755		The artists John Flaxman and Thomas Stothard born.
1756		
1757	William Blake born, 28 November, at 28 Broad (now Broadwick) Street, off Golden Square, Soho, London, to Catherine Harmitage and James Blake (hosier). Third of six sons and one daughter. Christened at St James's Church, Piccadilly (11 December). Parents probably Nonconformist (since buried later at Bunhill Fields, the Dissenters' cemetery).	Antonio Canova born, neo-classical sculptor of European fame. Edmund Burke: *A Philosophical Enquiry into the Sublime and Beautiful* (Blake disliked this as Newtonian). Gray: *Odes*.
1758		Thomas Taylor the Platonist born (key figure in the Greek Revival).
1759		Robert Burns and Mary Wollstonecraft born. Johnson: *Rasselas*. Voltaire: *Candide*. Macpherson: *Fragments of Ancient Poetry* (the first Ossian poems and a major stylistic influence). Josiah Wedgwood starts his neoclassical pottery at Etruria, Staffs.
1760		
1761	Blake's first vision (as reported by the diarist Henry Crabb Robinson in Blake's wife's own words: 'You know, dear, the first time you saw God was when	

xl

Start of Seven Years' War against Austria, France, Sweden and Russia. England allied with Frederick the Great of Prussia. The last major European conflict prior to the French Revolution, at the end of which England's empire position is established, Prussia's as a European power. In America and India, collisions with France over colonies and frontiers. The War conducted by William Pitt the Elder, Secretary of State.

General Wolfe in Canada. Capture of Quebec from the French.

Death of George II (Hanoverian). Accession of George III. Continuation of Methodist Revival (from 1739) under Whitefield and the Wesleys.

DATE	AUTHOR'S LIFE	LITERARY CONTEXT
1761 cont	you were four years old and "he put his head to the window and set you a-screaming..." ").	
1762		Rousseau: *Du contrat social*. Cobbett born. The radical newspaper *The North Briton*, ed. John Wilkes and Charles Churchill. Stuart & Revett: *The Antiquities of Athens*.
1763		Christopher Smart: *Song to David*. Wilkes arrested for having attacked the government in No. 45 of *The North Briton*.
1764		Hogarth dies. Voltaire: *Dictionnaire philosophique*. William Law: *The Works of Jacob Behmen* (Boehme), 4 vols., until 1781, with illustrations by Dionysius Freher greatly admired by Blake.
1764-70		
1765	Other contrastive visions in pastoral settings: one of 'haymakers at work, and amid them angelic figures walking'; another at Peckham Rye of 'a tree filled with angels, bright angelic wings, bespangling the boughs like stars' (Gilchrist). At his own wish, parents decide not to send him to school. Instead, is sent to train as an artist, since remarkable drawing talent shown. Visits to salerooms; begins to collect prints of Old Masters ('his little connoisseur', as the Covent Garden art-dealer, Abraham Langford, dubbed him). Blake later: 'I cannot say that Rafael Ever was, from my Earliest Childhood, hidden from Me. I Saw & I Knew	Horace Walpole: *The Castle of Otranto* (first Gothic novel and, together with his Strawberry Hill, Twickenham, Gothicized between 1747-76, a major source of the Gothic Revival). Percy: *Reliques of Ancient English Poetry*. John Wesley's *Journal*, 4 vols., until 1790 (the rise of Methodism, open-air preaching, and 'enthusiasm').

CHRONOLOGY

HISTORICAL EVENTS

End of Seven Years' War with the Treaty of Paris.

James Hargreaves invents the spinning jenny.

Period of comparative peace (during Blake's boyhood). But growing tensions between England and the American colonies.

DATE	AUTHOR'S LIFE	LITERARY CONTEXT
1765 cont	immediately the difference between Rafael and Rubens.' Already strong preference shown for the linear Florentine over the Venetian and Baroque.	
1766		Rousseau visits England. Goldsmith: *The Vicar of Wakefield*.
1767	Attends Henry Pars' Academy in the Strand for five years, drawing plaster casts from the antique (not from life). Starts writing verse. Blake's favourite brother Robert, also gifted, born.	
1768		Gray: *Poems* (with Norse- and Celtic-based lyrics). Sterne: *A Sentimental Journey*.
1769		Reynolds: *Discourses* 1.
1770		Wordsworth, Beethoven and Hegel born. Chatterton dies. Mallet: *Northern Antiquities* (trans. Percy) (important source-book on Norse myth for Blake).
1771		Gray dies. Scott born.
1772	Apprenticed to master-engraver, James Basire, of Stationers' Hall, probably boarding with him at his house in Lincoln's Inn Fields. Inherits Basire's 'firm and correct outline', not the fashionably soft stipple engraving of the day. Buys and reads Fuseli's translation of Winckelmann's *Reflections on the Painting and Sculpture of the Greeks*, a key work of the period influencing both Goethe and Schiller. Sent by Basire to study and draw Westminster Abbey tombs for engravings for the Society of Antiquaries, to whom Basire was official engraver. Blake's love of Gothic ('living form') starts here.	Swedenborg, Swedish scientist and visionary, dies in London.

xliv

CHRONOLOGY

Royal Academy founded, with Reynolds as President.

James Watt patents the steam engine.
Lord North as Prime Minister abolishes all import duties payable by the
colonists (to conciliate them), but retains the tea-duty.

DATE	AUTHOR'S LIFE	LITERARY CONTEXT
1773	First original engraving, titled *Joseph of Arimathea among the Rocks of Albion* (after Michelangelo), expressing interest in 'native British mythology' of Bryant's *Ancient Mythology* (1774–6), for which Blake engraved plates.	*The Works in Architecture of Robert and James Adam*, Vol. 1. Adam interiors at their height (cf. Osterley Park, Middlesex, with its picturesque concaves and convexes and its 'Etruscan' room based on Greek vases).
1774		Goethe: *Werther* – a central document of the 'Sturm und Drang' ('Storm and Stress') movement: anti-rational and moulded by Rousseau, Shakespeare, Edward Young, and Macpherson's 'Ossian'.
1775		The landscape painters Turner and Girtin born.
1775–83		
1776		Gibbon: *Decline and Fall of the Roman Empire*, Vol. 1.
1777		Chatterton: *Poems* (Blake owned a 1778 copy).
1778		Rousseau and Voltaire die. First Swedenborgian Church built. *Heaven and Hell* translated.
1779	Apprenticeship ends. Admitted to the Royal Academy Schools (8 October). Historical pictures painted: *The Ordeal of Queen Emma* and *The Penance of Jane Shore*. Engraves for booksellers, including Joseph Johnson.	Cowper: *Olney Hymns*. Hume: *Dialogues Concerning Natural Religion*.
1780	Exhibits *The Death of Earl Goodwin* at Royal Academy. Meets several like-minded artists: Thomas Stothard (a Swedenborgian), John Flaxman (also interested in Swedenborg), the Swiss Henry Fuseli, and George Cumberland. Engraves *The Dance of Albion* (modelled on cosmic Vitruvian man and often called *Glad Day* after its 1794 colour-print version).	Beginning of Sunday Schools.

CHRONOLOGY

HISTORICAL EVENTS

The Boston Tea-Party. Ships of the India Company are boarded and tea-chests thrown into the harbour. As a result England revokes its charter to the colony.

Declaration of Rights proclaimed at Philadelphia, with delegates from most colonies refusing all British imports until Boston's charter is restored.

American War of Independence, with Washington as commander-in-chief.

France allies itself with America by recognizing its independence. England declares war on France, who is supported by Spain. At home, the Roman Catholic Relief Bill passed, repealing the most repressive anti-Catholic laws.

The Gordon Riots in London: ostensibly anti-Catholic demonstrations led by Lord George Gordon, President of the Protestant Association, but masking much social discontent; 60,000 held the city for a week (in June), sacking and burning so-called 'Papist' chapels and houses, and breaking open prisons such as Newgate. The young Blake was swept along in one of the crowds, witnessing the above.

DATE	AUTHOR'S LIFE	LITERARY CONTEXT
1781		Rousseau: *Confessions*. Kant: *Critique of Pure Reason*.
1782	Marries Catherine Sophia Boucher, daughter of a local market-gardener, at St Mary's Church, Battersea (18 August). They set up house at 23 Green Street, Leicester Fields (now Square).	William Gilpin: *Observations on the Wye* (the rise of the picturesque). Fuseli's painting *The Nightmare*. John & Charles Wesley: *Hymns for the Nation* (copy owned by Blake).
1783	First and only volume of verse published, *Poetical Sketches*, at the expense of Rev. A. S. Mathew and Flaxman, showing remarkable skill with Elizabethan and eighteenth-century poetic models. Blake, like the penniless Flaxman before him, 'taken up' by Mrs Harriet Mathew and her circle of Blue Stockings (Hannah More, Hester Chapone, Elizabeth Montagu).	
1784	Blake's father dies. Together with a colleague from his Basire days (James Parker) sets up a print-shop at 27 Broad Street. Robert Blake joins them. Possibly under Flaxman's guidance, a thorough study of Swedenborg undertaken.	
1785	Exhibits four large watercolours of the Biblical Joseph story at the Royal Academy. Writes (from the previous autumn) the unfinished prose satire *An Island in the Moon*, containing in embryo some *Songs of Innocence*.	Gainsborough: *The Morning Walk*. Sir Charles Wilkins (trans.): *The Bhagavad-Gita* (see Blake's *A Descriptive Catalogue*: 'The subject is, Mr Wilkin translating the Geeta' – of a lost drawing, *The Bramins*).
1786		Mozart: *The Marriage of Figaro* (based on Beaumarchais).
1787	Flaxman leaves for study tour of Italy. Prior to this, Thomas Taylor the Platonist holds a series of lectures at Flaxman's	

CHRONOLOGY

HISTORICAL EVENTS

The British are finally defeated by the Americans at Yorktown, Virginia.

End of American War. The Treaty of Versailles, whereby England formally recognizes American independence.

DATE	AUTHOR'S LIFE	LITERARY CONTEXT
1787 *cont*	house (with Blake almost certainly present). Blake moves in the autumn to 28 Poland Street (off Oxford Street). Robert Blake dies of consumption, his brother nursing him for a fortnight without sleep, then sleeping non-stop for three days. At the moment of death Blake sees his brother's soul rising through the ceiling 'clapping its hand for joy', and later attributes to him his discovery of illuminated printing.	Thomas Taylor's translation of Plotinus: *Concerning the Beautiful*.
1788	First attempts at this new process (relief-etched with pen and colour-washes added) in the two tractates *There is No Natural Religion* and *All Religions Are One* – aphoristic statements of fundamental beliefs: e.g. 'That the Poetic Genius is the true Man, and that the body or outward form of Man is derived from the Poetic Genius'. Annotates J. C. Lavater's *Aphorisms on Man* (Swiss theologian and physiognomist) and Swedenborg's *Divine Love and Wisdom*.	Byron born. *The Times* started.
1788–9	Thomas Taylor's translation of the *Philosophical and Mathematical Commentaries of Proclus on the first Book of Euclid's Elements. To which are Added, a History of the Restoration of the Platonic Theology, by the Later Platonists: and a Translation from the Greek of Proclus's Theological Elements*, Vol. II, 1789. The full text of Porphyry's *De Antro Nympharum*, theme of Blake's Arlington Court tempera entitled (provisionally) 'The Sea of Time and Space', is based on	

1

CHRONOLOGY

Power-looms invented. First hot-air balloon crosses the Channel.

DATE	AUTHOR'S LIFE	LITERARY CONTEXT
1788–9 cont	this text. Taylor's essay was probably based on a series of lectures given at the house of Flaxman in 1787, which Blake probably attended.	
1789	*Songs of Innocence* – first major product of illuminated printing, with new beauties of text and design recalling medieval manuscripts. *The Book of Thel* – a Neoplatonic account of the soul's descent with alchemical dimensions. William and Catherine Blake attend the first conference and sign the manifesto of the Swedenborgian New Jerusalem Church, Great Eastcheap (13 April). *Tiriel* written and illustrated, though left unpublished (a symbolic narrative of parental tyranny that heralds later work).	
1790	Associates with the radical publisher, Joseph Johnson, whose weekly dinners near St Paul's he in part probably attended, and where he would have met Joseph Priestley the chemist and Unitarian, Thomas Paine, Fuseli, the feminist Mary Wollstonecraft, and Thomas Holcroft the 'English Jacobin' novelist. Begins *The Marriage of Heaven and Hell* with its satire on Swedenborg under a sense of political imminence and the impact of reading the German mystic, Jakob Boehme, whose theory of spiritual dialectics (Blake's 'contraries') infuses the whole work as it did that of the German idealists; cf. Hegel's own dialectic (*c.*1800). The Blakes leave for 13 Hercules Buildings, Lambeth.	Burke: *Reflections on the French Revolution.*

CHRONOLOGY

The French Revolution, with the storming of the Bastille (in July). A National Assembly is formed and Louis XVI put in prison. Washington becomes first American President.

DATE	AUTHOR'S LIFE	LITERARY CONTEXT
1791	Provides engravings for Mary Wollstonecraft's *Original Stories from Real Life* and Erasmus Darwin's *The Botanic Garden* (both published by Johnson). Johnson also sets up in proof Bk 1 of Blake's poem, *The French Revolution*; but this gets no further, from fear of prosecution (perhaps on Blake's side). Thomas Taylor: *Eleusinian and Bacchic Mysteries*, on which Blake's poems *The Little Girl Lost & Found* appear to be based.	In reply to Burke, Paine's *The Rights of Man*, Pt 1.
1792	Mother dies (9 September).	Mary Wollstonecraft: *Vindication of the Rights of Woman*. Wordsworth in France. Shelley born.
1793	Finishes *The Marriage of Heaven and Hell*, plus its appendix, *A Song of Liberty*, containing Blake's entire myth in embryo. First of the Lambeth Books: *Visions of the Daughters of Albion*; then *America*, a political allegory addressing 'the spiritual causes behind history' and subtitled 'A Prophecy'. *For Children: The Gates of Paradise*, a small book of emblems, reissued and extended as *For the Sexes* (1818). Issues *Prospectus to the Public* (10 October), in which he unsuccessfully tries to regain contact with a wider audience, talking of 'a method of printing which combines the Painter and the Poet'. Begins to use a MS. book belonging to Robert Blake for verse and drawings intermittently till 1818. Many of the *Songs of Experience* here in draft form. Originally called *The Rossetti MS*, because it previously belonged to D. G.	William Godwin: *Political Justice* (influenced the young Shelley).

HISTORICAL EVENTS

Austria and Prussia invade France to try and put Louis back in power, but are repulsed. September massacre of royalists. A National Convention is set up, replacing the Assembly; the monarchy is abolished and France declared a republic.

Louis and Marie Antoinette are guillotined (21 January and 16 October). Millennarial fantasies resurface at home and elsewhere (cf. the religious prophet, Richard Brothers, self-proclaimed 'Prince of the Hebrews', whose *Knowledge of the Prophecies and Times* (1794) is symptomatic). The Reign of Terror begins under Robespierre and St Just, with the Jacobins victorious over the Girondins. England, under the premiership of William Pitt the Younger, declares war on France, who is supported by Holland..

DATE	AUTHOR'S LIFE	LITERARY CONTEXT
1793 *cont*	Rossetti, the Pre-Raphaelite poet and painter, it is now referred to as Blake's *Notebook* and, like the *Vala MS* of 1795–1804, gives access to Blake's creative workshop.	
1794–6	*Songs and Innocence and of Experience* (Shewing the Two Contrary States of the Human Soul). Flaxman returns from Italy. *Europe*, another and darker political 'Prophecy'; also the powerfully disturbing creation-myth, *The First Book of Urizen* (no other books issued).	Taylor (trans.): *Five Books of Plotinus*.
1795	Three smaller illuminated books: *The Book of Ahania*, *The Book of Los*, and *The Song of Los* (the first two intaglio etching). Magnificent series of large colour-prints (rich mottled textures and sombre backgrounds indicating the 'Fallen world'), e.g. *Elohim Creating Adam*, *Newton*, *Nebuchadnezzar*, *Pity*, *The House of Death*. (*Note* the expressionist features of this art.) Blake acquires the patronage of Captain Thomas Butts of Fitzroy Square, a clerk at the War Office, who continues to commission work up to Blake's death. Illustrations to Edward Young's *Night Thoughts* (Graveyard School of verse: cf. Gray's *Elegy*). Begins *Vala* or *The Four Zoas*, subtitling it 'A Dream of Nine Nights', a Romantic epic of inner worlds. Proof-pages of Young used as MS. (left unpublished).	Keats and Carlyle born.
1796	Provides engravings for his friend George Cumberland's *Thoughts on Outline*, a neoclassical treatise on art; cf. Blake in 1799: 'the purpose for	William Beckford, author of *Vathek* (1786), a popular oriental-Gothic novel, builds Fonthill Abbey.

CHRONOLOGY

West Indian campaigns against the French; 40,000 British troops killed. At home, a run of bad harvests, financial crises, and loss of continental markets make for social unrest, which Pitt holds down with policies of repression.

Spain then declares war on England. Pitt, alarmed by the general sympathy shown in various radical clubs and societies at home for the Revolution and Republic, suspends Habeas Corpus (preventing arbitrary imprisonment), sets up informers and curtails freedom of the press. Because of the war, heavy taxation is necessary. A stagnant economy and year of famine.

DATE	AUTHOR'S LIFE	LITERARY CONTEXT
1796 cont	which I alone live, is, in conjunction with such men as my friend Cumberland, to renew the lost art of the Greeks'.	
1797	*Night Thoughts*, Vol. 1, published by bookseller Richard Edwards, a disaster; Blake saying later: 'Since my Young's Night Thoughts have been publish'd, Even Johnson & Fuseli have discarded my Graver'. His work is found 'eccentric', and his reputation begins to decline.	Burke, Horace Walpole and Mary Wollstonecraft die. Friendship between Wordsworth and Coleridge. *The Anti-Jacobin* published. Schelling: *Ideas Towards a Philosophy of Nature*. Hölderlin: *Hyperion*.
1798	Starts his critical annotations to Reynolds' *Discourses* and Bacon's *Essays*.	Wordsworth and Coleridge: *Lyrical Ballads*; both poets in Germany. Goya's dark and macabre series of etchings, *Los caprichos*; cf. Fuseli and Blake.
1799	Butts commissions fifty small pictures at a guinea each, illustrating Biblical texts. Experiments with 'tempera'.	Religious Tract Society founded (Evangelical). Novalis: *Hymnen an die Nacht* (mystical German Romantic poems).
1800	Through Flaxman, Blake moves to Felpham on the Sussex coast to work for a literary squire, William Hayley. At first, the change is wholly beneficial, but he soon discovers that Hayley's patronage is irksome and condescending. The cottage he, his wife, and his sister rent also proves cold and damp, causing 'My Wife & Myself ... Ague & Rheumatism'.	Wordsworth: *Preface to 'Lyrical Ballads'* (with its attack on poetic diction). The Schlegel brothers first apply the term 'romantic' to literature.
1801	Watercolours to Milton's *Comus* and *Paradise Lost*.	
1802	Engravings for Hayley's *Ballads* and *Life of Cowper*. The move to the country and presence of the sea liberate, resulting in impulses and ideas for the next major prophetic book, *Milton* (engraved 1804–8). cf. the	Victor Hugo born. Scott: *Minstrelsy of the Scottish Border*. Cobbett's *Weekly Political Register* (until 1835).

HISTORICAL EVENTS

Fears of invasion by France. The rise of Napoleon (French invasion of Italy). Mutinies in the British navy, with brutalities at large in the army. High prices and low wages contribute to a tinderbox situation. Towards the end of the year, things improve somewhat, with the rise of Nelson causing shifts in the balance of sea-power.

First Coalition of England, Austria, and Russia against France. The Battle of the Nile, whereby the French fleet is crushed. A rebellion in Ireland is also put down. Blake notes in his copy of Bishop Watson's *Apology for the Bible*: 'To defend the Bible in this year 1798 would cost a man his life. The Beast & the Whore rule without control'.

Second Coalition. Napoleon dissolves the Republican Directory (which had arrogated power to itself from the National Convention) and becomes first Consul (9 November).

A year of famine. Act of Union between Great Britain and Ireland, announcing a communal parliament at Westminster. Byron later described this as 'a Union of the shark with its prey' (1812, in Parliament).

The population of London doubled to a million since 1700; trade also doubles from 1750; and the export of pig-iron doubles from 1760. The Peace of Amiens signed (27 March), remaining unstable.

DATE	AUTHOR'S LIFE	LITERARY CONTEXT
1802 *cont*	splendid letter-poem to Butts (2 October 1800): 'To my Friend Butts I write/My first Vision of Light/On the yellow sands sitting.'	
1803	Encounter and scuffle with the dragoon John Scofield in the garden of the Blakes' cottage (12 August). To Butts (16 August): 'I am at Present in a Bustle to defend myself against a very unwarrantable warrant ... which was taken out against me by a Private in Capt. Leathes's troop of 1st. or Royal Dragoons for an assault & Seditious words.' Return to London in September to an apartment on the first floor of 17 South Molton Street, off Oxford Street.	Emerson born. Humphrey Repton: *Theory and Practice of Landscape Gardening* (the picturesque).
1804	Tried for sedition at the Guildhall, Chichester (11–12 January), and acquitted. Visits 'the Truchsessian Gallery of pictures' near Marylebone (a collection of largely dubious old masters brought to England by Count Joseph Truchsess), where he nevertheless 'was again enlightened with the light I enjoyed in my youth' (letter to Hayley). The title-pages of both *Milton* and *Jerusalem* designed.	Beethoven: *Eroica Symphony* (a cardinal musical statement of the age, dedicated to Napoleon, then withdrawn as he becomes Emperor: cf. the heroic in J.-L. David, Delacroix, and indeed Blake).
1805	R. H. Cromek commissions Blake to illustrate Robert Blair's *The Grave* (another Graveyard School product), but bypasses him for the engravings, giving these to Louis Schiavonetti, a soft-style engraver of the day.	First version of Wordsworth's *The Prelude* completed (subtitled 'The Growth of the Poet's Mind') – Romantic inner autobiography.
1806		Beethoven: *Fidelio* (first version): note its prison scenario. Kant dies.
1807	Thomas Phillips' fine portrait of Blake exhibited at the Royal Academy.	

CHRONOLOGY

Renewal of war against Napoleon, for invading Switzerland and annexing Piedmont, plus other Italian states (10 May). Growing fears of invasion at home.

Pitt Prime Minister again. Napoleon becomes Emperor.

The Battle of Trafalgar fought among hectic preparations for the invasion of England. Death of Nelson. Third Coalition against France. Austria and Russia defeated at the Battle of Austerlitz.

Death of Pitt. Economic blockade of England by Napoleon.

Abolition of the Slave Trade.

DATE	AUTHOR'S LIFE	LITERARY CONTEXT
1808	Blake exhibits three pictures at the Royal Academy: *Christ in the Sepulchre*, *Jacob's Dream* and *The Last Judgement*.	Goethe: *Faust*, Pt 1.
1809	Makes a desperate bid to gain public recognition by holding a one-man exhibition at his parents' old home (now a hosiery owned by his brother James). Opening in September and publicized by *A Descriptive Catalogue*, it continues into the following year, but is a disastrous failure. Henry Crabb Robinson and Charles Lamb attend. For almost a decade Blake's reputation remains in obscurity.	Tennyson and Darwin born. Paine dies.
1810		Coleridge lectures on Shakespeare.
1811		Jane Austen: *Sense and Sensibility* (anti-Jacobin novel). With the Regency, Greek-type fashions come into their own.
1812		Dickens and Browning born. Byron: *Childe Harold's Pilgrimage*, Cantos 1–2, turns its author and his hero into society idols. Cary's translation of Dante (last two parts).
1813		Wagner born. Southey poet laureate. Madame de Staël: *De l'Allemagne* translated (important work familiarizing France and England with the 'German Renaissance').
1814		Wordsworth: *The Excursion* (read and annotated by Blake, 1826). Scott: *Waverley* (first historical novel).

CHRONOLOGY

The Peninsular Wars against the French, led by Wellington and (in part) Sir John Moore through Portugal and Spain in two campaigns (1808-9 and 1809-14). Goya records the horrors of these in his very Blakean *Les desastres de la guerra* (1810-14). Parallel to this, Napoleon's 'Grande Armée' invades Russia (1812).

George III declared insane (October). The Prince Regent takes over (until 1820), thereby initiating the Regency Period, with Nash's terraces and crescents replacing the older, more solid, Georgian town architecture. Luddite riots in the Midlands and the North.

First steam vessel, the *Comet*, launched on the Clyde.

Westminster Bridge lighted with gas.

The allies (i.e. England, Austria, Russia, Prussia) enter Paris, forcing Napoleon to abdicate. The Vienna Congress established under Prince Metternich of Austria.

DATE	AUTHOR'S LIFE	LITERARY CONTEXT
1815	He is reduced to engraving designs for Wedgwood's chinaware catalogues.	
1816		Byron ostracized, leaves England. Coleridge: *Christabel* and *Kubla Khan*. T. L. Peacock: *Headlong Hall* (Socratic dialogue adapted to cultural satire). Shelley: *Alastor*. Elgin Marbles bought for nation. Charlotte Brontë born.
1817		Coleridge: *Biographia Literaria*.
1818	An upturn in Blake's career, though not financially, with Cumberland introducing him to the young painter John Linnell, who further introduces him to John Varley and Constable. A set of watercolours to *The Book of Job*, commissioned by Butts (one of his finest works). MS. poem *The Everlasting Gospel*.	Marx and Emily Brontë born. Shelley leaves England for Italy: *The Revolt of Islam*. Mary Shelley: *Frankenstein* (serious Gothic novel with Faustian-Promethean dimensions). Keats: *Endymion*. Thomas Bowdler: *The Family Shakespeare* (expurgated edition; hence 'bowdlerize').
1819		Queen Victoria, Ruskin and George Eliot born. Byron: *Don Juan*, Cantos 1-2. Keats: *Odes*.
1820	Engraves the *Laocoön Group* of Greek statuary (after an 1815 drawing made of a plaster-cast in the Royal Academy Schools), surrounding the design with cardinal beliefs: e.g. 'All that we See is Vision, from Generated Organs gone as soon as come,	Shelley: *Prometheus Unbound*. Keats: *Lamia, Isabella, Eve of St Agnes, Hyperion, and Other Poems*. John Clare: *Poems Descriptive of Rural Life*.

CHRONOLOGY

Napoleon escapes from exile on Elba. The Battle of Waterloo – where the French are finally defeated by the combined forces of the British under Wellington and the Prussians under Blücher. The Holy Alliance formed between France, Russia, Austria, Prussia, and Spain 'to promote peace and goodwill among nations on Christian principles' – in fact, to stifle all liberal reform. England not a party to this. Its national debt, due to the wars, now £860 million.

Agricultural riots, resulting from increased use of machinery and a very bad harvest, together with trade stagnation after the wars. Considerable poverty and social distress.

Continued existence of secret republican societies agitating for reform. The March of the Blanketeers: distressed operatives from Manchester, 'clad in blankets in which they intended to sleep', marched to London to petition the Prince Regent, but they were stopped and dispersed.

The Peterloo Massacre: a crowd of 50,000 collected on St Peter's Field, Manchester, to hear the popular reform agitator, Henry Hunt, when the yeomanry and hussars were summoned. Several were trampled to death and many injured during the charge (cf. Shelley's *The Mask of Anarchy*, which commemorates this). The Six Acts passed to counter such gatherings (prohibiting the assembling of seditious meetings, the publishing of seditious libels, and the uncontrolled possession of firearms in specific counties). The term 'Radical' first used (implying 'going to the *root* of distress'). Continued demands for Reform resisted in the main by Parliament.

Death of George III. Prince Regent becomes George IV. The Cato Street Conspiracy: a plot to assassinate the Cabinet Ministers of the day as they dined at Lord Harrowby's was foiled, some of the blame falling on the Radical Reformers. The trial of Queen Caroline. (In 1795 the Prince Regent had married Caroline of Brunswick, and, since the marriage had not worked, she had spent the Regency in Italy. On the Regent's accession, she returned to claim the throne with him, but he tried to get the marriage dissolved via Lord Liverpool and the House of Lords.)

DATE	AUTHOR'S LIFE	LITERARY CONTEXT
1820 cont	Permanent in The Imagination, Consider'd as Nothing by the Natural Man., One-leaf plate engraved, titled *On Homer's Poetry & On Virgil*.	
1821	Forced to sell his precious collection of Old Master prints assembled over fifty years. Major tempera painting on the theme of the Neoplatonist Porphyry's *On the Cave of the Nymphs* (in the *Odyssey*), now at Arlington Court, Devon. A series of seventeen tiny woodcuts for Dr R. J. Thornton's school edition of Virgil's *Eclogues* (a major influence on Samuel Palmer and Edward Calvert, the former finding 'in all such a mystic and dreamy glimmer as penetrates and kindles the innermost soul'). The Blakes move to 3 Fountain Court, Strand – their last residence.	Shelley: *A Defence of Poetry* written in reply to Peacock's *Four Ages of Poetry* (1820). Keats dies in Rome. Shelley's elegy, *Adonais*. De Quincey: *Confessions of an English Opium Eater*.
1822	Receives a Royal Academy donation of £25: 'Blake an able Designer & Engraver laboring under great distress'. A short 'play' etched: *The Ghost of Abel*, dedicated 'To Lord Byron in the Wilderness'.	Shelley drowned.
1823	Agrees to engrave his *Job Illustrations* for Linnell.	
1824	The latter brings the young Samuel Palmer to Fountain Court, who, as one of 'The Ancients' – a group of young artists in revolt against 'the	Byron dies while taking part in the Greek War of Liberation. *Westminster Review* started, mouthpiece of the

CHRONOLOGY

Faraday discovers the principle of the electric motor.

Lord Sidmouth retires as Home Secretary; Sir Robert Peel succeeds him. Lord Castlereagh commits suicide, succeeded by George Canning. The Greek War of Liberation against the Turks.

William Huskisson becomes President of the Board of Trade. This and the above two changes of office mark a shift away from the landed aristocracy to a more upper-middle-class government; hence non-repressive and reform-oriented, unlike Castlereagh and the Peterloo Massacre. Huskisson passes the Reciprocity of Duties Bill, whereby foreign ships entering British ports, instead of paying high import duties, are allowed the same as British ships, provided similar allowances are then made by the respective foreign countries. This signals the beginning of free trade. Peel introduces a bill to waive the death penalty for more than a hundred former crimes (e.g. theft, shoplifting, pickpocketing, forgery, etc.)

Three Labour Acts passed: i) to repeal the law allowing JPs to fix wages; ii) to repeal the law preventing workmen going to other parts of the country to seek employment; iii) the passing of the Combination Laws, permitting masters and men to combine to fix wages, but not for other purposes.

POEMS AND PROPHECIES

DATE	AUTHOR'S LIFE	LITERARY CONTEXT
1824 cont	moderns of the day' – introduces him to George Richmond, Edward Calvert, Arthur and Frederick Tatham, all based at Shoreham, Kent. Watercolours to Bunyan's *The Pilgrim's Progress* (and with reference to Bunyan, Fountain Court became known among the admiring Ancients as 'The House of the Interpreter'). Begins a series of drawings to Dante's *Divine Comedy*, commissioned by Linnell (102 unfinished watercolours, plus 7 unfinished engravings).	Utilitarians and influential during the Victorian period. James Hogg: *Confessions of a Justified Sinner*.
1825	The *Job Engravings* completed. The Blakes visit Palmer at Shoreham. Crabb Robinson visits Fountain Court (10 December).	Hazlitt: *The Spirit of the Age* (retrospective).
1826	Visit to Edward Calvert at Brixton.	
1827	Blake dies at Fountain Court (12 August) – singing, it is said – and is buried on the 17th near his parents in Bunhill Fields. His wife Catherine survives him till 1831.	University of London founded. Thomas Arnold headmaster of Rugby.
1828		Balzac: *La Comédie humaine* (until 1848).
1829		Carlyle: *Signs of the Times* (prophetic social critique with Blakean overtones in its attack on Locke and inner and outer 'Mechanism').
1830		Hugo: *Hernani* (first French Romantic drama). Coleridge: *On the Constitution of Church and State* (with its idea of the 'clerisy' as cultured elite). Tennyson: *Poems, Chiefly Lyrical*.

CHRONOLOGY

The Great Money Panic: a time of wild speculation and the founding of joint-stock companies on the basis of the most reckless schemes abroad. Many insolvencies, with banks overstretching themselves by issuing too much paper money. The government steps in to stem the tide and also make corn available on the market from the warehouses in order to mitigate social distress contingent on the financial débâcle. This latter as anticipating the Repeal of the Corn Laws (1846).

Wellington becomes Prime Minister, with Sir Robert Peel as Home Secretary. The Repeal of the Test and Corporation Acts (resisted by Lord Eldon and the Tories), enabling both Catholics and Nonconformists to hold civil and military office.
The Catholic Emancipation Bill – whereby Catholics were allowed to become MPs. This greatly assisted by the Catholic Association in Ireland under Daniel O'Connell (formed 1823). London watchmen abolished; 'Peelers' (policemen) introduced.

First railway opened between Liverpool and Manchester; Huskisson accidentally killed. The First Reform Bill introduced by Lord John Russell, advocating the abolition of 'rotten boroughs', the manufacturing cities allowed to vote, and with this the widening of the franchise to include all £10 per annum householders in such areas. The Victorian Age is underway.

I

WORKS
PRINTED AND ILLUSTRATED
BY BLAKE

THERE

is

NO NATURAL RELIGION

(1788)

[a]

The Argument

Man has no notion of moral fitness but from Education. Naturally he is only a natural organ subject to Sense.

I

Man cannot naturally Percieve but through his natural or bodily organs.

II

Man by his reasoning power can only compare & judge of what he has already perciev'd.

III

From a perception of only 3 senses or 3 elements none could deduce a fourth or fifth.

IV

None could have other than natural or organic thoughts if he had none but organic perceptions.

V

Man's desires are limited by his perceptions: none can desire what he has not perciev'd.

VI

The desires & perceptions of man untaught by any thing but organs of sense, must be limited to objects of sense.

Conclusion

If it were not for the Poetic or Prophetic Character, the Philosophic & Experimental would soon be at the ratio of all things & stand still, unable to do other than repeat the same dull round over again.

[♭]

I

Man's perceptions are not bounded by organs of perception: he percieves more than sense (tho' ever so acute) can discover.

II

Reason, or the ratio of all we have already known, is not the same that it shall be when we know more.

III

[This proposition is missing.]

IV

The bounded is loathed by its possessor. The same dull round, even of a universe, would soon become a mill with complicated wheels.

V

If the many become the same as the few when possess'd, More! More! is the cry of a mistaken soul: less than All cannot satisfy Man.

VI

If any could desire what he is incapable of possessing, despair must be his eternal lot.

VII

The desire of Man being Infinite, the possession is Infinite & himself Infinite.

Application

He who sees the Infinite in all things, sees God. He who sees the Ratio only, sees himself only.

Therefore God becomes as we are, that we may be as he is.

ALL RELIGIONS are ONE
(1788)

The Voice of one crying in the Wilderness.

The Argument

As the true method of knowledge is experiment, the true faculty of knowing must be the faculty which experiences. This faculty I treat of.

Principle 1st

That the Poetic Genius is the true Man, and that the body or outward form of Man is derived from the Poetic Genius. Likewise that the forms of all things are derived from their Genius, which by the Ancients was call'd an Angel & Spirit & Demon.

Principle 2^d

As all men are alike in outward form, So (and with the same infinite variety) all are alike in the Poetic Genius.

Principle 3^d

No man can think, write, or speak from his heart, but he must intend truth. Thus all sects of Philosophy are from the Poetic Genius adapted to the weaknesses of every individual.

Principle 4

As none by traveling over known lands can find out the unknown, So, from already acquired knowledge, Man could not acquire more; therefore an universal Poetic Genius exists.

Principle 5

The Religions of all Nations are derived from each Nation's different reception of the Poetic Genius, which is every where call'd the Spirit of Prophecy.

Principle 6
The Jewish & Christian Testaments are An original derivation from the Poetic Genius: this is necessary from the confined nature of bodily sensation.

Principle 7
As all men are alike (tho' infinitely various), So all Religions, &, as all similars, have one source.

The true Man is the source, he being the Poetic Genius.

SONGS

Of

INNOCENCE

and Of

EXPERIENCE

*Shewing the Two Contrary States
of the Human Soul*
(1794)

SONGS of INNOCENCE
(1789)

Introduction

PIPING down the valleys wild,
Piping songs of pleasant glee,
On a cloud I saw a child,
And he laughing said to me:

" Pipe a song about a Lamb! "
So I piped with merry chear.
" Piper, pipe that song again; "
So I piped: he wept to hear.

" Drop thy pipe, thy happy pipe,
Sing thy songs of happy chear."
So I sung the same again
While he wept with joy to hear.

" Piper, sit thee down and write
In a book that all may read."
So he vanish'd from my sight,
And I pluck'd a hollow reed,

WILLIAM BLAKE

And I made a rural pen,
And I stain'd the water clear,
And I wrote my happy songs
Every child may joy to hear.

The Shepherd

How sweet is the Shepherd's sweet lot!
From the morn to the evening he strays;
He shall follow his sheep all the day,
And his tongue shall be filled with praise.

For he hears the lambs' innocent call,
And he hears the ewes' tender reply;
He is watchful, while they are in peace
For they know when their Shepherd is nigh.

The Ecchoing Green

THE Sun does arise
And make happy the skies,
The merry bells ring
To welcome the Spring,
The sky-lark and thrush,
The birds of the bush,
Sing louder around
To the bells' chearful sound,
While our sports shall be seen
On the Ecchoing Green.

Old John with white hair
Does laugh away care,
Sitting under the oak
Among the old folk.
They laugh at our play,
And soon they all say:
" Such, such were the joys
When we all, girls & boys,

In our youth-time were seen
On the Ecchoing Green.''

Till the little ones, weary,
No more can be merry;
The sun does descend,
And our sports have an end.
Round the laps of their mothers
Many sisters and brothers,
Like birds in their nest,
Are ready for rest,
And sport no more seen
On the darkening Green.

The Lamb

LITTLE Lamb, who made thee:
Dost thou know who made thee?
Gave thee life & bid thee feed
By the stream & o'er the mead;
Gave thee clothing of delight,
Softest clothing, wooly, bright;
Gave thee such a tender voice
Making all the vales rejoice?
Little Lamb, who made thee?
Dost thou know who made thee?

Little Lamb, I'll tell thee,
Little Lamb, I'll tell thee:
He is called by thy name,
For he calls himself a Lamb.
He is meek & he is mild;
He became a little child:
I a child & thou a lamb,
We are called by his name.
Little Lamb, God bless thee.
Little Lamb, God bless thee.

The Little Black Boy

My mother bore me in the southern wild,
And I am black, but O! my soul is white;
White as an angel is the English child,
But I am black, as if bereav'd of light.

My mother taught me underneath a tree,
And sitting down before the heat of day
She took me on her lap and kissed me,
And pointing to the east, began to say:

" Look on the rising sun! there God does live,
And gives his light and gives his heat away;
And flowers and trees and beasts and men recieve
Comfort in morning, joy in the noon day.

" And we are put on earth a little space
That we may learn to bear the beams of love;
And these black bodies and this sun-burnt face
Is but a cloud, and like a shady grove;

" For when our souls have learn'd the heat to bear,
The cloud will vanish: we shall hear his voice,
Saying: ' come out from the grove, my love & care,
And round my golden tent like lambs rejoice.' "

Thus did my mother say, and kissed me.
And thus I say to little English boy:
When I from black and he from white cloud free
And round the tent of God like lambs we joy,

I'll shade him from the heat, till he can bear
To lean in joy upon our father's knee;
And then I'll stand and stroke his silver hair,
And be like him, and he will then love me.

The Blossom

MERRY Merry Sparrow,
Under leaves so green,
A happy Blossom
Sees you swift as arrow
Seek your cradle narrow
Near my Bosom.

Pretty Pretty Robin,
Under leaves so green,
A happy Blossom
Hears you sobbing, sobbing.
Pretty Pretty Robin
Near my Bosom.

The Chimney Sweeper

WHEN my mother died I was very young,
And my father sold me while yet my tongue
Could scarcely cry ' weep, weep, weep, weep,'
So your chimneys I sweep & in soot I sleep.

There's little Tom Dacre who cried when his head,
That curl'd like a lamb's back, was shav'd: so I said,
" Hush, Tom, never mind it, for when your head's bare
You know that the soot cannot spoil your white hair."

And so he was quiet, & that very night,
As Tom was a sleeping, he had such a sight,
That thousands of sweepers, Dick, Joe, Ned & Jack,
Were all of them lock'd up in coffins of black.

And by came an Angel who had a bright key,
And he open'd the coffins & set them all free;
Then down a green plain, leaping, laughing, they run,
And wash in a river, and shine in the Sun.

Then naked & white, all their bags left behind,
They rise upon clouds, and sport in the wind;
And the Angel told Tom, if he'd be a good boy,
He'd have God for his father & never want joy.

And so Tom awoke; and we rose in the dark,
And got with our bags & our brushes to work.
Tho' the morning was cold, Tom was happy & warm;
So if all do their duty they need not fear harm.

The Little Boy lost

" FATHER, father, where are you going?
O do not walk so fast.
Speak father, speak to your little boy,
Or else I shall be lost."

The night was dark, no father was there;
The child was wet with dew;
The mire was deep, & the child did weep,
And away the vapour flew.

The Little Boy found

THE little boy lost in the lonely fen,
Led by the wand'ring light,
Began to cry, but God ever nigh,
Appear'd like his father in white.

He kissed the child & by the hand led
And to his mother brought,
Who in sorrow pale, thro' the lonely dale,
Her little boy weeping sought.

Laughing Song

WHEN the green woods laugh with the voice of joy,
And the dimpling stream runs laughing by,
When the air does laugh with our merry wit,
And the green hill laughs with the noise of it,

When the meadows laugh with lively green,
And the grasshopper laughs in the merry scene,
When Mary and Susan and Emily
With their sweet round mouths sing " Ha, Ha, He! "

When the painted birds laugh in the shade
Where our table with cherries and nuts is spread,
Come live & be merry and join with me,
To sing the sweet chorus of " Ha, Ha, He! "

A CRADLE SONG

SWEET dreams, form a shade
O'er my lovely infant's head,
Sweet dreams of pleasant streams
By happy silent moony beams.

Sweet sleep, with soft down
Weave thy brows an infant crown.
Sweet sleep, Angel mild,
Hover o'er my happy child.

Sweet smiles, in the night
Hover over my delight;
Sweet smiles, Mother's smiles,
All the livelong night beguiles.

Sweet moans, dovelike sighs
Chase not slumber from thy eyes.
Sweet moans, sweeter smiles
All the dovelike moans beguiles.

Sleep, sleep, happy child,
All creation slept and smil'd;
Sleep, sleep, happy sleep,
While o'er thee thy mother weep.

Sweet babe, in thy face
Holy image I can trace.
Sweet babe, once like thee
Thy maker lay and wept for me:

Wept for me, for thee, for all,
When he was an infant small.
Thou his image ever see,
Heavenly face that smiles on thee:

Smiles on thee, on me, on all,
Who became an infant small.
Infant smiles are his own smiles,
Heaven & earth to peace beguiles.

The Divine Image

To Mercy Pity Peace and Love
All pray in their distress,
And to these virtues of delight
Return their thankfulness.

For Mercy Pity Peace and Love
Is God our father dear,
And Mercy Pity Peace and Love
Is Man his child and care.

For Mercy has a human heart,
Pity, a human face,
And Love, the human form divine,
And Peace, the human dress.

Then every man of every clime
That prays in his distress,
Prays to the human form divine,
Love Mercy Pity Peace.

And all must love the human form
In heathen, turk or jew.
Where Mercy Love & Pity dwell
There God is dwelling too.

HOLY THURSDAY

'Twas on a Holy Thursday, their innocent faces clean,
The children walking two & two, in red & blue & green,
Grey headed beadles walk'd before, with wands as white as snow,
Till into the high dome of Paul's they like Thames' waters flow.

O what a multitude they seem'd, these flowers of London town!
Seated in companies they sit with radiance all their own.
The hum of multitudes was there, but multitudes of lambs,
Thousands of little boys & girls raising their innocent hands.

Now like a mighty wind they raise to heaven the voice of song,
Or like harmonious thunderings the seats of heaven among.
Beneath them sit the aged men, wise guardians of the poor;
Then cherish pity, lest you drive an angel from your door.

Night

THE sun descending in the west
The evening star does shine,
The birds are silent in their nest
And I must seek for mine,
The moon, like a flower
In heaven's high bower,
With silent delight
Sits and smiles on the night.

Farewell green fields and happy groves
Where flocks have took delight;
Where lambs have nibbled, silent moves
The feet of angels bright;
Unseen they pour blessing
And joy without ceasing
On each bud and blossom
And each sleeping bosom.

They look in every thoughtless nest
Where birds are cover'd warm,
They visit caves of every beast
To keep them all from harm;
If they see any weeping
That should have been sleeping,
They pour sleep on their head
And sit down by their bed.

When wolves and tygers howl for prey
They pitying stand and weep,
Seeking to drive their thirst away
And keep them from the sheep;
But if they rush dreadful,
The angels most heedful
Recieve each mild spirit
New worlds to inherit.

And there the lion's ruddy eyes
Shall flow with tears of gold,
And pitying the tender cries
And walking round the fold
Saying, "wrath, by his meekness,
And by his health, sickness
Is driven away
From our immortal day.

" And now beside thee, bleating lamb,
I can lie down and sleep,
Or think on him who bore thy name,
Graze after thee and weep;
For, wash'd in life's river,
My bright mane for ever
Shall shine like the gold
As I guard o'er the fold."

Spring

SOUND the Flute!
Now it's mute.
Birds delight
Day and Night;
Nightingale
In the dale,
Lark in Sky,
Merrily,
Merrily, Merrily, to welcome in the Year.

Little Boy
Full of joy,
Little Girl
Sweet and small,
Cock does crow,
So do you;
Merry voice,
Infant noise,
Merrily, Merrily, to welcome in the Year.

Little Lamb
Here I am,
Come and lick
My white neck,
Let me pull
Your soft Wool,
Let me kiss
Your soft face;
Merrily, Merrily we welcome in the Year.

Nurse's Song

WHEN the voices of children are heard on the green
And laughing is heard on the hill,
My heart is at rest within my breast
And every thing else is still.

" Then come home, my children, the sun is gone down
And the dews of night arise;
Come, come, leave off play, and let us away
Till the morning appears in the skies."

" No, no, let us play, for it is yet day
And we cannot go to sleep;
Besides, in the sky the little birds fly
And the hills are all cover'd with sheep."

" Well, well, go & play till the light fades away
And then go home to bed."
The little ones leaped & shouted & laugh'd
And all the hills ecchoed.

Infant Joy

" I have no name:
I am but two days old."
What shall I call thee?
" I happy am,
Joy is my name."
Sweet joy befall thee!

Pretty joy!
Sweet joy but two days old,
Sweet joy I call thee:
Thou dost smile,
I sing the while
Sweet joy befall thee.

A Dream

ONCE a dream did weave a shade
O'er my Angel-guarded bed,
That an Emmet lost its way
Where on grass methought I lay.

Troubled, 'wilder'd and folorn,
Dark, benighted, travel-worn,
Over many a tangled spray,
All heart-broke I heard her say:

"O my children! do they cry?
Do they hear their father sigh?
Now they look abroad to see,
Now return and weep for me."

Pitying, I dropp'd a tear;
But I saw a glow-worm near,
Who replied: "What wailing wight
Calls the watchman of the night?

"I am set to light the ground,
While the beetle goes his round:
Follow now the beetle's hum;
Little wanderer, hie thee home."

On Another's Sorrow

CAN I see another's woe
And not be in sorrow too?
Can I see another's grief
And not seek for kind relief?

Can I see a falling tear
And not feel my sorrow's share?
Can a father see his child
Weep, nor be with sorrow fill'd?

Can a mother sit and hear
An infant groan an infant fear?
No, no never can it be,
Never, never can it be.

And can he who smiles on all
Hear the wren with sorrows small,
Hear the small bird's grief & care,
Hear the woes that infants bear,

And not sit beside the nest
Pouring pity in their breast,
And not sit the cradle near
Weeping tear on infant's tear,

And not sit both night & day
Wiping all our tears away?
O! no never can it be,
Never, never can it be.

He doth give his joy to all,
He becomes an infant small,
He becomes a man of woe,
He doth feel the sorrow too.

Think not thou canst sigh a sigh
And thy maker is not by;
Think not thou canst weep a tear
And thy maker is not near.

O! he gives to us his joy
That our grief he may destroy;
Till our grief is fled & gone
He doth sit by us and moan.

SONGS of EXPERIENCE

(1794)

Introduction

HEAR the voice of the Bard!
Who Present, Past, & Future sees,
Whose ears have heard
The Holy Word
That walk'd among the ancient trees,

Calling the lapsed Soul,
And weeping in the evening dew,
That might controll
The starry pole
And fallen fallen light renew!

" O Earth, O Earth return!
Arise from out the dewy grass;
Night is worn
And the morn
Rises from the slumberous mass.

" Turn away no more:
Why wilt thou turn away?
The starry floor
The wat'ry shore
Is giv'n thee till the break of day."

EARTH'S Answer

EARTH rais'd up her head
From the darkness dread & drear.
Her light fled:
Stony dread!
And her locks cover'd with grey despair.

" Prison'd on wat'ry shore,
Starry Jealousy does keep my den
Cold and hoar;
Weeping o'er,
I hear the father of the ancient men.

" Selfish father of men,
Cruel, jealous, selfish fear:
Can delight,
Chain'd in night,
The virgins of youth and morning bear?

" Does spring hide its joy
When buds and blossoms grow?
Does the sower
Sow by night?
Or the plowman in darkness plow?

" Break this heavy chain
That does freeze my bones around.
Selfish! vain!
Eternal bane!
That free Love with bondage bound."

The CLOD & the PEBBLE

" Love seeketh not Itself to please
Nor for itself hath any care,
But for another gives its ease
And builds a Heaven in Hell's despair.''

So sung a little Clod of Clay
Trodden with the cattle's feet,
But a Pebble of the brook
Warbled out these metres meet:

" Love seeketh only Self to please,
To bind another to Its delight,
Joys in another's loss of ease,
And builds a Hell in Heaven's despite."

HOLY THURSDAY

Is this a holy thing to see
In a rich and fruitful land,
Babes reduc'd to misery,
Fed with cold and usurous hand?

Is that trembling cry a song?
Can it be a song of joy?
And so many children poor?
It is a land of poverty!

And their sun does never shine,
And their fields are bleak & bare,
And their ways are fill'd with thorns:
It is eternal winter there.

For where-e'er the sun does shine,
And where-e'er the rain does fall,
Babe can never hunger there,
Nor poverty the mind appall.

The Little Girl Lost

IN futurity
I prophetic see
That the earth from sleep
(Grave the sentence deep)

Shall arise and seek
For her maker meek,
And the desart wild
Become a garden mild.

In the southern clime
Where the summer's prime
Never fades away,
Lovely Lyca lay.

Seven summers old
Lovely Lyca told;
She had wander'd long
Hearing wild birds' song.

" Sweet sleep, come to me
Underneath this tree.
Do father, mother, weep,
Where can Lyca sleep?

" Lost in desart wild
Is your little child.
How can Lyca sleep
If her mother weep?

" If her heart does ake
Then let Lyca wake;
If my mother sleep,
Lyca shall not weep.

" Frowning frowning night,
O'er this desart bright
Let thy moon arise
While I close my eyes."

Sleeping Lyca lay
While the beasts of prey,
Come from caverns deep,
View'd the maid asleep.

The kingly lion stood
And the virgin view'd,
Then he gambol'd round
O'er the hallow'd ground.

Leopards, tygers play
Round her as she lay,
While the lion old
Bow'd his mane of gold,

And her bosom lick,
And upon her neck
From his eyes of flame
Ruby tears there came;

While the lioness
Loos'd her slender dress,
And naked they convey'd
To caves the sleeping maid.

The Little Girl Found

ALL the night in woe
Lyca's parents go
Over vallies deep,
While the desarts weep.

Tired and woe-begone,
Hoarse with making moan,
Arm in arm seven days
They trac'd the desart ways.

Seven nights they sleep
Among shadows deep,
And dream they see their child
Starv'd in desart wild.

Pale, thro' pathless ways
The fancied image strays,
Famish'd, weeping, weak
With hollow piteous shriek.

Rising from unrest,
The trembling woman prest
With feet of weary woe:
She could no further go.

In his arms he bore
Her arm'd with sorrow sore,
Till before their way
A couching lion lay.

Turning back was vain:
Soon his heavy mane
Bore them to the ground,
Then he stalk'd around

Smelling to his prey,
But their fears allay
When he licks their hands
And silent by them stands.

They look upon his eyes
Fill'd with deep surprise,
And wondering behold
A spirit arm'd in gold.

On his head a crown,
On his shoulders down
Flow'd his golden hair.
Gone was all their care.

" Follow me," he said;
" Weep not for the maid;
In my palace deep
Lyca lies asleep."

Then they followed
Where the vision led,
And saw their sleeping child
Among tygers wild.

To this day they dwell
In a lonely dell,
Nor fear the wolvish howl
Nor the lion's growl.

The Chimney Sweeper

A LITTLE black thing among the snow,
Crying ' weep, weep,' in notes of woe!
" Where are thy father & mother, say? "
" They are both gone up to the church to pray.

" Because I was happy upon the heath,
And smil'd among the winter's snow,
They clothed me in the clothes of death,
And taught me to sing the notes of woe.

" And because I am happy, & dance & sing,
They think they have done me no injury,
And are gone to praise God & his Priest & King,
Who make up a heaven of our misery."

NURSE'S Song

WHEN the voices of children are heard on the green
And whisp'rings are in the dale,
The days of my youth rise fresh in my mind:
My face turns green and pale.

Then come home my children, the sun is gone down
And the dews of night arise;
Your spring & your day are wasted in play,
And your winter and night in disguise.

The SICK ROSE

O ROSE, thou art sick:
The invisible worm
That flies in the night
In the howling storm,

Has found out thy bed
Of crimson joy,
And his dark secret love
Does thy life destroy.

THE FLY

LITTLE Fly,
Thy summer's play
My thoughtless hand
Has brush'd away.

Am not I
A fly like thee?
Or art not thou
A man like me?

For I dance
And drink & sing,
Till some blind hand
Shall brush my wing.

If thought is life
And strength & breath,
And the want
Of thought is death,

Then am I
A happy fly
If I live
Or if I die.

The Angel

I DREAMT a Dream! what can it mean?
And that I was a maiden Queen
Guarded by an Angel mild:
Witless woe was ne'er beguil'd!

And I wept both night and day,
And he wip'd my tears away,
And I wept both day and night,
And hid from him my heart's delight.

So he took his wings and fled;
Then the morn blush'd rosy red;
I dried my tears & arm'd my fears
With ten thousand shields and spears.

Soon my Angel came again:
I was arm'd, he came in vain,
For the time of youth was fled
And grey hairs were on my head.

The Tyger

TYGER, Tyger, burning bright
In the forests of the night,
What immortal hand or eye
Could frame thy fearful symmetry?

In what distant deeps or skies
Burnt the fire of thine eyes?
On what wings dare he aspire?
What the hand dare sieze the fire?

And what shoulder, & what art,
Could twist the sinews of thy heart?
And when thy heart began to beat,
What dread hand? & what dread feet?

What the hammer? what the chain,
In what furnace was thy brain?
What the anvil? what dread grasp
Dare its deadly terrors clasp?

When the stars threw down their spears
And water'd heaven with their tears,
Did he smile his work to see?
Did he who made the Lamb make thee?

Tyger, Tyger, burning bright
In the forests of the night,
What immortal hand or eye
Dare frame thy fearful symmetry?

My Pretty ROSE TREE

A FLOWER was offer'd to me,
Such a flower as May never bore;
But I said " I've a Pretty Rose-tree,"
And I passed the sweet flower o'er.

Then I went to my Pretty Rose-tree,
To tend her by day and by night;
But my Rose turn'd away with jealousy,
And her thorns were my only delight.

AH! SUN-FLOWER

Ah Sun-flower! weary of time,
Who countest the steps of the Sun,
Seeking after that sweet golden clime
Where the traveller's journey is done:

Where the Youth pined away with desire,
And the pale Virgin shrouded in snow,
Arise from their graves and aspire
Where my Sun-flower wishes to go.

THE LILLY

THE modest Rose puts forth a thorn,
The humble Sheep a threat'ning horn,
While the Lilly white shall in Love delight,
Nor a thorn nor a threat stain her beauty bright.

The GARDEN of LOVE

I WENT to the Garden of Love,
And saw what I never had seen:
A Chapel was built in the midst,
Where I used to play on the green.

And the gates of this Chapel were shut,
And ' Thou shalt not ' writ over the door;
So I turn'd to the Garden of Love
That so many sweet flowers bore;

And I saw it was filled with graves,
And tomb-stones where flowers should be;
And Priests in black gowns were walking their rounds,
And binding with briars my joys & desires.

The Little Vagabond

DEAR Mother, dear Mother, the Church is cold,
But the Ale-house is healthy & pleasant & warm;
Besides I can tell where I am used well,
Such usage in heaven will never do well.

But if at the Church they would give us some Ale
And a pleasant fire our souls to regale,
We'd sing and we'd pray all the live-long day,
Nor ever once wish from the Church to stray.

Then the Parson might preach & drink & sing,
And we'd be as happy as birds in the spring;
And modest dame Lurch, who is always at Church,
Would not have bandy children, nor fasting, nor birch.

And God, like a father rejoicing to see
His children as pleasant and happy as he,
Would have no more quarrel with the Devil or the Barrel,
But kiss him & give him both drink and apparel.

LONDON

I WANDER thro' each charter'd street
Near where the charter'd Thames does flow,
And mark in every face I meet
Marks of weakness, marks of woe.

In every cry of every Man,
In every Infant's cry of fear,
In every voice, in every ban,
The mind-forg'd manacles I hear.

How the Chimney-sweeper's cry
Every black'ning Church appalls,
And the hapless Soldier's sigh
Runs in blood down Palace walls.

But most thro' midnight streets I hear
How the youthful Harlot's curse
Blasts the new born Infant's tear,
And blights with plagues the Marriage hearse.

The Human Abstract

PITY would be no more
If we did not make somebody Poor;
And Mercy no more could be
If all were as happy as we.

And mutual fear brings peace,
Till the selfish loves increase:
Then Cruelty knits a snare
And spreads his baits with care

He sits down with holy fears
And waters the ground with tears:
Then Humility takes its root
Underneath his foot.

Soon spreads the dismal shade
Of Mystery over his head,
And the Catterpiller and Fly
Feed on the Mystery.

And it bears the fruit of Deceit,
Ruddy and sweet to eat,
And the Raven his nest has made
In its thickest shade.

The Gods of the earth and sea
Sought thro' Nature to find this Tree,
But their search was all in vain:
There grows one in the Human Brain.

INFANT SORROW

My mother groan'd! my father wept,
Into the dangerous world I leapt,
Helpless, naked, piping loud,
Like a fiend hid in a cloud.

Struggling in my father's hands,
Striving against my swadling bands,
Bound and weary, I thought best
To sulk upon my mother's breast.

A POISON TREE

I was angry with my friend,
I told my wrath, my wrath did end;
I was angry with my foe,
I told it not, my wrath did grow.

And I water'd it in fears,
Night & morning with my tears;
And I sunned it with smiles,
And with soft deceitful wiles.

And it grew both day and night,
Till it bore an apple bright;
And my foe beheld it shine,
And he knew that it was mine,

And into my garden stole
When the night had veil'd the pole:
In the morning glad I see
My foe outstretch'd beneath the tree.

Little BOY Lost [1]

" NOUGHT loves another as itself,
Nor venerates another so,
Nor is it possible to Thought
A greater than itself to know:

" And Father, how can I love you
Or any of my brothers more?
I love you like the little bird
That picks up crumbs around the door."

The Priest sat by and heard the child,
In trembling zeal he siez'd his hair:
He led him by his little coat,
And all admir'd the Priestly care.

And standing on the altar high,
" Lo, what a fiend is here! " said he,
" One who sets reason up for judge
Of our most holy Mystery."

The weeping child could not be heard,
The weeping parents wept in vain;
They strip'd him to his little shirt,
And bound him in an iron chain;

And burn'd him in a holy place,
Where many had been burn'd before:
The weeping parents wept in vain.
Are such things done on Albion's shore?

[1] See note on p. 381.

A Little GIRL Lost

Children of the future Age
Reading this indignant page,
Know that in a former time
Love! sweet Love! was thought a crime.

In the Age of Gold,
Free from winter's cold,
Youth and maiden bright
To the holy light,
Naked in the sunny beams delight.

Once a youthful pair,
Fill'd with softest care,
Met in garden bright
Where the holy light
Had just remov'd the curtains of the night.

There, in rising day,
On the grass they play;
Parents were afar,
Strangers came not near,
And the maiden soon forgot her fear.

Tired with kisses sweet,
They agree to meet
When the silent sleep
Waves o'er heaven's deep,
And the weary tired wanderers weep.

To her father white
Came the maiden bright;
But his loving look,
Like the holy book,
All her tender limbs with terror shook.

"Ona! pale and weak!
To thy father speak:
O the trembling fear!
O the dismal care!
That shakes the blossoms of my hoary hair."

To Tirzah

WHATE'ER is Born of Mortal Birth
Must be consumed with the Earth
To rise from Generation free:
Then what have I to do with thee?

The Sexes sprung from Shame & Pride,
Blow'd in the morn, in evening died;
But Mercy chang'd Death into Sleep;
The Sexes rose to work & weep.

Thou Mother of my Mortal part,
With cruelty didst mould my Heart,
And with false self-decieving tears
Didst bind my Nostrils Eyes & Ears:

Didst close my Tongue in senseless clay,
And me to Mortal Life betray.
The Death of Jesus set me free:[1]
Then what have I to do with thee?

The School Boy

I LOVE to rise in a summer morn
When the birds sing on every tree;
The distant huntsman winds his horn,
And the sky-lark sings with me.
O! what sweet company.

But to go to school in a summer morn,
O! it drives all joy away;
Under a cruel eye outworn
The little ones spend the day
In sighing and dismay.

[1] It is Raised a Spiritual Body.

This quotation from I. Corinth. xv. 44, is inscribed by Blake on one of the figures of the illustration to this poem.

Ah! then at times I drooping sit,
And spend many an anxious hour,
Nor in my book can I take delight,
Nor sit in learning's bower,
Worn thro' with the dreary shower.

How can the bird that is born for joy
Sit in a cage and sing?
How can a child when fears annoy
But droop his tender wing
And forget his youthful spring?

O! father & mother, if buds are nip'd
And blossoms blown away,
And if the tender plants are strip'd
Of their joy in the springing day,
By sorrow and care's dismay,

How shall the summer arise in joy,
Or the summer fruits appear?
Or how shall we gather what griefs destroy,
Or bless the mellowing year
When the blasts of winter appear?

The Voice of the Ancient Bard

YOUTH of delight, come hither
And see the opening morn,
Image of truth new born.
Doubt is fled & clouds of reason,
Dark disputes & artful teazing.
Folly is an endless maze,
Tangled roots perplex her ways,
How many have fallen there!
They stumble all night over bones of the dead,
And feel they know not what but care,
And wish to lead others when they should be led.

NOTE.—*Blake etched the following poem upon a copper plate in his usual manner, but as he never included the verses in any copy of the Songs of Experience they may safely be regarded as having been rejected by him.*

A Divine Image

CRUELTY has a Human Heart,
And Jealousy a Human Face;
Terror the Human Form Divine,
And Secrecy the Human Dress.

The Human Dress is forged Iron,
The Human Form a fiery Forge,
The Human Face a Furnace seal'd,
The Human Heart its hungry Gorge.

THE

BOOK OF THEL

(1789)

THEL'S Motto

DOES the Eagle know what is in the pit?
Or wilt thou go ask the Mole:
Can Wisdom be put in a silver rod?
Or Love in a golden bowl?

I

THE daughters of [1] Mne Seraphim led round their sunny flocks,
All but the youngest: she in paleness sought the secret air,
To fade away like morning beauty from her mortal day;
Down by the river of Adona her soft voice is heard,
And thus her gentle lamentation falls like morning dew: 5

" O life of this our spring! why fades the lotus of the water?
Why fade these children of the spring? born but to smile & fall.
Ah! Thel is like a wat'ry bow, and like a parting cloud,
Like a reflection in a glass, like shadows in the water,
Like dreams of infants, like a smile upon an infant's face,   10
Like the dove's voice, like transient day, like music in the air.
Ah! gentle may I lay me down and gentle rest my head,
And gentle sleep the sleep of death, and gentle hear the voice
Of him that walketh in the garden in the evening time."

The Lilly of the Valley, breathing in the humble grass,   15
Answer'd the lovely maid and said: "I am a wat'ry weed,
And I am very small and love to dwell in lowly vales,
So weak the gilded butterfly scarce perches on my head;

[1] " In the list of spirits in Agrippa's *Occult Philosophy*, II. xxii., from which Blake took the names *Tiriel* and *Zazel*, occurs the name *Bne Seraphim* (the sons of the Seraphim), who represent ' the Intelligencies of Venus.' It is reasonable to suppose that Blake intended to use this name, but made a mistake in the engraving which he could not correct. The change of *Bne* to *Mne* is apparently meaningless."—S. FOSTER DAMON, *William Blake: His Philosophy and Symbols*.

Yet I am visited from heaven, and he that smiles on all   19
Walks in the valley, and each morn over me spreads his hand
Saying, ' rejoice, thou humble grass, thou new-born lilly flower,
Thou gentle maid of silent valleys and of modest brooks;
For thou shalt be clothed in light, and fed with morning manna,
Till summer's heat melts thee beside the fountains and the springs
To flourish in eternal vales ': then why should Thel complain?
Why should the mistress of the vales of Har utter a sigh? ''   26

She ceas'd & smil'd in tears, then sat down in her silver shrine.

Thel answer'd: '' O thou little virgin of the peaceful valley,
Giving to those that cannot crave, the voiceless, the o'ertired;
Thy breath doth nourish the innocent lamb, he smells thy milky
          garments,
He crops thy flowers while thou sittest smiling in his face,   31
Wiping his mild and meekin mouth from all contagious taints.
Thy wine doth purify the golden honey; thy perfume,
Which thou dost scatter on every little blade of grass that springs,
Revives the milked cow, & tames the fire-breathing steed.   35
But Thel is like a faint cloud kindled at the rising sun:
I vanish from my pearly throne, and who shall find my place? ''

'' Queen of the vales,'' the Lilly answer'd, '' ask the tender cloud
And it shall tell thee why it glitters in the morning sky,
And why it scatters its bright beauty thro' the humid air.   40
Descend, O little cloud, & hover before the eyes of Thel.''

The Cloud descended, and the Lilly bow'd her modest head
And went to mind her numerous charge among the verdant grass.

II

'' O little Cloud,'' the virgin said, '' I charge thee tell to me
Why thou complainest not when in one hour thou fade away:
Then we shall seek thee, but not find: ah! Thel is like to thee:
I pass away: yet I complain, and no one hears my voice.''

The Cloud then shew'd his golden head & his bright form emerg'd,
Hovering and glittering on the air before the face of Thel.   6

'' O virgin, know'st thou not, our steeds drink of the golden springs
Where Luvah doth renew his horses: look'st thou on my youth,
And fearest thou, because I vanish and am seen no more,
Nothing remains? O maid, I tell thee, when I pass away,   10
It is to tenfold life, to love, to peace, and raptures holy
Unseen descending weigh my light wings upon balmy flowers

And court the fair eyed dew to take me to her shining tent:
The weeping virgin, trembling kneels before the risen sun,
Till we arise, link'd in a golden band, and never part,   15
But walk united, bearing food to all our tender flowers."

" Dost thou, O little Cloud? I fear that I am not like thee,
For I walk thro' the vales of Har, and smell the sweetest flowers,
But I feed not the little flowers. I hear the warbling birds,
But I feed not the warbling birds: they fly and seek their food:
But Thel delights in these no more, because I fade away;   21
And all shall say, ' without a use this shining woman liv'd,
Or did she only live to be at death the food of worms? ' "

The Cloud reclin'd upon his airy throne and answer'd thus:

" Then if thou art the food of worms, O virgin of the skies,   25
How great thy use, how great thy blessing! every thing that lives
Lives not alone, nor for itself: fear not, and I will call
The weak worm from its lowly bed, and thou shalt hear its voice.
Come forth, worm of the silent valley, to thy pensive queen."

The helpless worm arose and sat upon the Lilly's leaf,   30
And the bright Cloud sail'd on, to find his partner in the vale.

III

Then Thel astonish'd view'd the Worm upon its dewy bed.

" Art thou a Worm? image of weakness, art thou but a Worm?
I see thee like an infant wrapped in the Lilly's leaf.
Ah, weep not, little voice, thou canst not speak, but thou canst
     weep.
Is this a Worm? I see thee lay helpless & naked, weeping   5
And none to answer, none to cherish thee with mother's smiles."

The Clod of Clay heard the Worm's voice & rais'd her pitying head.
She bow'd over the weeping infant, and her life exhal'd
In milky fondness: then on Thel she fix'd her humble eyes.

" O beauty of the vales of Har, we live not for ourselves.   10
Thou seest me the meanest thing, and so I am indeed:
My bosom of itself is cold and of itself is dark,
But he that loves the lowly, pours his oil upon my head
And kisses me, and binds his nuptial bands around my breast,
And says: ' Thou mother of my children, I have loved thee,   15
And I have given thee a crown that none can take away.'
But how this is, sweet maid, I know not, and I cannot know;
I ponder, and I cannot ponder; yet I live and love."

The daughter of beauty wip'd her pitying tears with her white
    veil,
And said: " Alas! I knew not this, and therefore did I weep.   20
That God would love a Worm I knew, and punish the evil foot
That wilful bruis'd its helpless form; but that he cherish'd it
With milk and oil I never knew, and therefore did I weep;
And I complain'd in the mild air, because I fade away   24
And lay me down in thy cold bed, and leave my shining lot."

" Queen of the vales," the matron Clay answer'd, " I heard thy
    sighs,
And all thy moans flew o'er my roof, but I have call'd them down.
Wilt thou, O Queen, enter my house? 'tis given thee to enter
And to return: fear nothing, enter with thy virgin feet."   29

IV

The eternal gates' terrific porter lifted the northern bar.
Thel enter'd in & saw the secrets of the land unknown.
She saw the couches of the dead, & where the fibrous roots
Of every heart on earth infixes deep its restless twists:
A land of sorrows & of tears where never smile was seen.   5

She wander'd in the land of clouds thro' valleys dark, list'ning
Dolours and lamentations; waiting oft beside a dewy grave
She stood in silence, list'ning to the voices of the ground,
Till to her own grave plot she came, & there she sat down,
And heard this voice of sorrow breathed from the hollow pit: 10

" Why cannot the Ear be closed to its own destruction?
Or the glist'ning Eye to the poison of a smile!
Why are Eyelids stor'd with arrows ready drawn,
Where a thousand fighting men in ambush lie,
Or an Eye of gifts & graces show'ring fruits & coined gold?   15
Why a Tongue impress'd with honey from every wind?
Why an Ear, a whirlpool fierce to draw creations in?
Why a Nostril wide inhaling terror trembling & affright?
Why a tender curb upon the youthful burning boy?
Why a little curtain of flesh on the bed of our desire? "   20

The Virgin started from her seat, & with a shriek
Fled back unhinder'd till she came into the vales of Har.

The End

THE MARRIAGE
OF
HEAVEN AND HELL

(About 1793)

The Argument

RINTRAH roars & shakes his fires in the burden'd air;
Hungry clouds swag on the deep.

Once meek, and in a perilous path,
The just man kept his course along
The vale of death.
Roses are planted where thorns grow,
And on the barren heath
Sing the honey bees.

Then the perilous path was planted,
And a river and a spring
On every cliff and tomb,
And on the bleached bones
Red clay brought forth;

Till the villain left the paths of ease,
To walk in perilous paths, and drive
The just man into barren climes.

Now the sneaking serpent walks
In mild humility,
And the just man rages in the wilds
Where lions roam.

Rintrah roars & shakes his fires in the burden'd air;
Hungry clouds swag on the deep.

As a new heaven is begun, and it is now thirty-three years since its advent, the Eternal Hell revives. And lo! Swedenborg is the Angel sitting at the tomb: his writings are the linen clothes folded up. Now is the dominion of Edom, & the return of Adam into Paradise: see Isaiah xxxiv & xxxv Chap.

Without Contraries is no progression. Attraction and Repulsion, Reason and Energy, Love and Hate, are necessary to Human existence.

From these contraries spring what the religious call Good & Evil. Good is the passive that obeys Reason. Evil is the active springing from Energy.

Good is Heaven. Evil is Hell.

The voice of the Devil

All Bibles or sacred codes have been the causes of the following Errors.

1. That Man has two real existing principles, Viz: a Body & a Soul.

2. That Energy, call'd Evil, is alone from the Body, & that Reason, call'd Good, is alone from the Soul.

3. That God will torment Man in Eternity for following his Energies.

But the following Contraries to these are True.

1. Man has no Body distinct from his Soul; for that call'd Body is a portion of Soul discern'd by the five Senses, the chief inlets of Soul in this age.

2. Energy is the only life and is from the Body, and Reason is the bound or outward circumference of Energy.

3. Energy is Eternal Delight.

Those who restrain desire, do so because theirs is weak enough to be restrained; and the restrainer or reason usurps its place & governs the unwilling.

And being restrain'd, it by degrees becomes passive, till it is only the shadow of desire.

The history of this is written in Paradise Lost, & the Governor or Reason is call'd Messiah.

And the original Archangel, or possessor of the command of the heavenly host, is call'd the Devil or Satan, and his children are call'd Sin & Death.

But in the Book of Job, Milton's Messiah is call'd Satan.

For this history has been adopted by both parties.

It indeed appear'd to Reason as if Desire was cast out; but the Devil's account is, that the Messiah fell, & formed a heaven of what he stole from the Abyss.

This is shewn in the Gospel, where he prays to the Father to send the comforter, or Desire, that Reason may have Ideas to build on, the Jehovah of the Bible being no other than he who dwells in flaming fire.

Know that after Christ's death, he became Jehovah.

But in Milton, the Father is Destiny, the Son a Ratio of the five senses, & the Holy-ghost Vacuum!

Note. The reason Milton wrote in fetters when he wrote of Angels & God, and at liberty when of Devils & Hell, is because he was a true Poet and of the Devil's party without knowing it.

A Memorable Fancy

As I was walking among the fires of hell, delighted with the enjoyments of Genius, which to Angels look like torment and insanity, I collected some of their Proverbs, thinking that as the sayings used in a nation mark its character, so the Proverbs of Hell shew the nature of Infernal wisdom better than any description of buildings or garments.

When I came home, on the abyss of the five senses, where a flat sided steep frowns over the present world, I saw a mighty Devil folded in black clouds hovering on the sides of the rock: with corroding fires he wrote the following sentence now percieved by the minds of men, & read by them on earth.

How do you know but ev'ry Bird that cuts the airy way,
Is an immense world of delight, clos'd by your senses five?

Proverbs of Hell

[1] 1. In seed time learn, in harvest teach, in winter enjoy.
2. Drive your cart and your plow over the bones of the dead.
3. The road of excess leads to the palace of wisdom.
4. Prudence is a rich ugly old maid courted by Incapacity.
5. He who desires but acts not, breeds pestilence.
6. The cut worm forgives the plow.
7. Dip him in the river who loves water.
8. A fool sees not the same tree that a wise man sees.
9. He whose face gives no light, shall never become a star.
10. Eternity is in love with the productions of time.
11. The busy bee has no time for sorrow.
12. The hours of folly are measur'd by the clock, but of wisdom no clock can measure.
13. All wholsom food is caught without a net or a trap.
14. Bring out number weight & measure in a year of dearth.
15. No bird soars too high if he soars with his own wings.
16. A dead body revenges not injuries.
17. The most sublime act is to set another before you.
18. If the fool would persist in his folly he would become wise.
19. Folly is the cloke of knavery.
20. Shame is Pride's cloke.
21. Prisons are built with stones of Law, Brothels with bricks of Religion.
22. The pride of the peacock is the glory of God.
23. The lust of the goat is the bounty of God.
24. The wrath of the lion is the wisdom of God.
25. The nakedness of woman is the work of God.
26. Excess of sorrow laughs. Excess of joy weeps.
27. The roaring of lions, the howling of wolves, the raging of the stormy sea, and the destructive sword, are portions of eternity too great for the eye of man.
28. The fox condemns the trap, not himself.
29. Joys impregnate. Sorrows bring forth.
30. Let man wear the fell of the lion, woman the fleece of the sheep.
31. The bird a nest, the spider a web, man friendship.

[1] Blake did not number these proverbs; numbers are added here for convenience in reference.

32. The selfish smiling fool, & the sullen frowning fool shall be both thought wise, that they may be a rod.

33. What is now proved was once only imagin'd.

34. The rat, the mouse, the fox, the rabbet, watch the roots; the lion, the tyger, the horse, the elephant, watch the fruits.

35. The cistern contains: the fountain overflows.

36. One thought fills immensity.

37. Always be ready to speak your mind and a base man will avoid you.

38. Every thing possible to be believ'd is an image of truth.

39. The eagle never lost so much time as when he submitted to learn of the crow.

40. The fox provides for himself, but God provides for the lion.

41. Think in the morning. Act in the noon. Eat in the evening. Sleep in the night.

42. He who has suffer'd you to impose on him knows you.

43. As the plow follows words, so God rewards prayers.

44. The tygers of wrath are wiser than the horses of instruction.

45. Expect poison from the standing water.

46. You never know what is enough unless you know what is more than enough.

47. Listen to the fool's reproach! it is a kingly title!

48. The eyes of fire, the nostrils of air, the mouth of water, the beard of earth.

49. The weak in courage is strong in cunning.

50. The apple tree never asks the beech how he shall grow, nor the lion the horse, how he shall take his prey.

51. The thankful reciever bears a plentiful harvest.

52. If others had not been foolish, we should be so.

53. The soul of sweet delight can never be defil'd.

54. When thou seest an Eagle, thou seest a portion of Genius. lift up thy head!

55. As the catterpiller chooses the fairest leaves to lay her eggs on, so the priest lays his curse on the fairest joys.

56. To create a little flower is the labour of ages.

57. Damn braces. Bless relaxes.

58. The best wine is the oldest, the best water the newest.

59. Prayers plow not! Praises reap not!

60. Joys laugh not! Sorrows weep not!

61. The head Sublime, the heart Pathos, the genitals Beauty, the hands & feet Proportion.

62. As the air to a bird or the sea to a fish, so is contempt to the contemptible.

63. The crow wish'd every thing was black, the owl that every thing was white.

64. Exuberance is Beauty.

65. If the lion was advised by the fox, he would be cunning.

66. Improvement makes strait roads, but the crooked roads without Improvement are roads of Genius.

67. Sooner murder an infant in its cradle than nurse unacted desires.

68. Where man is not, nature is barren.

69. Truth can never be told so as to be understood, and not be believ'd.

70. Enough! or Too much.

The ancient Poets animated all sensible objects with Gods or Geniuses, calling them by the names and adorning them with the properties of woods, rivers, mountains, lakes, cities, nations, and whatever their enlarged & numerous senses could percieve.

And particularly they studied the genius of each city & country, placing it under its mental deity;

Till a system was formed, which some took advantage of & enslav'd the vulgar by attempting to realize or abstract the mental deities from their objects: thus began Priesthood,

Choosing forms of worship from poetic tales.

And at length they pronounc'd that the Gods had order'd such things.

Thus men forgot that All deities reside in the human breast.

A Memorable Fancy

The Prophets Isaiah and Ezekiel dined with me, and I asked them how they dared so roundly to assert that God spoke to them; and whether they did not think at the time that they would be misunderstood, & so be the cause of imposition.

Isaiah answer'd: " I saw no God, nor heard any, in a finite organical perception; but my senses discover'd the infinite in every thing, and as I was then perswaded, & remain confirm'd, that the voice of honest indignation is the voice of God, I cared not for consequences, but wrote."

Then I asked: " does a firm perswasion that a thing is so, make it so? "

He replied: " All poets believe that it does, & in ages of imagination this firm perswasion removed mountains; but many are not capable of a firm perswasion of any thing."

Then Ezekiel said: " The philosophy of the east taught the first principles of human perception: some nations held one principle for the origin & some another: we of Israel taught that the Poetic Genius (as you now call it) was the first principle, and all the others merely derivative, which was the cause of our despising the Priests & Philosophers of other countries, and prophecying that all Gods would at last be proved to originate in ours & to be the tributaries of the Poetic Genius: it was this that our great poet, King David, desired so fervently & invokes so patheticly, saying by this he conquers enemies & governs kingdoms; and we so loved our God, that we cursed in his name all the deities of surrounding nations, and asserted that they had rebelled: from these opinions the vulgar came to think that all nations would at last be subject to the jews."

" This," said he, " like all firm perswasions, is come to pass; for all nations believe the jews' code and worship the jews' god, and what greater subjection can be? "

I heard this with some wonder, & must confess my own conviction. After dinner I ask'd Isaiah to favour the world with his lost works; he said none of equal value was lost. Ezekiel said the same of his.

I also asked Isaiah what made him go naked and barefoot three years? he answer'd, "the same that made our friend Diogenes the Grecian."

I then asked Ezekiel why he eat dung & lay so long on his right & left side? he answer'd, " the desire of raising other men into a perception of the infinite: this the North American tribes practise, & is he honest who resists his genius or conscience only for the sake of present ease or gratification? "

The ancient tradition that the world will be consumed in fire at the end of six thousand years is true, as I have heard from Hell;

For the cherub with his flaming sword is hereby commanded to leave his guard at tree of life, and when he does, the whole creation will be consumed and appear infinite and holy, whereas it now appears finite & corrupt.

This will come to pass by an improvement of sensual enjoyment.

But first the notion that man has a body distinct from his soul is to be expunged: this I shall do, by printing in the infernal method, by corrosives, which in Hell are salutary and medicinal, melting apparent surfaces away, and displaying the infinite which was hid.

If the doors of perception were cleansed, every thing would appear to man as it is, infinite.

For man has closed himself up, till he sees all things thro' narrow chinks of his cavern.

A Memorable Fancy

I was in a Printing house in Hell & saw the method in which knowledge is transmitted from generation to generation.

In the first chamber was a Dragon-Man, clearing away the rubbish from a cave's mouth: within, a number of Dragons were hollowing the cave.

In the second chamber was a Viper folding round the rock & the cave, and others adorning it with gold silver and precious stones.

In the third chamber was an Eagle with wings and feathers of air: he caused the inside of the cave to be infinite: around were numbers of Eagle like men, who built palaces in the immense cliffs.

In the fourth chamber were Lions of flaming fire, raging around & melting the metals into living fluids.

In the fifth chamber were Unnam'd forms, which cast the metals into the expanse.

There they were reciev'd by Men who occupied the sixth chamber, and took the forms of books & were arranged in libraries.

The Giants who formed this world into its sensual existence and now seem to live in it in chains, are in truth the causes of its life & the sources of all activity; but the chains are the cunning of weak and tame minds which have power to resist energy: according to the proverb, the weak in courage is strong in cunning.

Thus one portion of being is the Prolific; the other, the

Devouring: to the devourer it seems as if the producer was in his chains; but it is not so, he only takes portions of existence and fancies that the whole.

But the Prolific would cease to be Prolific unless the Devourer as a sea recieved the excess of his delights.

Some will say, "Is not God alone the Prolific?" I answer, "God only Acts and Is, in existing beings or Men."

These two classes of men are always upon earth, & they should be enemies: whoever tries to reconcile them seeks to destroy existence.

Religion is an endeavour to reconcile the two.

Note. Jesus Christ did not wish to unite, but to separate them, as in the Parable of sheep and goats! & he says, " I came not to send Peace but a Sword."

Messiah or Satan or Tempter was formerly thought to be one of the Antediluvians who are our Energies.

A Memorable Fancy

An Angel came to me and said: " O pitiable foolish young man! O horrible! O dreadful state! consider the hot burning dungeon thou art preparing for thyself to all eternity, to which thou art going in such career."

I said, " perhaps you will be willing to shew me my eternal lot & we will contemplate together upon it, and see whether your lot or mine is most desirable."

So he took me thro' a stable & thro' a church & down into the church vault, at the end of which was a mill: thro' the mill we went, and came to a cave: down the winding cavern we groped our tedious way till a void boundless as a nether sky appear'd beneath us, & we held by the roots of trees and hung over this immensity; but I said, " if you please we will commit ourselves to this void, and see whether providence is here also: if you will not, I will? " but he answer'd, " do not presume, O young man, but as we here remain, behold thy lot which will soon appear when the darkness passes away."

So I remain'd with him, sitting in the twisted root of an oak: he was suspended in a fungus, which hung with the head downward into the deep.

By degrees we beheld the infinite Abyss, fiery as the smoke of a burning city; beneath us at an immense distance was the sun, black but shining: round it were fiery tracks on which revolv'd vast spiders crawling after their prey, which flew, or rather swum in the infinite deep, in the most terrific shapes of animals sprung from corruption; & the air was full of them & seem'd composed of them: these are Devils, and are called Powers of the air. I now asked my companion which was my eternal lot? he said, " between the black & white spiders."

But now, from between the black & white spiders, a cloud and fire burst and rolled thro' the deep, blackning all beneath, so that the nether deep grew black as a sea & rolled with a terrible noise: beneath us was nothing now to be seen but a black tempest, till looking east between the clouds & the waves, we saw a cataract of blood mixed with fire, and not many stone's throw from us appear'd and sunk again the scaly fold of a monstrous serpent: at last, to the east, distant about three degrees, appear'd a fiery crest above the waves: slowly it reared like a ridge of golden rocks till we discover'd two globes of crimson fire, from which the sea fled away in clouds of smoke; and now we saw it was the head of Leviathan; his forehead was divided into streaks of green & purple like those on a tyger's forehead: soon we saw his mouth & red gills hang just above the raging foam, tinging the black deep with beams of blood, advancing toward us with all the fury of a spiritual existence.

My friend the Angel climb'd up from his station into the mill; I remain'd alone, & then this appearance was no more, but I found myself sitting on a pleasant bank beside a river by moonlight, hearing a harper who sung to the harp, & his theme was: "The man who never alters his opinion is like standing water, & breeds reptiles of the mind."

But I arose and sought for the mill & there I found my Angel, who surprised asked me how I escaped?

I answer'd: " All that we saw was owing to your metaphysics; for when you ran away, I found myself on a bank by moonlight hearing a harper.   But now we have seen my eternal lot, shall I shew you yours? " he laugh'd at my proposal; but I by force suddenly caught him in my arms, & flew westerly thro' the night, till we were elevated above the earth's shadow; then I flung myself with him directly into the body of the sun: here I clothed myself in white, & taking in my hand Swedenborg's volumes, sunk from the glorious clime, and passed all the planets till we

came to saturn: here I staid to rest, & then leap'd into the void
between saturn and the fixed stars.

"Here," said I, "is your lot, in this space, if space it may be
call'd." Soon we saw the stable and the church, & I took him to
the altar and open'd the Bible, and lo! it was a deep pit, into
which I descended driving the Angel before me: soon we saw
seven houses of brick: one we enter'd; in it were a number of
monkeys, baboons, & all of that species, chain'd by the middle,
grinning and snatching at one another, but withheld by the short-
ness of their chains: however, I saw that they sometimes grew
numerous, and then the weak were caught by the strong, and
with a grinning aspect, first coupled with & then devour'd, by
plucking off first one limb and then another, till the body was
left a helpless trunk: this, after grinning & kissing it with seeming
fondness, they devour'd too; and here & there I saw one savourily
picking the flesh off of his own tail: as the stench terribly annoy'd
us both, we went into the mill, & I in my hand brought the
skeleton of a body, which in the mill was Aristotle's Analytics.

So the Angel said: "thy phantasy has imposed upon me & thou
oughtest to be ashamed."

I answer'd: "we impose on one another, & it is but lost time
to converse with you whose works are only Analytics." [1]

―――――――

I have always found that Angels have the vanity to speak of
themselves as the only wise: this they do with a confident
insolence sprouting from systematic reasoning.

Thus Swedenborg boasts that what he writes is new, tho' it is
only the Contents or Index of already publish'd books.

A man carried a monkey about for a shew, & because he was
a little wiser than the monkey, grew vain, and conciev'd himself
as much wiser than seven men. It is so with Swedenborg: he
shews the folly of churches & exposes hypocrites, till he imagines
that all are religious, & himself the single one on earth that ever
broke a net.

Now hear a plain fact: Swedenborg has not written one new
truth. Now hear another: he has written all the old falshoods.

And now hear the reason. He conversed with Angels who are

[1] The words "Opposition is true Friendship" are discoverable here in
some copies of "The Marriage of Heaven and Hell." Blake afterwards
painted them out, perhaps because he considered they were not universally
applicable.

all religious, & conversed not with Devils who all hate religion, for he was incapable thro' his conceited notions.

Thus Swedenborg's writings are a recapitulation of all superficial opinions, and an analysis of the more sublime, but no further.

Have now another plain fact. Any man of mechanical talents may, from the writings of Paracelsus or Jacob Behmen, produce ten thousand volumes of equal value with Swedenborg's, and from those of Dante or Shakespear an infinite number.

But when he has done this, let him not say that he knows better than his master, for he only holds a candle in sunshine.

A Memorable Fancy

Once I saw a Devil in a flame of fire, who arose before an Angel that sat on a cloud, and the Devil utter'd these words:

"The worship of God is, Honouring his gifts in other men, each according to his genius, and loving the greatest men best: those who envy or calumniate great men hate God, for there is no other God."

The Angel hearing this became almost blue; but mastering himself he grew yellow, & at last white pink & smiling, and then replied:

"Thou Idolater: is not God One? & is not he visible in Jesus Christ? and has not Jesus Christ given his sanction to the law of ten commandments? and are not all other men fools, sinners, & nothings? "

The Devil answer'd: " bray a fool in a morter with wheat, yet shall not his folly be beaten out of him: if Jesus Christ is the greatest man, you ought to love him in the greatest degree: now hear how he has given his sanction to the law of ten commandments: did he not mock at the sabbath, and so mock the sabbath's God? murder those who were murder'd because of him? turn away the law from the woman taken in adultery? steal the labor of others to support him? bear false witness when he omitted making a defence before Pilate? covet when he pray'd for his disciples, and when he bid them shake off the dust of their feet against such as refused to lodge them? I tell you, no virtue can exist without breaking these ten commandments. Jesus was all virtue, and acted from impulse, not from rules."

When he had so spoken, I beheld the Angel, who stretched out his arms embracing the flame of fire, & he was consumed and arose as Elijah.

Note. This Angel, who is now become a Devil, is my particular friend: we often read the Bible together in its infernal or diabolical sense, which the world shall have if they behave well.

I have also, The Bible of Hell, which the world shall have whether they will or no.

One Law for the Lion & Ox is Oppression.[1]

A Song of Liberty

1. The Eternal Female groan'd! it was heard over all the Earth.

2. Albion's coast is sick silent: the American meadows faint!

3. Shadows of Prophecy shiver along by the lakes and the rivers and mutter across the ocean: " France, rend down thy dungeon.

4. " Golden Spain, burst the barriers of old Rome.

5. " Cast thy keys, O Rome, into the deep down falling, even to eternity down falling,

6. " And weep."

7. In her trembling hands she took the new born terror howling.

8. On those infinite mountains of light, now barr'd out by the atlantic sea, the new born fire stood before the starry king!

9. Flag'd with grey brow'd snows and thunderous visages, the jealous wings wav'd over the deep.

10. The speary hand burned aloft, unbuckled was the shield; forth went the hand of jealousy among the flaming hair, and hurl'd the new born wonder thro' the starry night.

11. The fire, the fire, is falling!

12. Look up! look up! O citizen of London, enlarge thy countenance. O Jew, leave counting gold! return to thy oil and wine. O African! black African! (go, winged thought, widen his forehead.)

13. The fiery limbs, the flaming hair, shot like the sinking sun into the western sea.

[1] This aphorism appears beneath a picture of Nebuchadnezzar going as a beast.

14. Wak'd from his eternal sleep, the hoary element roaring fled away.

15. Down rush'd, beating his wings in vain, the jealous king; his grey brow'd councellors, thunderous warriors, curl'd veterans, among helms, and shields, and chariots, horses, elephants, banners, castles, slings and rocks,

16. Falling, rushing, ruining! buried in the ruins, on Urthona's dens.

17. All night beneath the ruins, then their sullen flames faded emerge round the gloomy king.

18. With thunder and fire, leading his starry hosts thro' the waste wilderness, he promulgates his ten commands, glancing his beamy eyelids over the deep in dark dismay,

19. Where the son of fire in his eastern cloud, while the morning plumes her golden breast,

20. Spurning the clouds written with curses, stamps the stony law to dust, loosing the eternal horses from the dens of night, crying,

" Empire is no more ! and now the lion & wolf shall cease."

Chorus

Let the Priests of the Raven of dawn, no longer, in deadly black, with hoarse note, curse the sons of joy. Nor his accepted brethren, whom, tyrant, he calls free, lay the bound or build the roof. Nor pale religious letchery call that Virginity that wishes but acts not! For every thing that lives is Holy.

VISIONS

OF

THE DAUGHTERS OF ALBION

The Eye sees more than the Heart knows.

(1793)

The Argument

" I loved Theotormon
And I was not ashamed.
I trembled in my virgin fears
And I hid in Leutha's vale.

" I plucked Leutha's flower,
And I rose up from the vale;
But the terrible thunders tore
My virgin mantle in twain."

VISIONS

ENSLAV'D, the Daughters of Albion weep: a trembling lamentation
Upon their mountains: in their valleys, sighs toward America.

For the soft soul of America, Oothoon, wander'd in woe
Along the vales of Leutha seeking flowers to comfort her;
And thus she spoke to the bright Marygold of Leutha's vale: 5

" Art thou a flower? art thou a nymph? I see thee now a flower,
Now a nymph! I dare not pluck thee from thy dewy bed! "

The Golden nymph replied: " pluck thou my flower, Oothoon the
  mild,
Another flower shall spring, because the soul of sweet delight
Can never pass away: " she ceas'd & clos'd her golden shrine.   10

Then Oothoon pluck'd the flower, saying, " I pluck thee from thy
  bed,

56

Sweet flower, and put thee here to glow between my breasts,
And thus I turn my face to where my whole soul seeks."

Over the waves she went in wing'd exulting swift delight,
And over Theotormon's reign took her impetuous course.   15

Bromion rent her with his thunders; on his stormy bed
Lay the faint maid, and soon her woes appall'd his thunders hoarse.

Bromion spoke: " behold this harlot here on Bromion's bed,
And let the jealous dolphins sport around the lovely maid.
Thy soft American plains are mine, and mine thy north & south:
Stampt with my signet are the swarthy children of the sun;   21
They are obedient, they resist not, they obey the scourge;
Their daughters worship terrors and obey the violent.
Now thou maist marry Bromion's harlot, and protect the child
Of Bromion's rage that Oothoon shall put forth in nine moons'
    time."   25

Then storms rent Theotormon's limbs: he roll'd his waves around
And folded his black jealous waters round the adulterate pair.
Bound back to back in Bromion's caves, terror & meekness dwell.

At entrance Theotormon sits, wearing the threshold hard
With secret tears; beneath him sound like waves on a desart shore
The voice of slaves beneath the sun, and children bought with
    money   31
That shiver in religious caves beneath the burning fires
Of lust, that belch incessant from the summits of the earth.

Oothoon weeps not; she cannot weep! her tears are locked up;
But she can howl incessant writhing her soft snowy limbs   35
And calling Theotormon's Eagles to prey upon her flesh:

" I call with holy voice! kings of the sounding air,
Rend away this defiled bosom that I may reflect
The image of Theotormon on my pure transparent breast."

The Eagles at her call descend & rend their bleeding prey.   40
Theotormon severely smiles: her soul reflects the smile,
As the clear spring mudded with feet of beasts grows pure & smiles.

The Daughters of Albion hear her woes, & eccho back her sighs.

" Why does my Theotormon sit weeping upon the threshold,
And Oothoon hovers by his side, perswading him in vain?   45
I cry: arise, O Theortormon, for the village dog
Barks at the breaking day, the nightingale has done lamenting,
The lark does rustle in the ripe corn, and the Eagle returns

From nightly prey and lifts his golden beak to the pure east,
Shaking the dust from his immortal pinions to awake   50
The sun that sleeps too long. Arise, my Theotormon. I am pure,
Because the night is gone that clos'd me in its deadly black.
They told me that the night & day were all that I could see.
They told me that I had five senses to inclose me up;
And they inclos'd my infinite brain into a narrow circle,   55
And sunk my heart into the Abyss, a red round globe, hot burning,
Till all from life I was obliterated and erased.
Instead of morn arises a bright shadow, like an eye
In the eastern cloud; instead of night a sickly charnel house.
That Theotormon hears me not! to him the night and morn   60
Are both alike: a night of sighs, a morning of fresh tears;
And none but Bromion can hear my lamentations.

" With what sense is it that the chicken shuns the ravenous hawk?
With what sense does the tame pigeon measure out the expanse?
With what sense does the bee form cells? have not the mouse
     & frog   65
Eyes and ears and sense of touch? yet are their habitations
And their pursuits as different as their forms and as their joys.
Ask the wild ass why he refuses burdens, and the meek camel
Why he loves man: is it because of eye, ear, mouth, or skin,
Or breathing nostrils? No, for these the wolf and tyger have.   70
Ask the blind worm the secrets of the grave, and why her spires
Love to curl round the bones of death; and ask the rav'nous snake
Where she gets poison, & the wing'd eagle why he loves the sun,
And then tell me the thoughts of man that have been hid of old.

" Silent I hover all the night, and all day could be silent,   75
If Theotormon once would turn his loved eyes upon me.
How can I be defil'd when I reflect thy image pure?
Sweetest the fruit that the worm feeds on, & the soul prey'd on
     by woe.
The new wash'd lamb ting'd with the village smoke & the bright
     swan
By the red earth of our immortal river. I bathe my wings,   80
And I am white and pure to hover round Theotormon's breast."

Then Theotormon broke his silence, and he answered:

" Tell me what is the night or day to one o'erflow'd with woe?
Tell me what is a thought? & of what substance is it made?
Tell me what is a joy? & in what gardens do joys grow?   85
And in what rivers swim the sorrows? and upon what mountains
Wave shadows of discontent? and in what houses dwell the
     wretched,
Drunken with woe forgotten, and shut up from cold despair?

" Tell me where dwell the thoughts forgotten till thou call them
    forth?   89
Tell me where dwell the joys of old? & where the ancient loves?
And when will they renew again & the night of oblivion past?
That I might traverse times & spaces far remote and bring
Comforts into a present sorrow and a night of pain.
Where goest thou, O thought? to what remote land is thy flight?
If thou returnest to the present moment of affliction   95
Wilt thou bring comforts on thy wings, and dews and honey and
    balm,
Or poison from the desart wilds, from the eyes of the envier? "

Then Bromion said, and shook the cavern with his lamentation:

" Thou knowest that the ancient trees seen by thine eyes have fruit,
But knowest thou that trees and fruits flourish upon the earth 100
To gratify senses unknown? trees, beasts and birds unknown:
Unknown, not unperciev'd, spread in the infinite microscope,
In places yet unvisited by the voyager, and in worlds
Over another kind of seas, and in atmospheres unknown.
Ah! are there other wars beside the wars of sword and fire?   105
And are there other sorrows beside the sorrows of poverty?
And are there other joys beside the joys of riches and ease?
And is there not one law for both the lion and the ox?
And is there not eternal fire and eternal chains
To bind the phantoms of existence from eternal life? "   110

Then Oothoon waited silent all the day and all the night.
But when the morn arose, her lamentation renew'd.
The Daughters of Albion hear her woes, & eccho back her sighs.

" O Urizen! Creator of men! mistaken Demon of heaven,
Thy joys are tears! thy labour vain to form men to thine image.
How can one joy absorb another? are not different joys   116
Holy, eternal, infinite? and each joy is a Love.

" Does not the great mouth laugh at a gift? & the narrow eyelids
    mock
At the labour that is above payment? and wilt thou take the ape
For thy counsellor? or the dog for a schoolmaster to thy children?
Does he who contemns poverty, and he who turns with abhorrence
From usury, feel the same passion, or are they moved alike?
How can the giver of gifts experience the delights of the merchant?
How the industrious citizen the pains of the husbandman?
How different far the fat fed hireling with hollow drum,   125
Who buys whole corn fields into wastes, and sings upon the heath:
How different their eye and ear! how different the world to them!
With what sense does the parson claim the labour of the farmer?

What are his nets & gins & traps, & how does he surround him
With cold floods of abstraction, and with forests of solitude,   130
To build him castles and high spires, where kings & priests may
      dwell,
Till she who burns with youth and knows no fixed lot, is bound
In spells of law to one she loaths? and must she drag the chain
Of life in weary lust? must chilling murderous thoughts obscure
The clear heaven of her eternal spring? to bear the wintry rage
Of a harsh terror driv'n to madness, bound to hold a rod   136
Over her shrinking shoulders all the day, & all the night
To turn the wheel of false desire, and longings that wake her womb
To the abhorred birth of cherubs in the human form
That live a pestilence & die a meteor & are no more;   140
Till the child dwell with one he hates, and do the deed he loaths,
And the impure scourge force his seed into its unripe birth
E'er yet his eyelids can behold the arrows of the day.

"Does the whale worship at thy footsteps as the hungry dog?
Or does he scent the mountain prey, because his nostrils wide   145
Draw in the ocean? does his eye discern the flying cloud
As the raven's eye? or does he measure the expanse like the
      vulture?
Does the still spider view the cliffs where eagles hide their young?
Or does the fly rejoice because the harvest is brought in?
Does not the eagle scorn the earth, & despise the treasures
      beneath?   150
But the mole knoweth what is there, & the worm shall tell it
      thee.
Does not the worm erect a pillar in the mouldering church yard?
And a palace of eternity in the jaws of the hungry grave?
Over his porch these words are written: ' Take thy bliss, O Man!
And sweet shall be thy taste & sweet thy infant joys renew! '   155

"Infancy, fearless, lustful, happy! nestling for delight
In laps of pleasure. Innocence! honest, open, seeking
The vigorous joys of morning light, open to virgin bliss.
Who taught thee modesty, subtil modesty? child of night & sleep
When thou awakest, wilt thou dissemble all thy secret joys,   16c
Or wert thou not awake when all this mystery was disclos'd?
Then com'st thou forth a modest virgin knowing to dissemble,
With nets found under thy night pillow, to catch virgin joy
And brand it with the name of whore, & sell it in the night,
In silence, ev'n without a whisper, and in seeming sleep.   165
Religious dreams and holy vespers light thy smoky fires:
Once were thy fires lighted by the eyes of honest morn;
And does my Theotormon seek this hypocrite modesty?
This knowing, artful, secret, fearful, cautious, trembling hypocrite!
Then is Oothoon a whore indeed! and all the virgin joys   170

Of life are harlots, and Theotormon is a sick man's dream,
And Oothoon is the crafty slave of selfish holiness.

" But Oothoon is not so: a virgin fill'd with virgin fancies
Open to joy and to delight where ever beauty appears.
If in the morning sun I find it, there my eyes are fix'd   175
In happy copulation; if in evening mild, wearied with work,
Sit on a bank and draw the pleasures of this free born joy.

" The moment of desire! the moment of desire! The virgin
That pines for man shall awaken her womb to enormous joys
In the secret shadows of her chamber: the youth shut up from
 The lustful joy shall forget to generate, & create an amorous image
In the shadows of his curtains and in the folds of his silent pillow.
Are not these the places of religion? the rewards of continence?
The self enjoyings of self denial? Why dost thou seek religion?
Is it because acts are not lovely that thou seekest solitude,   185
Where the horrible darkness is impressed with reflections of desire?

" Father of Jealousy, be thou accursed from the earth!
Why hast thou taught my Theotormon this accursed thing?
Till beauty fades from off my shoulders, darken'd and cast out,
A solitary shadow wailing on the margin of non-entity.   190

" I cry: Love! Love! Love! happy happy Love! free as the
     mountain wind!
Can that be Love, that drinks another as a sponge drinks water?
That clouds with jealousy his nights, with weepings all the day,
To spin a web of age around him, grey and hoary! dark!
Till his eyes sicken at the fruit that hangs before his sight.   195
Such is self-love that envies all! a creeping skeleton
With lamplike eyes watching around the frozen marriage bed.

" But silken nets and traps of adamant will Oothoon spread,
And catch for thee girls of mild silver, or of furious gold.
I'll lie beside thee on a bank & view their wanton play   200
In lovely copulation, bliss on bliss, with Theotormon.
Red as the rosy morning, lustful as the first born beam,
Oothoon shall view his dear delight, nor e'er with jealous cloud
Come in the heaven of generous love, nor selfish blightings bring.

" Does the sun walk in glorious raiment on the secret floor   205
Where the cold miser spreads his gold? or does the bright cloud
     drop
On his stone threshold? does his eye behold the beam that brings
Expansion to the eye of pity? or will he bind himself
Beside the ox to thy hard furrow? does not that mild beam blot
The bat, the owl, the glowing tyger, and the king of night?   210
     D 792

The sea fowl takes the wintry blast for a cov'ring to her limbs,
And the wild snake the pestilence to adorn him with gems & gold;
And trees & birds & beasts & men behold their eternal joy.
Arise, you little glancing wings, and sing your infant joy!
Arise and drink your bliss, for every thing that lives is holy! " 215

Thus every morning wails Oothoon, but Theotormon sits
Upon the margin'd ocean conversing with shadows dire.

The Daughters of Albion hear her woes, & eccho back her sighs.

The End

AMERICA

A

PROPHECY

(1793)

Preludium

THE shadowy daughter of Urthona stood before red Orc
When fourteen suns had faintly journey'd o'er his dark abode:
His food she brought in iron baskets, his drink in cups of iron.
Crown'd with a helmet & dark hair the nameless female stood;
A quiver with its burning stores, a bow like that of night   5
When pestilence is shot from heaven: no other arms she need,
Invulnerable tho' naked, save where clouds roll round her loins
Their awful folds in the dark air: silent she stood as night,
For never from her iron tongue could voice or sound arise,
But dumb till that dread day when Orc assay'd his fierce embrace.

"Dark Virgin," said the hairy Youth, "thy father stern abhorr'd,
Rivets my tenfold chains while still on high my spirit soars: 12
Sometimes an eagle screaming in the sky, sometimes a lion
Stalking upon the mountains, & sometimes a whale I lash
The raging fathomless abyss, anon a serpent folding   15
Around the pillars of Urthona, and round thy dark limbs
On the Canadian wilds I fold; feeble my spirit folds,
For chain'd beneath I rend these caverns: when thou bringest food
I howl my joy, and my red eyes seek to behold thy face.
In vain! these clouds roll to & fro, & hide thee from my sight."

Silent as despairing love, and strong as jealousy,   21
The hairy shoulders rend the links; free are the wrists of fire;
Round the terrific loins he siez'd the panting struggling womb;
It joy'd: she put aside her clouds & smiled her first-born smile,
As when a black cloud shews its lightnings to the silent deep.   25

Soon as she saw the terrible boy then burst the virgin cry:

"I know thee, I have found thee, & I will not let thee go.
Thou art the image of God who dwells in darkness of Africa,

And thou art fall'n to give me life in regions of dark death.
On my American plains I feel the struggling afflictions   30
Endur'd by roots that writhe their arms into the nether deep:
I see a serpent in Canada who courts me to his love,
In Mexico an Eagle, and a Lion in Peru;
I see a Whale in the South-sea, drinking my soul away.
O what limb rending pains I feel; thy fire & my frost   35
Mingle in howling pains, in furrows by thy lightnings rent.
This is eternal death, and this the torment long foretold.''

A PROPHECY

THE Guardian Prince of Albion burns in his nightly tent:
Sullen fires across the Atlantic glow to America's shore,
Piercing the souls of warlike men who rise in silent night.
Washington, Franklin, Paine & Warren, Gates, Hancock & Green
Meet on the coast glowing with blood from Albion's fiery Prince.

Washington spoke: '' Friends of America, look over the Atlantic
    sea;   6
A bended bow is lifted in heaven, & a heavy iron chain
Descends link by link from Albion's cliffs across the sea to bind
Brothers & sons of America, till our faces pale and yellow,
Heads deprest, voices weak, eyes downcast, hands work-bruis'd, 10
Feet bleeding on the sultry sands, and the furrows of the whip
Descend to generations that in future times forget.''

The strong voice ceas'd; for a terrible blast swept over the heaving
    sea:
The eastern cloud rent: on his cliffs stood Albion's wrathful Prince,
A dragon form clashing his scales at midnight he arose,   15
And flam'd red meteors round the land of Albion beneath;
His voice, his locks, his awful shoulders, and his glowing eyes
Appear to the Americans upon the cloudy night.

Solemn heave the Atlantic waves between the gloomy nations,
Swelling, belching from its deeps red clouds & raging fires.   20
Albion is sick, America faints! enrag'd the Zenith grew.
As human blood shooting its veins all round the orbed heaven,
Red rose the clouds from the Atlantic in vast wheels of blood,
And in the red clouds rose a Wonder o'er the Atlantic sea,
Intense! naked! a Human fire, fierce glowing as the wedge   25
Of iron heated in the furnace; his terrible limbs were fire,
With myriads of cloudy terrors, banners dark, & towers
Surrounded: heat but not light went thro' the murky atmosphere.

The King of England looking westward trembles at the vision.

Albion's Angel stood beside the Stone of night, and saw   30
The terror like a comet, or more like the planet red
That once inclos'd the terrible wandering comets in its sphere.
Then, Mars, thou wast our center, & the planets three flew round
Thy crimson disk; so, e'er the Sun was rent from thy red sphere,
The Spectre glow'd his horrid length staining the temple long   35
With beams of blood; & thus a voice came forth, and shook the
    temple:

" The morning comes, the night decays, the watchmen leave their
    stations;
The grave is burst, the spices shed, the linen wrapped up;
The bones of death, the cov'ring clay, the sinews shrunk & dry'd
Reviving shake, inspiring move, breathing! awakening!   40
Spring like redeemed captives when their bonds & bars are burst.
Let the slave grinding at the mill run out into the field,
Let him look up into the heavens & laugh in the bright air:
Let the inchained soul, shut up in darkness and in sighing,
Whose face has never seen a smile in thirty weary years,   45
Rise and look out; his chains are loose, his dungeon doors are open,
And let his wife and children return from the opressor's scourge.
They look behind at every step & believe it is a dream,
Singing: ' The Sun has left his blackness, & has found a fresher
    morning,
And the fair Moon rejoices in the clear & cloudless night;   50
For Empire is no more, and now the Lion & Wolf shall cease.' "

In thunders ends the voice. Then Albion's Angel wrathful burn
Beside the Stone of Night, and like the Eternal Lion's howl
In famine & war reply'd: " Art thou not Orc, who serpent-form'd
Stands at the gate of Enitharmon to devour her children,   55
Blasphemous Demon, Antichrist, hater of Dignities,
Lover of wild rebellion, and transgressor of God's Law,
Why dost thou come to Angel's eyes in this terrific form? "

The terror answer'd: " I am Orc, wreath'd round the accursed tree.
The times are ended: shadows pass, the morning 'gins to break:
The fiery joy that Urizen perverted to ten commands   61
What night he led the starry hosts thro' the wide wilderness,
That stony law I stamp to dust, and scatter religion abroad
To the four winds as a torn book, & none shall gather the leaves,
But they shall rot on desart sands & consume in bottomless deeps,
To make the desarts blossom & the deeps shrink to their fountains,
And to renew the fiery joy, and burst the stony roof;   67
That pale religious letchery, seeking Virginity,
May find it in a harlot, and in coarse-clad honesty
The undefil'd tho' ravish'd in her cradle night and morn;   70
For every thing that lives is holy, life delights in life;

Because the soul of sweet delight can never be defil'd.
Fires inwrap the earthly globe, yet man is not consum'd;
Amidst the lustful fires he walks; his feet become like brass,
His knees and thighs like silver, & his breast and head like gold." 75

" Sound! sound! my loud war-trumpets & alarm my Thirteen
  Angels!
Loud howls the eternal Wolf! the eternal Lion lashes his tail!
America is dark'ned, and my punishing Demons terrified
Crouch howling before their caverns deep like skins dry'd in the
  wind. 79
They cannot smite the wheat, nor quench the fatness of the earth,
They cannot smite with sorrows, nor subdue the plough and spade,
They cannot wall the city, nor moat round the castle of princes,
They cannot bring the stubbed oak to overgrow the hills,
For terrible men stand on the shores, & in their robes I see
Children take shelter from the lightnings: there stands Washington
And Paine and Warren with their foreheads rear'd toward the east,
But clouds obscure my aged sight. A vision from afar! 87
Sound! sound! my loud war-trumpets & alarm my thirteen Angels.
Ah vision from afar! Ah rebel form that rent the ancient
Heavens! Eternal Viper self-renew'd, rolling in clouds, 90
I see thee in thick clouds and darkness on America's shore
Writhing in pangs of abhorred birth; red flames the crest rebellious
And eyes of death; the harlot womb, oft opened in vain,
Heaves in enormous circles; now the times are return'd upon thee,
Devourer of thy parent; now thy unutterable torment renews. 95
Sound! sound! my loud war trumpets & alarm my thirteen Angels.
Ah, terrible birth! a young one bursting! where is the weeping
  mouth?
And where the mother's milk? instead, those ever-hissing jaws
And parched lips drop with fresh gore: now roll thou in the clouds;
Thy mother lays her length outstretch'd upon the shore beneath.
Sound! sound! my loud war-trumpets & alarm my thirteen Angels!
Loud howls the eternal Wolf! the eternal Lion lashes his tail!" 102

Thus wept the Angel voice, & as he wept, the terrible blasts
Of trumpets blew a loud alarm across the Atlantic deep.
No trumpets answer; no reply of clarions or of fifes; 105
Silent the Colonies remain and refuse the loud alarm.

On those vast shady hills between America & Albion's shore
Now barr'd out by the Atlantic sea, call'd Atlantean hills
Because from their bright summits you may pass to the Golden
  world,
An ancient palace, archetype of mighty Emperies, 110
Rears its immortal pinnacles, built in the forest of God
By Ariston the king of beauty for his stolen bride.

Here on their magic seats the thirteen Angels sat perturb'd,
For clouds from the Atlantic hover o'er the solemn roof.

Fiery the Angels rose, & as they rose deep thunder roll'd   115
Around their shores, indignant burning with the fires of Orc;
And Boston's Angel cried aloud as they flew thro' the dark night.

He cried: " Why trembles honesty and like a murderer
Why seeks he refuge from the frowns of his immortal station?
Must the generous tremble & leave his joy to the idle, to the
       pestilence,   120
That mock him? who commanded this? what God? what Angel?
To keep the gen'rous from experience till the ungenerous
Are unrestrain'd performers of the energies of nature:
Till pity is become a trade, and generosity a science   124
That men get rich by, & the sandy desart is giv'n to the strong.
What God is he writes laws of peace & clothes him in a tempest?
What pitying Angel lusts for tears and fans himself with sighs?
What crawling villain preaches abstinence & wraps himself
In fat of lambs? no more I follow, no more obedience pay."

So cried he, rending off his robe & throwing down his scepter
In sight of Albion's Guardian; and all the thirteen Angels   131
Rent off their robes to the hungry wind & threw their golden
       scepters
Down on the land of America; indignant they descended
Headlong from out their heav'nly heights, descending swift as fires
Over the land; naked & flaming are their lineaments seen   135
In the deep gloom; by Washington & Paine & Warren they stood;
And the flame folded, roaring fierce within the pitchy night
Before the Demon red who burnt towards America,
In black smoke thunders and loud winds rejoicing in its terror,
Breaking in smoky wreaths from the wild deep, & gath'ring thick
In flames as of a furnace on the land from North to South.   141

What time the thirteen Governors that England sent, convene
In Bernard's house, the flames cover'd the land; they rouze, they
       cry.

Shaking their mental chains, they rush in fury to the sea.
To quench their anguish; at the feet of Washington down fall'n
They grovel on the sand and writhing lie, while all   146
The British soldiers thro' the thirteen states sent up a howl
Of anguish, threw their swords & muskets to the earth & ran
From their encampments and dark castles, seeking where to hide
From the grim flames and from the visions of Orc, in sight   150
Of Albion's Angel, who enrag'd, his secret clouds open'd
From north to south, and burnt outstretch'd on wings of wrath
       cov'ring

The eastern sky, spreading his awful wings across the heavens.
Beneath him roll'd his num'rous hosts, all Albion's Angels camp'd
Darken'd the Atlantic mountains, & their trumpets shook the
    valleys   155
Arm'd with diseases of the earth to cast upon the Abyss,
Their numbers forty millions, must'ring in the eastern sky.

In the flames stood & view'd the armies drawn out in the sky,
Washington, Franklin, Paine & Warren, Allen, Gates & Lee,
And heard the voice of Albion's Angel give the thunderous
    command.   160
His plagues, obedient to his voice, flew forth out of their clouds,
Falling upon America, as a storm to cut them off
As a blight cuts the tender corn when it begins to appear.
Dark is the heaven above, & cold & hard the earth beneath:
And as a plague wind fill'd with insects cuts off man & beast,
And as a sea o'erwhelms a land in the day of an earthquake,   166
Fury! rage! madness! in a wind swept through America,
And the red flames of Orc that folded, roaring fierce around
The angry shores and the fierce rushing of th' inhabitants together.
The citizens of New-York close their books & lock their chests;
The mariners of Boston drop their anchors and unlade;   171
The scribe of Pensylvania casts his pen upon the earth;
The builder of Virginia throws his hammer down in fear.

Then had America been lost, o'erwhelm'd by the Atlantic,
And Earth had lost another portion of the infinite,   175
But all rush together in the night in wrath and raging fire.
The red fires rag'd! the plagues recoil'd! then roll'd they back
    with fury
On Albion's Angels: then the Pestilence began in streaks of red
Across the limbs of Albion's Guardian; the spotted plague smote
    Bristol's,
And the Leprosy London's Spirit, sickening all their bands.   180
The millions sent up a howl of anguish and threw off their
    hammer'd mail,
And cast their swords & spears to earth, & stood, a naked multi-
    tude.
Albion's Guardian writhed in torment on the eastern sky,
Pale quiv'ring toward the brain his glimmering eyes, teeth
    chattering,
Howling & shuddering, his legs quivering; convuls'd each muscle
    & sinew.   185
Sick'ning lay London's Guardian and the ancient miter'd York,
Their heads on snowy hills, their ensigns sick'ning in the sky.

The plagues creep on the burning winds driven by flames of Orc
And by the fierce Americans rushing together in the night,

Driven o'er the Guardians of Ireland and Scotland and Wales.
They, spotted with plagues, forsook the frontiers, & their banners sear'd   191
With fires of hell, deform their ancient heavens with shame & woe.
Hid in his caves the Bard of Albion felt the enormous plagues,
And a cowl of flesh grew o'er his head, & scales on his back & ribs;
And, rough with black scales, all his Angels fright their ancient heavens.   195
The doors of marriage are open, and the Priests in rustling scales
Rush into reptile coverts, hiding from the fires of Orc
That play around the golden roofs in wreaths of fierce desire
Leaving the females naked and glowing with the lusts of youth.

For the female spirits of the dead, pining in bonds of religion, 200
Run from their fetters reddening, & in long drawn arches sitting
They feel the nerves of youth renew, and desires of ancient times
Over their pale limbs, as a vine when the tender grape appears.

Over the hills, the vales, the cities, rage the red flames fierce. 204
The Heavens melted from north to south; and Urizen, who sat
Above all heavens in thunders wrap'd, emerg'd his leprous head
From out his holy shrine, his tears in deluge piteous
Falling into the deep sublime; flag'd with grey-brow'd snows
And thunderous visages, his jealous wings wav'd over the deep;
Weeping in dismal howling woe, he dark descended, howling 210
Around the smitten bands, clothed in tears & trembling shudd'ring cold.
His stored snows he poured forth, and his icy magazines
He open'd on the deep and on the Atlantic sea white shiv'ring.
Leprous his limbs, all over white, and hoary was his visage,
Weeping in dismal howlings before the stern Americans,   215
Hiding the Demon red with clouds & cold mists from the earth,
Till Angels & weak men twelve years should govern o'er the strong,
And then their end should come, when France reciev'd the Demon's light.

Stiff shudderings shook the heav'nly thrones! France, Spain & Italy
In terror view'd the bands of Albion and the ancient Guardians
Fainting upon the elements, smitten with their own plagues.   221
They slow advance to shut the five gates of their law-built heaven
Filled with blasting fancies and with mildews of despair,
With fierce disease and lust, unable to stem the fires of Orc.
But the five gates were consum'd & their bolts and hinges melted,
And the fierce flames burnt round the heavens & round the abodes of men.   226

FINIS

*D 792

EUROPE

A

PROPHECY

(1794)

" FIVE windows light the cavern'd Man: thro' one he breathes
    the air,
Thro' one hears music of the spheres, thro' one the eternal vine
Flourishes that he may recieve the grapes, thro' one can look
And see small portions of the eternal world that ever groweth,
Thro' one himself pass out what time he please; but he will not,
For stolen joys are sweet & bread eaten in secret pleasant."   6

So sang a Fairy, mocking, as he sat on a streak'd Tulip
Thinking none saw him: when he ceas'd, I started from the trees
And caught him in my hat as boys knock down a butterfly.
" How know you this," said I, " small Sir? where did you learn
    this song? "   10
Seeing himself in my possession, thus he answer'd me:
" My Master, I am yours! command me, for I must obey."

" Then tell me what is the material world, and is it dead? "
He, laughing answer'd: " I will write a book on leaves of flowers
If you will feed me on love-thoughts & give me now and then
A cup of sparkling poetic fancies; so, when I am tipsie,   16
I'll sing to you to this soft lute, and shew you all alive
The world, where every particle of dust breathes forth its joy."

I took him home in my warm bosom: as we went along   19
Wild flowers I gather'd, & he shew'd me each eternal flower.
He laugh'd aloud to see them whimper because they were pluck'd.
They hover'd round me like a cloud of incense: when I came
Into my parlour and sat down and took my pen to write,
My Fairy sat upon the table and dictated ' Europe.' [1]

---

[1] These explanatory lines are to be found only in one of the nine existing
copies of *Europe*.

PRELUDIUM

THE nameless shadowy female rose from out the breast of Orc,
Her snaky hair brandishing in the winds of Enitharmon,
And thus her voice arose:

" O mother Enitharmon, wilt thou bring forth other sons?
To cause my name to vanish, that my place may not be found,   5
For I am faint with travel! [1]
Like the dark cloud disburden'd in the day of dismal thunder.

" My roots are brandish'd in the heavens, my fruits in earth
    beneath
Surge, foam and labour into life, first born & first consum'd!
Consumed and consuming!   10
Then why shouldst thou, accursed mother, bring me into life?

" I wrap my turban of thick clouds around my lab'ring head
And fold the sheety waters as a mantle round my limbs,
Yet the red sun and moon
And all the overflowing stars rain down prolific pains.   15

" Unwilling I look up to heaven! unwilling count the stars
Sitting in fathomless abyss of my immortal shrine;
I sieze their burning power
And bring forth howling terrors, all devouring fiery kings:

" Devouring & devoured roaming on dark and desolate mountains,
In forests of eternal death shrieking in hollow trees.   21
Ah mother Enitharmon!
Stamp not with solid form this vig'rous progeny of fires.

" I bring forth from my teeming bosom myriads of flames,
And thou dost stamp them with a signet; then they roam abroad
And leave me void as death.   26
Ah! I am drown'd in shady woe and visionary joy.

" And who shall bind the infinite with an eternal band?
To compass it with swaddling bands? and who shall cherish it
With milk and honey?   30
I see it smile & I roll inward & my voice is past."

She ceast & roll'd her shady clouds
Into the secret place.

[1] So spelt, but meaning *travail*.

A PROPHECY

THE deep of winter came
What time the secret child
Descended thro' the orient gates of the eternal day.
War ceas'd, & all the troops like shadows fled to their abodes.

Then Enitharmon saw her sons & daughters rise around,   5
Like pearly clouds they meet together in the crystal house;
And Los, possessor of the moon, joy'd in the peaceful night,
Thus speaking, while his num'rous sons shook their bright fiery
    wings:

" Again the night is come
That strong Urthona takes his rest,   10
And Urizen unloos'd from chains
Glows like a meteor in the distant north.
Stretch forth your hands and strike the elemental strings!
Awake the thunders of the deep.

" The shrill winds wake!   15
Till all the sons of Urizen look out and envy Los.
Sieze all the spirits of life and bind
Their warbling joys to our loud strings:
Bind all the nourishing sweets of earth
To give us bliss, that we may drink the sparkling wine of Los, 20
And let us laugh at war,
Despising toil and care,
Because the days and nights of joy in lucky hours renew.

" Arise, O Orc, from thy deep den,
First born of Enitharmon, rise!   25
And we will crown thy head with garlands of the ruddy vine;
For now thou art bound,
And I may see thee in the hour of bliss, my eldest born."

The horrent Demon rose surrounded with red stars of fire
Whirling about in furious circles round the immortal fiend. 30

Then Enitharmon down descended into his red light,
And thus her voice rose to her children: the distant heavens reply.

" Now comes the night of Enitharmon's joy!
Who shall I call? Who shall I send?
That Woman, lovely Woman! may have dominion?   35
Arise, O Rintrah, thee I call! & Palamabron, thee!
Go! tell the human race that Woman's love is Sin:

That an Eternal life awaits the worms of sixty winters
In an allegorical abode where existence hath never come.
Forbid all Joy, & from her childhood shall the little female   40
Spread nets in every secret path.

" My weary eyelids draw towards the evening, my bliss is yet but
    new!

" Arise, O Rintrah eldest born, second to none but Orc:
O lion Rintrah, raise thy fury from thy forests black:
Bring Palamabron, horned priest, skipping upon the mountains,
And silent Elynittria, the silver bowed queen.   46
Rintrah, where hast thou hid thy bride?
Weeps she in desart shades?
Alas my Rintrah! bring the lovely jealous Ocalythron.

"Arise, my son! bring all thy brethren, O thou king of fire: 50
Prince of the sun, I see thee with thy innumerable race,
Thick as the summer stars;
But each, ramping, his golden mane shakes,
And thine eyes rejoice because of strength, O Rintrah, furious
    king."

Enitharmon slept   55
Eighteen hundred years. Man was a Dream!
The night of Nature and their harps unstrung.
She slept in middle of her nightly song,
Eighteen hundred years, a female dream!

Shadows of men in fleeting bands upon the winds   60
Divide the heavens of Europe,
Till Albion's Angel, smitten with his own plagues, fled with his
    bands.
The cloud bears hard on Albion's shore,
Fill'd with immortal demons of futurity.
In council gather the smitten Angels of Albion;   65
The cloud bears hard upon the council house, down rushing
On the heads of Albion's Angels.

One hour they lay buried beneath the ruins of that hall;
But as the stars rise from the salt lake, they arise in pain,   69
In troubled mists, o'erclouded by the terrors of strugling times.

In thoughts perturb'd they rose from the bright ruins, silent
    following
The fiery King, who sought his ancient temple serpent-form'd
That stretches out its shady length along the Island white.
Round him roll'd his clouds of war; silent the Angel went

Along the infinite shores of Thames to golden Verulam.   75
There stand the venerable porches that high-towering rear
Their oak-surrounded pillars form'd of massy stones uncut
With tool, stones precious: such eternal in the heavens,
Of colours twelve, few known on earth, give light in the opake,
Plac'd in the order of the stars when the five senses whelm'd   80
In deluge o'er the earth-born man: then turn'd the fluxile eyes
Into two stationary orbs, concentrating all things.
The ever-varying spiral ascents to the heavens of heavens
Were bended downward, and the nostrils' golden gates shut,
Turn'd outward, barr'd and petrify'd against the infinite.   85

Thought chang'd the infinite to a serpent, that which pitieth
To a devouring flame, and man fled from its face and hid
In forests of night: then all the eternal forests were divided
Into earths rolling in circles of space, that like an ocean rush'd
And overwhelmed all except this finite wall of flesh.   90
Then was the serpent temple form'd, image of infinite
Shut up in finite revolutions, and man became an Angel,
Heaven a mighty circle turning, God a tyrant crown'd.

Now arriv'd the ancient Guardian at the southern porch
That planted thick with trees of blackest leaf, & in a vale   95
Obscure, inclos'd the Stone of Night; oblique it stood, o'erhung
With purple flowers and berries red, image of that sweet south
Once open to the heavens and elevated on the human neck,
Now overgrown with hair and cover'd with a stony roof:
Downward 'tis sunk beneath th' attractive north, that round the
      feet   100
.: raging whirlpool draws the dizzy enquirer to his grave.

Albion's Angel rose upon the Stone of Night.
He saw Urizen on the Atlantic,
And his brazen Book
That Kings & Priests had copied on Earth   105
Expanded from North to South.

And the clouds & fires pale roll'd round in the night of Enitharmon,
Round Albion's cliffs & London's walls: still Enitharmon slept.
Rolling volumes of grey mist involve Churches, Palaces, Towers;
For Urizen unclasp'd his Book, feeding his soul with pity.   110
The youth of England, hid in gloom, curse the pain'd heavens,
      compell'd
Into the deadly night to see the form of Albion's Angel;
Their parents brought them forth, & aged ignorance preaches,
      canting,
On a vast rock perciev'd by those senses that are clos'd from
      thought:

Bleak, dark, abrupt it stands & overshadows London city.   115
They saw his boney feet on the rock, the flesh consum'd in flames;
They saw the Serpent temple lifted above, shadowing the Island
    white;
They heard the voice of Albion's Angel howling in flames of Orc
Seeking the trump of the last doom.

Above the rest the howl was heard from Westminster louder and
    louder.   120
The Guardian of the secret codes forsook his ancient mansion,
Driven out by the flames of Orc; his furr'd robes & false locks
Adhered and grew one with his flesh, and nerves & veins shot
    thro' them.
With dismal torment sick, hanging upon the wind, he fled
Groveling along Great George Street, thro' the Park gate: all
    the soldiers   125
Fled from his sight: he drag'd his torments to the wilderness.

Thus was the howl thro' Europe,
For Orc rejoic'd to hear the howling shadows,
But Palamabron shot his lightnings, trenching down his wide back,
And Rintrah hung with all his legions in the nether deep.   130

Enitharmon laugh'd in her sleep to see (O woman's triumph)
Every house a den, every man bound, the shadows are fill'd
With spectres, and the windows wove over with curses of iron;
Over the doors 'Thou shalt not,' & over the chimneys 'Fear'
    is written;
With bands of iron round their necks, fasten'd into the walls   135
The citizens; in leaden gyves the inhabitants of suburbs
Walk heavy; soft and bent are the bones of villagers.

Between the clouds of Urizen the flames of Orc roll heavy
Around the limbs of Albion's Guardian, his flesh consuming.
Howlings & hissings, shrieks & groans & voices of despair
Arise around him in the cloudy Heavens of Albion. Furious,   141
The red limb'd Angel siez'd in horror and torment
The Trump of the last doom, but he could not blow the iron tube!
Thrice he assay'd presumptuous to awake the dead to Judgment.

A mighty Spirit leap'd from the land of Albion,   145
Nam'd Newton: he siez'd the Trump & blow'd the enormous blast!
Yellow as leaves of Autumn, the myriads of Angelic hosts
Fell thro' the wintry skies, seeking their graves,
Rattling their hollow bones in howling and lamentation.

Then Enitharmon woke, nor knew that she had slept   150
And eighteen hundred years were fled

As if they had not been.
She call'd her sons & daughters
To the sports of night
Within her crystal house,   155
And thus her song proceeds:

"Arise, Ethinthus! tho' the earth-worm call,
Let him call in vain,
Till the night of holy shadows
And human solitude is past!   160

"Ethinthus, queen of waters, how thou shinest in the sky!
My daughter, how do I rejoice! for thy children flock around
Like the gay fishes on the wave when the cold moon drinks the dew.
Ethinthus! thou art sweet as comforts to my fainting soul,
For now thy waters warble round the feet of Enitharmon.   165

"Manathu-Varcyon! I behold thee flaming in my halls,
Light of thy mother's soul! I see thy lovely eagles round;
Thy golden wings are my delight, & thy flames of soft delusion.

"Where is my lureing bird of Eden? Leutha, silent love!
Leutha, the many colour'd bow delights upon thy wings,   17c
Soft soul of flowers, Leutha!
Sweet smiling pestilence! I see thy blushing light;
Thy daughters, many changing,
Revolve like sweet perfumes ascending, O Leutha, silken queen!

"Where is the youthful Antamon, prince of the pearly dew?   175
O Antamon, why wilt thou leave thy mother Enitharmon?
Alone I see thee, crystal form,
Floating upon the bosom'd air
With lineaments of gratified desire.
My Antamon, the seven churches of Leutha seek thy love.   180

"I hear the soft Oothoon in Enitharmon's tents.
Why wilt thou give up woman's secrecy, my melancholy child?
Between two moments bliss is ripe.
O Theotormon robb'd of joy, I see thy salt tears flow
Down the steps of my crystal house.   185

"Sotha & Thiralatha, secret dwellers of dreamful caves,
Arise and please the horrent fiend with your melodious songs.
Still all your thunders, golden hoof'd, & bind your horses black.
Orc! smile upon my children!
Smile, son of my afflictions.   190
Arise, O Orc, and give our mountains joy of thy red light."

She ceas'd; for All were forth at sport beneath the solemn moon
Waking the stars of Urizen with their immortal songs,
That nature felt thro' all her pores the enormous revelry,
Till morning oped the eastern gate;   195
Then every one fled to his station, & Enitharmon wept.

But terrible Orc, when he beheld the morning in the east,
Shot from the heights of Enitharmon
And in the vineyards of red France appear'd the light of his fury.

The sun glow'd fiery red!   200
The furious terrors flew around!
On golden chariots raging with red wheels dropping with blood.
The Lions lash their wrathful tails!
The Tigers couch upon the prey & suck the ruddy tide,
And Enitharmon groans & cries in anguish and dismay.   205

Then Los arose: his head he rear'd, in snaky thunders clad,
And with a cry that shook all nature to the utmost pole,
Call'd all his sons to the strife of blood.

FINIS

THE
FIRST BOOK
OF
URIZEN

(1794)

PRELUDIUM
TO
THE BOOK OF URIZEN

Of the primeval Priest's assum'd power
When Eternals spurn'd back his religion
And gave him a place in the north,
Obscure, shadowy, void, solitary.

Eternals, I hear your call gladly.
Dictate swift winged words, & fear not
To unfold your dark visions of torment

Chap: I

1. Lo, a shadow of horror is risen
In Eternity! Unknown, unprolific,
Self-clos'd, all-repelling: what Demon
Hath form'd this abominable void,
This soul-shudd'ring vacuum? Some said   5
" It is Urizen." But unknown, abstracted,
Brooding secret, the dark power hid.

2. Times on times he divided, & measur'd
Space by space in his ninefold darkness,
Unseen, unknown: changes appear'd   10
Like desolate mountains rifted furious
By the black winds of perturbation.

3. For he strove in battles dire,
In unseen conflictions with shapes
Bred from his forsaken wilderness   15
Of beast, bird, fish, serpent & element,
Combustion, blast, vapour and cloud.

4. Dark revolving in silent activity,
Unseen in tormenting passions,
An activity unknown and horrible,   20
A self-contemplating shadow
In enormous labours occupied.

5. But Eternals beheld his vast forests.
Age on ages he lay, clos'd, unknown,
Brooding, shut in the deep; all avoid   25
The petrific abominable chaos.

6. His cold horrors silent,[1] dark Urizen
Prepar'd; his ten thousands of thunders
Rang'd in gloom'd array, stretch out across
The dread world; & the rolling of wheels   30
As of swelling seas, sound in his clouds,
In his hills of stor'd snows, in his mountains
Of hail & ice: voices of terror
Are heard like thunders of autumn
When the cloud blazes over the harvests.   35

Chap: II

1. Earth was not, nor globes of attraction.
The will of the Immortal expanded
Or contracted his all flexible senses.
Death was not, but eternal life sprung.

2. The sound of a trumpet the heavens   5
Awoke, & vast clouds of blood roll'd
Round the dim rocks of Urizen, so nam'd
That solitary one in Immensity.

[2]3. Shrill the trumpet; & myriads of Eternity
Muster around the bleak desarts   10
Now fill'd with clouds, darkness & waters
That roll'd perplex'd lab'ring, & utter'd
Words articulate bursting in thunders
That roll'd on the tops of his mountains

---

[1] Probably an adverbial use, like the " gentle " of " The Book of Thel."
[2] This line is crossed out in Baron Dimsdale's copy.

4. From the depths of dark solitude: '' From   15
The eternal abode, in my holiness
Hidden, set apart in my stern counsels
Reserv'd for the days of futurity,
I have sought for a joy without pain,
For a solid without fluctuation.   20
Why will you die, O Eternals?
Why live in unquenchable burnings?

5. '' First I fought with the fire, consum'd
Inwards into a deep world within,
A void immense, wild, dark & deep,   25
Where nothing was, Nature's wide womb:
And self-balanc'd, stretch'd o'er the void,
I alone, even I! the winds merciless
Bound; but condensing in torrents
They fall and fall; strong I repell'd   30
The vast waves, & arose on the waters
A wide world of solid obstruction.

6. '' Here alone I, in books form'd of metals,
Have written the secrets of wisdom,
The secrets of dark contemplation,   35
By fightings and conflicts dire
With terrible monsters Sin-bred
Which the bosoms of all inhabit,
Seven deadly Sins of the soul.

7. ''Lo! I unfold my darkness, and on   40
This rock place with strong hand the Book
Of eternal brass, written in my solitude:

8. '' Laws of peace, of love, of unity,
Of pity, compassion, forgiveness.
Let each chuse one habitation,   45
His ancient infinite mansion,
One command, one joy, one desire,
One curse, one weight, one measure,
One King, one God, one Law.''

Chap: III

1. The voice ended: they saw his pale visage
Emerge from the darkness, his hand
On the rock of eternity unclasping
The Book of brass. Rage siez'd the strong,

2. Rage, fury, intense indignation.   5
In cataracts of fire, blood & gall,
In whirlwinds of sulphurous smoke
And enormous forms of energy,
[1] All the seven deadly sins of the soul
In living creations appear'd   10
In the flames of eternal fury.

3. Sund'ring, dark'ning, thund'ring!
Rent away with a terrible crash,
Eternity roll'd wide apart,
Wide asunder rolling   15
Mountainous, all around
Departing, departing, departing,
Leaving ruinous fragments of life
Hanging, frowning cliffs, & all between
An ocean of voidness unfathomable.   20

4. The roaring fires ran o'er the heav'ns
In whirlwinds & cataracts of blood,
And o'er the dark desarts of Urizen
Fires pour thro' the void on all sides
On Urizen's self-begotten armies.   25

5. But no light from the fires, all was darkness
In the flames of Eternal fury.

6. In fierce anguish & quenchless flames
To the desarts and rocks he ran raging
To hide, but he could not: combining,   30
He dug mountains & hills in vast strength,
He piled them in incessant labour,
In howlings & pangs & fierce madness,
Long periods in burning fires labouring,
Till hoary and age-broke and aged,   35
In despair and the shadows of death.

7. And a roof vast, petrific, around
On all sides he fram'd, like a womb,
Where thousands of rivers in veins
Of blood pour down the mountains to cool   40
The eternal fires beating without
From Eternals; & like a black globe
View'd by sons of Eternity, standing
On the shore of the infinite ocean,

[1] This line is erased from Baron Dimsdale's copy and the two following
are crossed out.

Like a human heart strugling & beating   45
The vast world of Urizen appear'd.

8. And Los round the dark globe of Urizen
Kept watch for Eternals to confine
The obscure separation alone;
For Eternity stood wide apart   50
As the stars are apart from the earth.

9. Los wept howling around the dark Demon,
And cursing his lot; for in anguish
Urizen was rent from his side,
And a fathomless void for his feet,   55
And intense fires for his dwelling.

10. But Urizen laid in a stony sleep,
Unorganiz'd, rent from Eternity.

11. The Eternals said, " What is this? Death.
Urizen is a clod of clay."   60

12. Los howl'd in a dismal stupor,
Groaning! gnashing! groaning!
Till the wrenching apart was healed.

13. But the wrenching of Urizen heal'd not.
Cold, featureless, flesh or clay   65
Rifted with direful changes,
He lay in a dreamless night,

14. Till Los rouz'd his fires, affrighted
At the formless unmeasurable death.

Chap : IV

1. Los, smitten with astonishment,
Frighten'd at the hurtling bones

2. And at the surging sulphureous
Perturbed Immortal, mad raging

3. In whirlwinds & pitch & nitre
Round the furious limbs of Los.

4. And Los formed nets & gins
And threw the nets round about.

5. He watch'd in shudd'ring fear
The dark changes, & bound every change   10
With rivets of iron & brass.

6. And these were the changes of Urizen:

Chap: IV [a]

1. Ages on ages roll'd over him,
In stony sleep ages roll'd over him,
Like a dark waste stretching chang'able
By earthquakes riv'n, belching sullen fires:
On ages roll'd ages in ghastly   5
Sick torment; around him in whirlwinds
Of darkness the eternal Prophet howl'd,
Beating still on his rivets of iron,
Pouring sodor of iron, dividing
The horrible night into watches.   10

2. And Urizen (so his eternal name)
His prolific delight obscur'd more & more
In dark secresy, hiding in surgeing
Sulphureous fluid his phantasies.
The Eternal Prophet heav'd the dark bellows   15
And turn'd restless the tongs, and the hammer
Incessant beat, forging chains new & new,
Numb'ring with links hours, days & years.

3. The Eternal mind bounded began to roll
Eddies of wrath ceaseless round & round,   20
And the sulphureous foam, surgeing thick,
Settled, a lake bright & shining clear,
White as the snow on the mountains cold.

4. Forgetfulness, dumbness, necessity!
In chains of the mind locked up,   25
Like fetters of ice shrinking together,
Disorganiz'd, rent from Eternity.
Los beat on his fetters of iron,
And heated his furnaces & pour'd
Iron sodor and sodor of brass.   30

5. Restless turn'd the immortal inchain'd,
Heaving dolorous! anguish'd unbearable,
Till a roof, shaggy wild, inclos'd
In an orb his fountain of thought.

6. In a horrible dreamful slumber,　　35
Like the linked infernal chain
A vast Spine writh'd in torment
Upon the winds, shooting pain'd
Ribs, like a bending cavern;
And bones of solidness froze　　40
Over all his nerves of joy.
And a first Age passed over,
And a state of dismal woe.

7. From the caverns of his jointed Spine
Down sunk with fright a red　　45
Round globe, hot burning, deep
Deep down into the Abyss,
Panting, Conglobing, Trembling,
Shooting out ten thousand branches
Around his solid bones.　　50
And a second Age passed over,
And a state of dismal woe.

8. In harrowing fear rolling round,
His nervous brain shot branches
Round the branches of his heart　　55
On high into two little orbs,
And fixed in two little caves
Hiding carefully from the wind,
His Eyes beheld the deep.
And a third Age passed over,　　60
And a state of dismal woe.

9. The pangs of hope began.
In heavy pain, striving, struggling,
Two Ears in close volutions
From beneath his orbs of vision　　65
Shot spiring out and petrified
As they grew. And a fourth Age passed,
And a state of dismal woe.

10. In ghastly torment sick,
Hanging upon the wind,　　70
Two Nostrils bent down to the deep.
And a fifth Age passed over,
And a state of dismal woe.

11. In ghastly torment sick,
Within his ribs bloated round　　75
A craving Hungry Cavern.
Thence arose his channel'd Throat,

And like a red flame, a Tongue
Of thirst & of hunger appear'd.
And a sixth Age passed over,   80
And a state of dismal woe.

12. Enraged & stifled with torment,
He threw his right Arm to the north,
His left Arm to the south
Shooting out in anguish deep,   85
And his Feet stamp'd the nether Abyss
In trembling & howling & dismay.
And a seventh [1] Age passed over,
And a state of dismal woe.

Chap: V

1. In terrors Los shrunk from his task:
His great hammer fell from his hand.
His fires beheld, and sickening
Hid their strong limbs in smoke;
For with noises ruinous loud,   5
With hurtlings & clashings & groans,
The Immortal endur'd his chains,
Tho' bound in a deadly sleep.

2. All the myriads of Eternity,
All the wisdom & joy of life   10
Roll like a sea around him,
Except what his little orbs
Of sight by degrees unfold.

3. And now his eternal life
Like a dream was obliterated.   15

4. Shudd'ring, the Eternal Prophet smote
With a stroke from his north to south region.
The bellows & hammer are silent now,
A nerveless silence his prophetic voice
Siez'd; a cold solitude & dark void   20
The Eternal Prophet & Urizen clos'd.

5. Ages on ages roll'd over them,
Cut off from life & light, frozen
Into horrible forms of deformity.

[1] In the British Museum copy this word is " second," but in Baron
Dimsdale's copy the word is clearly " seventh."

Los suffer'd his fires to decay;   25
Then he look'd back with anxious desire,
But the space, undivided by existence,
Struck horror into his soul.

6. Los wept, obscur'd with mourning,
His bosom earthquak'd with sighs;   30
He saw Urizen deadly black,
In his chains bound, & Pity began

7. In anguish dividing & dividing,
For pity divides the soul.
In pangs, eternity on eternity,   35
Life in cataracts pour'd down his cliffs.
The void shrunk the lymph into Nerves
Wand'ring wide on the bosom of night,
And left a round globe of blood
Trembling upon the void.   40

Thus the Eternal Prophet was divided
Before the death image of Urizen;
For in changeable clouds and darkness,
In a winterly night beneath,
The Abyss of Los stretch'd immense,   45
And now seen, now obscur'd, to the eyes
Of Eternals the visions remote
Of the dark seperation appear'd.
As glasses discover Worlds
In the endless Abyss of space,   50
So the expanding eyes of Immortals
Beheld the dark visions of Los
And the globe of life blood trembling.

8. The globe of life blood trembled
Branching out into roots   55
Fibrous, writhing upon the winds,
Fibres of blood, milk and tears,
In pangs, eternity on eternity.
At length, in tears & cries imbodied,
A female form trembling and pale   60
Waves before his deathy face.

9. All Eternity shudder'd at sight
Of the first female now separate,
Pale as a cloud of snow
Waving before the face of Los.   65

10. Wonder, awe, fear, astonishment
Petrify the eternal myriads

At the first female form now separate.
They call'd her Pity, and fled.

11. " Spread a Tent with strong curtains around them.
Let cords & stakes bind in the Void,   71
That Eternals may no more behold them."

12. They began to weave curtains of darkness,
They erected large pillars round the Void,
With golden hooks fasten'd in the pillars;   75
With infinite labour the Eternals
A woof wove, and called it Science.

Chap: VI

1. But Los saw the Female & pitied;
He embrac'd her; she wept, she refus'd;
In perverse and cruel delight
She fled from his arms, yet he follow'd.

2. Eternity shudder'd when they saw   5
Man begetting his likeness
On his own divided image.

3. A time passed over: the Eternals
Began to erect the tent,
When Enitharmon sick   10
Felt a Worm within her womb.

4. Yet helpless it lay like a Worm
In the trembling womb
To be moulded into existence.

5. All day the worm lay on her bosom;   15
All night within her womb
The worm lay, till it grew to a serpent
With dolorous hissings & poisons
Round Enitharmon's loins folding.

6. Coil'd within Enitharmon's womb   20
The serpent grew, casting its scales;
With sharp pangs the hissings began
To change to a grating cry.
Many sorrows and dismal throes,
Many forms of fish, bird & beast   25
Brought forth an Infant form
Where was a worm before.

7. The Eternals their tent finished
Alarm'd with these gloomy visions,
When Enitharmon groaning   30
Produc'd a man Child to the light.

8. A shriek ran thro' Eternity
And a paralytic stroke
At the birth of the Human shadow.

9. Delving earth in his resistless way,   35
Howling, the Child with fierce flames
Issu'd from Enitharmon.

10. The Eternals closed the tent;
They beat down the stakes, the cords
Stretch'd for a work of eternity.   40
No more Los beheld Eternity.

11. In his hands he siez'd the infant;
He bathed him in springs of sorrow;
He gave him to Enitharmon.

Chap: VII

1. They named the child Orc; he grew,
Fed with milk of Enitharmon.

2. Los awoke her. O sorrow & pain!
A tight'ning girdle grew
Around his bosom. In sobbings   5
He burst the girdle in twain,
But still another girdle
Oppress'd his bosom. In sobbings
Again he burst it. Again
Another girdle succeeds.   10
The girdle was form'd by day,
By night was burst in twain.

3. These falling down on the rock
Into an iron Chain,
In each other link by link lock'd.   15

4. They took Orc to the top of a mountain.
O how Enitharmon wept!
They chain'd his young limbs to the rock
With the Chain of Jealousy
Beneath Urizen's deathful shadow.   20

5. The dead heard the voice of the child
And began to awake from sleep;
All things heard the voice of the child
And began to awake to life.

6. And Urizen, craving with hunger,   25
Stung with the odours of Nature,
Explor'd his dens around.

7. He form'd a line & a plummet
To divide the Abyss beneath;
He form'd a dividing rule.   30

8. He formed scales to weigh,
He formed massy weights,
He formed a brazen quadrant,
He formed golden compasses,
And began to explore the Abyss;   35
And he planted a garden of fruits.

9. But Los encircled Enitharmon
With fires of Prophecy
From the sight of Urizen & Orc,

10. And she bore an enormous race.   40

Chap: VIII

1. Urizen explor'd his dens,
Mountain, moor & wilderness,
With a globe of fire lighting his journey,
A fearful journey, annoy'd
By cruel enormities, forms   5
Of life on his forsaken mountains.

2. And his world teem'd vast enormities,
Fright'ning, faithless, fawning
Portions of life, similitudes
Of a foot or a hand or a head   10
Or a heart or an eye; they swam, mischevous
Dread terrors, delighting in blood.

3. Most Urizen sicken'd to see
His eternal creations appear
Sons & daughters of sorrow on mountains   15
Weeping! wailing! first Thiriel appear'd,

WILLIAM BLAKE

Astonish'd at his own existence,
Like a man from a cloud born, & Utha
From the waters emerging, laments.
Grodna rent the deep earth, howling   20
Amaz'd; his heavens immense cracks
Like the ground parch'd with heat: then Fuzon
Flam'd out, first begotten, last born.[1]
All his eternal sons in like manner,
His daughters from green herbs & cattle,   25
From monsters & worms of the pit.

4. He, in darkness clos'd, view'd all his race,
And his soul sicken'd! he curs'd
Both sons and daughters, for he saw
That no flesh nor spirit could keep   30
His iron laws one moment.

5. For he saw that life liv'd upon death:
The Ox in the slaughter house moans,
The Dog at the wintry door.
And he wept & he called it Pity,   35
And his tears flowed down on the winds.

6. Cold he wander'd on high, over their cities
In weeping & pain & woe;
And where-ever he wander'd in sorrows
Upon the aged heavens   40
A cold shadow follow'd behind him
Like a spider's web, moist, cold & dim,
Drawing out from his sorrowing soul,
The dungeon-like heaven dividing,
Where ever the footsteps of Urizen   45
Walk'd over the cities in sorrow;

7. Till a Web, dark & cold, throughout all
The tormented element stretch'd
From the sorrows of Urizen's soul;
And the Web is a Female in embrio: 50
None could break the Web, no wings of fire,

8. So twisted the cords & so knotted
The meshes, twisted like to the human brain.

9. And all call'd it The Net of Religion.

[1] The Clarendon Edition of the Prophetic Books gives the word "of" at
the end of this line, but this does not appear either in Baron Dimsdale's
copy or in the British Museum copy of the book.

Chap: IX

1. Then the Inhabitants of those Cities
Felt their Nerves change into Marrow,
And hardening Bones began
In swift diseases and torments,
In throbbings & shootings & grindings   5
Thro' all the coasts, till weaken'd
The Senses inward rush'd shrinking
Beneath the dark net of infection;

2. Till the shrunken eyes, clouded over,
Discern'd not the woven hipocrisy,   10
But the streaky slime in their heavens,
Brought together by narrowing perceptions,
Appear'd transparent air; for their eyes
Grew small like the eyes of a man,
And in reptile forms shrinking together,   15
Of seven feet stature they remain'd.

3. Six days they shrunk up from existence
And on the seventh day they rested,
And they bless'd the seventh day, in sick hope,
And forgot their eternal life.   20

4. And their thirty cities divided
In form of a human heart.
No more could they rise at will
In the infinite void, but bound down
To earth by their narrowing perceptions,   25
They lived a period of years,
Then left a noisom body
To the jaws of devouring darkness.

5. And their children wept, & built
Tombs in the desolate places,   30
And form'd laws of prudence and call'd them
The eternal laws of God.

6. And the thirty cities remain'd
Surrounded by salt floods, now call'd
Africa: its name was then Egypt.   35

7. The remaining sons of Urizen
Beheld their brethren shrink together
Beneath the Net of Urizen.
Perswasion was in vain,

For the ears of the inhabitants   40
Were wither'd & deafn'd & cold,
And their eyes could not discern
Their brethren of other cities.

8. So Fuzon call'd all together
The remaining children of Urizen,
And they left the pendulous earth: 45
They called it Egypt, & left it.

9. And the salt ocean rolled englob'd.

The End of the
book of Urizen

THE
SONG of
LOS

(1795)

AFRICA

I will sing you a song of Los, the Eternal Prophet:
He sung it to four harps at the tables of Eternity.
In heart-formed Africa
Urizen faded! Ariston shudder'd!
And thus the Song began: 5

ADAM stood in the garden of Eden
And Noah on the mountains of Ararat;
They saw Urizen give his Laws to the Nations
By the hands of the children of Los.

Adam shudder'd! Noah faded! black grew the sunny African   10
When Rintrah gave Abstract Philosophy to Brama in the East.
    (Night spoke to the Cloud!
" Lo, these Human form'd spirits, in smiling hipocrisy War
Against one another; so let them War on, slaves to the eternal
    Elements.")
Noah shrunk beneath the waters;   15
Abram fled in fires from Chaldea;
Moses beheld upon Mount Sinai forms of dark delusion.

To Trismegistus Palamabron gave an abstract Law;
To Pythagoras, Socrates & Plato.

Times rolled on o'er all the sons of Har, time after time.   20
Orc on Mount Atlas howl'd, chain'd down with the Chain of
    Jealousy.
Then Oothoon hover'd over Judah & Jerusalem,
And Jesus heard her voice (a man of sorrows); he reciev'd
A Gospel from wretched Theotormon.

E 792   93

The human race began to wither, for the healthy built   25
Secluded places, fearing the joys of Love,
And the diseased only propagated.
So Antamon call'd up Leutha from her valleys of delight
And to Mahomet a loose Bible gave.

But in the North, to Odin Sotha gave a Code of War,   30
Because of Diralada, thinking to reclaim his joy.

These were the Churches, Hospitals, Castles, Palaces,
Like nets & gins & traps to catch the joys of Eternity,
          And all the rest a desart,
Till like a dream Eternity was obliterated & erased,   35

Since that dread day when Har and Heva fled
Because their brethren & sisters liv'd in War & Lust;
And as they fled, they shrunk
Into two narrow doleful forms
Creeping in reptile flesh upon   40
The bosom of the ground,
And all the vast of Nature shrunk
Before their shrunken eyes.

Thus the terrible race of Los & Enitharmon gave
Laws & Religions to the sons of Har, binding them more   45
And more to Earth: closing and restraining,
Till a Philosophy of Five Senses was complete.
Urizen wept & gave it into the hands of Newton & Locke.

Clouds roll heavy upon the Alps round Rousseau & Voltaire,
And on the mountains of Lebanon round the deceased Gods   50
Of Asia, & on the desarts of Africa round the Fallen Angels.
The Guardian Prince of Albion burns in his nightly tent.

ASIA

THE Kings of Asia heard
The howl rise up from Europe!
And each ran out from his Web,
From his ancient woven Den;
For the darkness of Asia was startled   5
At the thick-flaming, thought-creating fires of Orc.

And the Kings of Asia stood
And cried in bitterness of soul:

" Shall not the King call for Famine from the heath,
Nor the Priest for Pestilence from the fen?　　　　10
To restrain! to dismay! to thin!
The inhabitants of mountain and plain
In the day of full-feeding prosperity
And the night of delicious songs.

" Shall not the Councellor throw his curb　　　　15
Of Poverty on the laborious?
To fix the price of labour,
To invent allegoric riches,

" And the privy admonishers of men
Call for fires in the City,　　　　20
For heaps of smoking ruins
In the night of prosperity & wantonness,

" To turn man from his path,
To restrain the child from the womb,
To cut off the bread from the city,　　　　25
That the remnant may learn to obey,

" That the pride of the heart may fail,
That the lust of the eyes may be quench'd,
That the delicate ear in its infancy
May be dull'd, and the nostrils clos'd up,　　　　30
To teach mortal worms the path
That leads from the gates of the Grave."

　　　Urizen heard them cry,
And his shudd'ring waving wings
Went enormous above the red flames　　　　35
Drawing clouds of despair thro' the heavens
Of Europe as he went.
And his Books of brass, iron & gold
Melted over the land as he flew
Heavy-waving, howling, weeping.　　　　40

　　　　And he stood over Judea,
　　　　And stay'd in his ancient place,
　　　　And stretch'd his clouds over Jerusalem;

　　　　For Adam, a mouldering skeleton,
　　　　Lay bleach'd on the garden of Eden,　　　　45
　　　　And Noah, as white as snow,
　　　　On the mountains of Ararat.

Then the thunders of Urizen bellow'd aloud
From his woven darkness above.

Orc, raging in European darkness,   50
Arose like a pillar of fire above the Alps,
Like a serpent of fiery flame!

        The sullen Earth
        Shrunk!

Forth from the dead dust, rattling bones to bones   55
Join: shaking convuls'd, the shiv'ring clay breathes
And all flesh naked stands: Fathers and Friends,
Mothers & Infants, Kings & Warriors.

    The Grave shrieks with delight, & shakes
    Her hollow womb, & clasps the solid stem.   60
    Her bosom swells with wild desire,
    And milk & blood & glandous wine
    In rivers rush & shout & dance
    On mountain, dale and plain.

        The SONG of LOS is Ended

            Urizen Wept.

THE
BOOK of
AHANIA

(1795)

Chap: Ist

1. FUZON on a chariot iron-wing'd
On spiked flames rose: his hot visage
Flam'd furious; sparkles his hair & beard
Shot down his wide bosom and shoulders.
On clouds of smoke rages his chariot,   5
And his right hand burns red in its cloud,
Moulding into a vast globe his wrath
As the thunder-stone is moulded,
Son of Urizen's silent burnings.

2. "Shall we worship this Demon of smoke,"   10
Said Fuzon, "this abstract non-entity,
This cloudy God seated on waters,
Now seen, now obscur'd, King of Sorrow?"

3. So he spoke in a fiery flame,
On Urizen frowning indignant,   15
The Globe of wrath shaking on high.
Roaring with fury, he threw
The howling Globe; burning it flew,
Length'ning into a hungry beam. Swiftly

4. Oppos'd to the exulting flam'd beam   20
The broad Disk of Urizen upheav'd
Across the Void many a mile.

5. It was forg'd in mills where the winter
Beats incessant: ten winters the disk
Unremitting endur'd the cold hammer.   25

6. But the strong arm that sent it remember'd
The sounding beam: laughing, it tore through
That beaten mass, keeping its direction,
The cold loins of Urizen dividing.

7. Dire shriek'd his invisible Lust.   30
Deep groan'd Urizen! stretching his awful hand,
Ahania (so name his parted soul)
He siez'd on his mountains of Jealousy.
He groan'd, anguish'd, & called her Sin,
Kissing her and weeping over her;   35
Then hid her in darkness, in silence,
Jealous tho' she was invisible.

8. She fell down, a faint shadow wand'ring
In chaos and circling dark Urizen
As the moon, anguish'd, circles the earth: 40
Hopeless! abhorr'd! a death-shadow
Unseen, unbodied, unknown,
The mother of Pestilence.

9. But the fiery beam of Fuzon
Was a pillar of fire to Egypt   45
Five hundred years wand'ring on earth
Till Los siez'd it and beat in a mass
With the body of the sun.

Chap: II^d

1. But the forehead of Urizen gathering,
And his eyes pale with anguish, his lips
Blue & changing, in tears and bitter
Contrition, he prepar'd his Bow

2. Form'd of Ribs that in his dark solitude,   5
When obscur'd in his forests, fell monsters
Arose. For his dire Contemplations
Rush'd down like floods from his mountains,
In torrents of mud settling thick
With Eggs of unnatural production: 10
Forthwith hatching, some howl'd on his hills,
Some in vales, some aloft flew in air.

3. Of these, an enormous dread Serpent,
Scaled and poisonous horned,
Approach'd Urizen even to his knees   15
As he sat on his dark rooted Oak.

4. With his horns he push'd furious:
Great the conflict & great the jealousy
In cold poisons: but Urizen smote him.

5. First he poison'd the rocks with his blood,   20
Then polish'd his ribs, and his sinews
Dried, laid them apart till winter;
Then a Bow black prepar'd; on this Bow
A poisoned rock plac'd in silence.
He utter'd these words to the Bow: 25

6. "O Bow of the clouds of secrecy,
O nerve of that lust form'd monster!
Send this rock swift invisible thro'
The black clouds on the bosom of Fuzon."

7. So saying, In torment of his wounds,   3c
He bent the enormous ribs slowly:
A circle of darkness! then fixed
The sinew in its rest; then the Rock,
Poisonous source! plac'd with art, lifting difficult
Its weighty bulk: silent the rock lay,   35

8. While Fuzon, his tygers unloosing,
Thought Urizen slain by his wrath.
"I am God," said he, " eldest of things!"

9. Sudden sings the rock: swift & invisible
On Fuzon flew: enter'd his bosom.   40
His beautiful visage, his tresses
That gave light to the mornings of heaven,
Were smitten with darkness, deform'd
And outstretch'd on the edge of the forest.

10. But the rock fell upon the Earth,   45
Mount Sinai in Arabia.

Chap: III

1. The Globe shook, and Urizen, seated
On black clouds, his sore wound anointed;
The ointment flow'd down on the void
Mix'd with blood: here the snake gets her poison.

2. With difficulty & great pain Urizen   5
Lifted on high the dead corse:
On his shoulders he bore it to where
A Tree hung over the Immensity.

3. For when Urizen shrunk away
From Eternals, he sat on a rock   10
Barren: a rock which himself
From redounding fancies had petrified.
Many tears fell on the rock,
Many sparks of vegetation.
Soon shot the pained root   15
Of Mystery under his heel.
It grew a thick tree: he wrote
In silence his book of iron,
Till the horrid plant, bending its boughs,
Grew to roots when it felt the earth   20
And again sprung to many a tree.

4. Amaz'd started Urizen! when
He beheld himself compassed round
And high roofed over with trees.
He arose, but the stems stood so thick   25
He with difficulty and great pain
Brought his Books, all but the Book
Of iron, from the dismal shade.

5. The Tree still grows over the Void,
Enrooting itself all around,   30
And endless labyrinth of woe!

6. The corse of his first begotten
On the accursed Tree of Mystery,
On the topmost stem of this Tree
Urizen nail'd Fuzon's corse.   35

Chap: IV

1. Forth flew the arrows of pestilence
Round the pale living Corse on the tree;

2. For in Urizen's slumbers of abstraction
In the infinite ages of Eternity,
When his Nerves of Joy melted and flow'd   5
A white Lake on the dark blue air,
In perturb'd pain and dismal torment
Now stretching out, now swift conglobing,

3. Effluvia vapour'd above
In noxious clouds; these hover'd thick   10
Over the disorganiz'd Immortal,
Till petrific pain scurf'd o'er the Lakes
As the bones of man, solid & dark.

4. The clouds of disease hover'd wide
Around the Immortal in torment,   15
Perching around the hurtling bones,
Disease on disease, shape on shape,
Winged, screaming in blood & torment.

5. The Eternal Prophet beat on his anvils,
Enrag'd in the desolate darkness,   20
He forg'd nets of iron around
And Los threw them around the bones.

6. The shapes screaming flutter'd vain:
Some combin'd into muscles & glands,
Some organs for craving and lust;   25
Most remain'd on the tormented void,
Urizen's army of horrors.

7. Round the pale living Corse on the Tree
Forty years flew the arrows of pestilence.

8. Wailing and terror and woe   30
Ran thro' all his dismal world
Forty years; all his sons & daughters
Felt their skulls harden; then Asia
Arose in the pendulous deep.

9. They reptilize upon the Earth.   35

10. Fuzon groan'd on the Tree.

Chap: V

1. The lamenting voice of Ahania
Weeping upon the void
And round the Tree of Fuzon:
Distant in solitary night
Her voice was heard, but no form   5
Had she; but her tears from clouds
Eternal fell round the Tree.

2. And the voice cried: " Ah, Urizen! Love!
Flower of morning! I weep on the verge
Of Non-entity: how wide the Abyss   10
Between Ahania and thee!

*E 792

3. "I lie on the verge of the deep,
I see thy dark clouds ascend,
I see thy black forests and floods
A horrible waste to my eyes!   15

4. "Weeping I walk over rocks,
Over dens & thro' valleys of death.
Why didst thou despise Ahania,
To cast me from thy bright presence
Into the World of Loneness?   20

5. "I cannot touch his hand,
Nor weep on his knees, nor hear
His voice & bow, nor see his eyes
And joy, nor hear his footsteps and
My heart leap at the lovely sound!   25
I cannot kiss the place
Whereon his bright feet have trod,
But I wander on the rocks
With hard necessity.

6. "Where is my golden palace?   30
Where my ivory bed?
Where the joy of my morning hour?
Where the sons of eternity singing

7. "To awake bright Urizen, my king,
To arise to the mountain sport,   35
To the bliss of eternal valleys:

8. "To awake my king in the morn
To embrace Ahania's joy
On the bredth of his open bosom,
From my soft cloud of dew to fall   40
In showers of life on his harvests?

9. "When he gave my happy soul
To the sons of eternal joy:
When he took the daughters of life
Into my chambers of love: 45

10. "When I found babes of bliss on my beds,
And bosoms of milk in my chambers
Fill'd with eternal seed,
O! eternal births sung round Ahania
In interchange sweet of their joys.   50

11. "Swell'd with ripeness & fat with fatness,
Bursting on winds my odors,
My ripe figs and rich pomegranates
In infant joy at thy feet
O Urizen, sported and sang. 55

12. "Then thou with thy lap full of seed,
With thy hand full of generous fire,
Walked forth from the clouds of morning,
On the virgins of springing joy,
On the human soul to cast 60
The seed of eternal science.

13. "The sweat poured down thy temples
To Ahania return'd in evening;
The moisture awoke to birth
My mother's-joys, sleeping in bliss. 65

14. "But now, alone, over rocks, mountains,
Cast out from thy lovely bosom,
Cruel jealousy, selfish fear,
Self-destroying: how can delight
Renew in these chains of darkness 70
Where bones of beasts are strown
On the bleak and snowy mountains
Where bones from the birth are buried
Before they see the light? "

FINIS

THE
BOOK of
LOS

(1795)

Chap: I

1. *ENO, aged Mother*
Who the chariot of Leutha guides
Since the day of thunders in old time,

2. *Sitting beneath the eternal Oak,*
Trembled and shook the steadfast Earth,   5
And thus her speech broke forth:

3. *" O Times remote!*
When Love & Joy were adoration
And none impure were deem'd,
Not Eyeless Covet,   10
Nor Thin-lip'd Envy,
Nor Bristled Wrath,
Nor Curled Wantonness;

4. *" But Covet was poured full,*
Envy fed with fat of lambs,   15
Wrath with lion's gore,
Wantonness lull'd to sleep
With the virgin's lute
Or sated with her love,

5. *" Till Covet broke his locks & bars*   20
And slept with open doors,
Envy sung at the rich man's feast,
Wrath was follow'd up and down
By a little ewe lamb,
And Wantonness on his own true love   25
Begot a giant race.

6. Raging furious, the flames of desire
Ran thro' heaven & earth, living flames,
Intelligent, organiz'd, arm'd
With destruction & plagues. In the midst   30
The Eternal Prophet, bound in a chain,
Compell'd to watch Urizen's shadow,

7. Rag'd with curses & sparkles of fury.
Round the flames roll as Los hurls his chains,
Mounting up from his fury, condens'd,   35
Rolling round & round, mounting on high
Into vacuum, into non-entity
Where nothing was! dash'd wide apart,
His feet stamp the eternal fierce-raging
Rivers of wide flame; they roll round   40
And round on all sides, making their way
Into darkness and shadowy obscurity.

8. Wide apart stood the fires. Los remain'd
In the void between fire and fire.
In trembling and horror they beheld him;   45
They stood wide apart, driv'n by his hands
And his feet which the nether abyss
Stamp'd in fury and hot indignation.

9. But no light from the fires, all was
Darkness round Los; heat was not, for bound up   50
Into fiery spheres from his fury
The gigantic flames trembled and hid.

10. Coldness, darkness, obstruction, a Solid
Without fluctuation, hard as adamant,
Black as marble of Egypt impenetrable,   55
Bound in the fierce raging Immortal;
And the separated fires, froze in
A vast solid without fluctuation,
Bound in his expanding clear senses.

Chap: II

1. The Immortal stood frozen amidst
The vast rock of eternity times
And times, a night of vast durance,
Impatient, stifled, stiffen'd, hard'ned,

2. Till impatience no longe could bear   5
The hard bondage, rent, rent the vast solid,
With a crash from immense to immense

3. Crack'd across into numberless fragments.
The Prophetic wrath, strugling for vent,
Hurls apart, stamping furious to dust,   10
And crumbling with bursting sobs, heaves
The black marble on high into fragments.

4. Hurl'd apart on all sides as a falling
Rock, the innumerable fragments away
Fell asunder; and horrible vacuum   15
Beneath him & on all sides round.

5. Falling, falling! Los fell & fell,
Sunk precipitant, heavy, down, down,
Times on times, night on night, day on day:
Truth has bounds, Error none: falling, falling;   20
Years on years, and ages on ages
Still he fell thro' the void, still a void
Found for falling day & night without end;
For tho' day or night was not, their spaces
Were measur'd by his incessant whirls   25
In the horrid vacuity bottomless.

6. The Immortal revolving, indignant
First in wrath threw his limbs, like the babe
New born into our world: wrath subsided
And contemplative thoughts first arose.   30
Then aloft his head rear'd in the Abyss
And his downward-borne fall chang'd oblique.

7. Many ages of groans, till there grew
Branchy forms organizing the Human
Into finite inflexible organs,   35

8. Till in process from falling he bore
Sidelong on the purple air, wafting
The weak breeze in efforts o'erwearied.

9. Incessant the falling Mind labour'd
Organizing itself, till the Vacuum   40
Became element pliant to rise
Or to fall, or to swim, or to fly,
With ease searching the dire vacuity.

Chap: III

1. The Lungs heave incessant, dull and heavy,
For as yet were all other parts formless,
Shiv'ring, clinging around like a cloud,
Dim & glutinous as the white Polypus
Driv'n by waves & englob'd on the tide.   5

2. And the unformed part crav'd repose.
Sleep began; the Lungs heave on the wave,
Weary, overweigh'd, sinking beneath.
In a stifling black fluid he woke:

3. He arose on the waters, but soon   10
Heavy falling, his organs, like roots
Shooting out from the seed, shot beneath,
And a vast world of waters around him
In furious torrents began.

4. Then he sunk, & around his spent Lungs   15
Began intricate pipes that drew in
The spawn of the waters. Outbranching
An immense Fibrous form, stretching out
Thro' the bottoms of immensity, raging,

5. He rose on the floods; then he smote   20
The wild deep with his terrible wrath
Seperating the heavy and thin.

6. Down the heavy sunk, cleaving around
To the fragments of solid: up rose
The thin, flowing round the fierce fires   25
That glow'd furious in the expanse.

Chap: IV

1. Then Light first began: from the fires,
Beams, conducted by fluid so pure,
Flow'd around the Immense, Los beheld
Forthwith writhing upon the dark void
The Back bone of Urizen appear   5
Hurtling upon the wind
Like a serpent! like an iron chain
Whirling about in the Deep.

2. Upfolding his Fibres together
To a Form of impregnable strength,   10
Los, astonish'd and terrified, built
Furnaces; he formed an Anvil,
A Hammer of adamant: then began
The binding of Urizen day and night.

3. Circling round the dark Demon, with howlings   15
Dismay & sharp blightings, the Prophet
Of Eternity beat on his iron links.

4. And first, from those infinite fires,
The light that flow'd down on the winds
He siez'd, beating incessant, condensing   20
The subtil particles in an Orb.

5. Roaring indignant the bright sparks
Endur'd the vast Hammer; but unwearied
Los beat on the Anvil, till glorious
An immense Orb of fire he fram'd.   25

6. Oft he quench'd it beneath in the Deeps;
Then survey'd the all bright mass. Again
Siezing fires from the terrific Orbs,
He heated the round Globe; then beat,
While roaring his furnaces endur'd   30
The chain'd Orb in their infinite wombs.

7. Nine ages completed their circles
When Los heated the glowing mass, casting
It down into the Deeps: the Deeps fled
Away in redounding smoke: the Sun   35
Stood self-balanc'd. And Los smil'd with joy.
He the vast Spine of Urizen siez'd
And bound down to the glowing illusion.

8. But no light; for the Deep fled away
On all sides, and left an unform'd   40
Dark vacuity: here Urizen lay
In fierce torments on his glowing bed,

9. Till his Brain in a rock, & his Heart
In a fleshy slough formed four rivers
Obscuring the immense Orb of fire   45
Flowing down into night; till a Form
Was completed, a Human Illusion
In darkness and deep clouds involv'd.

The End of the
Book of LOS

MILTON

A

POEM

IN 2 BOOKS

To Justify the Ways of God to Men

(Begun 1804*)*

PREFACE

THE Stolen and Perverted Writings of Homer & Ovid, of Plato & Cicero, which all Men ought to contemn, are set up by artifice against the Sublime of the Bible; but when the New Age is at leisure to Pronounce, all will be set right, & those Grand Works of the more ancient & consciously & professedly Inspired Men will hold their proper rank, & the Daughters of Memory shall become the Daughters of Inspiration. Shakspeare & Milton were both curb'd by the general malady & infection from the silly Greek & Latin slaves of the Sword.

Rouze up, O Young Men of the New Age! set your foreheads against the ignorant Hirelings! For we have Hirelings in the Camp, the Court & the University, who would, if they could, for ever depress Mental & prolong Corporeal War. Painters! on you I call. Sculptors! Architects! Suffer not the fashionable Fools to depress your powers by the prices they pretend to give for contemptible works, or the expensive advertizing boasts that they make of such works: believe Christ & his Apostles that there is a Class of Men whose whole delight is in Destroying. We do not want either Greek or Roman Models if we are but just & true to our own Imaginations, those Worlds of Eternity in which we shall live for ever in Jesus our Lord.

> And did those feet in ancient time
> Walk upon England's mountains green:
> And was the holy Lamb of God
> On England's pleasant pastures seen!

And did the Countenance Divine
Shine forth upon our clouded hills?
And was Jerusalem builded here
Among these dark Satanic Mills?

Bring me my Bow of burning gold:
Bring me my Arrows of desire:
Bring me my Spear: O clouds unfold!
Bring me my Chariot of fire!

I will not cease from Mental Fight,
Nor shall my Sword sleep in my hand
Till we have built Jerusalem
In England's green & pleasant Land.

Would to God that all the Lord's people were Prophets.
Numbers XI. Ch. 29 v.

MILTON

Book the First

[2]
DAUGHTERS of Beulah! Muses who inspire the Poet's Song,
Record the journey of immortal Milton thro' your Realms
Of terror & mild moony lustre, in soft sexual delusions
Of varied beauty to delight the wanderer and repose
His burning thirst & freezing hunger! Come into my hand,   5
By your mild power descending down the Nerves of my right arm
From out the Portals of my Brain, where by your ministry
The Eternal Great Humanity Divine planted his Paradise
And in it caus'd the Spectres of the Dead to take sweet forms
In likeness of himself. Tell also of the False Tongue! vegetated
Beneath your land of shadows: of its sacrifices and   11
Its offerings, even till Jesus, the image of the Invisible God,
Became its prey, a curse, an offering and an atonement
For Death Eternal in the heavens of Albion & before the Gates
Of Jerusalem his Emanation in the heavens beneath Beulah.   15

Say first! what mov'd Milton, who walk'd about in Eternity
One hundred years, pond'ring the intricate mazes of Providence,
Unhappy tho' in heav'n—he obey'd, he murmur'd not, he was
          silent
Viewing his Sixfold Emanation scatter'd thro' the deep   19
In torment—To go into the deep, her to redeem & himself perish?

[1] What cause at length mov'd Milton to this unexampled deed?
A Bard's prophetic Song! for sitting at eternal tables,
Terrific among the Sons of Albion in chorus solemn & loud,
A Bard broke forth: all sat attentive to the awful man.

" Mark well my words! they are of your eternal salvation.   25

" Three Classes are Created by the Hammer of Los & Woven
[3]
" By Enitharmon's Looms when Albion was slain upon his
    Mountains
And in his Tent thro' envy of the Living Form, even of the
    Divine Vision,
And of the sports of Wisdom in the Human Imagination,
Which is the Divine Body of the Lord Jesus, blessed for ever.
Mark well my words! they are of your eternal salvation.   5

" Urizen lay in darkness & solitude, in chains of the mind lock'd
    up.
Los siez'd his Hammer & Tongs; he labour'd at his resolute Anvil
Among indefinite Druid rocks & snows of doubt & reasoning.

" Refusing all Definite Form, the Abstract Horror roof'd, stony
    hard;
And a first Age passed over, & a State of dismal woe.   10

" Down sunk with fright a red round Globe, hot burning, deep
Deep down into the Abyss, panting, conglobing, trembling;
And a second Age passed over, & a State of dismal woe.

" Rolling round into two little Orbs, & closed in two little Caves,
The Eyes beheld the Abyss, lest bones of solidness freeze over all;
And a third Age passed over, & a State of dismal woe.   16

" From beneath his Orbs of Vision, Two Ears in close volutions
Shot spiring out in the deep darkness & petrified as they grew;
And a fourth Age passed over, & a State of dismal woe.

" Hanging upon the wind, Two Nostrils bent down into the Deep;
And a fifth Age passed over, & a State of dismal woe.   21

" In ghastly torment sick, a Tongue of hunger & thirst flamed out;
And a sixth Age passed over, & a State of dismal woe.

---

[1] " What " is substituted for " That " in two of the four existing copies
of " Milton." " What " appears in the latest copy, of which this is a
transcript—except that the Preface has here been restored.

"Enraged & stifled without & within, in terror & woe he threw his
Right Arm to the north, his left Arm to the south, & his Feet   25
Stamp'd the nether Abyss in trembling & howling & dismay;
And a seventh Age passed over, & a State of dismal woe.

"Terrified, Los stood in the Abyss, & his immortal limbs
Grew deadly pale: he became what he beheld; for a red   29
Round Globe sunk down from his Bosom into the Deep; in pangs
He hover'd over it, trembling & weeping: suspended it shook
The nether Abyss: in tremblings he wept over it; he cherish'd it
In deadly sickening pain, till separated into a Female, pale
As the cloud that brings the snow; all the while from his Back
A blue fluid exuded in Sinews, hardening in the Abyss   35
Till it separated into a Male Form howling in Jealousy.

"Within labouring, beholding Without, from Particulars to
     Generals,
Subduing his Spectre, they Builded the Looms of Generations.
They Builded Great Golgonooza Times on Times, Ages on Ages.
First Orc was Born, then the Shadowy Female, then All Los's
     family.
At last Enitharmon brought forth Satan, Refusing Form in vain,
The Miller of Eternity made subservient to the Great Harvest
That he may go to his own Place, Prince of the Starry Wheels 43
[4]
"Beneath the Plow of Rintrah & the Harrow of the Almighty
In the hands of Palamabron, Where the Starry Mills of Satan
Are built beneath the Earth & Waters of the Mundane Shell.
Here the Three Classes of Men take their Sexual texture, Woven:
The Sexual is Threefold, the Human is Fourfold.   5

"'If you account it Wisdom when you are angry to be silent and
Not to shew it, I do not account that Wisdom, but Folly.
Every Man's Wisdom is peculiar to his own Individuality.
O Satan, my youngest born, art thou not Prince of the Starry
     Hosts
And of the Wheels of Heaven, to turn the Mills day & night? 10
Art thou not Newton's Pantocrator, weaving the Woof of Locke?
To Mortals thy Mills seem every thing, & the Harrow of Shaddai
A Scheme of Human conduct invisible & incomprehensible.
Get to thy Labours at the Mills & leave me to my wrath.'

"Satan was going to reply, but Los roll'd his loud thunders: 15

"'Anger me not! thou canst not drive the Harrow in pity's paths:
Thy Work is Eternal Death with Mills & Ovens & Cauldrons.
Trouble me no more; thou canst not have Eternal Life.'

" So Los spoke. Satan trembling obey'd, weeping along the way.
Mark well my words! they are of your eternal Salvation.   20

" Between South Molton Street & Stratford Place, Calvary's foot
Where the Victims were preparing for Sacrifice, their Cherubim
Around their loins pour'd forth their arrows, & their bosoms beam
With all colours of precious stones, & their inmost palaces
Resounded with preparation of animals wild & tame,   25
(Mark well my words: Corporeal Friends are Spiritual Enemies)
Mocking Druidical Mathematical Proportion of Length, Bredth,
      Highth:
Displaying Naked Beauty, with Flute & Harp & Song.

[5]
" Palamabron with the fiery Harrow in morning returning
From breathing fields, Satan fainted beneath the artillery.
Christ took on Sin in the Virgin's Womb, & put it off on the Cross.
All pitied the piteous & was wrath with the wrathful, & Los
      heard it.

" And this is the manner of the Daughters of Albion in their beauty:
Every one is threefold in Head & Heart & Reins, & every one   6
Has three Gates into the Three Heavens of Beulah which shine
Translucent in their Foreheads & their Bosoms & their Loins
Surrounded with fires unapproachable: but whom they please
They take up into their Heavens in intoxicating delight;   10
For the Elect cannot be Redeem'd, but Created continually
By Offering & Atonement in the cruelties of Moral Law.
Hence the three Classes of Men take their fix'd destinations.
They are the Two Contraries & the Reasoning Negative.   14

" While the Females prepare the Victims, the Males at Furnaces
And Anvils dance the dance of tears & pain: loud lightnings
Lash on their limbs as they turn the whirlwinds loose upon
The Furnaces, lamenting around the Anvils, & this their Song:

" ' Ah weak & wide astray! Ah shut in narrow doleful form
Creeping in reptile flesh upon the bosom of the ground!   20
The Eye of Man a little narrow orb clos'd up & dark,
Scarcely beholding the great light, conversing with the Void.
The Ear, a little shell in small volutions shutting out
All melodies & comprehending only Discord and Harmony.
The Tongue a little moisture fills, a little food it cloys,   25
A little sound it utters & its cries are faintly heard.
Then brings forth Moral Virtue the cruel Virgin Babylon.

" ' Can such an Eye judge of the stars? & looking thro' its tubes
Measure the sunny rays that point their spears on Udanadan?

Can such an Ear, fill'd with the vapours of the yawning pit,   30
Judge of the pure melodious harp struck by a hand divine?
Can such closed Nostrils feel a joy? or tell of autumn fruits
When grapes & figs burst their covering to the joyful air?
Can such a Tongue boast of the living waters? or take in
Ought but the Vegetable Ratio & loathe the faint delight?   35
Can such gross Lips percieve? alas! folded within themselves
They touch not ought, but pallid turn & tremble at every wind.'

" Thus they sing Creating, the Three Classes among Druid Rocks.
Charles calls on Milton for Atonement. Cromwell is ready.
James calls for fires in Golgonooza, for heaps of smoking ruins   40
In the night of prosperity and wantonness which he himself
    Created
Among the Daughters of Albion, among the Rocks of the Druids
When Satan fainted beneath the arrows of Elynittria,
And Mathematic Proportion was subdued by Living Proportion.

[6]
" From Golgonooza, the spiritual Four-fold London eternal,
In immense labours & sorrows, ever building, ever falling,
Thro' Albion's four Forests which overspread all the Earth
From London Stone to Blackheath east, to Hounslow west,
To Finchley north, to Norwood south; and the weights   5
Of Enitharmon's Loom play lulling cadences on the winds of
    Albion
From Caithness in the north to Lizard-point & Dover in the south.

" Loud sounds the Hammer of Los & loud his Bellows is heard
Before London to Hampstead's breadths & Highgate's heights, To
Stratford & old Bow & across to the Gardens of Kensington   10
On Tyburn's Brook: loud groans Thames beneath the iron Forge
Of Rintrah & Palamabron, of Theotorm & Bromion, to forge the
    instruments
Of Harvest, the Plow & Harrow to pass over the Nations.   13

" The Surrey hills glow like the clinkers of the furnace; Lam-
    beth's Vale
Where Jerusalem's foundations began, where they were laid in
    ruins,
Where they were laid in ruins from every Nation, & Oak Groves
    rooted,
Dark gleams before the Furnace-mouth a heap of burning ashes.
When shall Jerusalem return & overspread all the Nations?
Return, return to Lambeth's Vale, O building of human souls!
Thence stony Druid Temples overspread the Island white,   20
And thence from Jerusalem's ruins, from her walls of salvation
And praise, thro' the whole Earth were rear'd from Ireland

To Mexico & Peru west, & east to China, & Japan, till Babel
The Spectre of Albion frown'd over the Nations in glory & war.
All things begin & end in Albion's ancient Druid rocky shore: 25
But now the Starry Heavens are fled from the mighty limbs of
Albion.

"Loud sounds the Hammer of Los, loud turn the Wheels of
Enitharmon:
Her Looms vibrate with soft affections, weaving the Web of Life
Out from the ashes of the Dead. Los lifts his iron Ladles 29
With molten ore: he heaves the iron cliffs in his rattling chains
From Hyde Park to the Alms-houses of Mile-end & old Bow.
Here the Three Classes of Mortal Men take their fix'd destinations,
And hence they overspread the Nations of the whole Earth, &
hence
The Web of Life is woven & the tender sinews of life created 34
And the Three Classes of Men regulated by Los's Hammers:[1]
[7]
"The first, The Elect from before the foundation of the World:
The second, The Redeem'd: The Third, The Reprobate & form'd
To destruction from the mother's womb: . . .[2]
                    . . . follow with me my plow.

"Of the first class was Satan: with incomparable mildness 5
His primitive tyrannical attempts on Los, with most endearing
love
He soft intreated Los to give to him Palamabron's station,
For Palamabron return'd with labour wearied every evening.
Palamabron oft refus'd, and as often Satan offer'd
His service, till by repeated offers and repeated intreaties 10
Los gave to him the Harrow of the Almighty; alas, blamable,
Palamabron fear'd to be angry, lest Satan should accuse him of
Ingratitude & Los believe the accusation thro' Satan's extreme
Mildness. Satan labour'd all day: it was a thousand years:
In the evening returning terrified, overlabour'd & astonish'd, 15
Embrac'd soft with a brother's tears Palamabron, who also wept.

"Mark well my words! they are of your eternal salvation.

"Next morning Palamabron rose: the horses of the Harrow
Were madden'd with tormenting fury, & the servants of the
Harrow,
The Gnomes, accus'd Satan with indignation, fury and fire. 20
Then Palamabron, reddening like the Moon in an eclipse,

[1] In the first two copies of "Milton" the following phrase is to be found
here:
                          "and woven
    By Enitharmon's Looms & Spun beneath the Spindle of Tirzah."
[2] Indicates words erased from the plate.

Spoke, saying: ' You know Satan's mildness and his self-imposition
Seeming a brother, being a tyrant, even thinking himself a brother
While he is murdering the just: prophetic I behold   24
His future course thro' darkness and despair to eternal death.
But we must not be tyrants also: he hath assum'd my place
For one whole day under pretence of pity and love to me.
My horses hath he madden'd and my fellow servants injur'd.
How should he, he, know the duties of another? O foolish for-
          bearance!
Would I had told Los all my heart! but patience, O my friends,
All may be well: silent remain, while I call Los and Satan.'   31

'' Loud as the wind of Beulah that unroots the rocks & hills
Palamabron call'd, and Los & Satan came before him;
And Palamabron shew'd the horses & the servants. Satan wept,
And mildly cursing Palamabron, him accus'd of crimes   35
Himself had wrought. Los trembled: Satan's blandishments
          almost
Perswaded the Prophet of Eternity that Palamabron
Was Satan's enemy, & that the Gnomes, being Palamabron's
          friends,
Were leagued together against Satan thro' ancient enmity.   39
What could Los do? how could he judge, when Satan's self
          believ'd
That he had not oppres'd the horses of the Harrow nor the
          servants?

'' So Los said: ' Henceforth, Palamabron, let each his own station
Keep, nor in pity false, nor in officious brotherhood, where
None needs, be active.' Mean time Palamabron's horses   44
Rag'd with thick flames redundant, & the Harrow madden'd with
          fury.
Trembling Palamabron stood; the strongest of Demons trembled,
Curbing his living creatures: many of the strongest Gnomes
They bit in their wild fury, who also madden'd like wildest beasts.

'' Mark well my words! they are of your eternal salvation.   49

[8]
'' Mean while wept Satan before Los, accusing Palamabron,
Himself exculpating with mildest speech; for himself believ'd
That he had not opress'd nor injur'd the refractory servants.

'' But Satan returning to his Mills (for Palamabron had serv'd
The Mills of Satan as the easier task) found all confusion,   5
And back return'd to Los, not fill'd with vengeance but with tears,
Himself convinc'd of Palamabron's turpitude. Los beheld
The servants of the Mills drunken with wine and dancing wild

With shouts and Palamabron's songs, rending the forests green
With ecchoing confusion, tho' the Sun was risen on high.   10

" Then Los took off his left sandal, placing it on his head,
Signal of solemn mourning: when the servants of the Mills
Beheld the signal, they in silence stood, tho' drunk with wine.
Los wept! But Rintrah also came, and Enitharmon on
His arm lean'd tremblingly, observing all these things.   15

" And Los said: ' Ye Genii of the Mills, the Sun is on high,
Your labours call you. Palamabron is also in sad dilemma:
His horses are mad, his Harrow confounded, his companions
    enrag'd.
Mine is the fault! I should have remember'd that pity divides the
    soul   19
And man unmans: follow with me my Plow: this mournful day
Must be a blank in Nature: follow with me, and tomorrow again
Resume your labours, & this day shall be a mournful day.'

" Wildly they follow'd Los and Rintrah, & the Mills were silent.
They mourn'd all day, this mournful day of Satan & Palamabron:
And all the Elect & all the Redeem'd mourn'd one toward another
Upon the mountains of Albion among the cliffs of the Dead.   26

" They Plow'd in tears! incessant pour'd Jehovah's rain, &
    Molech's
Thick fires contending with the rain, thunder'd above, rolling
Terrible over their heads. Satan wept over Palamabron.
Theotormon & Bromion contended on the side of Satan,   30
Pitying his youth and beauty, trembling at eternal death.
Michael contended against Satan in the rolling thunder:
Thulloh, the friend of Satan, also reprov'd him: faint their reproof.

" But Rintrah, who is of the reprobate, of those form'd to
    destruction,
In indignation for Satan's soft dissimulation of friendship,   35
Flam'd above all the plowed furrows, angry, red and furious,
Till Michael sat down in the furrow, weary, dissolv'd in tears.
Satan, who drave the team beside him, stood angry & red:
He smote Thulloh & slew him, & he stood terrible over Michael
Urging him to arise: he wept. Enitharmon saw his tears,   40
But Los hid Thulloh from her sight, lest she should die of grief.
She wept, she trembled, she kissed Satan, she wept over Michael:
She form'd a Space for Satan & Michael & for the poor infected.
Trembling she wept over the Space & clos'd it with a tender Moon.

' Los secret buried Thulloh, weeping disconsolate over the moony
    Space.

" But Palamabron called down a Great Solemn Assembly,   46
That he who will not defend Truth, may be compelled to
Defend a Lie, that he may be snared & caught & taken.

[9]
" And all Eden descended into Palamabron's tent
Among Albion's Druids & Bards in the caves beneath Albion's
Death Couch, in the caverns of death, in the corner of the Atlantic.
And in the midst of the Great Assembly Palamabron pray'd: 4
' O God, protect me from my friends, that they have not power
     over me.
Thou hast giv'n me power to protect myself from my bitterest
     enemies.'

" Mark well my words! they are of your eternal salvation.

" Then rose the Two Witnesses, Rintrah & Palamabron;
And Palamabron appeal'd to all Eden and reciev'd
Judgment: and Lo! it fell on Rintrah and his rage,   10
Which now flam'd high & furious in Satan against Palamabron,
Till it became a proverb in Eden: Satan is among the Reprobate.

" Los in his wrath curs'd heaven & earth; he rent up Nations,
Standing on Albion's rocks among high-rear'd Druid temples
Which reach the stars of heaven & stretch from pole to pole.   15
He displac'd continents, the oceans fled before his face.
He alter'd the poles of the world, east, west & north & south,
But he clos'd up Enitharmon from the sight of all these things.

" For Satan, flaming with Rintrah's fury hidden beneath his own
     mildness,
Accus'd Palamabron before the Assembly of ingratitude, of malice.
He created Seven deadly Sins, drawing out his infernal scroll   21
Of Moral laws and cruel punishments upon the clouds of Jehovah,
To pervert the Divine voice in its entrance to the earth
With thunder of war & trumpet's sound, with armies of disease,
Punishments & deaths muster'd & number'd, Saying: ' I am
     God alone,
There is no other! let all obey my principles of moral individuality.
I have brought them from the uppermost innermost recesses
Of my Eternal Mind: transgressors I will rend off for ever
As now I rend this accursed Family from my covering.'

" Thus Satan rag'd amidst the Assembly, and his bosom grew 30
Opake against the Divine Vision: the paved terraces of
His bosom inwards shone with fires, but the stones becoming opake
Hid him from sight in an extreme blackness and darkness.
And there a World of deeper Ulro was open'd in the midst   34
Of the Assembly: In Satan's bosom, a vast unfathomable Abyss

" Astonishment held the Assembly in an awful silence, and tears
Fell down as dews of night, & a loud solemn universal groan
Was utter'd from the east & from the west & from the south
And from the north; and Satan stood opake immeasurable,
Covering the east with solid blackness round his hidden heart, 40
With thunders, utter'd from his hidden wheels, accusing loud
The Divine Mercy for protecting Palamabron in his tent.

" Rintrah rear'd up walls of rocks and pour'd rivers & moats
Of fire round the walls: columns of fire guard around
Between Satan and Palamabron in the terrible darkness.   45

" And Satan, not having the Science of Wrath, but only of Pity,
Rent them asunder, and wrath was left to wrath, & pity to pity.
He sunk down, a dreadful Death unlike the slumbers of Beulah.

" The Separation was terrible: the Dead was repos'd on his Couch
Beneath the Couch of Albion, on the seven mountains of Rome,
In the whole place of the Covering Cherub, Rome, Babylon & Tyre.
His Spectre, raging furious, descended into its Space.   52

[11]
" Then Los and Enitharmon knew that Satan is Urizen
Drawn down by Orc & the Shadowy Female into Generation.
Oft Enitharmon enter'd weeping into the Space, there appearing
An aged Woman raving along the Streets (the Space is named   4
Canaan): then she returned to Los, weary, frighted as from
    dreams.

" The nature of a Female Space is this: it shrinks the Organs
Of Life till they become Finite, & Itself seems Infinite.

" And Satan vibrated in the immensity of the Space, Limited
To those without, but Infinite to those within: it fell down and
Became Canaan, closing Los from Eternity in Albion's Cliffs,   10
A mighty Fiend against the Divine Humanity must'ring to War.

" ' Satan, Ah me! is gone to his own place,' said Los: ' their God
I will not worship in their Churches, nor King in their Theatres.
Elynittria! whence is this Jealousy running along the mountains?
British Women were not Jealous when Greek & Roman were
    Jealous.
Every thing in Eternity shines by its own Internal light, but thou
Darkenest every Internal light with the arrows of thy quiver,
Bound up in the horns of Jealousy to a deadly fading Moon,
And Ocalythron binds the Sun into a Jealous Globe,
That every thing is fix'd Opake, without Internal light.'   20

" So los lamented over Satan who triumphant divided the Nations.

[12]
" He set his face against Jerusalem to destroy the Eon of Albion

" But Los hid Enitharmon from the sight of all these things
Upon the Thames whose lulling harmony repos'd her soul,
Where Beulah lovely terminates in rocky Albion,
Terminating in Hyde Park on Tyburn's awful brook.   5

" And the Mills of Satan were separated into a moony Space
Among the rocks of Albion's Temples, and Satan's Druid sons
Offer the Human Victims throughout all the Earth, and Albion's
Dread Tomb, immortal on his Rock, overshadow'd the whole
    Earth,
Where Satan, making to himself Laws from his own identity,   10
Compell'd others to serve him in moral gratitude & submission,
Being call'd God, setting himself above all that is called God;
And all the Spectres of the Dead, calling themselves Sons of God,
In his Synagogues worship Satan under the Unutterable Name.

" And it was enquir'd Why in a Great Solemn Assembly   15
The Innocent should be condemn'd for the Guilty. Then an
    Eternal rose,

" Saying: ' If the Guilty should be condemn'd, he must be an
    Eternal Death,
And one must die for another throughout all Eternity.
Satan is fall'n from his station & never can be redeem'd
But must be new Created continually moment by moment.   20
And therefore the Class of Satan shall be call'd the Elect, & those
Of Rintrah the Reprobate, & those of Palamabron the Redeem'd;
For he is redeem'd from Satan's Law, the wrath falling on Rintrah.
And therefore Palamabron dared not to call a solemn Assembly
Till Satan had assum'd Rintrah's wrath in the day of mourning,   25
In a feminine delusion of false pride self-deciev'd.'

" So spake the Eternal and confirm'd it with a thunderous oath.

" But when Leutha (a Daughter of Beulah) beheld Satan's con-
    demnation,
She down descended into the midst of the Great Solemn Assembly,
Offering herself a Ransom for Satan, taking on her his Sin.   30

" Mark well my words! they are of your eternal salvation.

" And Leutha stood glowing with varying colours, immortal,
    heart-piercing
And lovely, & her moth-like elegance shone over the Assembly.

" At length, standing upon the golden floor of Palamabron,
She spake: ' I am the Author of this Sin! by my suggestion   35
My Parent power, Satan, has committed this transgression.
I loved Palamabron & I sought to approach his Tent.
But beautiful Elynittria with her silver arrows repell'd me,

[13]
" ' For her light is terrible to me: I fade before her immortal beauty
O wherefore doth a Dragon-form forth issue from my limbs
To sieze her new born son? Ah me! the wretched Leutha!
This to prevent, entering the doors of Satan's brain night after
    night
Like sweet perfumes, I stupified the masculine perceptions   5
And kept only the feminine awake: hence rose his soft
Delusory love to Palamabron, admiration join'd with envy,
Cupidity unconquerable! my fault, when at noon of day
The Horses of Palamabron call'd for rest and pleasant death,
I sprang out of the breast of Satan, over the Harrow beaming   10
In all my beauty, that I might unloose the flaming steeds
As Elynittria used to do; but too well those living creatures
Knew that I was not Elynittria, and they brake the traces.
But me the servants of the Harrow saw not but as a bow
Of varying colours on the hills; terribly rag'd the horses.   15
Satan astonish'd and with power above his own controll
Compell'd the Gnomes to curb the horses & to throw banks of sand
Around the fiery flaming Harrow in labyrinthine forms,
And brooks between to intersect the meadows in their course.
The Harrow cast thick flames: Jehovah thunder'd above.   20
Chaos & ancient night fled from beneath the fiery Harrow:
The Harrow cast thick flames & orb'd us round in concave fires,
A Hell of our own making; see, its flames still gird me round.
Jehovah thunder'd above. Satan in pride of heart
Drove the fierce Harrow among the constellations of Jehovah,   25
Drawing a third part in the fires as stubble north & south
To devour Albion and Jerusalem the Emanation of Albion,
Driving the Harrow in Pity's paths: 'twas then, with our dark fires
Which now gird round us (O eternal torment!) I form'd the Serpent
Of precious stones & gold, turn'd poisons on the sultry wastes.   30
The Gnomes in all that day spar'd not; they curs'd Satan bitterly.
To do unkind things in kindness, with power arm'd to say
The most irritating things in the midst of tears and love,
These are the stings of the Serpent! thus did we by them till thus
They in return retaliated, and the Living Creatures madden'd.   35
The Gnomes labour'd. I weeping hid in Satan's inmost brain.
But when the Gnomes refus'd to labour more, with blandishments
I came forth from the head of Satan: back the Gnomes recoil'd
And called me Sin, and for a sign portentous held me. Soon
Day sunk and Palamabron return'd; trembling I hid myself   40
In Satan's inmost Palace of his nervous fine wrought Brain:

For Elynittria met Satan with all her singing women,
Terrific in their joy & pouring wine of wildest power.
They gave Satan their wine: indignant at the burning wrath,
Wild with prophetic fury, his former life became like a dream. 45
Cloth'd in the Serpent's folds, in selfish holiness demanding purity,
Being most impure, self-condemn'd to eternal tears, he drove
Me from his inmost Brain & the doors clos'd with thunder's sound.
O Divine Vision, who didst create the Female to repose
The Sleepers of Beulah, pity the repentant Leutha! My   50
[14]
" ' Sick Couch bears the dark shades of Eternal Death infolding
The Spectre of Satan: he furious refuses to repose in sleep.
I humbly bow in all my Sin before the Throne Divine.
Not so the Sick-one. Alas, what shall be done him to restore
Who calls the Individual Law Holy and despises the Saviour,   5
Glorying to involve Albion's Body in fires of eternal War? '

" Now Leutha ceas'd: tears flow'd, but the Divine Pity supported
her.

" ' All is my fault! We are the Spectre of Luvah, the murderer
Of Albion. O Vala! O Luvah! O Albion! O lovely Jerusalem!
The Sin was begun in Eternity and will not rest to Eternity,   10
Till two Eternitys meet together. Ah! lost! lost! lost! for ever! '

" So Leutha spoke. But when she saw that Enitharmon had
Created a New Space to protect Satan from punishment,
She fled to Enitharmon's Tent & hid herself. Loud raging
Thunder'd the Assembly dark & clouded, and they ratify'd   15
The kind decision of Enitharmon & gave a Time to the Space,
Even Six Thousand years, and sent Lucifer for its Guard.
But Lucifer refus'd to die & in pride he forsook his charge:
And they elected Molech, and when Molech was impatient   19
The Divine hand found the Two Limits, first of Opacity, then of
    Contraction:
Opacity was named Satan, Contraction was named Adam.
Triple Elohim came: Elohim wearied fainted: they elected
    Shaddai:
Shaddai angry, Pahad descended: Pahad terrified, they sent
    Jehovah;
And Jehovah was leprous: loud he call'd, stretching his hand to
    Eternity,
For then the Body of Death was perfected in hypocritic holiness, 25
Around the Lamb, a Female Tabernacle woven in Cathedron's
    Looms.
He died as a Reprobate; he was Punish'd as a Transgressor.
Glory! Glory! Glory! to the Holy Lamb of God!
I touch the heavens as an instrument to glorify the Lord!   29

" The Elect shall meet the Redeem'd on Albion's rocks; they
shall meet
Astonish'd at the Transgressor, in him beholding the Saviour.
And the Elect shall say to the Redeem'd: ' We behold it is of
Divine
Mercy alone, of Free Gift and Election that we live:
Our Virtues & Cruel Goodnesses have deserv'd Eternal Death.'
Thus they weep upon the fatal Brook of Albion's River.   35

" But Elynittria met Leutha in the place where she was hidden
And threw aside her arrows and laid down her sounding Bow.
She sooth'd her with soft words & brought her to Palamabron's bed
In moments new created for delusion, interwoven round about. 39
In dreams she bore the shadowy Spectre of Sleep & nam'd him
Death:
In dreams she bore Rahab, the mother of Tirzah, & her sisters
In Lambeth's vales, in Cambridge & in Oxford, places of Thought,
Intricate labyrinths of Times and Spaces unknown, that Leutha
lived
In Palamabron's Tent, and Oothoon was her charming guard."

The Bard ceas'd. All consider'd and a loud resounding murmur
Continu'd round the Halls; and much they question'd the im-
mortal   46
Loud voic'd Bard; and many condemn'd the high toned Song,
Saying: " Pity and Love are too venerable for the imputation
Of Guilt." Others said: " If it is true, if the acts have been per-
form'd,
Let the Bard himself witness. Where hadst thou this terrible
Song? "

The Bard replied: " I am Inspired! I know it is Truth! for I Sing 51
[15]
" According to the inspiration of the Poetic Genius
Who is the eternal all-protecting Divine Humanity,
To whom be Glory & Power & Dominion Evermore. Amen."

Then there was great murmuring in the Heavens of Albion
Concerning Generation & the Vegetative power, & concerning   5
The Lamb, the Saviour. Albion trembled to Italy, Greece & Egypt,
To Tartary & Hindostan & China & to Great America,
Shaking the roots & fast foundations of the Earth in doubtfulness.
The loud voic'd Bard terrify'd took refuge in Milton's bosom.

Then Milton rose up from the heavens of Albion ardorous.   10
The whole Assembly wept prophetic, seeing in Milton's face
And in his lineaments divine the shades of Death & Ulro;
He took off the robe of the promise & ungirded himself from the
oath of God.

   And Milton said: " I go to Eternal Death! The Nations still
Follow after the detestable Gods of Priam, in pomp   15
Of warlike selfhood contradicting and blaspheming.
When will the Resurrection come to deliver the sleeping body
From corruptibility? O when, Lord Jesus, wilt thou come?
Tarry no longer, for my soul lies at the gates of death.
I will arise and look forth for the morning of the grave: 20
I will go down to the sepulcher to see if morning breaks:
I will go down to self annihilation and eternal death,
Lest the Last Judgment come & find me unannihilate
And I be siez'd & giv'n into the hands of my own Selfhood.
The Lamb of God is seen thro' mists & shadows, hov'ring   25
Over the sepulchers in clouds of Jehovah & winds of Elohim,
A disk of blood distant, & heav'ns & earths roll dark between.
What do I here before the Judgment? without my Emanation?
With the daughters of memory & not with the daughters of
    inspiration?
I in my Selfhood am that Satan: I am that Evil One!   30
He is my Spectre! in my obedience to loose him from my Hells,
To claim the Hells, my Furnaces, I go to Eternal Death."

   And Milton said: " I go to Eternal Death!" Eternity shudder'd,
For he took the outside course among the graves of the dead,   34
A mournful shade. Eternity shudder'd at the image of eternal
    death.

Then on the verge of Beulah he beheld his own Shadow,
A mournful form double, hermaphroditic, male & female
In one wonderful body; and he enter'd into it
In direful pain, for the dread shadow twenty-seven fold
Reach'd to the depths of direst Hell & thence to Albion's land,
Which is this earth of vegetation on which now I write.   41

The Seven Angels of the Presence wept over Milton's Shadow.

[17]
As when a man dreams, he reflects not that his body sleeps,
Else he would wake, so seem'd he entering his Shadow; but
With him the Spirits of the Seven Angels of the Presence
Entering, they gave him still perceptions of his Sleeping Body
Which now arose and walk'd with them in Eden, as an Eighth
Image, Divine tho' darken'd, and tho' walking, as one walks
In sleep; and the Seven comforted and supported him.

Like as a Polypus that vegetates beneath the deep,
They saw his Shadow vegetated underneath the Couch
Of death: for when he enter'd into his Shadow, Himself,   10
His real and immortal Self, was, as appear'd to those
Who dwell in immortality, as One sleeping on a couch

Of gold; and those in immortality gave forth their Emanations
Like Females of sweet beauty to guard round him & to feed
His lips with food of Eden in his cold and dim repose;   15
But to himself he seem'd a wanderer lost in dreary night.

Onwards his Shadow kept its course among the Spectres call'd
Satan, but swift as lightning passing them, startled the shades
Of Hell beheld him in a trail of light as of a comet
That travels into Chaos: so Milton went guarded within.   20

The nature of infinity is this: That every thing has its
Own Vortex, and when once a traveller thro' Eternity
Has pass'd that Vortex, he percieves it roll backward behind
His path, into a globe itself infolding like a sun,
Or like a moon, or like a universe of starry majesty,   25
While he keeps onwards in his wondrous journey on the earth,
Or like a human form, a friend with whom he liv'd benevolent.
As the eye of man views both the east & west encompassing
Its vortex, and the north & south with all their starry host,
Also the rising sun & setting moon he views surrounding   30
His corn-fields and his valleys of five hundred acres square,
Thus is the earth one infinite plane, and not as apparent
To the weak traveller confin'd beneath the moony shade.
Thus is the heaven a vortex pass'd already, and the earth
A vortex not yet pass'd by the traveller thro' Eternity.   35

First Milton saw Albion upon the Rock of Ages,
Deadly pale outstretch'd and snowy cold, storm cover'd,
A Giant form of perfect beauty outstretch'd on the rock
In solemn death: the Sea of Time & Space thunder'd aloud   39
Against the rock, which was inwrapped with the weeds of death.
Hovering over the cold bosom in its vortex Milton bent down
To the bosom of death: what was underneath soon seem'd above:
A cloudy heaven mingled with stormy seas in loudest ruin;
But as a wintry globe descends precipitant thro' Beulah, bursting
With thunders loud and terrible, so Milton's shadow fell   45
Precipitant, loud thund'ring into the Sea of Time & Space.

Then first I saw him in the Zenith as a falling star
Descending perpendicular, swift as the swallow or swift;
And on my left foot falling on the tarsus, enter'd there:
But from my left foot a black cloud redounding spread over
     Europe.

Then Milton knew that the Three Heavens of Beulah were beheld
By him on earth in his bright pilgrimage of sixty years [1]   52

---

[1] Plate 18 is occupied by a full-page illustration showing a strong nude figure (? Blake as Ololon) striding inwards, left foot foremost, to seize the giant Urizen who, with outstretched arms, supporting himself upon stones

[19]
In those three females whom his Wives, & those three whom his
    Daughters
Had represented and contain'd, that they might be resum'd
By giving up of Selfhood: & they distant view'd his journey
In their eternal spheres, now Human, tho' their Bodies remain
    clos'd
In the dark Ulro till the Judgment: also Milton knew they and   5
Himself was Human, tho' now wandering thro' Death's Vale
In conflict with those Female forms, which in blood & jealousy
Surrounded him, dividing & uniting without end or number.

He saw the Cruelties of Ulro and he wrote them down
In iron tablets; and his Wives' & Daughters' names were these:
Rahab and Tirzah & Milcah & Malah & Noah &Hoglah.   11
They sat rang'd round him as the rocks of Horeb round the land
Of Canaan, and they wrote in thunder, smoke and fire
His dictate; and his body was the Rock Sinai, that body
Which was on earth born to corruption; & the six Females   15
Are Hor & Peor & Bashan & Abarim & Lebanon & Hermon,
Seven rocky masses terrible in the Desarts of Midian.

But Milton's Human Shadow continu'd journeying above
The rocky masses of The Mundane Shell, in the Lands
Of Edom & Aram & Moab & Midian & Amalek.   20

The Mundane Shell is a vast Concave Earth, an immense
Harden'd shadow of all things upon our Vegetated Earth,
Enlarg'd into dimension & deform'd into indefinite space,
In Twenty-seven Heavens and all their Hells, with Chaos
And Ancient Night & Purgatory. It is a cavernous Earth   25
Of labyrinthine intricacy, twenty-seven-folds of opakeness,
And finishes where the lark mounts: here Milton journeyed
In that Region call'd Midian among the Rocks of Horeb;
For travellers from Eternity pass outward to Satan's seat,
But travellers to Eternity pass inward to Golgonooza.   30

Los, the Vehicular terror, beheld him, & divine Enitharmon
Call'd all her daughters, Saying: "Surely to unloose my bond
Is this Man come! Satan shall be unloos'd upon Albion!"

Los heard in terror Enitharmon's words: in fibrous strength
His limbs shot forth like roots of trees against the forward path
Of Milton's journey. Urizen beheld the immortal Man   36

---

of the law, wades in a river. Above, upon an arc of darkness, is a frieze of
juvenile figures advancing left, playing musical instruments. At the foot of
the design is the inscription: "To Annihilate the Self-hood of Deceit &
False Forgiveness."

[20]
And Tharmas, Demon of the Waters, & Orc, who is Luvah.

The Shadowy Female, seeing Milton, howl'd in her lamentation
Over the Deeps, outstretching her Twenty seven Heavens over
    Albion;

And thus the Shadowy Female howls in articulate howlings:

" I will lament over Milton in the lamentations of the afflicted: 5
My Garments shall be woven of sighs & heart broken lamentations:
The misery of unhappy Families shall be drawn out into its border,
Wrought with the needle with dire sufferings, poverty, pain & woe
Along the rocky Island & thence throughout the whole Earth.
There shall be the sick Father & his starving Family, there   10
The Prisoner in the stone Dungeon & the Slave at the Mill.
I will have writings written all over it in Human Words
That every Infant that is born upon the Earth shall read
And get by rote as a hard task of a life of sixty years.   14
I will have Kings inwoven upon it & Councellors & Mighty Men:
The Famine shall clasp it together with buckles & Clasps,
And the Pestilence shall be its fringe & the War its girdle,
To divide into Rahab & Tirzah that Milton may come to our tents.
For I will put on the Human Form & take the Image of God,
Even Pity & Humanity, but my Clothing shall be Cruelty: 20
And I will put on Holiness as a breastplate & as a helmet,
And all my ornaments shall be of the gold of broken hearts,
And the precious stones of anxiety & care & desperation & death
And repentance for sin & sorrow & punishment & fear,
To defend me from thy terrors, O Orc, my only beloved!"   25

Orc answer'd: " Take not the Human Form, O loveliest, Take not
Terror upon thee! Behold how I am, & tremble lest thou also
Consume in my Consummation; but thou maist take a Form
Female & lovely, that cannot consume in Man's consummation.
Wherefore dost thou Create & Weave this Satan for a Covering?
When thou attemptest to put on the Human Form, my wrath
Burns to the top of heaven against thee in Jealousy & fear;   32
Then I rend thee asunder; then I howl over thy clay & ashes.
When wilt thou put on the Female Form as in times of old,
With a Garment of Pity & Compassion like the Garment of God?
His garments are long sufferings for the Children of Men;   36
Jerusalem is his Garment, & not thy Covering Cherub, O lovely
Shadow of my delight who wanderest seeking for the prey."

So spoke Orc when Oothoon & Leutha hover'd over his Couch
Of fire, in interchange of Beauty & Perfection in the darkness   40
Opening interiorly into Jerusalem & Babylon, shining glorious
In the Shadowy Female's bosom. Jealous her darkness grew:

Howlings fill'd all the desolate places in accusations of Sin,
In Female beauty shining in the unform'd void; & Orc in vain
Stretch'd out his hands of fire & wooed: they triumph in his pain.

Thus darken'd the Shadowy Female tenfold, & Orc tenfold   46
Glow'd on his rocky Couch against the darkness: loud thunders
Told of the enormous conflict. Earthquake beneath, around,
Rent the Immortal Females, limb from limb & joint from joint,
And moved the fast foundations of the Earth to wake the Dead.

Urizen emerged from his Rocky Form & from his Snows,   51
[21]
And he also darken'd his brows, freezing dark rocks between
The footsteps, and infixing deep the feet in marble beds,
That Milton labour'd with his journey & his feet bled sore
Upon the clay now chang'd to marble; also Urizen rose
And met him on the shores of Arnon & by the streams of the
      brooks.

Silent they met and silent strove among the streams of Arnon 6
Even to Mahanaim, when with cold hand Urizen stoop'd down
And took up water from the river Jordan, pouring on
To Milton's brain the icy fluid from his broad cold palm.
But Milton took of the red clay of Succoth, moulding it with care
Between his palms and filling up the furrows of many years,   11
Beginning at the feet of Urizen, and on the bones
Creating new flesh on the Demon cold and building him,
As with new clay, a Human form in the Valley of Beth Peor.

Four Universes round the Mundane Egg remain Chaotic,   15
One to the North, named Urthona: One to the South, named
      Urizen:
One to the East, named Luvah: One to the West, named Tharmas;
They are the Four Zoas that stood around the Throne Divine.
But when Luvah assum'd the World of Urizen to the South
And Albion was slain upon his mountains & in his tent,   20
All fell towards the Center in dire ruin sinking down.
And in the South remains a burning fire: in the East, a void:
In the West, a world of raging waters: in the North, a solid,
Unfathomable, without end. But in the midst of these
Is built eternally the Universe of Los and Enitharmon,   25
Towards which Milton went, but Urizen oppos'd his path.

The Man and Demon strove many periods. Rahab beheld,
Standing on Carmel. Rahab and Tirzah trembled to behold
The enormous strife, one giving life, the other giving death
To his adversary; and they sent forth all their sons & daughters
In all their beauty to entice Milton across the river.   31

MILTON

The Twofold form Hermaphroditic, and the Double-sexed,
The Female-male & the Male-female, self-dividing stood
Before him in their beauty & in cruelties of holiness,
Shining in darkness, glorious upon the deeps of Entuthon,   35

Saying: " Come thou to Ephraim! behold the Kings of Canaan!
The beautiful Amalekites! behold the fires of youth
Bound with the Chain of Jealousy by Los & Enitharmon.
The banks of Cam, cold learning's streams, London's dark frown-
ing towers
Lament upon the winds of Europe in Rephaim's Vale,   40
Because Ahania, rent apart into a desolate night,
Laments, & Enion wanders like a weeping inarticulate voice,
And Vala labours for her bread & water among the Furnaces.
Therefore bright Tirzah triumphs, putting on all beauty
And all perfection in her cruel sports among the Victims.   45
Come, bring with thee Jerusalem with songs on the Grecian
Lyre!
In Natural Religion, in experiments on Men
Let her be Offer'd up to Holiness! Tirzah numbers her:
She numbers with her fingers every fibre ere it grow.   49
Where is the Lamb of God? where is the promise of his coming?
Her shadowy Sisters form the bones, even the bones of Horeb
Around the marrow, and the orbed scull around the brain.
His Images are born for War, for Sacrifice to Tirzah,
To Natural Religion! to Tirzah, the Daughter of Rahab the Holy!
She ties the knot of nervous fibres into a white brain!   55
She ties the knot of bloody veins into a red hot heart!
Within her bosom Albion lies embalm'd, never to awake.
Hand is become a rock: Sinai & Horeb is Hyle & Coban:
Scofield is bound in iron armour before Reuben's Gate.
She ties the knot of milky seed into two lovely Heavens,   60
[22]
" Two yet but one, each in the other sweet reflected; these
Are our Three Heavens beneath the shades of Beulah, land of rest.
Come then to Ephraim & Manasseh, O beloved-one!
Come to my ivory palaces, O beloved of thy mother!
And let us bind thee in the bands of War, & be thou King   5
Of Canaan, and reign in Hazor where the Twelve Tribes meet."

So spoke they as in one voice. Silent Milton stood before
The darken'd Urizen, as the sculptor silent stands before
His forming image; he walks round it patient labouring.
Thus Milton stood forming bright Urizen, while his Mortal part
Sat frozen in the rock of Horeb, and his Redeemed portion   11
Thus form'd the Clay of Urizen; but within that portion
His real Human walk'd above in power and majesty
Tho' darken'd, and the Seven Angels of the Presence attended him.

O how can I with my gross tongue that cleaveth to the dust 15
Tell of the Four-fold Man in starry numbers fitly order'd,
Or how can I with my cold hand of clay! But thou, O Lord,
Do with me as thou wilt! for I am nothing, and vanity.
If thou chuse to elect a worm, it shall remove the mountains.
For that portion nam'd the Elect, the Spectrous body of Milton,
Redounding from my left foot into Los's Mundane space, 21
Brooded over his Body in Horeb against the Resurrection,
Preparing it for the Great Consummation: red the Cherub on Sinai
Glow'd, but in terrors folded round his clouds of blood.

Now Albion's sleeping Humanity began to turn upon his Couch,
Feeling the electric flame of Milton's awful precipitate descent.
Seest thou the little winged fly, smaller than a grain of sand?
It has a heart like thee, a brain open to heaven & hell,
Withinside wondrous & expansive: its gates are not clos'd:
I hope thine are not: hence it clothes itself in rich array: 30
Hence thou art cloth'd with human beauty, O thou mortal man.
Seek not thy heavenly father then beyond the skies,
There Chaos dwells & ancient Night & Og & Anak old.
For every human heart has gates of brass & bars of adamant 34
Which few dare unbar, because dread Og & Anak guard the gates
Terrific; and each mortal brain is wall'd and moated round
Within, and Og & Anak watch here: here is the Seat
Of Satan in its Webs; for in brain and heart and loins
Gates open behind Satan's Seat to the City of Golgonooza,
Which is the spiritual fourfold London in the loins of Albion. 40

Thus Milton fell thro' Albion's heart, travelling outside of
    Humanity
Beyond the Stars in Chaos, in Caverns of the Mundane Shell.

But many of the Eternals rose up from eternal tables
Drunk with the Spirit; burning round the Couch of death they
    stood
Looking down into Beulah; wrathful, fill'd with rage 45
They rend the heavens round the Watchers in a fiery circle
And round the Shadowy Eighth: the Eight close up the Couch
Into a tabernacle and flee with cries down to the Deeps
Where Los opens his three wide gates surrounded by raging fires.
They soon find their own place & join the Watchers of the Ulro. 50

Los saw them, and a cold pale horror cover'd o'er his limbs.
Pondering he knew that Rintrah & Palamabron might depart,
Even as Reuben & as Gad: gave up himself to tears;
He sat down on his anvil-stock and lean'd upon the trough,
Looking into the black water, mingling it with tears. 55

At last when desperation almost tore his heart in twain
He recollected an old Prophecy, in Eden recorded
And often sung to the loud harp at the immortal feasts,
That Milton of the Land of Albion should up ascend
Forwards from Ulro from the Vale of Felpham, and set free   60
Orc from his Chain of Jealousy: he started at the thought
[23]
And down descended into Udan-Adan: it was night,
And Satan sat sleeping upon his Couch in Udan-Adan:
His Spectre slept, his Shadow woke; when one sleeps th'other
     wakes.

But Milton entering my Foot, I saw in the nether
Regions of the Imagination—also all men on Earth   5
And all in Heaven saw in the nether regions of the Imagination
In Ulro beneath Beulah—the vast breach of Milton's descent.
But I knew not that it was Milton, for man cannot know
What passes in his members till periods of Space & Time
Reveal the secrets of Eternity: for more extensive   10
Than any other earthly things are Man's earthly lineaments.
And all this Vegetable World appear'd on my left Foot
As a bright sandal form'd immortal of precious stones & gold.
I stooped down & bound it on to walk forward thro' Eternity.

There is in Eden a sweet River of milk & liquid pearl   15
Nam'd Ololon, on whose mild banks dwelt those who Milton drove
Down into Ulro: and they wept in long resounding song
For seven days of eternity, and the river's living banks,
The mountains, wail'd, & every plant that grew, in solemn sighs
     lamented.

When Luvah's bulls each morning drag the sulphur Sun out of
     the Deep
Harness'd with starry harness, black & shining, kept by black
     slaves
That work all night at the starry harness, Strong and vigorous
They drag the unwilling Orb, at this time all the Family
Of Eden heard the lamentation, and Providence began.   24
But when the clarions of day sounded, they drown'd the lamen-
     tations,
And when night came, all was silent in Ololon, & all refus'd to
     lament
In the still night, fearing lest they should others molest.

Seven mornings Los heard them, as the poor bird within the shell
Hears its impatient parent bird; and Enitharmon heard them   29
But saw them not, for the blue Mundane Shell inclos'd them in.

And they lamented that they had in wrath & fury & fire
Driven Milton into the Ulro; for now they knew too late
That it was Milton the Awakener: they had not heard the Bard
Whose song call'd Milton to the attempt; and Los heard these
    laments.
He heard them call in prayer all the Divine Family,   35
And he beheld the Cloud of Milton stretching over Europe.

But all the Family Divine collected as Four Suns
In the Four Points of heaven, East, West & North & South,
Enlarging and enlarging till their Disks approach'd each other,
And when they touch'd, closed together Southward in One Sun
Over Ololon; and as One Man who weeps over his brother   41
In a dark tomb, so all the Family Divine wept over Ololon,

Saying: "Milton goes to Eternal Death!" so saying they groan'd
    in spirit
And were troubled; and again the Divine Family groaned in spirit.

And Ololon said: "Let us descend also, and let us give   45
Ourselves to death in Ulro among the Transgressors.
Is Virtue a Punisher? O no! how is this wondrous thing,
This World beneath, unseen before, this refuge from the wars
Of Great Eternity! unnatural refuge! unknown by us till now?
Or are these the pangs of repentance? let us enter into them." 50

Then the Divine Family said: "Six Thousand Years are now
Accomplish'd in this World of Sorrow. Milton's Angel knew
The Universal Dictate, and you also feel this Dictate;
And now you know this World of Sorrow and feel Pity. Obey
The Dictate! Watch over this World, and with your brooding
    wings
Renew it to Eternal Life. Lo! I am with you alway.   56
But you cannot renew Milton: he goes to Eternal Death."

So spake the Family Divine as One Man, even Jesus,
Uniting in One with Ololon, & the appearance of One Man,
Jesus the Saviour, appear'd coming in the Clouds of Ololon.   60

[24]
Tho' driven away with the Seven Starry Ones into the Ulro,
Yet the Divine Vision remains Every-where For-ever. Amen.
And Ololon lamented for Milton with a great lamentation.

While Los heard indistinct in fear, what time I bound my sandals
On to walk forward thro' Eternity, Los descended to me: 5
And Los behind me stood, a terrible flaming Sun, just close
Behind my back. I turned round in terror, and behold!

Los stood in that fierce glowing fire, & he also stoop'd down
And bound my sandals on in Udan-Adan: trembling I stood
Exceedingly with fear & terror, standing in the Vale   10
Of Lambeth; but he kissed me and wish'd me health,
And I became One Man with him arising in my strength.
'Twas too late now to recede. Los had enter'd into my soul:
His terrors now posses'd me whole! I arose in fury & strength.

" I am that Shadowy Prophet who, Six Thousand Years ago,   15
Fell from my station in the Eternal bosom. Six Thousand Years
Are finish'd. I return! both Time & Space obey my will.
I in Six Thousand Years walk up and down; for not one Moment
Of Time is lost, nor one Event of Space unpermanent,
But all remain: every fabric of Six Thousand Years   20
Remains permanent, tho' on the Earth where Satan
Fell and was cut off, all things vanish & are seen no more,
They vanish not from me & mine, we guard them first & last.
The generations of men run on in the tide of Time,
But leave their destin'd lineaments permanent for ever & ever."

So spoke Los as we went along to his supreme abode.   26

Rintrah and Palamabron met us at the Gate of Golgonooza,
Clouded with discontent & brooding in their minds terrible things.

They said: " O Father most beloved! O merciful Parent!
Pitying and permitting evil, tho' strong & mighty to destroy,
Whence is this Shadow terrible? wherefore dost thou refuse   31
To throw him into the Furnaces? knowest thou not that he
Will unchain Orc & let loose Satan, Og, Sihon & Anak
Upon the Body of Albion? for this he is come! behold it written
Upon his fibrous left Foot black! most dismal to our eyes.   35
The Shadowy Female shudders thro' heaven in torment inex-
    pressible,
And all the Daughters of Los prophetic wail: yet in deceit
They weave a new Religion from new Jealousy of Theotormon.
Milton's Religion is the cause: there is no end to destruction.
Seeing the Churches at their Period in terror & despair,   40
Rahab created Voltaire, Tirzah created Rousseau,
Asserting the Self-righteousness against the Universal Saviour,
Mocking the Confessors & Martyrs, claiming Self-righteousness,
With cruel Virtue making War upon the Lamb's Redeemed
To perpetuate War & Glory, to perpetuate the Laws of Sin.   45
They perverted Swedenborg's Visions in Beulah & in Ulro
To destroy Jerusalem as a Harlot & her Sons as Reprobates,
To raise up Mystery the Virgin Harlot, Mother of War,
Babylon the Great, the Abomination of Desolation.   49
O Swedenborg! strongest of men, the Samson shorn by the
    Churches,

Shewing the Transgressors in Hell, the proud Warriors in Heaven,
Heaven as a Punisher, & Hell as One under Punishment,
With Laws from Plato & his Greeks to renew the Trojan Gods
In Albion, & to deny the value of the Saviour's blood.   54
But then I rais'd up Whitefield; Palamabron rais'd up Westley;
And these are the cries of the Churches before the two Witnesses:
Faith in God the dear Saviour who took on the likeness of men,
Becoming obedient to death, even the death of the Cross.
The Witnesses lie dead in the Street of the Grat City: 59
No Faith is in all the Earth: the Book of God is trodden under
     Foot.
He sent his two Servants, Whitefield & Westley: were they
     Prophets,
Or were they Idiots or Madmen? 'shew us Miracles!'
[25]
'' Can you have greater Miracles than these? Men who devote
Their life's whole comfort to intire scorn & injury & death?
Awake, thou sleeper on the Rock of Eternity! Albion awake!
The trumpet of Judgment hath twice sounded: all Nations are
     awake,
But thou art still heavy and dull. Awake, Albion awake!   5
Lo, Orc arises on the Atlantic. Lo, his blood and fire
Glow on America's shore. Albion turns upon his Couch:
His listens to the sounds of War, astonish'd and confounded:
He weeps into the Atlantic deep, yet still in dismal dreams
Unwaken'd, and the Covering Cherub advances from the East.
How long shall we lay dead in the Street of the Great City?   11
How long beneath the Covering Cherub give our Emanations?
Milton will utterly consume us & thee our beloved Father.
He hath enter'd into the Covering Cherub, becoming one with
Albion's dread Sons: Hand, Hyle & Coban surround him as   15
A girdle, Gwendolen & Conwenna as a garment woven
Of War & Religion: let us descend & bring him chained
To Bowlahoola, O father most beloved! O mild Parent!
Cruel in thy mildness, pitying and permitting evil,   19
Tho' strong and mighty to destroy, O Los our beloved Father! ''

Like the black storm coming out of Chaos beyond the stars
It issues thro' the dark & intricate caves of the Mundane Shell,
Passing the planetary visions & the well adorned Firmament,
The Sun rolls into Chaos & the Stars into the Desarts,
And then the storms, become visible audible & terrible   25
Covering the light of day & rolling down upon the mountains,
Deluge all the country round: Such is a vision of Los
When Rintrah & Palamabron spake, and such his stormy face
Appear'd as does the face of heaven when cover'd with thick
     storms,
Pitying and loving tho' in frowns of terrible perturbation.   30

But Los dispers'd the clouds, even as the strong winds of Jehovah,
And Los thus spoke: " O noble Sons, be patient yet a little.
I have embrac'd the falling Death; he is become One with me.
O Sons, we live not by wrath, by mercy alone we live!
I recollect an old Prophecy, in Eden recorded in gold, and oft 35
Sung to the harp, That Milton of the land of Albion
Should up ascend forward from Felpham's Vale & break the Chain
Of Jealousy from all its roots: be patient therefore, O my Sons!
These lovely Females form sweet night and silence and secret
Obscurities to hide from Satan's Watch-Fiends Human loves 40
And graces, lest they write them in their Books & in the Scroll
Of mortal life to condemn the accused, who at Satan's Bar
Tremble in Spectrous Bodies continually day and night
While on the Earth they live in sorrowful Vegetations.
O when shall we tread our Wine-presses in heaven and Reap 45
Our wheat with shoutings of joy, and leave the Earth in peace?
Remember how Calvin and Luther in fury premature
Sow'd War and stern division between Papists & Protestants.
Let it not be so now! O go not forth in Martyrdoms & Wars!
We were plac'd here by the Universal Brotherhood & Mercy 50
With powers fitted to circumscribe this dark Satanic death,
And that the Seven Eyes of God may have space for Redemption.
But how this is, as yet we know not, and we cannot know
Till Albion is arisen; then patient wait a little while.
Six Thousand years are pass'd away; the end approaches fast. 55
This mighty one is come from Eden; he is of the Elect
Who died from Earth & he is return'd before the Judgment. This
    thing
Was never known, that one of the holy dead should willing return.
Then patient wait a little while till the Last Vintage is over, 59
Till we have quench'd the Sun of Salah in the Lake of Udan-Adan.
O my dear Sons! leave not your Father as your brethren left me:
Twelve Sons successive fled away in that thousand years of sorrow

[26]
" Of Palamabron's Harrow & of Rintrah's wrath & fury:
Reuben & Manazzoth & Gad & Simeon & Levi
And Ephraim & Judah were Generated, because
They left me, wandering with Tirzah. Enitharmon wept
One thousand years, and all the Earth was in a wat'ry deluge. 5
We call'd him Menassheh because of the Generations of Tirzah,
Because of Satan, & the Seven Eyes of God continually
Guard round them; but I, the Fourth Zoa, am also set
The Watchman of Eternity: the Three are not, & I am preserved.
Still my four mighty ones are left to me in Golgonooza, 10
Still Rintrah fierce, and Palamabron mild & piteous,
Theotormon fill'd with care, Bromion loving Science.
You, O my Sons, still guard round Los. O wander not & leave me!
Rintrah, thou well rememberest when Amalek & Canaan

Fled with their Sister Moab into that abhorred Void: 15
They became Nations in our sight beneath the hands of Tirzah.
And Palamabron, thou rememberest when Joseph, an infant
Stolen from his nurse's cradle, wrap'd in needle-work
Of emblematic texture, was sold to the Amalekite
Who carried him down into Egypt where Ephraim & Menassheh
Gather'd my Sons together in the Sands of Midian;   21
And if you also flee away and leave your Father's side
Following Milton into Ulro, altho' your power is great,
Surely you also shall become poor mortal vegetations
Beneath the Moon of Ulro: pity then your Father's tears.   25
When Jesus rais'd Lazarus from the Grave, I stood & saw
Lazarus, who is the Vehicular Body of Albion the Redeem'd,
Arise into the Covering Cherub, who is the Spectre of Albion,
By martyrdoms to suffer, to watch over the Sleeping Body
Upon his Rock beneath his Tomb. I saw the Covering Cherub
Divide Four-fold into Four Churches when Lazarus arose,   31
Paul, Constantine, Charlemaine, Luther; behold, they stand be-
        fore us
Stretch'd over Europe & Asia! come O Sons, come, come away!
Arise, O Sons, give all your strength against Eternal Death,
Lest we are vegetated, for Cathedron's Looms weave only Death,
A Web of Death: & were it not for Bowlahoola & Allamanda   36
No Human Form but only a Fibrous Vegetation,
A Polypus of soft affections without Thought or Vision,
Must tremble in the Heavens & Earths thro' all the Ulro space.
Throw all the Vegetated Mortals into Bowlahoola: 40
But as to this Elected Form who is return'd again,
He is the Signal that the Last Vintage now approaches
Nor Vegetation may go on till all the Earth is reap'd.''

So Los spoke. Furious they descended to Bowlahoola & Allamanda,
Indignant, unconvinc'd by Los's arguments & thunders rolling:
They saw that wrath now sway'd and now pity absorb'd him.   46
As it was, so it remain'd, & no hope of an end.

Bowlahoola is nam'd Law by mortals. Tharmas founded it,
Because of Satan, before Luban in the City of Golgonooza;
But Golgonooza is nam'd Art & Manufacture by mortal men.   50

In Bowlahoola Los's Anvils stand & his Furnaces rage;
Thundering the Hammers beat & the Bellows blow loud,
Living, self moving, mourning, lamenting & howling incessantly.
Bowlahoola thro' all its porches feels, tho' too fast founded
Its pillars & porticoes to tremble at the force   55
Of mortal or immortal arm, and softly lilling flutes,
Accordant with the horrid labours, make sweet melody

The Bellows are the Animal Lungs: the Hammers the Animal
    Heart:
The Furnaces the Stomach for digestion: terrible their fury.
Thousands & thousands labour, thousands play on instruments
Stringed or fluted to ameliorate the sorrows of slavery.   61
Loud sport the dancers in the dance of death, rejoicing in carnage.
The hard dentant Hammers are lull'd by the flutes' lula lula,
The bellowing Furnaces' blare by the long sounding clarion, 64
The double drum drowns howls & groans, the shrill fife shrieks &
    cries,
The crooked horn mellows the hoarse raving serpent, terrible but
    harmonious.
Bowlahoola is the Stomach in every individual man.

Los is by mortals nam'd Time, Enitharmon is nam'd Space;
But they depict him bald & aged who is in eternal youth
All powerful and his locks flourish like the brows of morning: 70
He is the Spirit of Prophecy, the ever apparent Elias.
Time is the mercy of Eternity: without Time's swiftness,
Which is the swiftest of all things, all were eternal torment.
All the Gods of the Kingdoms of Earth labour in Los's Halls:
Every one is a fallen Son of the Spirit of Prophecy: 75
He is the Fourth Zoa that stood around the Throne Divine.

[27]
Loud shout the Sons of Luvah at the Wine-presses as Los
    descended
With Rintrah & Palamabron in his fires of resistless fury.

The Wine-press on the Rhine groans loud, but all its central beams
Act more terrific in the central Cities of the Nations   4
Where Human Thought is crush'd beneath the iron hand of Power:
There Los puts all into the Press, the Opressor & the Opressed
Together, ripe for the Harvest & Vintage & ready for the Loom.

They sang at the Vintage: " This is the Last Vintage, & Seed
Shall no more be sown upon Earth till all the Vintage is over
And all gather'd in, till the Plow has pass'd over the Nations   10
And the Harrow & heavy thundering Roller upon the mountains."

And loud the Souls howl round the Porches of Golgonooza,
Crying: " O God deliver us to the Heavens or to the Earths,
That we may preach righteousness & punish the sinner with
    death."
But Los refused, till all the Vintage of Earth was gather'd in. 15

And Los stood & cried to the Labourers of the Vintage in voice of
    awe:

" Fellow Labourers! The Great Vintage & Harvest is now upon
   Earth.
The whole extent of the Globe is explored. Every scatter'd Atom
Of Human Intellect now is flocking to the sound of the Trumpet.
All the Wisdom which was hidden in caves & dens from ancient 20
Time is now sought out from Animal & Vegetable & Mineral.
The Awakener is come, outstretch'd over Europe: the Vision of
   God is fulfilled.
The Ancient Man upon the Rock of Albion Awakes,
He listens to the sounds of War astonish'd & ashamed,
He sees his Children mock at Faith and deny Providence;   25
Therefore you must bind the Sheaves, not by Nations or Families,
You shall bind them in Three Classes, according to their Classes
So shall you bind them, Separating what has been Mixed
Since Men began to be Wove into Nations by Rahab & Tirzah,
Since Albion's Death & Satan's Cutting off from our awful Fields,
When under pretence to benevolence the Elect Subdu'd All   31
From the Foundation of the World. The Elect is one Class: You
Shall bind them separate: they cannot Believe in Eternal Life
Except by Miracle & a New Birth. The other two Classes,
The Reprobate who never cease to Believe, and the Redeem'd   35
Who live in doubts & fears, perpetually tormented by the Elect,
These you shall bind in a twin-bundle for the Consummation.
But the Elect must be saved [from] fires of Eternal Death,
To be formed into the Churches of Beulah that they destroy not
   the Earth.
For in every Nation & every Family the Three Classes are born, 40
And in every Species of Earth, Metal, Tree, Fish, Bird & Beast.
We form the Mundane Egg, that Spectres coming by fury or amity,
All is the same, & every one remains in his own energy.
Go forth Reapers with rejoicing; you sowed in tears,
But the time of your refreshing cometh: only a little moment 45
Still abstain from pleasure & rest in the labours of eternity,
And you shall Reap the whole Earth from Pole to Pole, from
   Sea to Sea,
Beginning at Jerusalem's Inner Court, Lambeth, ruin'd and given
To the detestable Gods of Priam, to Apollo, and at the Asylum
Given to Hercules, who labour in Tirzah's Looms for bread,   50
Who set Pleasure against Duty, who Create Olympic crowns
To make Learning a burden & the Work of the Holy Spirit, Strife:
The Thor & cruel Odin who first rear'd the Polar Caves.
Lambeth mourns, calling Jerusalem: she weeps & looks abroad   54
For the Lord's coming, that Jerusalem may overspread all Nations.
Crave not for the mortal & perishing delights, but leave them
To the weak, and pity the weak as your infant care. Break not
Forth in your wrath, lest you also are vegetated by Tirzah.
Wait till the Judgement is past, till the Creation is consumed,
And then rush forward with me into the glorious spiritual   60

Vegetation, the Supper of the Lamb & his Bride, and the
Awaking of Albion our friend and ancient companion.''

So Los spoke. But lightnings of discontent broke on all sides round
And murmurs of thunder rolling heavy long & loud over the
    mountains,
While Los call'd his Sons around him to the Harvest & the Vintage.

Thou seest the Constellations in the deep & wondrous Night: 66
They rise in order and continue their immortal courses
Upon the mountains & in vales with harp & heavenly song,
With flute & clarion, with cups & measures fill'd with foaming
    wine:
Glitt'ring the streams reflect the Vision of beatitude,   70
And the calm Ocean joys beneath & smooths his awful waves:
[28]
These are the Sons of Los, & these the Labourers of the Vintage.
Thou seest the gorgeous clothed Flies that dance & sport in
    summer
Upon the sunny brooks & meadows: every one the dance
Knows, in its intricate mazes of delight, artful to weave:
Each one to sound his instruments of music in the dance,   5
To touch each other & recede, to cross & change & return:
These are the Children of Los; thou seest the Trees on mountains,
The wind blows heavy, loud they thunder thro' the darksom sky,
Uttering prophecies & speaking instructive words to the sons
Of men: These are the Sons of Los : These the Visions of Eternity;
But we see only, as it were, the hem of their garments   11
When with our vegetable eyes we view these wondrous Visions.

There are Two Gates thro' which all Souls descend, One Southward
From Dover Cliff to Lizard Point, the other toward the North,
Caithness & rocky Durness, Pentland & John Groat's House.

The Souls descending to the Body wail on the right hand   16
Of Los, & those deliver'd from the Body on the left hand.
For Los against the east his force continually bends
Along the Valleys of Middlesex from Hounslow to Blackheath,
Lest those Three Heavens of Beulah should the Creation destroy,
And lest they should descend before the north & south Gates.
Groaning with pity, he among the wailing Souls laments.   22

And these the Labours of the Sons of Los in Allamanda
And in the City of Golgonooza & in Luban & around
The Lake of Udan-Adan in the Forests of Entuthon Benython, 25
Where Souls incessant wail, being piteous Passions & Desires
With neither lineament nor form, but like to wat'ry clouds:
The Passions & Desires descend upon the hungry winds,

For such alone Sleepers remain, meer passion & appetite;
The Sons of Los clothe them & feed & provide houses & fields.   30

And every Generated Body in its inward form
Is a garden of delight & a building of magnificence
Built by the Sons of Los in Bowlahoola & Allamanda;
And the herbs & flowers & furniture & beds & chambers
Continually woven in the Looms of Enitharmon's Daughters, 35
In bright Cathedron's golden Dome with care & love & tears.
For the various Classes of Men are all mark'd out determinate
In Bowlahoola, & as the Spectres choose their affinities
So they are born on Earth, & every Class is determinate:
But not by Natural, but by Spiritual power alone, Because   40
The Natural power continually seeks & tends to Destruction,
Ending in Death, which would of itself be Eternal Death.
And all are Class'd by Spiritual & not by Natural power.

And every Natural Effect has a Spiritual Cause, and Not
A Natural; for a Natural Cause only seems: it is a Delusion   45
Of Ulro & a ratio of the perishing Vegetable Memory.

[29]
But the Wine-press of Los is eastward of Golgonooza before the
    Seat
Of Satan: Luvah laid the foundation & Urizen finish'd it in
    howling woe.
How red the sons & daughters of Luvah! here they tread the
    grapes.
Laughing & shouting, drunk with odours many fall o'erwearied;
Drown'd in the wine is many a youth & maiden: those around 5
Lay them on skins of Tygers & of the spotted Leopard & the
    Wild Ass
Till they revive, or bury them in cool grots, making lamentation.

This Wine-press is call'd War on Earth: it is the Printing-Press
Of Los, and here he lays his words in order above the mortal brain,
As cogs are form'd in a wheel to turn the cogs of the adverse wheel.

Timbrels and violins sport round the Wine-presses; the little Seed,
The sportive Root, the Earth-worm, the gold Beetle, the wise
    Emmet,   12
Dance round the Wine-presses of Luvah: the Centipede is there,
The ground Spider with many eyes, the Mole clothed in velvet,
The ambitious Spider in his sullen web, the lucky golden Spinner,
The Earwig arm'd, the tender Maggot, emblem of immortality, 16
The Flea, Louse, Bug, the Tape-Worm, all the Armies of Disease
Visible or invisible to the slothful vegetating Man:
The slow Slug, the Grasshopper that sings & laughs & drinks:

Winter comes, he folds his slender bones without a murmur: 20
The cruel Scorpion is there, the Gnat, Wasp, Hornet & the Honey
    Bee,
The Toad & venomous Newt, the Serpent cloth'd in gems & gold:
They throw off their gorgeous raiment: they rejoice with loud
    jubilee
Around the Wine-presses of Luvah, naked & drunk with wine.

There is the Nettle that stings with soft down, and there 25
The indignant Thistle whose bitterness is bred in his milk,
Who feeds on contempt of his neighbour: there all the idle Weeds
That creep around the obscure places shew their various limbs
Naked in all their beauty dancing round the Wine-presses.

But in the Wine-presses the Human grapes sing not nor dance: 30
They howl and writhe in shoals of torment, in fierce flames
    consuming,
In chains of iron & in dungeons circled with ceaseless fires,
In pits & dens & shades of death, in shapes of torment & woe:
The plates & screws & wracks & saws & cords & fires & cisterns,
The cruel joys of Luvah's Daughters, lacerating with knives 35
And whips their Victims, & the deadly sport of Luvah's Sons.

They dance around the dying & they drink the howl & groan,
They catch the shrieks in cups of gold, they hand them to one
    another:
These are the sports of love, & these the sweet delights of amorous
    play,
Tears of the grape, the death sweat of the cluster, the last sigh 40
Of the mild youth who listens to the lureing songs of Luvah.

But Allamanda, call'd on Earth Commerce, is the Cultivated land
Around the City of Golgonooza in the Forests of Entuthon:
Here the Sons of Los labour against Death Eternal, through all
The Twenty-seven Heavens of Beulah in Ulro, Seat of Satan, 45
Which is the False Tongue beneath Beulah: it is the Sense of
    Touch.
The Plow goes forth in tempests & lightnings, & the Harrow cruel
In blights of the east; the heavy Roller follows in howlings of woe.

Urizen's sons here labour also, & here are seen the Mills
Of Theotormon on the verge of the Lake of Udan-Adan. 50
These are the starry voids of night & the depths & caverns of earth.
These Mills are oceans, clouds & waters ungovernable in their fury:
Here are the stars created & the seeds of all things planted,
And here the Sun & Moon recieve their fixed destinations.

But in Eternity the Four Arts, Poetry, Painting, Music 55
And Architecture, which is Science, are the Four Faces of Man.

Not so in Time & Space: there, Three are shut out, and only
Science remains thro' Mercy; & by means of Science the Three
Become apparent in Time & Space in the Three Professions,   59
[1] Poetry in Religion: Music, Law: Painting, in Physic & Surgery:
That Man may live upon Earth till the time of his awaking.
And from these Three Science derives every Occupation of Men,
And Science is divided into Bowlahoola & Allamanda.

[30]
Some Sons of Los surround the Passions with porches of iron &
    silver,
Creating form & beauty around the dark regions of sorrow,
Giving to airy nothing a name and a habitation
Delightful, with bounds to the Infinite, putting off the Indefinite
Into most holy forms of Thought (such is the power of inspiration)
They labour incessant, with many tears & afflictions,   6
Creating the beautiful House for the piteous sufferer.

Others Cabinets richly fabricate of gold & ivory
For Doubts & fears: unform'd & wretched & melancholy,
The little weeping Spectre stands on the threshold of Death   10
Eternal, and sometimes two Spectres like lamps quivering,
And often malignant they combat (heart-breaking sorrowful &
    piteous).
Antamon takes them into his beautiful flexible hands
As the Sower takes the seed or as the Artist his clay
Or fine wax to mould artful a model for golden ornaments.   15
The soft hands of Antamon draw the indelible line,
Form immortal, with golden pen, such as the Spectre admiring
Puts on the sweet form; then smiles Antamon bright thro' his
    windows,
The Daughters of beauty look up from their Loom & prepare
The integument soft for its clothing with joy & delight.   20

But Theotormon & Sotha stand in the Gate of Luban anxious:
Their numbers are seven million & seven thousand & seven
    hundred.
They contend with the weak Spectres, they fabricate soothing
    forms.
The Spectre refuses, he seeks cruelty: they create the crested Cock.[2]

---

[1] In the latest copy of " Milton " Blake deleted this line, presumably be-
cause of its inadequacy. It is retained here merely to preserve continuity.
    [2] " Theotormon and Sotha are the two sons who snare the wandering
Spectres, that they may be circumscribed by Antamon, and then take on
the flesh. If the Spectres cannot be lured by ' soothing forms,' they must be
terrified by animal forms, from which they recoil into ' Human lineaments.'
    " The device of revealing to some the animal forms of the Cock, and to
others the Lion, is explained by the magical antipathy between these two
animals. . . . Blake probably found the tradition in Cornelius Agrippa: ' As

Terrified the Spectre screams & rushes in fear into their Net   25
Of kindness & compassion, & is born a weeping terror.
Or they create the Lion & Tyger in compassionate thunderings.
Howling the Spectres flee: they take refuge in Human lineaments.

The Sons of Ozoth within the Optic Nerve stand fiery glowing,
And the number of his Sons is eight millions & eight.   30
They give delights to the man unknown; artificial riches
They give to scorn, & their possessors to trouble & sorrow & care,
Shutting the sun & moon & stars & trees & clouds & waters
And hills out from the Optic Nerve, & hardening it into a bone
Opake and like the black pebble on the enraged beach,   35
While the poor indigent is like the diamond which, tho' cloth'd
In rugged covering in the mine, is open all within
And in his hallow'd center holds the heavens of bright eternity.
Ozoth here builds walls of rocks against the surging sea,
And timbers crampt with iron cramps bar in the joys of life   40
From fell destruction in the Spectrous cunning or rage. He Creates
The speckled Newt, the Spider & Beetle, the Rat & Mouse,
The Badger & Fox: they worship before his feet in trembling fear.

But others of the Sons of Los build Moments & Minutes & Hours
And Days & Months & Years & Ages & Periods, wondrous
    buildings;
And every Moment has a Couch of gold for soft repose,   46
(A Moment equals a pulsation of the artery),
And between every two Moments stands a Daughter of Beulah
To feed the Sleepers on their Couches with maternal care.
And every Minute has an azure Tent with silken Veils;
And every Hour has a bright golden Gate carved with skill;   51
And every Day & Night has Walls of brass & Gates of adamant,
Shining like precious stones & ornamented with appropriate signs;
And every Month a silver paved Terrace builded high;
And every Year invulnerable Barriers with high Towers;   55
And every Age is Moated deep with Bridges of silver & gold;
And every Seven Ages is Incircled with a Flaming Fire.
Now Seven Ages is amounting to Two Hundred Years.
Each has its Guard, each Moment, Minute, Hour, Day, Month &
    Year:
All are the work of Fairy hands of the Four Elements: 60
The Guard are Angels of Providence on duty evermore.
Every Time less than a pulsation of the artery
Is equal in its period & value to Six Thousand Years,

Proclus gives an example in a spirit, which was wont to appear in the form
of a Lion, but by the setting of a Cock before it, vanished away, because
there is a contrariety betwixt a Cock and a Lion and so the like con-
sideration ' (I. xliii.). Agrippa refers thrice again to this peculiar antipathy
(I. xlviii.; I. liv.; III. xxxiii.)."—S. FOSTER DAMON, *W. Blake: His
Philosophy and Symbols.*

[31]
For in this Period the Poet's Work is Done, and all the Great
Events of Time start forth & are conciev'd in such a Period,
Within a Moment, a Pulsation of the Artery.

The Sky is an immortal Tent built by the Sons of Los;
And every Space that a Man views around his dwelling-place
Standing on his own roof or in his garden on a mount   6
Of twenty-five cubits in height, such space is his Universe;
And on its verge the Sun rises & sets, the Clouds bow
To meet the flat Earth & the Sea in such an order'd Space.
The Starry heavens reach no further, but here bend and set
On all sides, & the two Poles turn on their valves of gold;   11
And if he move his dwelling-place, his heavens also move
Where'er he goes, & all his neighbourhood bewail his loss.
Such are the Spaces called Earth & such its dimension.
As to that false appearance, which appears to the reasoner,   15
As of a Globe rolling thro' Voidness, it is a delusion of Ulro.
The Microscope knows not of this, nor the Telescope: they alter
The ratio of the Spectator's Organs, but leave Objects untouch'd.
For every Space larger than a red Globule of Man's blood
Is visionary, and is created by the Hammer of Los;   20
And every Space smaller than a Globule of Man's blood opens
Into Eternity, of which this vegetable Earth is but a shadow.
The red Globule is the unwearied Sun by Los created
To measure Time and Space to mortal Men every morning.
Bowlahoola & Allamanda are placed on each side   25
Of that Pulsation & that Globule; terrible their power.

But Rintrah & Palamabron govern over Day & Night
In Allamanda & Entuthon Benython where Souls wail,
Where Orc incessant howls, burning in fires of Eternal Youth
Within the vegetated mortal Nerves; for every Man born is joined
Within into One mighty Polypus, and this Polypus is Orc.   31

But in the Optic vegetative Nerves, Sleep was transformed
To Death in old time by Satan the father of Sin & Death:
And Satan is the Spectre of Orc, & Orc is the generate Luvah.

But in the Nerves of the Nostrils, Accident being formed   35
Into Substance & Principle by the cruelties of Demonstration,
It became Opake & Indefinite; but the Divine Saviour
Formed it into a Solid by Los's Mathematic power.
He named the Opake, Satan: he named the Solid, Adam.   39

And in the Nerves of the Ear (for the Nerves of the Tongue are
    closed)
On Albion's Rock Los stands creating the glorious Sun each
    morning;

And when unwearied in the evening, he creates the Moon,
Death to delude, who all in terror at their splendour leaves
His prey, while Los appoints & Rintrah & Palamabron guide   44
The Souls clear from the Rock of Death, that Death himself may
    wake
In his appointed season when the ends of heaven meet.

Then Los conducts the Spirits to be Vegetated into
Great Golgonooza, free from the four iron pillars of Satan's Throne,
(Temperance, Prudence, Justice, Fortitude, the four pillars of
    tyranny)   49
That Satan's Watch-Fiends touch them not before they Vegetate.

But Enitharmon and her Daughters take the pleasant charge
To give them to their lovely heavens till the Great Judgment Day:
Such is their lovely charge. But Rahab & Tirzah pervert
Their mild influences; therefore the Seven Eyes of God walk round
The Three Heavens of Ulro where Tirzah & her Sisters   55
Weave the black Woof of Death upon Entuthon Benython,
In the Vale of Surrey where Horeb terminates in Rephaim.
The stamping feet of Zelophehad's Daughters are cover'd with
    Human gore
Upon the treddles of the Loom: they sing to the winged shuttle.
The River rises above his banks to wash the Woof: 60
He takes it in his arms; he passes it in strength thro' his current;
The veil of human miseries is woven over the Ocean
From the Atlantic to the Great South Sea, the Erythrean.

Such is the World of Los, the labour of six thousand years.
Thus Nature is a Vision of the Science of the Elohim.[1]   65

End of the First Book

[1] Plate 32 is a full-page illustration showing the nude figure of a man
advancing right, left foot foremost, in an attitude of complete astonish-
ment, the head being far thrown back and the arms outstretched; while, like
a meteor, a star is falling upon his left foot. Behind the figure are three
stone steps; above it is the inscription " WILLIAM."

¹*MILTON*

Book the Second

[33]
There is a place where Contrarieties are equally True:
This place is called Beulah. It is a pleasant lovely Shadow
Where no dispute can come, Because of those who sleep.
Into this place the Sons & Daughters of Ololon descended
With solemn mourning, into Beulah's moony shades & hills   5
Weeping for Milton: mute wonder held the Daughters of Beulah,
Enraptur'd with affection sweet and mild benevolence.

Beulah is evermore Created around Eternity, appearing
To the Inhabitants of Eden around them on all sides.
But Beulah to its Inhabitants appears within each district   10
As the beloved infant in his mother's bosom round incircled
With arms of love & pity & sweet compassion. But to
The Sons of Eden the moony habitations of Beulah
Are from Great Eternity a mild & pleasant Rest.

And it is thus Created. Lo, the Eternal Great Humanity,   15
To whom be Glory & Dominion Evermore, Amen,
Walks among all his awful Family seen in every face:
As the breath of the Almighty, such are the words of man to man
In the great Wars of Eternity, in fury of Poetic Inspiration,
To build the Universe stupendous, Mental forms Creating.   20

But the Emanations trembled exceedingly, nor could they
Live, because the life of Man was too exceeding unbounded.
His joy became terrible to them; they trembled & wept,
Crying with one voice: '' Give us a habitation & a place
In which we may be hidden under the shadow of wings: 25
For if we, who are but for a time & who pass away in winter,
Behold these wonders of Eternity we shall consume:
But you, O our Fathers & Brothers, remain in Eternity.
But grant us a Temporal Habitation; do you speak
To us, we will obey your words as you obey Jesus   30
The Eternal who is blessed for ever & ever. Amen.''

¹ On the original plate, written in reverse around the Title, are the
following sentences:
"How wide the Gulf & Unpassable! between Simplicity & Insipidity."
"Contraries are Positives. A Negation is not a Contrary."

So spake the lovely Emanations, & there appear'd a pleasant
Mild Shadow above, beneath, & on all sides round.

[34]
Into this pleasant Shadow all the weak & weary
Like Women & Children were taken away as on wings
Of dovelike softness, & shadowy habitations prepared for them.
But every Man return'd & went still going forward thro'
The Bosom of the Father in Eternity on Eternity,   5
Neither did any lack or fall into Error without
A Shadow to repose in all the Days of happy Eternity.

Into this pleasant Shadow, Beulah, all Ololon descended;
And when the Daughters of Beulah heard the lamentation
All Beulah wept, for they saw the Lord coming in the Clouds.
And the Shadows of Beulah terminate in rocky Albion.   11

And all Nations wept in affliction, Family by Family:
Germany wept towards France & Italy, England wept & trembled
Towards America, India rose up from his golden bed
As one awaken'd in the night; they saw the Lord coming
In the Clouds of Ololon with Power & Great Glory.   16

And all the Living Creatures of the Four Elements wail'd
With bitter wailing; these in the aggregate are named Satan
And Rahab: they know not of Regeneration, but only of Genera-
     tion:
The Fairies, Nymphs, Gnomes & Genii of the Four Elements,
Unforgiving & unalterable, these cannot be Regenerated   21
But must be Created, for they know only of Generation:
These are the Gods of the Kingdoms of the Earth, in contrarious
And cruel opposition, Element against Element, opposed in War
Not Mental, as the Wars of Eternity, but a Corporeal Strife   25
In Los's Halls, continual labouring in the Furnaces of Golgonooza.
Orc howls on the Atlantic: Enitharmon trembles: All Beulah
     weeps.

Thou hearest the Nightingale begin the Song of Spring.
The Lark sitting upon his earthly bed, just as the morn
Appears, listens silent; then springing from the waving Corn-field,
     loud
He leads the Choir of Day: trill, trill, trill, trill,   31
Mounting upon the wings of light into the Great Expanse,
Reecchoing against the lovely blue & shining heavenly Shell,
His little throat labours with inspiration, every feather
On throat & breast & wings vibrates with the effluence Divine,
All Nature listens silent to him, & the awful Sun   36

Stands still upon the Mountain looking on this little Bird
With eyes of soft humility & wonder, love & awe.
Then loud from their green covert all the Birds begin their Song:
The Thrush, the Linnet & the Goldfinch, Robin & the Wren
Awake the Sun from his sweet reverie upon the Mountain.   41
The Nightingale again assays his song, & thro' the day
And thro' the night warbles luxuriant, every Bird of Song
Attending his loud harmony with admiration & love.
This is a Vision of the lamentation of Beulah over Ololon.   45

Thou percievest the Flowers put forth their precious Odours,
And none can tell how from so small a center comes such sweets,
Forgetting that within that Center Eternity expands
Its ever during doors that Og & Anak fiercely guard.   49
First, e'er the morning breaks, joy opens in the flowery bosoms,
Joy even to tears, which the Sun rising dries: first the Wild Thyme
And Meadow-sweet, downy & soft, waving among the reeds,
Light springing on the air, lead the sweet Dance: they wake
The Honeysuckle sleeping on the Oak; the flaunting beauty
Revels along upon the wind; the White-thorn, lovely May,   55
Opens her many lovely eyes: listening the Rose still sleeps,
None dare to wake her; soon she bursts her crimson curtain'd bed
And comes forth in the majesty of beauty: every Flower,
The Pink, the Jessamine, the Wall-flower, the Carnation,
The Jonquil, the mild Lilly opes her heavens; every Tree   60
And Flower & Herb soon fill the air with an innumerable Dance,
Yet all in order sweet & lovely. Men are sick with Love.
Such is a Vision of the lamentation of Beulah over Ololon.

[35]
And Milton oft sat upon the Couch of Death & oft conversed
In vision & dream beatific with the Seven Angels of the Presence.

" I have turned my back upon these Heavens builded on cruelty;
My Spectre, still wandering thro' them, follows my Emanation,
He hunts her footsteps thro' the snow & the wintry hail & rain.
The idiot Reasoner laughs at the Man of Imagination,   6
And from laughter proceeds to murder by undervaluing calumny."

Then Hillel, who is Lucifer, replied over the Couch of Death,
And thus the Seven Angels instructed him, & thus they converse:

"We are not Individuals but States, Combinations of Individuals.
We were Angels of the Divine Presence, & were Druids in Annan-
          dale,   11
Compell'd to combine into Form by Satan, the Spectre of Albion
Who made himself a God & destroyed the Human Form Divine.

But the Divine Humanity & Mercy gave us a Human Form [1]
Because we were combin'd in Freedom & holy Brotherhood,   15
While those combin'd by Satan's Tyranny, first in the blood of War
And Sacrifice, & next in Chains of imprisonment, are Shapeless
    Rocks
Retaining only Satan's Mathematic Holiness, Length, Bredth &
    Highth,
Calling the Human Imagination, which is the Divine Vision &
    Fruition
In which Man liveth eternally, madness & blasphemy against 20
Its own Qualities, which are Servants of Humanity, not Gods or
    Lords.
Distinguish therefore States from Individuals in those States.
States change, but Individual Identities never change nor cease.
You cannot go to Eternal Death in that which can never Die.
Satan & Adam are States Created into Twenty-seven Churches,
And thou, O Milton, art a State, about to be Created   26
Called Eternal Annihilation, that none but the Living shall
Dare to enter, & they shall enter triumphant over Death
And Hell & the Grave: States that are not, but ah! Seem to be.

" Judge then of thy Own Self: thy Eternal Lineaments explore,
What is Eternal & what Changeable & what Annihilable?   31
The Imagination is not a State: it is the Human Existence itself.
Affection or Love becomes a State when divided from Imagination,
The Memory is a State always, & the Reason is a State
Created to be Annihilated & a new Ratio Created.   35
Whatever can be Created can be Annihilated: Forms cannot:
The Oak is cut down by the Ax, the Lamb falls by the Knife,
But their Forms Eternal Exist For-ever. Amen. Hallelujah!"

Thus they converse with the Dead, watching round the Couch of
    Death;
For God himself enters Death's Door always with those that enter
And lays down in the Grave with them, in Visions of Eternity, 41
Till they awake & see Jesus & the Linen Clothes lying
That the Females had Woven for them, & the Gates of their
    Father's House.

[36]
And the Divine Voice was heard in the Songs of Beulah, Saying:

"When I first Married you, I gave you all my whole Soul.
I thought that you would love my loves & joy in my delights,

---

1 At the end of the lines 14, 15, Blake wrote in the margin:

"כרבים *
as multitudes
    Vox Populi."

* i.e. among the many.

Seeking for pleasures in my pleasures, O Daughter of Babylon.
Then thou wast lovely, mild & gentle; now thou art terrible
In jealousy & unlovely in my sight, because thou hast cruelly
Cut off my loves in fury till I have no love left for thee.
Thy love depends on him thou lovest, & on his dear loves
Depend thy pleasures, which thou has cut off by jealousy.
Therefore I shew my Jealousy & set before you Death.   10
Behold Milton descended to Redeem the Female Shade
From Death Eternal; such your lot, to be continually Redeem'd
By death & misery of those you love & by Annihilation.
When the Sixfold Female percieves that Milton annihilates
Himself, that, seeing all his loves by her cut off, he leaves   15
Her also, intirely abstracting himself from Female loves.
She shall relent in fear of death; She shall begin to give
Her maidens to her husband, delighting in his delight.
And then & then alone begins the happy Female joy   19
As it is done in Beulah; & thou, O Virgin Babylon, Mother of
      Whoredoms,
Shalt bring Jerusalem in thine arms in the night watches, and
No longer turning her a wandering Harlot in the streets,
Shalt give her into the arms of God your Lord & Husband.''

Such are the Songs of Beulah in the Lamentations of Ololon.[1]   24

[38]
And all the Songs of Beulah sounded comfortable notes
To comfort Ololon's lamentation, for they said:
'' Are you the Fiery Circle that late drove in fury & fire
The Eight Immortal Starry-Ones down into Ulro dark,
Rending the Heavens of Beulah with your thunders & lightnings?
And can you thus lament, & can you pity & forgive?   6
Is terror chang'd to pity? O wonder of Eternity! ''

And the Four States of Humanity in its Repose
Were shewed them. First of Beulah, a most pleasant Sleep
On Couches soft with mild music, tended by Flowers of Beulah,
Sweet Female forms, winged or floating in the air spontaneous.
The Second State is Alla, & the third State Al-Ulro;
But the Fourth State is dreadful, it is named Or-Ulro.
The First State is in the Head, the Second is in the Heart,
The Third in the Loins & Seminal Vessels, & the Fourth   15
In the Stomach & Intestines terrible, deadly, unutterable.
And he whose Gates are open'd in those Regions of his Body
Can from those Gates view all these wondrous Imaginations.

[1] Plate 37 is occupied by a full-page illustration that is an almost exact
counterpart of Plate 32. The figure here faces left and the star is descending
upon the advancing right foot. The inscription above is '' ROBFRT.''

But Ololon sought the Or-Ulro & its fiery Gates ¹⁹
And the Couches of the Martyrs, & many Daughters of Beulah
Accompany them down to the Ulro with soft melodious tears,
A long journey & dark thro' Chaos in the track of Milton's course,
To where the Contraries of Beulah War beneath Negation's
    Banner.

Then view'd from Milton's Track they see the Ulro, a vast Polypus
Of living fibres down into the Sea of Time & Space growing,   25
A self-devouring monstrous Human Death Twenty seven fold.
Within it sit Five Females & the nameless Shadowy Mother,
Spinning it from their bowels with songs of amorous delight
And melting cadences that lure the Sleepers of Beulah down
The River Storge (which is Arnon) into the Dead Sea.   30
Around this Polypus Los continual builds the Mundane Shell.

Four Universes round the Universe of Los remain Chaotic,
Four intersecting Globes, & the Egg form'd World of Los
In midst, stretching from Zenith to Nadir in midst of Chaos.
One of these Ruin'd Universes is to the North, named Urthona:
One to the South, this was the glorious World of Urizen: 36
One to the East, of Luvah: One to the West, of Tharmas.
But when Luvah assumed the World of Urizen in the South
All fell towards the Center, sinking downward in dire Ruin.

Here in these Chaoses the Sons of Ololon took their abode,   40
In Chasms of the Mundane Shell which open on all sides round,
Southward & by the East within the Breach of Milton's descent,¹
To watch the time, pitying & gentle to awaken Urizen.
They stood in a dark land of death, of fiery corroding waters,
Where lie in evil death the Four Immortals pale and cold   45
And the Eternal Man, even Albion, upon the Rock of Ages.
Seeing Milton's Shadow, some Daughters of Beulah trembling
Return'd, but Ololon remain'd before the Gates of the Dead.

And Ololon looked down into the Heavens of Ulro in fear.
They said: " How are the Wars of man, which in Great Eternity
Appear around in the External Spheres of Visionary Life,   51
Here render'd Deadly within the Life & Interior Vision?
How are the Beasts & Birds & Fishes & Plant & Minerals
Here fix'd into a frozen bulk, subject to decay & death?
Those Visions of Human Life & Shadows of Wisdom & Knowledge

---

¹ On the lower half of Plate 36 is a geometric design of four intersecting
circles sustained in the centre by an inverted egg. The circles are inscribed
" Urthona (N)," " Urizen (S)," " Luvah (E)," and " Tharmas (W"; the
upper part of the egg bears the title " Adam " and the lower part " Satan."
A line passing through the point where the circles of Urizen and Luvah in-
tersect, is described as " Milton's Track." The design is enveloped in flames.

[39]
" Are here frozen to unexpansive deadly destroying terrors,
And War & Hunting, the Two Fountains of the River of Life,
Are become Fountains of bitter Death & of corroding Hell,
Till Brotherhood is chang'd into a Curse & a Flattery
By Differences between Ideas, that Ideas themselves (which are
The Divine Members) may be slain in offerings for sin.   6
O dreadful Loom of Death! O piteous Female forms compell'd
To weave the Woof of Death! On Camberwell Tirzah's Courts,
Malah's on Blackheath, Rahab & Noah dwell on Windsor's heights,
Where once the Cherubs of Jerusalem spread to Lambeth's Vale.
Milcah's Pillars shine from Harrow to Hampstead, where Hoglah
On Highgate's heights magnificent Weaves over trembling Thames
To Shooters' Hill and thence to Blackheath, the dark Woof. Loud,
Loud roll the Weights & Spindles over the whole Earth, let down
On all sides round to the Four Quarters of the World, eastward on
Europe to Euphrates & Hindu to Nile, & back in Clouds   16
Of Death across the Atlantic to America North & South."

So spake Ololon in reminiscence astonish'd, but they
Could not behold Golgonooza without passing the Polypus,
A wondrous journey not passable by Immortal feet, & none
But the Divine Saviour can pass it without annihilation;   21
For Golgonooza cannot be seen till, having pass'd the Polypus,
It is viewed on all sides round in a Four-fold Vision,
Or till you become Mortal & Vegetable in Sexuality,
Then you behold its mighty Spires & Domes of ivory & gold.

And Ololon examined all the Couches of the Dead,   26
Even of Los & Enitharmon & all the Sons of Albion
And his Four Zoas terrified & on the verge of Death.
In midst of these was Milton's Couch, & when they saw Eight
Immortal Starry-Ones guarding the Couch in flaming fires,
They thunderous utter'd all a universal groan, falling down   31
Prostrate before the Starry Eight, asking with tears forgiveness,
Confessing their crime with humiliation and sorrow.

O how the Starry Eight rejoic'd to see Ololon descended,
And now that a wide road was open to Eternity   35
By Ololon's descent thro' Beulah to Los & Enitharmon!
For mighty were the multitudes of Ololon, vast the extent
Of their great sway, reaching from Ulro to Eternity,
Surrounding the Mundane Shell outside in its Caverns
And through Beulah; and all silent forbore to contend   40
With Ololon, for they saw the Lord in the Clouds of Ololon.

There is a Moment in each Day that Satan cannot find,
Nor can his Watch Fiends find it; but the Industrious find

This Moment & it multiply; & when it once is found
It renovates every Moment of the Day if rightly placed.   45
In this Moment Ololon descended to Los & Enitharmon
Unseen beyond the Mundane Shell, Southward in Milton's track.

Just in this Moment, when the morning odours rise abroad
And first from the Wild Thyme, stands a Fountain in a rock
Of crystal flowing into two Streams: one flows thro' Golgonooza
And thro' Beulah to Eden beneath Los's western wall: 51
The other flows thro' the Aerial Void & all the Churches,
Meeting again in Golgonooza beyond Satan's Seat.

The Wild Thyme is Los's Messenger to Eden, a mighty Demon,
Terrible, deadly & poisonous his presence in Ulro dark;   55
Therefore he appears only a small Root creeping in grass
Covering over the Rock of Odours his bright purple mantle
Beside the Fount above the Lark's Nest in Golgonooza.
Luvah slept here in death, & here is Luvah's empty Tomb.
Ololon sat beside this Fountain on the Rock of Odours.   60

Just at the place to where the Lark mounts is a Crystal Gate:
It is the enterance of the First Heaven, named Luther; for
The Lark is Los's Messenger thro' the Twenty-seven Churches,
That the Seven Eyes of God, who walk even to Satan's Seat
Thro' all the Twenty-seven Heavens, may not slumber nor sleep.
But the Lark's Nest is at the Gate of Los, at the eastern   66
Gate of wide Golgonooza, & the Lark is Los's Messenger.

[40]
When on the highest lift of his light pinions he arrives
At that bright Gate, another Lark meets him, & back to back
They touch their pinions, tip tip, and each descend
To their respective Earths & there all night consult with Angels
Of Providence & with the eyes of God all night in slumber   5
Inspired, & at the dawn of day send out another Lark
Into another Heaven to carry news upon his wings.
Thus are the Messengers dispatch'd till they reach the Earth again
In the East Gate of Golgonooza; & the Twenty-eighth bright
Lark met the Female Ololon descending into my Garden.   10
Thus it appears to Mortal eyes & those of the Ulro Heavens;
But not thus to Immortals: the Lark is a mighty Angel.

For Ololon step'd into the Polypus within the Mundane Shell—
They could not step into Vegetable Worlds without becoming
The enemies of Humanity, except in a Female Form—   15
And as One Female, Ololon and all its mighty Hosts
Appear'd a Virgin of twelve years: nor time nor space was
To the perception of the Virgin Ololon, but as the

Flash of lightning, but more quick, the Virgin in my Garden
Before my Cottage stood; for the Satanic Space is delusion.   20

For when Los join'd with me he took me in his fi'ry whirlwind:
My Vegetated portion was hurried from Lambeth's shades,
He set me down in Felpham's Vale & prepar'd a beautiful
Cottage for me, that in three years I might write all these Visions
To display Nature's cruel holiness, the deceits of Natural Religion.
Walking in my Cottage Garden, sudden I beheld   26
The Virgin Ololon & address'd her as a Daughter of Beulah:

" Virgin of Providence, fear not to enter into my Cottage.
What is thy message to thy friend? what am I now to do?
Is it again to plunge into deeper affliction? behold me   30
Ready to obey; but pity thou my Shadow of Delight:
Enter my Cottage, comfort her, for she is sick with fatigue." ¹

[41]
The Virgin answer'd: " Knowest thou of Milton who descended
Driven from Eternity? him I seek! terrified at my Act
In Great Eternity which thou knowest, I come him to seek."

So Ololon utter'd in words distinct the anxious thought:
Mild was the voice, but more distinct than any earthly   5
That Milton's Shadow heard; & condensing all his Fibres
Into a strength impregnable of majesty & beauty infinite,
I saw he was the Covering Cherub & within him Satan
And Rahab, in an outside which is fallacious, within
Beyond the outline of Identity, in the Selfhood deadly: 10
And he appear'd the Wicker Man of Scandinavia, in whom
Jerusalem's children consume in flames among the Stars.

Descending down into my Garden, a Human Wonder of God
Reaching from heaven to earth, a Cloud & Human Form,
I beheld Milton with astonishment, & in him beheld   15
The Monstrous Churches of Beulah, the Gods of Ulro dark,
Twelve monstrous dishumaniz'd terrors, Synagogues of Satan,
A Double Twelve & Thrice Nine: such their divisions.

And these their Names & their Places within the Mundane Shell:

In Tyre & Sidon I saw Baal & Ashtaroth: In Moab Chemosh: 20
In Ammon Molech, loud his Furnaces rage among the Wheels
Of Og, & pealing loud the cries of the Victims of Fire,

¹ At the foot of Plate 40 Blake has drawn a picture of himself walking in
his garden while the wingless angel Ololon descends. The illustration is
inscribed:

" Blake's Cottage at Felpham."

And pale his Priestesses infolded in Veils of Pestilence border'd
With War, Woven in Looms of Tyre & Sidon by beautiful Ash-
     taroth:
In Palestine Dagon, Sea Monster, worship'd o'er the Sea: 25
Thammuz in Lebanon & Rimmon in Damascus curtain'd:
Osiris, Isis, Orus in Egypt, dark their Tabernacles on Nile
Floating with solemn songs & on the Lakes of Egypt nightly
With pomp even till morning break & Osiris appear in the sky:
But Belial of Sodom & Gomorrha, obscure Demon of Bribes   30
And secret Assasinations, not worship'd nor ador'd but
With the finger on the lips & the back turn'd to the light:
And Saturn, Jove & Rhea of the Isles of the Sea remote.
These Twelve Gods are the Twelve Spectre Sons of the Druid
     Albion.

And these the names of the Twenty-seven Heavens & their
     Churches:
Adam, Seth, Enos, Cainan, Mahalaleel, Jared, Enoch,   36
Methuselah, Lamech, these are Giants mighty, Hermaphroditic;
Noah, Shem, Arphaxad, Cainan the second, Salah, Heber,
Peleg, Reu, Serug, Nahor, Terah, these are the Female-Males,
A Male within a Female hid as in an Ark & Curtains;   40
Abraham, Moses, Solomon, Paul, Constantine, Charlemaine,
Luther, these seven are the Male-Females, the Dragon Forms,
Religion hid in War, a Dragon red & hidden Harlot.

All these are seen in Milton's Shadow, who is the Covering Cherub,
The Spectre of Albion in which the Spectre of Luvah inhabits 45
In the Newtonian Voids between the Substances of Creation.

For the Chaotic Voids outside of the Stars are measured by
The Stars, which are the boundaries of Kingdoms, Provinces
And Empires of Chaos invisible to the Vegetable Man.
The Kingdom of Og is in Orion: Sihon is in Ophiucus.   50
Og has Twenty-seven Districts: Sihon's Districts Twenty-one,
From Star to Star, Mountains & Valleys, terrible dimension
Stretch'd out, compose the Mundane Shell, a mighty Incrustation
Of Forty-eight deformed Human Wonders of the Almighty,
With Caverns whose remotest bottoms meet again beyond   55
The Mundane Shell in Golgonooza; but the Fires of Los rage
In the remotest bottoms of the Caves, that none can pass
Into Eternity that way, but all descend to Los,
To Bowlahoola & Allamanda & to Entuthon Benython.

The Heavens are the Cherub: the Twelve Gods are Satan,   60
[43]
And the Forty-eight Starry Regions are Cities of the Levites,
The Heads of the Great Polypus, Four-fold twelve enormity,

In mighty & mysterious comingling, enemy with enemy,
Woven by Urizen into Sexes from his mantle of years.   4
And Milton, collecting all his fibres into impregnable strength,
Descended down a Paved work of all kinds of precious stones
Out from the eastern sky; descending down into my Cottage
Garden, clothed in black, severe & silent he descended.

The Spectre of Satan stood upon the roaring sea & beheld   9
Milton within his sleeping Humanity; trembling & shudd'ring
He stood upon the waves a Twenty-seven-fold mighty Demon
Gorgeous & beautiful: loud roll his thunders against Milton:
Loud Satan thunder'd; loud & dark upon mild Felpham shore,
Not daring to touch one fibre, he howl'd round upon the Sea.

I also stood in Satan's bosom & beheld its desolations: 15
A ruin'd Man, a ruin'd building of God not made with hands:
Its plains of burning sand, its mountains of marble terrible:
Its pits & declivities flowing with molten ore & fountains
Of pitch & nitre: its ruin'd palaces & cities & mighty works:
Its furnaces of affliction, in which his Angels & Emanations   20
Labour with blacken'd visages among its stupendous ruins,
Arches & pyramids & porches, colonades & domes,
In which dwells Mystery, Babylon; here is her secret place,
From hence she comes forth on the Churches in delight;   24
Here is her Cup fill'd with its poisons in these horrid vales,
And here her scarlet Veil woven in pestilence & war;
Here is Jerusalem bound in chains in the Dens of Babylon.

In the Eastern porch of Satan's Universe Milton stood & said:

" Satan! my Spectre! I know my power thee to annihilate
And be a greater in thy place & be thy Tabernacle,   30
A covering for thee to do thy will, till one greater comes
And smites me as I smote thee & becomes my covering.
Such are the Laws of thy false Heav'ns; but Laws of Eternity
Are not such; know thou, I come to Self Annihilation.
Such are the Laws of Eternity, that each shall mutually   35
Annihilate himself for other's good, as I for thee.
Thy purpose & the purpose of thy Priests & of thy Churches
Is to impress on men the fear of death, to teach
Trembling & fear, terror, constriction, abject selfishness:
Mine is to teach Men to despise death & to go on   40
In fearless majesty annihilating Self, laughing to scorn
Thy Laws & terrors, shaking down thy Synagogues as webs.
I come to discover before Heav'n & Hell the Self righteousness
In all its Hypocritic turpitude, opening to every eye
These wonders of Satan's holiness, shewing to the Earth   45
The Idol Virtues of the Natural Heart, & Satan's Seat

Explore in all its Selfish Natural Virtue, & put off
In Self annihilation all that is not of God alone,
To put off Self & all I have, ever & ever. Amen."   49

Satan heard, Coming in a cloud with trumpets & flaming fire,
Saying: " I am God the judge of all, the living & the dead.
Fall therefore down & worship me; submit thy supreme
Dictate to my eternal Will, & to my dictate bow.
I hold the Balances of Right & Just, & mine the Sword.
Seven Angels bear my Name & in those Seven I appear,   55
But I alone am God, & I alone in Heav'n & Earth
Of all that live dare utter this, others tremble & bow,
[44]
" Till All Things become One Great Satan, in Holiness
Oppos'd to Mercy, and the Divine Delusion, Jesus, be no more."

Suddenly around Milton on my Path the Starry Seven
Burn'd terrible: my Path became a solid fire, as bright
As the clear Sun, & Milton silent came down on my Path.   5
And there went forth from the Starry limbs of the Seven, Forms
Human, with Trumpets innumerable, sounding articulate
As the Seven spake; and they stood in a mighty Column of Fire
Surrounding Felpham's Vale, reaching to the Mundane Shell,
    Saying:

" Awake, Albion awake! reclaim thy Reasoning Spectre. Subdue
Him to the Divine Mercy. Cast him down into the Lake   11
Of Los that ever burneth with fire, ever & ever, Amen!
Let the Four Zoas awake from Slumbers of Six Thousand Years."

Then loud the Furnaces of Los were heard, & seen as Seven
    Heavens
Stretching from south to north over the mountains of Albion.   15

Satan heard: trembling round his Body, he incircled it:
He trembled with exceeding great trembling & astonishment,
Howling in his Spectre round his Body, hung'ring to devour
But fearing for the pain, for if he touches a Vital
His torment is unendurable: therefore he cannot devour   20
But howls round it as a lion round his prey continually.
Loud Satan thunder'd, loud & dark upon mild Felpham's Shore,
Coming in a Cloud with Trumpets & with Fiery Flame,
An awful Form eastward from midst of a bright Paved-work
Of precious stones by Cherubim surrounded, so permitted   25
(Lest he should fall apart in his Eternal Death) to imitate
The Eternal Great Humanity Divine surrounded by
His Cherubim & Seraphim in ever happy Eternity.
Beneath sat Chaos: Sin on his right hand, Death on his left;   29

And Ancient Night spread over all the heav'n his Mantle of Laws.
He trembled with exceeding great trembling & astonishment.

Then Albion rose up in the Night of Beulah on his Couch
Of dread repose; seen by the visionary eye, his face is toward
The east, toward Jerusalem's Gates: groaning he sat above
His rocks. London & Bath & Legions & Edinburgh   35
Are the four pillars of his Throne: his left foot near London
Covers the shades of Tyburn: his instep from Windsor
To Primrose Hill stretching to Highgate & Holloway.
London is between his knees, its basements fourfold;
His right foot stretches to the sea on Dover cliffs, his heel   40
On Canterbury's ruins; his right hand covers lofty Wales,
His left Scotland; his bosom girt with gold involves
York, Edinburgh, Durham & Carlisle, & on the front
Bath, Oxford, Cambridge, Norwich; his right elbow
Leans on the Rocks of Erin's Land, Ireland, ancient nation.   45
His head bends over London; he sees his embodied Spectre
Trembling before him with exceeding great trembling & fear.
He views Jerusalem & Babylon, his tears flow down.
He mov'd his right foot to Cornwall, his left to the˙Rocks of
   Bognor,
He strove to rise to walk into the Deep, but strength failing   50
Forbad, & down with dreadful groans he sunk upon his Couch
In moony Beulah. Los, his strong Guard, walks round beneath
   the Moon.

Urizen faints in terror, striving among the Brooks of Arnon
With Milton's Spirit; as the Plowman or Artificer or Shepherd
While in the labours of his Calling sends his Thought abroad   55
To labour in the ocean or in the starry heaven, So Milton
Labour'd in Chasms of the Mundane Shell, tho' here before
My Cottage midst the Starry Seven where the Virgin Ololon
Stood trembling in the Porch: loud Satan thunder'd on the
   stormy Sea
Circling Albion's Cliffs, in which the Four-fold World resides,
Tho' seen in fallacy outside, a fallacy of Satan's Churches.   61

[46]
Before Ololon Milton stood & perciev'd the Eternal Form
Of that mild Vision: wondrous were their acts, by me unknown
Except remotely; and I heard Ololon say to Milton:

" I see thee strive upon the Brooks of Arnon: there a dread
And awful Man I see, o'ercover'd with the mantle of years.   5
I behold Los & Urizen, I behold Orc & Tharmas,
The Four Zoas of Albion, & thy Spirit with them striving,
In Self annihilation giving thy life to thy enemies.

Are those who contemn Religion & seek to annihilate it   9
Become in their Feminine [1] portions the causes & promoters
Of these Religions? how is this thing, this Newtonian Phantasm,
This Voltaire & Rousseau, this Hume & Gibbon & Bolingbroke,
This Natural Religion, this impossible absurdity?
Is Ololon the cause of this? O where shall I hide my face?
These tears fall for the little ones, the Children of Jerusalem,
Lest they be annihilated in thy annihilation."   16

No sooner she had spoke but Rahab Babylon appear'd
Eastward upon the Paved work across Europe & Asia,
Glorious as the midday Sun, in Satan's bosom glowing,
A Female hidden in a Male, Religion hidden in War,   20
Nam'd Moral Virtue, cruel two-fold Monster shining bright,
A Dragon red & hidden Harlot which John in Patmos saw.

And all beneath the Nations innumerable of Ulro
Appear'd the Seven Kingdoms of Canaan & Five Baalim
Of Philistea into Twelve divided, call'd after the Names   25
Of Israel, as they are in Eden, Mountain, River & Plain,
City & sandy Desert intermingled beyond mortal ken.

But turning toward Ololon in terrible majesty, Milton
Replied: " Obey thou the Words of the Inspired Man.
All that can be annihilated must be annihilated   30
That the Children of Jerusalem may be saved from slavery.
There is a Negation, & there is a Contrary:
The Negation must be destroy'd to redeem the Contraries.
The Negation is the Spectre, the Reasoning Power in Man:
This is a false Body, an Incrustation over my Immortal   35
Spirit, a Selfhood which must be put off & annihilated alway.
To cleanse the Face of my Spirit by Self-examination,
[48]
" To bathe in the Waters of Life, to wash off the Not Human,
I come in Self-annihilation & the grandeur of Inspiration,
To cast off Rational Demonstration bv Faith in the Saviour,
To cast off the rotten rags of Memory by Inspiration,   4
To cast off Bacon, Locke & Newton from Albion's covering,
To take off his filthy garments & clothe him with Imagination;
To cast aside from Poetry all that is not Inspiration,
That it no longer shall dare to mock with the aspersion of Madness
Cast on the Inspired by the tame high finisher of paltry Blots
Indefinite, or paltry Rhymes, or paltry Harmonies,   10
Who creeps into State Government like a catterpiller to destroy;
To cast off the idiot Questioner who is always questioning
But never capable of answering, who sits with a sly grin

---

1 "Feminine." Blake actually wrote " Femine," both here and on Plate
48, l. 30.

Silent plotting when to question, like a thief in a cave,   14
Who publishes doubt & calls it knowledge, whose Science is
    Despair,
Whose pretence to knowledge is Envy, whose whole Science is
To destroy the wisdom of ages to gratify ravenous Envy
That rages round him like a Wolf day & night without rest:
He smiles with condescension, he talks of Benevolence & Virtue,
And those who act with Benevolence & Virtue they murder time
    on time.
These are the destroyers of Jerusalem, these are the murderers
Of Jesus, who deny the Faith & mock at Eternal Life,   22
Who pretend to Poetry that they may destroy Imagination
By imitation of Nature's Images drawn from Remembrance.
These are the Sexual Garments, the Abomination of Desolation,
Hiding the Human Lineaments as with an Ark & Curtains
Which Jesus rent & now shall wholly purge away with Fire
Till Generation is swallow'd up in Regeneration."

Then trembled the Virgin Ololon & reply'd in clouds of despair:

" Is this our Feminine Portion, the Six-fold Miltonic Female?
Terribly this Portion trembles before thee, O awful Man.   31
Altho' our Human Power can sustain the severe contentions
Of Friendship, our Sexual cannot, but flies into the Ulro.
Hence arose all our terrors in Eternity; & now remembrance
Returns upon us: are we Contraries, O Milton, Thou & I?
O Immortal! how were we led to War the Wars of Death?
Is this the Void Outside of Existence, which if enter'd into   37
[49]
" Becomes a Womb? & is this the Death Couch of Albion?
Thou goest to Eternal Death & all must go with thee."

So saying, the Virgin divided Six-fold, & with a shriek
Dolorous that ran thro' all Creation, a Double Six-fold Wonder,
Away from Ololon she divided & fled into the depths   5
Of Milton's Shadow, as a Dove upon the stormy Sea.

Then as a Moony Ark Ololon descended to Felpham's Vale
In clouds of blood, in streams of gore, with dreadful thunderings
Into the Fires of Intellect that rejoic'd in Felpham's Vale
Around the Starry Eight: with one accord the Starry Eight
    became
One Man, Jesus the Saviour, wonderful! round his limbs   11
The Clouds of Ololon folded as a Garment dipped in blood,
Written within & without in woven letters, & the Writing
Is the Divine Revelation in the Litteral expression,
A Garment of War. I heard it nam'd the Woof of Six Thousand
    Years.

And I beheld the Twenty-four Cities of Albion   16
Arise upon their Thrones to Judge the Nations of the Earth;
And the Immortal Four in whom the Twenty-four appear Four-
    fold
Arose around Albion's body. Jesus wept & walked forth
From Felpham's Vale clothed in Clouds of blood, to enter into
Albion's Bosom, the bosom of death, & the Four surrounded him
In the Column of Fire in Felpham's Vale; then to their mouths
    the Four
Applied their Four Trumpets & then [1] sounded to the Four winds.

Terror struck in the Vale I stood at that immortal sound.
My bones trembled, I fell outstretch'd upon the path   25
A moment, & my Soul return'd into its mortal state
To Resurrection & Judgment in the Vegetable Body,
And my sweet Shadow of Delight stood trembling by my side.

Immediately the Lark mounted with a loud trill from Felpham's
    Vale,
And the Wild Thyme from Wimbleton's green & impurpled Hills,
And Los & Enitharmon rose over the Hills of Surrey: 31
Their clouds roll over London with a south wind; soft Oothoon
Pants in the Vales of Lambeth, weeping o'er her Human Harvest.
Los listens to the Cry of the Poor Man, his Cloud
Over London, in volume terrific, low bended in anger.   35

Rintrah & Palamabron view the Human Harvest beneath:
Their Wine-presses & Barns stand open, the Ovens are prepar'd,
The Waggons ready; terrific Lions & Tygers sport & play:
All Animals upon the Earth are prepar'd in all their strength
[50]
To go forth to the Great Harvest & Vintage of the Nations.   40

Finis

---

[1] " then." The word is indistinct and might be " them."

JERUSALEM

The EMANATION of

THE GIANT ALBION

(*Begun* 1804)

[3]

SHEEP   GOATS

To the Public

AFTER my three years' slumber on the banks of the Ocean, I again display my Giant forms to the Public. My former Giants & Fairies having reciev'd the highest reward possible, the . [1] . and . . . of those with whom to be connected is to be . . ., I cannot doubt that this more consolidated & extended Work will be as kindly recieved. The Enthusiasm of the following Poem, the Author hopes. . . . I also hope the Reader will be with me, wholly One in Jesus our Lord, who is the God . . . and Lord . . . to whom the Ancients look'd, and saw his day afar off with trembling & amazement.

The Spirit of Jesus is continual forgiveness of Sin: he who waits to be righteous before he enters into the Saviour's kingdom, the Divine Body, will never enter there. I am perhaps the most sinful of men. I pretend not to holiness: yet I pretend to love, to see, to converse with daily as man with man, & the more to have an interest in the Friend of Sinners. Therefore, . . . Reader, . . . what you do not approve, & . . . me for this energetic exertion of my talent.

> Reader! . . . of books! . . . of heaven,
> And of that God from whom . . .,
> Who in mysterious Sinai's awful cave
> To Man the wondrous art of writing gave:
> Again he speaks in thunder and in fire!

[1] Blake erased a number of words and sentences, as here indicated.

Thunder of Thought, & flames of fierce desire:
Even from the depths of Hell his voice I hear
Within the unfathom'd caverns of my Ear.
Therefore I print; nor vain my types shall be:
Heaven, Earth & Hell henceforth shall live in harmony.

Of the Measure in which
the following Poem is written.

We who dwell on Earth can do nothing of ourselves; every
thing is conducted by Spirits, no less than Digestion or Sleep.
. . . When this Verse was first dictated to me, I consider'd a
Monotonous Cadence like that used by Milton & Shakspeare &
all writers of English Blank Verse, derived from the modern
bondage of Rhyming, to be a necessary and indispensible part
of Verse. But I soon found that in the mouth of a true Orator
such monotony was not only awkward, but as much a bondage
as rhyme itself. I therefore have produced a variety in every
line, both of cadences & number of syllables. Every word and
every letter is studied and put into its fit place; the terrific
numbers are reserved for the terrific parts, the mild & gentle for
the mild & gentle parts, and the prosaic for inferior parts; all
are necessary to each other. Poetry Fetter'd Fetters the Human
Race. Nations are Destroy'd or Flourish in proportion as Their
Poetry, Painting and Music are Destroy'd or Flourish! The
Primeval State of Man was Wisdom, Art and Science.

Μονος ο Ιεσους[1]

JERUSALEM

Chap: 1

Of the Sleep of Ulro! and of the passage through
Eternal Death! and of the awaking to Eternal Life.

This theme calls me in sleep night after night, & ev'ry morn
Awakes me at sun-rise; then I see the Saviour over me
Spreading his beams of love & dictating the words of this mild song.

" Awake! awake O sleeper of the land of shadows, wake! expand!
I am in you and you in me, mutual in love divine:
Fibres of love from man to man thro' Albion's pleasant land.
In all the dark Atlantic vale down from the hills of Surrey
A black water accumulates; return Albion! return!   10
Thy brethren call thee, and thy fathers and thy sons,
Thy nurses and thy mothers, thy sisters and thy daughters
Weep at thy soul's disease, and the Divine Vision is darken'd;
Thy Emanation that was wont to play before thy face,
Beaming forth with her daughters into the Divine bosom: 15
Where hast thou hidden thy Emanation, lovely Jerusalem,
From the vision and fruition of the Holy-one?
I am not a God afar off, I am a brother and friend;
Within your bosoms I reside, and you reside in me:
Lo! we are One, forgiving all Evil, Not seeking recompense: 20
Ye are my members, O ye sleepers of Beulah, land of shades! "

But the perturbed Man away turns down the valleys dark:

" Phantom of the over heated brain! shadow of immortality!
Seeking to keep my soul a victim to thy Love! which binds
Man, the enemy of man, into deceitful friendships,   25
Jerusalem is not! her daughters are indefinite:
By demonstration man alone can live, and not by faith.
My mountains are my own, and I will keep them to myself:
The Malvern and the Cheviot, the Wolds, Plinlimmon & Snowdon

---

[1] i.e. " Jesus alone." The editors of the Clarendon Edition of the *Prophetic Writings* supply the important reference to John viii. 9.

Are mine: here will I build my Laws of Moral Virtue.   30
Humanity shall be no more, but war & princedom & victory!''

So spoke Albion in jealous fears, hiding his Emanation
Upon the Thames and Medway, rivers of Beulah, dissembling
His jealousy before the throne divine, darkening, cold!

[5]
The banks of the Thames are clouded! the ancient porches of
    Albion are
Darken'd! they are drawn thro' unbounded space, scatter'd upon
The Void in incoherent despair! Cambridge & Oxford & London
Are driven among the starry Wheels, rent away and dissipated
In Chasms & Abysses of sorrow, enlarg'd without dimension,
    terrible.
Albion's mountains run with blood, the cries of war & of tumult 6
Resound into the unbounded night, every Human perfection
Of mountain & river & city are small & wither'd & darken'd.
Cam is a little stream! Ely is almost swallow'd up!
Lincoln & Norwich stand trembling on the brink of Udan-Adan! 10
Wales and Scotland shrink themselves to the west and to the north!
Mourning for fear of the warriors in the Vale of Entuthon-
    Benython
Jerusalem is scatter'd abroad like a cloud of smoke thro' non-
    entity.
Moab & Ammon & Amalek & Canaan & Egypt & Aram
Recieve her little-ones for sacrifices and the delights of cruelty. 15

Trembling I sit day and night, my friends are astonish'd at me,
Yet they forgive my wanderings. I rest not from my great task!
To open the Eternal Worlds, to open the immortal Eyes
Of Man inwards into the Worlds of Thought, into Eternity 19
Ever expanding in the Bosom of God, the Human Imagination.
O Saviour pour upon me thy Spirit of meekness & love:
Annihilate the Selfhood in me: be thou all my life!
Guide thou my hand, which trembles exceedingly upon the rock
    of ages,
While I write of the building of Golgonooza, & of the terrors of
    Entuthon,
Of Hand & Hyle & Coban, of Kwantok, Peachey, Brereton, Slayd
    & Hutton,
Of the terrible sons & daughters of Albion, and their Generations.

Scofield, Kox, Kotope and Bowen revolve most mightily upon
The Furnace of Los; before the eastern gate bending their fury
They war to destroy the Furnaces, to desolate Golgonooza 29
And to devour the Sleeping Humanity of Albion in rage & hunger.

They revolve into the Furnaces Southward & are driven forth
    Northward,
Divided into Male and Female forms time after time.
From these Twelve all the Families of England spread abroad.

The Male is a Furnace of beryll; the Female is a golden Loom.
I behold them, and their rushing fires overwhelm my Soul   35
In London's darkness, and my tears fall day and night
Upon the Emanations of Albion's Sons, the Daughters of Albion,
Names anciently remember'd, but now contemn'd as fictions
Although in every bosom they controll our Vegetative powers.

These are united into Tirzah and her Sisters, on Mount Gilead, 40
Cambel & Gwendolen & Conwenna & Cordella & Ignoge.
And these united into Rahab in the Covering Cherub on Euphrates,
Gwiniverra & Gwinefred & Gonorill & Sabrina beautiful,
Estrild, Mehetabel & Ragan, lovely Daughters of Albion,
They are the beautiful Emanations of the Twelve Sons of Albion.

The Starry Wheels revolv'd heavily over the Furnaces,   46
Drawing Jerusalem in anguish of maternal love
Eastward, a pillar of a cloud with Vala upon the mountains
Howling in pain, redounding from the arms of Beulah's Daughters
Out from the Furnaces of Los above the head of Los,   50
A pillar of smoke writhing afar into Non-Entity, redounding
Till the cloud reaches afar outstretch'd among the Starry Wheels
Which revolve heavily in the mighty Void above the Furnaces.

O what avail the loves & tears of Beulah's lovely Daughters!
They hold the Immortal Form in gentle bands & tender tears, 55
But all within is open'd into the deeps of Entuthon Benython,
A dark and unknown night, indefinite, unmeasurable, without end,
Abstract Philosophy warring in enmity against Imagination
(Which is the Divine Body of the Lord Jesus, blessed for ever),
And there Jerusalem wanders with Vala upon the mountains. 60
Attracted by the revolutions of those Wheels, the Cloud of smoke
Immense, and Jerusalem & Vala weeping in the Cloud
Wander away into the Chaotic Void, lamenting with her Shadow
Among the Daughters of Albion, among the Starry Wheels,
Lamenting for her children, for the sons & daughters of Albion. 65

Los heard her lamentations in the deeps afar! his tears fall
Incessant before the Furnaces, and his Emanation divided in pain
Eastward toward the Starry Wheels. But Westward, a black
    Horror,
[6]
His Spectre driv'n by the Starry Wheels of Albion's sons, black and
Opake divided from his back; he labours and he mourns!

For as his Emanation divided, his Spectre also divided
In terror of those starry wheels: and the Spectre stood over Los
Howling in pain, a black'ning Shadow, black'ning dark & opake,
Cursing the terrible Los, bitterly cursing him for his friendship   6
To Albion, suggesting murderous thoughts against Albion.

Los rag'd and stamp'd the earth in his might & terrible wrath!
He stood and stamp'd the earth; then he threw down his hammer
    in rage &
In fury; then he sat down and wept, terrified! Then arose   10
And chaunted his song, labouring with the tongs and hammer;
But still the Spectre divided, and still his pain increas'd!

In pain the Spectre divided, in pain of hunger and thirst
To devour Los's Human Perfection; but when he saw that Los
[7]
Was living, panting like a frighted wolf and howling
He stood over the Immortal in the solitude and darkness
Upon the dark'ning Thames, across the whole Island westward,
A horrible Shadow of Death among the Furnaces beneath
The pillar of folding smoke; and he sought by other means   5
To lure Los, by tears, by arguments of science & by terrors,
Terrors in every Nerve, by spasms & extended pains,
While Los answer'd unterrified to the opake blackening Fiend.

And thus the Spectre spoke: "Wilt thou still go on to destruc-
    tion?
Till thy life is all taken away by this deceitful Friendship?
He drinks thee up like water, like wine he pours thee   11
Into his tuns; thy Daughters are trodden in his vintage,
He makes thy Sons the trampling of his bulls, they are plow'd
And harrow'd for his profit; lo! thy stolen Emanation
Is his garden of pleasure! all the Spectres of his Sons mock thee;
Look how they scorn thy once admired palaces, now in ruins
Because of Albion! because of deceit and friendship! For Lo!
Hand has peopled Babel & Nineveh: Hyle, Ashur & Aram:
Coban's son is Nimrod: his son Cush is adjoin'd to Aram   19
By the Daughter of Babel in a woven mantle of pestilence & war.
They put forth their spectrous cloudy sails which drive their
    immense
Constellations over the deadly deeps of indefinite Udan-Adan.
Kox is the Father of Shem & Ham & Japheth, he is the Noah
Of the Flood of Udan-Adan: Hut'n is the Father of the Seven
From Enoch to Adam: Schofield is Adam who was New-   25
Created in Edom. I saw it indignant, & thou art not moved!
This has divided thee in sunder, and wilt thou still forgive?
O! thou seest not what I see, what is done in the Furnaces.
Listen, I will tell thee what is done in moments to thee unknown:

Luvah was cast into the Furnaces of affliction and sealed,   30
And Vala fed in cruel delight the Furnaces with fire.
Stern Urizen beheld, urg'd by necessity to keep
The evil day afar, and if perchance with iron power
He might avert his own despair, in woe & fear he saw   34
Vala incircle round the Furnaces where Luvah was clos'd.
With joy she heard his howlings & forgot he was her Luvah,
With whom she liv'd in bliss in times of innocence & youth.
Vala comes from the Furnace in a cloud, but wretched Luvah
Is howling in the Furnaces, in flames among Albion's Spectres,
To prepare the Spectre of Albion to reign over thee, O Los,   40
Forming the Spectres of Albion according to his rage:
To prepare the Spectre sons of Adam, who is Scofield, the Ninth
Of Albion's sons & the father of all his brethren in the Shadowy
Generation. Cambel & Gwendolen wove webs of war & of
Religion to involve all Albion's sons, and when they had   45
Involv'd Eight, their webs roll'd outwards into darkness,
And Scofield the Ninth remain'd on the outside of the Eight,
And Kox, Kotope & Bowen, One in him, a Fourfold Wonder,
Involv'd the Eight. Such are the Generations of the Giant Albion,
To separate a Law of Sin, to punish thee in thy members."   50

Los answer'd: " Altho' I know not this, I know far worse than this:
I know that Albion hath divided me, and that thou, O my Spectre,
Hast just cause to be irritated; but look stedfastly upon me;
Comfort thyself in my strength; the time will arrive
When all Albion's injuries shall cease, and when we shall   55
Embrace him, tenfold bright, rising from his tomb in immortality.
They have divided themselves by Wrath, they must be united by
Pity; let us therefore take example & warning, O my Spectre.
O that I could abstain from wrath! O that the Lamb
Of God would look upon me and pity me in my fury!   60
In anguish of regeneration, in terrors of self annihilation,
Pity must join together those whom wrath has torn in sunder,
And the Religion of Generation, which was meant for the de-
     struction
Of Jerusalem, become her covering till the time of the End.
O holy Generation, Image of regeneration!   65
O point of mutual forgiveness between Enemies!
Birthplace of the Lamb of God incomprehensible!
The Dead despise & scorn thee & cast thee out as accursed,
Seeing the Lamb of God in thy gardens & thy palaces
Where they desire to place the Abomination of Desolation.   70
Hand sits before his furnace: scorn of others & furious pride
Freeze round him to bars of steel & to iron rocks beneath
His feet; indignant self-righteousness like whirlwinds of the north
[8]
Rose up against me thundering, from the Brook of Albion's River,

From Ranelagh & Strumbolo, from Cromwell's gardens & Chelsea
The place of wounded Soldiers; but when he saw my Mace
Whirl'd round from heaven to earth, trembling he sat; his cold
Poisons rose up, & his sweet deceits cover'd them all over   5
With a tender cloud. As thou art now, such was he, O Spectre.
I know thy deceit & thy revenges, and unless thou desist
I will certainly create an eternal Hell for thee. Listen!
Be attentive! be obedient! Lo, the Furnaces are ready to recieve
    thee!
I will break thee into shivers & melt thee in the furnaces of death,
I will cast thee into forms of abhorrence & torment if thou   11
Desist not from thine own will & obey not my stern command.
I am clos'd up from my children: my Emanation is dividing,
And thou, my Spectre, art divided against me. But mark,
I will compell thee to assist me in my terrible labours. To beat
These hypocritic Selfhoods on the Anvils of bitter Death   16
I am inspired. I act not for myself; for Albion's sake
I now am what I am! a horror and an astonishment,
Shudd'ring the heavens to look upon me. Behold what cruelties
Are practised in Babel & Shinar, & have approach'd to Zion's
    Hill.''

While Los spoke the terrible Spectre fell shudd'ring before him,
Watching his time with glowing eyes to leap upon his prey.   22
Los open'd the Furnaces in fear, the Spectre saw to Babel & Shinar
Across all Europe & Asia, he saw the tortures of the Victims,
He saw now from the outside what he before saw & felt from
    within;
He saw that Los was the sole, uncontroll'd Lord of the Furnaces.
Groaning he kneel'd before Los's iron-shod feet on London Stone,
Hung'ring & thirsting for Los's life, yet pretending obedience,
While Los pursu'd his speech in threat'nings loud & fierce: 29

'' Thou art my Pride & Self-righteousness: I have found thee out.
Thou art reveal'd before me in all thy magnitude & power.
Thy Uncircumcised pretences to Chastity must be cut in sunder.
Thy holy wrath & deep deceit cannot avail against me,
Nor shalt thou ever assume the triple-form of Albion's Spectre,
For I am one of the living: dare not to mock my inspired fury.   35
If thou wast cast forth from my life, if I was dead upon the
    mountains,
Thou mightest be pitied & lov'd; but now I am living, unless
Thou abstain ravening I will create an eternal Hell for thee.
Take thou this Hammer & in patience heave the thundering
    Bellows;
Take thou these Tongs, strike thou alternate with me, labour
    obedient.
Hand & Hyle & Koban, Skofeld, Kox & Kotope labour mightily

In the Wars of Babel & Shinar; all their Emanations were   42
Condens'd. Hand has absorb'd all his Brethren in his might;
All the infant Loves & Graces were lost, for the mighty Hand
[9]
" Condens'd his Emanations into hard opake substances,
And his infant thoughts & desires into cold dark cliffs of death.
His hammer of gold he siez'd, and his anvil of adamant;
He siez'd the bars of condens'd thoughts to forge them
Into the sword of war, into the bow and arrow,   5
Into the thundering cannon and into the murdering gun.
I saw the limbs form'd for exercise contemn'd, & the beauty of
Eternity look'd upon as deformity, & loveliness as a dry tree.
I saw disease forming a Body of Death around the Lamb
Of God to destroy Jerusalem & to devour the body of Albion,   10
By war and stratagem to win the labour of the husbandman:
Awkwardness arm'd in steel, folly in a helmet of gold,
Weakness with horns & talons, ignorance with a rav'ning beak,
Every Emanative joy forbidden as a Crime   14
And the Emanations buried alive in the earth with pomp of
     religion,
Inspiration deny'd, Genius forbidden by laws of punishment,
I saw terrified. I took the sighs & tears & bitter groans,
I lifted them into my Furnaces to form the spiritual sword
That lays open the hidden heart. I drew forth the pang
Of sorrow red hot: I work'd it on my resolute anvil: 20
I heated it in the flames of Hand & Hyle & Coban
Nine times. Gwendolen & Cambel & Gwineverra
Are melted into the gold, the silver, the liquid ruby,
The crysolite, the topaz, the jacinth & every precious stone.
Loud roar my Furnaces and loud my hammer is heard.   25
I labour day and night. I behold the soft affections
Condense beneath my hammer into forms of cruelty,
But still I labour in hope, tho' still my tears flow down:
That he who will not defend Truth may be compell'd to defend
A Lie: that he may be snared and caught and snared and taken:
That Enthusiasm and Life may not cease; arise Spectre, arise!"

Thus they contended among the Furnaces with groans & tears.
Groaning the Spectre heav'd the bellows, obeying Los's frowns,
Till the Spaces of Erin were perfected in the furnaces   34
Of affliction; and Los drew them forth, compelling the harsh Spectre
[10]
Into the Furnaces & into the valleys of the Anvils of Death
And into the mountains of the Anvils & of the heavy Hammers,
Till he should bring the Sons & Daughters of Jerusalem to be
The Sons & Daughters of Los, that he might protect them from
Albion's dread Spectres; storming, loud, thunderous & mighty
The Bellows & the Hammers move compell'd by Los's hand.

   And this is the manner of the Sons of Albion in their strength:
They take the Two Contraries, which are call'd Qualities, with
      which
Every Substance is clothed: they name them Good & Evil;
From them they make an Abstract, which is a Negation   10
Not only of the Substance from which it is derived,
A murderer of its own Body, but also a murderer
Of every Divine Member: it is the Reasoning Power,
An Abstract objecting power that Negatives every thing.
This is the Spectre of Man, the Holy Reasoning Power,   15
And in its Holiness is closed the Abomination of Desolation.

Therefore Los stands in London building Golgonooza,
Compelling his Spectre to labours mighty; trembling in fear
The Spectre weeps, but Los unmov'd by tears or threats remains.

"I must Create a System or be enslav'd by another Man's.   20
I will not Reason & Compare: my business is to Create."

So Los in fury & strength, in indignation & burning wrath.
Shudd'ring the Spectre howls, his howlings terrify the night.
He stamps around the Anvil, beating blows of stern despair,
He curses Heaven & Earth, Day & Night & Sun & Moon,   25
He curses Forest, Spring & River, Desart & sandy Waste,
Cities & Nations, Families & Peoples, Tongues & Laws,
Driven to desperation by Los's terrors & threat'ning fears.

Los cries, "Obey my voice & never deviate from my will
And I will be merciful to thee: be thou invisible to all   30
To whom I make thee invisible, but chief to my own Children.
O Spectre of Urthona! Reason not against their dear approach
Not them obstruct with thy temptations of doubt & despair.
O Shame, O strong & mighty Shame, I break thy brazen fetters.
If thou refuse, thy present torments will seem southern breezes 35
To what thou shalt endure if thou obey not my great will."

The Spectre answer'd: "Art thou not asham'd of those thy Sins
That thou callest thy Children? lo, the Law of God commands
That they be offered upon his Altar. O cruelty & torment,
For thine are also mine! I have kept silent hitherto   40
Concerning my chief delight, but thou hast broken silence.
Now I will speak my mind! Where is my lovely Enitharmon?
O thou my enemy, where is my Great Sin? She is also thine.
I said: now is my grief at worst, incapable of being   44
Surpassed; but every moment it accumulates more & more,
It continues accumulating to eternity: the joys of God advance,
For he is Righteous, he is not a Being of Pity & Compassion,
He cannot feel Distress, he feeds on Sacrifice & Offering,

Delighting in cries & tears & clothed in holiness & solitude;
But my griefs advance also, for ever & ever without end.   50
O that I could cease to be! Despair! I am Despair,
Created to be the great example of horror & agony; also my
Prayer is vain. I called for compassion: compassion mock'd;
Mercy & pity threw the grave stone over me, & with lead
And iron bound it over me for ever. Life lives on my   55
Consuming, & the Almighty hath made me his Contrary
To be all evil, all reversed & for ever dead, knowing
And seeing life, yet living not; how can I then behold
And not tremble? how can I be beheld & not abhorr'd? ''   59

So spoke the Spectre shudd'ring, & dark tears ran down his
    shadowy face,
Which Los wiped off, but comfort none could give, or beam of
    hope.
Yet ceas'd he not from labouring at the roarings of his Forge,
With iron & brass Building Golgonooza in great contendings,
Till his Sons & Daughters came forth from the Furnaces   64
At the sublime Labours: for Los compell'd the invisible Spectre
[11]
To labours mighty with vast strength, with his mighty chains,
In pulsations of time, & extensions of space like Urns of Beulah,
With great labour upon his anvils, & in his ladles the Ore
He lifted, pouring it into the clay ground prepar'd with art,
Striving with Systems to deliver Individuals from those Systems,
That whenever any Spectre began to devour the Dead,   6
He might feel the pain as if a man gnaw'd his own tender nerves.

Then Erin came forth from the Furnaces, & all the Daughters of
    Beulah
Came from the Furnaces, by Los's mighty power for Jerusalem's
Sake, walking up and down among the Spaces of Erin.   10
And the Sons and Daughters of Los came forth in perfection lovely,
And the Spaces of Erin reach'd from the starry heighth to the
    starry depth.

Los wept with exceeding joy & all wept with joy together.
They fear'd they never more should see their Father who
Was built in from Eternity in the Cliffs of Albion.   15

But when the joy of meeting was exhausted in loving embrace,
Again they lament: "O what shall we do for lovely Jerusalem,
To protect the Emanations of Albion's mighty ones from cruelty?
Sabrina & Ignoge begin to sharpen their beamy spears
Of light and love: their little children stand with arrows of gold.
Ragan is wholly cruel, Scofield is bound in iron armour,   21
He is like a mandrake in the earth before Reuben's gate,

He shoots beneath Jerusalem's walls to undermine her founda-
 tions.
Vala is but thy shadow, O thou loveliest among women,
A shadow animated by thy tears, O mournful Jerusalem!   25
[12]
" Why wilt thou give to her a Body whose life is but a Shade?
Her joy and love, a shade, a shade of sweet repose;
But animated and vegetated she is a devouring worm.
What shall we do for thee, O lovely mild Jerusalem? "

And Los said, " I behold the finger of God in terrors!   5
Albion is dead! his Emanation is divided from him!
But I am living! yet I feel my Emanation also dividing.
Such thing was never known! O pity me, thou all-piteous-one!
What shall I do, or how exist, divided from Enitharmon?
Yet why despair? I saw the finger of God go forth   10
Upon my Furnaces from within the Wheels of Albion's Sons,
Fixing their Systems permanent, by mathematic power
Giving a body to Falshood that it may be cast off for ever,
With Demonstrative Science piercing Apollyon with his own bow.
God is within & without: he is even in the depths of Hell! "   15

Such were the lamentations of the Labourers in the Furnaces.

And they appear'd within & without, incircling on both sides
The Starry Wheels of Albion's Sons, with Spaces for Jerusalem
And for Vala the shadow of Jerusalem, the ever mourning Shade,
On both sides, within & without, beaming gloriously.   20

Terrified at the sublime Wonder, Los stood before his Furnaces.
And they stood around, terrified with admiration at Erin's Spaces,
For the Spaces reach'd from the starry heighth to the starry depth:
And they builded Golgonooza: terrible eternal labour!

What are those golden builders doing? where was the burying-
 place
Of soft Ethinthus? near Tyburn's fatal Tree? is that   26
Mild Zion's hill's most ancient promontory, near mournful
Ever weeping Paddington? is that Calvary and Golgotha
Becoming a building of pity and compassion? Lo!
The stones are pity, and the bricks, well wrought affections   30
Enamel'd with love & kindness, & the tiles engraven gold,
Labour of merciful hands: the beams & rafters are forgiveness:
The mortar & cement of the work, tears of honesty: the nails
And the screws & iron braces are well wrought blandishments
And well contrived words, firm fixing, never forgotten,   35
Always comforting the remembrance: the floors, humility:
The cielings, devotion: the hearths, thanksgiving.

Prepare the furniture, O Lambeth, in thy pitying looms!
The curtains, woven tears & sighs wrought into lovely forms
For comfort; there the secret furniture of Jerusalem's chamber
Is wrought. Lambeth! the Bride, the Lamb's Wife, loveth thee.
Thou art one with her & knowest not of self in thy supreme joy.
Go on, builders, in hope, tho' Jerusalem wanders far away
Without the gate of Los, among the dark Satanic wheels.

Fourfold the Sons of Los in their divisions, and fourfold   45
The great City of Golgonooza: fourfold toward the north,
And toward the south fourfold, & fourfold toward the east & west,
Each within other toward the four points: that toward
Eden, and that toward the World of Generation,
And that toward Beulah, and that toward Ulro: 50
Ulro is the space of the terrible starry wheels of Albion's sons;
But that toward Eden is walled up till time of renovation,
Yet it is perfect in its building, ornaments & perfection.

And the Four Points are thus beheld in Great Eternity:
West, the Circumference: South, the Zenith: North,   55
The Nadir: East, the Center, unapproachable for ever.
These are the four Faces towards the Four Worlds of Humanity
In every Man. Ezekiel saw them by Chebar's flood.
And the Eyes are the South, and the Nostrils are the East,
And the Tongue is the West, and the Ear is the North.   60

And the North Gate of Golgonooza toward Generation
Has four sculptur'd Bulls terrible before the Gate of iron,
And iron the Bulls; and that which looks toward Ulro,
Clay bak'd & enamel'd, eternal glowing as four furnaces,
Turning upon the Wheels of Albion's sons with enormous power:
And that toward Beulah four, gold, silver, brass & iron;   66
[13]
And that toward Eden, four, form'd of gold, silver, brass & iron.

The South, a golden Gate, has four Lions terrible, living:
That towards Generation, iron: that toward Beulah, stone:
That toward Ulro, four, clay bak'd, laborious workmanship:
That toward Eden, four, immortal gold, silver, brass & iron.   5

The Western Gate fourfold is clos'd, having four Cherubim
Its guards, living, the work of elemental hands, laborious task,
Like Men hermaphroditic, each winged with eight wings.
That towards Generation, iron: that toward Beulah, stone:
That toward Ulro, clay: that toward Eden, metals: 10
But all clos'd up till the last day, when the graves shall yield
　　their dead.

The Eastern Gate fourfold, terrible & deadly its ornaments,
Taking their forms from the Wheels of Albion's sons, as cogs
Are form'd in a wheel to fit the cogs of the adverse wheel.

That toward Eden, eternal ice frozen in seven folds   15
Of forms of death: and that toward Beulah, stone,
The seven diseases of the earth are carved terrible:
And that toward Ulro, forms of war, seven enormities:
And that toward Generation, seven generative forms.

And every part of the City is fourfold; & every inhabitant, four-
    fold.
And every pot & vessel & garment & utensil of the houses,   21
And every house, fourfold; but the third Gate in every one
Is clos'd as with a threefold curtain of ivory & fine linen & ermine.
And Luban stands in middle of the City; a moat of fire
Surrounds Luban, Los's Palace & the golden Looms of Cathedron.

And sixty-four thousand Genii guard the Eastern Gate,   26
And sixty-four thousand Gnomes guard the Northern Gate,
And sixty-four thousand Nymphs guard the Western Gate,
And sixty-four thousand Fairies guard the Southern Gate.

Around Golgonooza lies the land of death eternal, a Land   30
Of pain and misery and despair and ever brooding melancholy
In all the Twenty-seven Heavens, number'd from Adam to Luther,
From the blue Mundane Shell reaching to the Vegetative Earth.

The Vegetative Universe opens like a flower from the Earth's
    center
In which is Eternity. It expands in Stars to the Mundane Shell
And there it meets Eternity again, both within and without,   36
And the abstract Voids between the Stars are the Satanic Wheels.

There is the Cave, the Rock, the Tree, the Lake of Udan Adan,
The Forest and the Marsh and the Pits of bitumen deadly,
The Rocks of solid fire, the Ice valleys, the Plains   40
Of burning sand, the rivers, cataract & Lakes of Fire,
The Islands of the fiery Lakes, the Trees of Malice, Revenge
And black Anxiety, and the Cities of the Salamandrine men,
(But whatever is visible to the Generated Man
Is a Creation of mercy & love from the Satanic Void).   45
The land of darkness flamed, but no light & no repose:
The land of snows of trembling & of iron hail incessant:
The land of earthquakes, and the land of woven labyrinths:
The land of snares & traps & wheels & pit-falls & dire mills: 49
The Voids, the Solids, & the land of clouds & regions of waters

With their inhabitants, in the Twenty-seven Heavens beneath
    Beulah:
Self-righteousness conglomerating against the Divine Vision:
A Concave Earth wondrous, Chasmal, Abyssal, Incoherent,
Forming the Mundane Shell, above, beneath, on all sides sur-
    rounding
Golgonooza. Los walks round the walls night and day.   55

He views the City of Golgonooza & its smaller Cities,
The Looms & Mills & Prisons & Work-houses of Og & Anak,
The Amalekite, the Canaanite, the Moabite, the Egyptian,
And all that has existed in the space of six thousand years,
Permanent & not lost, not lost nor vanish'd, & every little act,
Word, work & wish that has existed, all remaining still
In those Churches ever consuming & ever building by the Spectres
Of all the inhabitants of Earth wailing to be Created,
Shadowy to those who dwell not in them, meer possibilities,
But to those who enter into them they seem the only substances;
For every thing exists, & not one sigh nor smile nor tear,   66
[14]
One hair nor particle of dust, not one can pass away.

He views the Cherub at the Tree of Life, also the Serpent
Orc, the first born, coil'd in the south, the Dragon Urizen,
Tharmas the Vegetated Tongue, even the Devouring Tongue,
A threefold region, a false brain, a false heart   5
And false bowels, altogether composing the False Tongue
Beneath Beulah, as a wat'ry flame revolving every way,
And as dark roots and stems, a Forest of affliction, growing
In seas of sorrow. Los also views the Four Females,
Ahania and Enion and Vala and Enitharmon lovely,   10
And from them, all the lovely beaming Daughters of Albion
Ahania & Enion & Vala are three evanescent shades:
Enitharmon is a vegetated mortal Wife of Los,
His Emanation, yet his Wife till the sleep of death is past.

Such are the Buildings of Los, & such are the Woofs of Enitharmon.

And Los beheld his Sons and he beheld his Daughters,   16
Every one a translucent Wonder, a Universe within,
Increasing inwards into length and breadth and heighth,
Starry & glorious; and they every one in their bright loins
Have a beautiful golden gate, which opens into the vegetative
    world;
And every one a gate of rubies & all sorts of precious stones   21
In their translucent hearts, which opens into the vegetative world;
And every one a gate of iron dreadful and wonderful
In their translucent heads, which opens into the vegetative world;

And every one has the three regions, Childhood, Manhood & Age;
But the gate of the tongue, the western gate, in them is clos'd,
Having a wall builded against it, and thereby the gates
Eastward & Southward & Northward are incircled with flaming
    fires.
And the North is Breadth, the South is Heighth & Depth,
The East is Inwards, & the West is Outwards every way.   30

And Los beheld the mild Emanation, Jerusalem, eastward
    bending
Her revolutions toward the Starry Wheels in maternal anguish,
Like a pale cloud arising from the arms of Beulah's Daughters
In Entuthon Benython's deep Vales beneath Golgonooza.

[15]
And Hand & Hyle rooted into Jerusalem by a fibre
Of strong revenge, & Skofeld Vegetated by Reuben's Gate
In every Nation of the Earth, till the Twelve Sons of Albion
Enrooted into every Nation, a mighty Polypus growing
From Albion over the whole Earth: such is my awful Vision   5

I see the Four-fold Man, The Humanity in deadly sleep
And its fallen Emanation, The Spectre & its cruel Shadow.
I see the Past, Present & Future existing all at once
Before me. O Divine Spirit, sustain me on thy wings!
That I may awake Albion from his long & cold repose;   10
For Bacon & Newton, sheath'd in dismal steel, their terrors hang
Like iron scourges over Albion. Reasonings like vast Serpents
Infold around my limbs, bruising my minute articulations.

I turn my eyes to the Schools & Universities of Europe
And there behold the Loom of Locke, whose Woof rages dire, 15
Wash'd by the Water-wheels of Newton: black the cloth
In heavy wreathes folds over every Nation: cruel Works
Of many Wheels I view, wheel without wheel, with cogs tyrannic
Moving by compulsion each other, not as those in Eden, which,
Wheel within Wheel, in freedom revolve in harmony & peace. 20

I see in deadly fear in London, Los raging round his Anvil
Of death, forming an Ax of gold; the Four Sons of Los
Stand round him cutting the Fibres from Albion's hills
That Albion's Sons may roll apart over the Nations,   24
While Reuben enroots his brethren in the narrow Canaanite
From the Limit Noah to the Limit Abram, in whose Loins
Reuben in his Twelve-fold majesty & beauty shall take refuge
As Abraham flees from Chaldea shaking his goary locks.
But first Albion must sleep, divided from the Nations.

I see Albion sitting upon his Rock in the first Winter,   30
And thence I see the Chaos of Satan & the World of Adam
When the Divine Hand went forth on Albion in the mid Winter
And at the place of Death, when Albion sat in Eternal Death
Among the Furnaces of Los in the Valley of the Son of Hinnom.

[16]
Hampstead, Highgate, Finchley, Hendon, Muswell hill rage loud
Before Bromion's iron Tongs & glowing Poker reddening fierce;
Hertfordshire glows with fierce Vegetation; in the Forests
The Oak frowns terrible, the Beech & Ash & Elm enroot   4
Among the Spiritual fires; loud the Corn-fields thunder along,
The Soldier's fife, the Harlot's shriek, the Virgin's dismal groan,
The Parent's fear, the Brother's jealousy, the Sister's curse,
Beneath the Storms of Theotormon, & the thund'ring Bellows
Heaves in the hand of Palamabron, who in London's darkness
Before the Anvil watches the bellowing flames: thundering   10
The Hammer loud rages in Rintrah's strong grasp, swinging loud
Round from heaven to earth, down falling with heavy blow
Dead on the Anvil, where the red hot wedge groans in pain.
He quenches it in the black trough of his Forge: London's River
Feeds the dread Forge, trembling & shuddering along the Valleys.

Humber & Trent roll dreadful before the Seventh Furnace,
And Tweed & Tyne anxious give up their Souls for Albion's sake.
Lincolnshire, Derbyshire, Nottinghamshire, Leicestershire,
From Oxfordshire to Norfolk on the Lake of Udan Adan,
Labour within the Furnaces, walking among the Fires   20
With Ladles huge & iron Pokers over the Island white.

Scotland pours out his Sons to labour at the Furnaces;
Wales gives his Daughters to the Looms; England, nursing
      Mothers
Gives to the Children of Albion & to the Children of Jerusalem.
From the blue Mundane Shell even to the Earth of Vegetation, 25
Throughout the whole Creation, which groans to be deliver'd,
Albion groans in the deep slumbers of Death upon his Rock.

Here Los fix'd down the Fifty-two Counties of England & Wales,
The Thirty-six of Scotland & the Thirty-four of Ireland,
With mighty power, when they fled out at Jerusalem's Gates   30
Away from the Conflict of Luvah & Urizen, fixing the Gates
In the Twelve Counties of Wales, & thence Gates looking every way
To the Four Points conduct to England & Scotland & Ireland,
And thence to all the Kingdoms & Nations & Families of the Earth.
The Gate of Reuben in Carmarthenshire: the Gate of Simeon in
Cardiganshire, & the Gate of Levi in Montgomeryshire: 36
The Gate of Judah, Merionethshire: the Gate of Dan, Flintshire:

The Gate of Napthali, Radnorshire: the Gate of Gad, Pembroke-
shire:
The Gate of Asher, Carnarvonshire: the Gate of Issachar, Breck-
nokshire:
The Gate of Zebulun in Anglesea & Sodor; so is Wales divided: 40
The Gate of Joseph, Denbighshire: the Gate of Benjamin,
Glamorganshire:
For the protection of the Twelve Emanations of Albion's Sons.

And the Forty Counties of England are thus divided in the Gates:
Of Reuben: Norfolk, Suffolk, Essex; Simeon: Lincoln, York,
Lancashire;
Levi: Middlesex, Kent, Surrey; Judah: Somerset, Glouster,
Wiltshire; 45
Dan: Cornwal, Devon, Dorset; Napthali: Warwick, Leicester,
Worcester;
Gad: Oxford, Bucks, Harford; Asher: Sussex, Hampshire,
Berkshire;
Issachar: Northampton, Rutland, Nottgham; Zebulun: Bedford,
Huntgn, Camb;
Joseph: Stafford, Shrops, Heref; Benjamin: Derby, Cheshire,
Monmouth;
And Cumberland, Northumberland, Westmoreland & Durham are
Divided in the Gates of Reuben, Judah, Dan & Joseph. 51

And the Thirty-six Counties of Scotland, divided in the Gates:
Of Reuben: Kincard, Haddntn, Forfar; Simeon: Ayr, Argyll, Banff;
Levi: Edinburh, Roxbro, Ross; Judah: Abrdeen, Berwik, Dum-
fries;
Dan: Bute, Caitnes, Clakmanan; Napthali: Nairn, Invernes,
Linlithgo; 55
Gad: Peebles, Perth, Renfru; Asher: Sutherlan, Sterling, Wigtoun;
Issachar: Selkirk, Dumbartn, Glasgo; Zebulun: Orkney, Shetland,
Skye;
Joseph: Elgin, Lanerk, Kinros; Benjamin: Kromarty, Murra,
Kirkubriht;
Governing all by the sweet delights of secret amorous glances
In Enitharmon's Halls builded by Los & his mighty Children. 60

All things acted on Earth are seen in the bright Sculptures of
Los's Halls, & every Age renews its powers from these Works
With every pathetic story possible to happen from Hate or
Wayward Love; & every sorrow & distress is carved here,
Every Affinity of Parents, Marriages & Friendships are here 5
In all their various combinations wrought with wondrous Art,
All that can happen to Man in his pilgrimage of seventy years.
Such is the Divine Written Law of Horeb & Sinai,
And such the Holy Gospel of Mount Olivet & Calvary

[17]
  His Spectre divides & Los in fury compells it to divide,
To labour in the fire, in the water, in the earth, in the air,
To follow the Daughters of Albion as the hound follows the scent
Of the wild inhabitant of the forest to drive them from his own,
To make a way for the Children of Los to come from the Furnaces.
But Los himself against Albion's Sons his fury bends, for he   6
Dare not approach the Daughters openly, lest he be consumed
In the fires of their beauty & perfection, & be Vegetated beneath
Their Looms in a Generation of death & resurrection to forget-
    fulness.
They wooe Los continually to subdue his strength; he continually
Shews them his Spectre, sending him abroad over the four points
    of heaven   11
In the fierce desires of beauty & in the tortures of repulse. He is
The Spectre of the Living pursuing the Emanations of the Dead.
Shudd'ring they flee: they hide in the Druid Temples in cold
    chastity,
Subdued by the Spectre of the Living & terrified by undisguis'd
    desire.

For Los said: "Tho' my Spectre is divided, as I am a Living Man
I must compell him to obey me wholly, that Enitharmon may not
Be lost, & lest he should devour Enitharmon. Ah me!   18
Piteous image of my soft desires & loves, O Enitharmon!
I will compell my Spectre to obey. I will restore to thee thy
    Children.
No one bruises or starves himself to make himself fit for labour.

" Tormented with sweet desire for these beauties of Albion,
They would never love my power if they did not seek to destroy
Enitharmon. Vala would never have sought & loved Albion
If she had not sought to destroy Jerusalem; such is that false
And Generating Love, a pretence of love to destroy love,   26
Cruel hipocrisy, unlike the lovely delusions of Beulah,
And cruel forms, unlike the merciful forms of Beulah's Night.

" They know not why they love nor wherefore they sicken & die,
Calling that Holy Love which is Envy, Revenge & Cruelty,
Which separated the stars from the mountains, the mountains
    from Man
And left Man a little grovelling Root outside of Himself.
Negations are not Contraries: Contraries mutually Exist,
But Negations Exist Not. Exceptions & Objections & Unbeliefs
Exist not, nor shall they ever be Organized for ever & ever.   35
If thou separate from me, thou art a Negation, a meer
Reasoning & Derogation from me, an Objecting & cruel Spite
And Malice & Envy; but my Emanation, Alas! will become

My Contrary. O thou Negation, I will continually compell
Thee to be invisible to any but whom I please, & when   40
And where & how I please, and never! never! shalt thou be
    Organized
But as a distorted & reversed Reflexion in the Darkness
And in the Non Entity: nor shall that which is above
Ever descend into thee, but thou shalt be a Non Entity for ever;
And if any enter into thee, thou shalt be an Unquenchable Fire
And he shall be a never dying Worm, mutually tormented by
Those that thou tormentest: a Hell & Despair for ever & ever."

So Los in secret with himself communed, & Enitharmon heard
In her darkness & was comforted; yet still she divided away
In gnawing pain from Los's bosom in the deadly Night;   50
First as a red Globe of blood trembling beneath his bosom,
Suspended over her he hung: he infolded her in his garments
Of wool: he hid her from the Spectre in shame & confusion of
Face; in terrors & pains of Hell & Eternal Death, the   54
Trembling Globe shot forth Self-living, & Los howl'd over it
Feeding it with his groans & tears, day & night without ceasing:
And the Spectrous Darkness from his back divided in temptations
And in grinding agonies, in threats, stiflings & direful strugglings.

" Go thou to Skofield: ask him if he is Bath or if he is Canterbury.
Tell him to be no more dubious: demand explicit words.   60
Tell him I will dash him into shivers where & at what time
I please; tell Hand & Skofield they are my ministers of evil
To those I hate, for I can hate also as well as they."

[18]
From every-one of the Four Regions of Human Majesty
There is an Outside spread Without & an Outside spread Within,
Beyond the Outline of Identity both ways, which meet in One,
An orbed Void of doubt, despair, hunger & thirst & sorrow.
Here the Twelve Sons of Albion, join'd in dark Assembly,   5
Jealous of Jerusalem's children, asham'd of her little-ones,
(For Vala produc'd the Bodies, Jerusalem gave the Souls)
Became as Three Immense Wheels turning upon one-another
Into Non-Entity, and their thunders hoarse appall the Dead
To murder their own Souls, to build a Kingdom among the Dead.

" Cast! Cast ye Jerusalem forth! The Shadow of delusions!
The Harlot daughter! Mother of pity and dishonourable for-
    giveness!
Our Father Albion's sin and shame! But father now no more,
Nor sons, nor hateful peace & love, nor soft complacencies,   14
With transgressors meeting in brotherhood around the table
Or in the porch or garden. No more the sinful delights

Of age and youth, and boy and girl, and animal and herb,
And river and mountain, and city & village, and house & family
Beneath the Oak & Palm, beneath the Vine and Fig-tree,
In self-denial! But War and deadly contention, Between   20
Father and Son, and light and love! All bold asperities
Of Haters met in deadly strife, rending the house & garden,
The unforgiving porches, the tables of enmity, and beds
And chambers of trembling & suspition, hatreds of age & youth,
And boy & girl, & animal & herb, & river & mountain,   25
And city & village, and house & family, That the Perfect
May live in glory, redeem'd by Sacrifice of the Lamb
And of his children before sinful Jerusalem, To build
Babylon the City of Vala, the Goddess Virgin-Mother.
She is our Mother! Nature! Jerusalem is our Harlot-Sister   30
Return'd with Children of pollution to defile our House
With Sin and Shame. Cast! Cast her into the Potter's field!
Her little-ones She must slay upon our Altars, and her aged
Parents must be carried into captivity, to redeem her Soul,
To be for a Shame & a Curse, and to be our Slaves for ever.''   35

So cry Hand & Hyle, the eldest of the fathers of Albion's
Little-ones, to destroy the Divine Saviour, the Friend of Sinners,
Building Castles in desolated places and strong Fortifications.
Soon Hand mightily devour'd & absorb'd Albion's Twelve Sons;
Out from his bosom a mighty Polypus, vegetating in darkness;
And Hyle & Coban were his two chosen ones for Emissaries
In War: forth from his bosom they went and return'd,   42
Like Wheels from a great Wheel reflected in the Deep.
Hoarse turn'd the Starry Wheels rending a way in Albion's Loins
Beyond the Night of Beulah. In a dark & unknown Night
Outstretch'd his Giant beauty on the ground in pain & tears:
[19]
His Children exil'd from his breast pass to and fro before him,
His birds are silent on his hills, flocks die beneath his branches,
His tents are fall'n; his trumpets and the sweet sound of his harp
Are silent on his clouded hills that belch forth storms & fire.
His milk of Cows & honey of Bees & fruit of golden harvest
Is gather'd in the scorching heat & in the driving rain.   6
Where once he sat, he weary walks in misery and pain,
His Giant beauty and perfection fallen into dust,
Till, from within his wither'd breast, grown narrow with his woes,
The corn is turn'd to thistles & the apples into poison,   10
The birds of song to murderous crows, his joys to bitter groans,
The voices of children in his tents to cries of helpless infants,
And self-exiled from the face of light & shine of morning,
In the dark world, a narrow house! he wanders up and down
Seeking for rest and finding none! and hidden far within,
His Eon weeping in the cold and desolated Earth.   16

All his Affections now appear withoutside: all his Sons,
Hand, Hyle & Coban, Guantok, Peachey, Brereton, Slayd &
     Hutton,
Scofeld, Kox, Kotope & Bowen: his Twelve Sons, Satanic Mill,
Who are the Spectres of the Twenty-four, each Double-form'd,
Revolve upon his mountains groaning in pain beneath   21
The dark incessant sky, seeking for rest and finding none,
Raging against their Human natures, rav'ning to gormandize
The Human majesty and beauty of the Twentyfour,
Condensing them into solid rocks with cruelty and abhorrence,
Suspition & revenge; & the seven diseases of the Soul   26
Settled around Albion and around Luvah in his secret cloud.
Willing the Friends endur'd for Albion's sake and for
Jerusalem his Emanation shut within his bosom,
Which harden'd against them more and more as he builded
     onwards
On the Gulph of Death in self-righteousness that roll'd   31
Before his awful feet, in pride of virtue for victory:
And Los was roof'd in from Eternity in Albion's Cliffs
Which stand upon the ends of Beulah, and withoutside all
Appear'd a rocky form against the Divine Humanity.   35

Albion's Circumference was clos'd: his Center began dark'ning
Into the Night of Beulah, and the Moon of Beulah rose
Clouded with storms. Los, his strong Guard, walk'd round beneath
     the Moon,
And Albion fled inward among the currents of his rivers.

He found Jerusalem upon the River of his City, soft repos'd
In the arms of Vala, assimilating in one with Vala   41
The Lilly of Havilah; and they sang soft thro' Lambeth's vales
In a sweet moony night & silence that they had created
With a blue sky spread over with wings and a mild moon,
Dividing & uniting into many female forms, Jerusalem
Trembling! then in one comingling in eternal tears,
Sighing to melt his Giant beauty on the moony river.   17

[20]
But when they saw Albion fall'n upon mild Lambeth's vale,
Astonish'd! Terrified! they hover'd over his Giant limbs.
Then thus Jerusalem spoke while Vala wove the veil of tears,
Weeping in pleadings of Love, in the web of despair: 4

" Wherefore hast thou shut me into the winter of human life
And clos'd up the sweet regions of youth and virgin innocence,
Where we live, forgetting error, not pondering on evil,
Among my lambs & brooks of water, among my warbling birds:
Where we delight in innocence before the face of the Lamb,
Going in and out before him in his love and sweet affection? "

Vala replied weeping & trembling, hiding in her veil: 11

"When winter rends the hungry family and the snow falls
Upon the ways of men, hiding the paths of man and beast,
Then mourns the wanderer: then he repents his wanderings & eyes
The distant forest: then the slave groans in the dungeon of stone,
The captive in the mill of the stranger, sold for scanty hire.
They view their former life: they number moments over and over,
Stringing them on their remembrance as on a thread of sorrow.
Thou art my sister and my daughter: thy shame is mine also:
Ask me not of my griefs! thou knowest all my griefs." 20

Jerusalem answer'd with soft tears over the valleys:

"O Vala, what is Sin? that thou shudderest and weepest
At sight of thy once lov'd Jerusalem! What is Sin but a little
Error & fault that is soon forgiven; but mercy is not a Sin,
Nor pity nor love nor kind forgiveness. O! if I have Sinned 25
Forgive & pity me! O! unfold thy Veil in mercy & love!
Slay not my little ones, beloved Virgin daughter of Babylon,
Slay not my infant loves & graces, beautiful daughter of Moab.
I cannot put off the human form. I strive but strive in vain.
When Albion rent thy beautiful net of gold and silver twine—
Thou hadst woven it with art, thou hadst caught me in the bands
Of love, thou refusedst to let me go—Albion beheld thy beauty,
Beautiful thro' our Love's comeliness, beautiful thro' pity. 33
The Veil shone with thy brightness in the eyes of Albion
Because it inclos'd pity & love, because we lov'd one-another.
Albion lov'd thee! he rent thy Veil! he embrac'd thee! he lov'd
    thee!
Astonish'd at his beauty & perfection, thou forgavest his furious
    love.
I redounded from Albion's bosom in my virgin loveliness:
The Lamb of God reciev'd me in his arms, he smil'd upon us:
He made me his Bride & Wife: he gave thee to Albion. 40
Then was a time of love. O why is it passed away!"

Then Albion broke silence and with groans reply'd:
[21]
"O Vala! O Jerusalem! do you delight in my groans!
You, O lovely forms, you have prepared my death-cup.
The disease of Shame covers me from head to feet. I have no hope.
Every boil upon my body is a separate & deadly Sin.
Doubt first assail'd me, then Shame took possession of me. 5
Shame divides Families. Shame hath divided Albion in sunder.
First fled my Sons & then my Daughters, then my Wild Anima-
    tions,
My Cattle next, last ev'n the Dog of my Gate; the Forests fled,

The Corn-fields & the breathing Gardens outside separated,
The Sea, the Stars, the Sun, the Moon, driv'n forth by my disease.
All is Eternal Death unless you can weave a chaste   11
Body over an unchaste Mind! Vala! O that thou wert pure!
That the deep wound of Sin might be clos'd up with the Needle
And with the Loom, to cover Gwendolen & Ragan with costly Robes
Of Natural Virtue, for their Spiritual forms without a Veil   15
Wither in Luvah's Sepulcher. I thrust him from my presence,
And all my Children follow'd his loud howlings into the Deep.
Jerusalem! dissembler Jerusalem! I look into thy bosom:
I discover thy secret places. Cordella! I behold   19
Thee whom I thought pure as the heavens in innocence & fear,
Thy Tabernacle taken down, thy secret Cherubim disclosed.
Art thou broken? Ah me, Sabrina, running by my side,
In childhood what wert thou? unutterable anguish! Conwenna!
Thy cradled infancy is most piteous. O hide, O hide!
Their secret gardens were made paths to the traveller.   25
I knew not of their secret loves with those I hated most,
Nor that their every thought was Sin & secret appetite.
Hyle sees in fear, he howls in fury over them. Hand sees
In jealous fear: in stern accusation with cruel stripes
He drives them thro' the Streets of Babylon before my face.   30
Because they taught Luvah to rise into my clouded heavens,
Battersea and Chelsea mourn for Cambel & Gwendolen,
Hackney and Holloway sicken for Estrild & Ignoge:
Because the Peak, Malvern & Cheviot Reason in Cruelty,
Penmaenmawr & Dhinas-bran Demonstrate in Unbelief,   35
Manchester & Liverpool are in tortures of Doubt and Despair,
Malden & Colchester Demonstrate. I hear my Children's voices,
I see their piteous faces gleam out upon the cruel winds
From Lincoln & Norwich, from Edinburgh & Monmouth.
I see them distant from my bosom scourg'd along the roads,
Then lost in clouds. I hear their tender voices! clouds divide:
I see them die beneath the whips of the Captains; they are taken
In solemn pomp into Chaldea across the bredths of Europe.
Six months they lie embalm'd in silent death, worshipped,
Carried in Arks of Oak before the armies: in the spring   45
Bursting their Arks they rise again to life: they play before
The Armies. I hear their loud cymbals & their deadly cries.
Are the Dead cruel? are those who are infolded in moral Law
Revengeful? O that Death & Annihilation were the same!"

Then Vala answer'd spreading her scarlet Veil over Albion: 50
[22]
"Albion, thy fear has made me tremble; thy terrors have sur-
     rounded me:
Thy Sons have nail'd me on the Gates, piercing my hands & feet,
Till Skofield's Nimrod, the mighty Huntsman Jehovah, came

With Cush his Son & took me down. He in a golden Ark
Bears me before his Armies, tho' my shadow hovers here.   5
The flesh of multitudes fed & nouris'd me in my childhood,
My morn & evening food were prepar'd in Battles of Men.
Great is the cry of the Hounds of Nimrod along the Valley
Of Vision, they scent the odor of War in the Valley of Vision.
All Love is lost! terror succeeds, & Hatred instead of Love,
And stern demands of Right & Duty instead of Liberty.   11
Once thou wast to me the loveliest Son of heaven, but now
Where shall I hide from thy dread countenance & searching eyes?
I have looked into the secret Soul of him I loved
And in the dark recesses found Sin & can never return."   15

Albion again utter'd his voice beneath the silent Moon:

"I brought Love into light of day, to pride in chaste beauty,
I brought Love into light, & fancied Innocence is no more."

Then spoke Jerusalem: "O Albion! my Father Albion!
Why wilt thou number every little fibre of my Soul,   20
Spreading them out before the Sun like stalks of flax to dry?
The Infant Joy is beautiful, but its anatomy
Horrible, ghast & deadly! nought shalt thou find in it
But dark despair & everlasting brooding melancholy!"

Then Albion turn'd his face toward Jerusalem & spoke: 25

"Hide thou, Jerusalem, in impalpable voidness, not to be
Touch'd by the hand nor seen with the eye. O Jerusalem,
Would thou wert not & that thy place might never be found!
But come, O Vala, with knife & cup, drain my blood
To the last drop, then hide me in thy Scarlet Tabernacle;   30
For I see Luvah whom I slew, I behold him in my Spectre
As I behold Jerusalem in thee, O Vala, dark and cold."

Jerusalem then stretch'd her hand toward the Moon & spoke:

"Why should Punishment Weave the Veil with Iron Wheels of
     War
When Forgiveness might it Weave with Wings of Cherubim?"

Loud groan'd Albion from mountain to mountain & replied:
[23]
"Jerusalem! Jerusalem! deluding shadow of Albion!
Daughter of my phantasy! unlawful pleasure! Albion's curse!
I came here with intention to annihilate thee, But
My soul is melted away, inwoven within the Veil.
Hast thou again knitted the Veil of Vala which I for thee   5

Pitying rent in ancient times? I see it whole and more
Perfect and shining with beauty! But thou!—O wretched Father!"

Jerusalem reply'd, like a voice heard from a sepulcher,
" Father once piteous! Is Pity a Sin? Embalm'd in Vala's bosom
In an Eternal Death for Albion's sake, our best beloved,   10
Thou art my Father & my Brother. Why hast thou hidden me
Remote from the divine Vision my Lord and Saviour? "

Trembling stood Albion at her words in jealous dark despair;
He felt that Love and Pity are the same, a soft repose,
Inward complacency of Soul, a Self-annihilation.   15

" I have erred! I am ashamed! and will never return more.
I have taught my children sacrifices of cruelty: what shall I
      answer?
I will hide it from Eternals! I will give myself for my Children!
Which way soever I turn, I behold Humanity and Pity!"   19

He recoil'd: he rush'd outwards: he bore the Veil whole away.
His fires redound from his Dragon Altars in Errors returning.
He drew the Veil of Moral Virtue, woven for Cruel Laws,
And cast it into the Atlantic Deep to catch the Souls of the Dead.
He stood between the Palm tree & the Oak of Weeping   24
Which stand upon the edge of Beulah; and there Albion sunk
Down in sick pallid languor. These were his last words, relapsing
Hoarse from his rocks, from caverns of Derbyshire & Wales
And Scotland, utter'd from the Circumference into Eternity:

" Blasphemous Sons of Feminine delusion! God in the dreary Void
Dwells from Eternity, wide separated from the Human Soul.   30
But thou, deluding Image, by whom imbu'd the Veil I rent,
Lo, here is Vala's Veil whole, for a Law, a Terror & a Curse!
And therefore God takes vengeance on me: from my clay-cold
      bosom
My children wander, trembling victims of his Moral Justice:
His snows fall on me and cover me, while in the Veil I fold   35
My dying limbs. Therefore O Manhood, if thou art aught
But a meer Phantasy, hear dying Albion's Curse!
May God,who dwells in this dark Ulro & voidness, vengeance take,
And draw thee down into this Abyss of sorrow and torture,   39
Like me thy Victim. O that Death & Annihilation were the same!

[24]
"What have I said? What have I done? O all-powerful Human
      Words!
You recoil back upon me in the blood of the Lamb slain in his
      Children.
Two bleeding Contraries, equally true, are his Witnesses against me.

We reared mighty Stones, we danced naked around them,   4
Thinking to bring Love into light of day, to Jerusalem's shame
Displaying our Giant limbs to all the winds of heaven. Sudden
Shame siez'd us, we could not look on one-another for abhorrence:
    the Blue
Of our immortal Veins & all their Hosts fled from our Limbs
And wander'd distant in a dismal Night clouded & dark.   9
The Sun fled from the Briton's forehead, the Moon from his
    mighty loins,
Scandinavia fled with all his mountains fill'd with groans.

" O what is Life & what is Man? O what is Death? Wherefore
Are you, my Children, natives in the Grave to where I go?
Or are you born to feed the hungry ravenings of Destruction,
To be the sport of Accident, to waste in Wrath & Love a weary   15
Life, in brooding cares & anxious labours that prove but chaff?
O Jerusalem, Jerusalem, I have forsaken thy Courts,
Thy Pillars of ivory & gold, thy Curtains of silk & fine
Linen, thy Pavements of precious stones, thy Walls of pearl
And gold, thy Gates of Thanksgiving, thy Windows of Praise, 20
Thy Clouds of Blessing, thy Cherubims of Tender-mercy
Stretching their Wings sublime over the Little-ones of Albion!
O Human Imagination, O Divine Body I have Crucified,
I have turned my back upon thee into the Wastes of Moral Law.
There Babylon is builded in the Waste, founded in Human desola-
    tion.   25
O Babylon, thy Watchman stands over thee in the night,
Thy severe Judge all the day long proves thee, O Babylon,
With provings of destruction, with giving thee thy heart's desire;
But Albion is cast forth to the Potter, his Children to the Builders
To build Babylon because they have forsaken Jerusalem.   30
The Walls of Babylon are Souls of Men, her Gates the Groans
Of Nations, her Towers are the Miseries of once happy Families,
Her Streets are paved with Destruction, her Houses built with
    Death,
Her Palaces with Hell & the Grave, her Synagogues with Torments
Of ever-hardening Despair, squar'd & polish'd with cruel skill.
Yet thou wast lovely as the summer cloud upon my hills   36
When Jerusalem was thy heart's desire, in times of youth & love.
Thy Sons came to Jerusalem with gifts: she sent them away
With blessings on their hands & on their feet, blessings of gold
And pearl & diamond: thy Daughters sang in her Courts.
They came up to Jerusalem: they walked before Albion: 41
In the Exchanges of London every Nation walk'd,
And London walk'd in every Nation, mutual in love & harmony.
Albion cover'd the whole Earth, England encompass'd the Nations,
Mutual each within other's bosom in Visions of Regeneration.
Jerusalem cover'd the Atlantic Mountains & the Erythrean   46

From bright Japan & China to Hesperia, France & England.
Mount Zion lifted his head in every Nation under heaven,
And the Mount of Olives was beheld over the whole Earth.
The footsteps of the Lamb of God were there; but now no more,
No more shall I behold him; he is clos'd in Luvah's Sepulcher.
Yet why these smitings of Luvah, the gentlest mildest Zoa?
If God was Merciful, this could not be. O Lamb of God,   53
Thou art a delusion and Jerusalem is my Sin! O my Children,
I have educated you in the crucifying cruelties of Demonstration
Till you have assum'd the Providence of God & slain your Father.
Dost thou appear before me, who liest dead in Luvah's Sepulcher?
Dost thou forgive me? thou who was Dead & art Alive?
Look not so merciful upon me, O thou Slain Lamb of God!
I die! I die in thy arms, tho' Hope is banish'd from me."   60

Thund'ring the Veil rushes from his hand, Vegetating Knot by
Knot, Day by Day, Night by Night: loud roll the indignant
    Atlantic
Waves & the Erythrean, turning up the bottoms of the Deeps.

[25]
And there was heard a great lamenting in Beulah: all the Regions
Of Beulah were moved as the tender bowels are moved, & they
    said:
" Why did you take Vengeance, O ye sons of the mighty Albion?
Planting these Oaken Groves, Erecting these Dragon Temples.
Injury the Lord heals, but Vengeance cannot be healed.   5
As the Sons of Albion have done to Luvah, so they have in him
Done to the Divine Lord & Saviour, who suffers with those that
    suffer;
For not one sparrow can suffer & the whole Universe not suffer also
In all its Regions, & its Father & Saviour not pity and weep.
But Vengeance is the destroyer of Grace & Repentance in the
    bosom
Of the Injurer, in which the Divine Lamb is cruelly slain.   11
Descend, O Lamb of God, & take away the imputation of Sin
By the Creation of States & the deliverance of Individuals Ever-
    more. Amen."

Thus wept they in Beulah over the Four Regions of Albion;
But many doubted & despair'd & imputed Sin & Righteousness
To Individuals & not to States, and these Slept in Ulro.[1]   16

[1] The pull-page illustration which concludes this chapter and occupies
Plate 26 is of " Hand," a naked man walking in flames, beheld by " Jerusa-
lem," an awe-struck woman. Interspersed among the figures are the words:

        " SUCH VISIONS HAVE APPEAR'D TO ME
        AS I MY ORDER'D RACE HAVE RUN.
        JERUSALEM IS NAMED LIBERTY
        AMONG THE SONS OF ALBION."

[27]   To The Jews

JERUSALEM the Emanation of the Giant Albion! Can it be? Is it
a Truth that the Learned have explored? Was Britain the Primi-
tive Seat of the Patriarchal Religion? If it is true, my title-page
is also True, that Jerusalem was & is the Emanation of the Giant
Albion. It is True and cannot be controverted. Ye are united, O
ye Inhabitants of Earth, in One Religion, The Religion of Jesus,
the most Ancient, the Eternal & the Everlasting Gospel. The
Wicked will turn it to Wickedness, the Righteous to Righteous-
ness. Amen! Huzza! Selah!
" All things Begin & End in Albion's Ancient Druid Rocky Shore."

   Your Ancestors derived their origin from Abraham, Heber,
Shem and Noah, who were Druids, as the Druid Temples (which
are the Patriarchal Pillars & Oak Groves) over the whole Earth
witness to this day.
   You have a tradition, that Man anciently contain'd in his
mighty limbs all things in Heaven & Earth: this you recieved
from the Druids.
" But now the Starry Heavens are fled from the mighty limbs
   of Albion."

   Albion was the Parent of the Druids, & in his Chaotic State of
Sleep, Satan & Adam & the whole World was Created by the
Elohim.

           The fields from Islington to Marybone,
        To Primrose Hill and Saint John's Wood,
           Were builded over with pillars of gold,
        And there Jerusalem's pillars stood.   4

           Her Little-ones ran on the fields.
        The Lamb of God among them seen,
           And fair Jerusalem, his Bride,
        Among the little meadows green.   8

           Pancrass & Kentish-town repose
        Among her golden pillars high,
           Among her golden arches which
        Shine upon the starry sky.   12

           The Jew's-harp-house & the Green Man,
        The Ponds where Boys to bathe delight,
           The fields of Cows by Willan's farm,
        Shine in Jerusalem's pleasant sight.   16

She walks upon our meadows green,
The Lamb of God walks by her side,
    And every English Child is seen
Children of Jesus & his Bride.   20

Forgiving trespasses and sins
Lest Babylon with cruel Og
    With Moral & Self-righteous Law
Should Crucify in Satan's Synagogue!   24

What are those golden Builders doing
Near mournful ever-weeping Paddington,
    Standing above that mighty Ruin
Where Satan the first victory won,   28

Where Albion slept beneath the Fatal Tree,
And the Druids' golden Knife
    Rioted in human gore,
In Offerings of Human Life?   32

They groan'd aloud on London Stone,
They groan'd aloud on Tyburn's Brook,
    Albion gave his deadly groan,
And all the Atlantic Mountains shook.   36

Albion's Spectre from his Loins
Tore forth in all the pomp of War:
    Satan his name: in flames of fire
He stretch'd his Druid Pillars far.   40

Jerusalem fell from Lambeth's Vale
Down thro' Poplar & Old Bow,
    Thro' Malden & acros the Sea,
In War & howling, death & woe.   44

The Rhine was red with human blood,
The Danube roll'd a purple tide,
    On the Euphrates Satan stood,
And over Asia stretch'd his pride.   48

He wither'd up sweet Zion's Hill
From every Nation of the Earth;
    He wither'd up Jerusalem's Gates,
And in a dark Land gave her birth.   52

He wither'd up the Human Form
By laws of sacrifice for sin,
    Till it became a Mortal Worm,
But O! translucent all within,   56

The Divine Vision still was seen,
Still was the Human Form Divine,
   Weeping in weak & mortal clay,
O Jesus, still the Form was thine.   60

And thine the Human Face, & thine
The Human Hands & Feet & Breath
   Entering thro' the Gates of Birth
And passing thro' the Gates of Death.   64

And O thou Lamb of God, whom I
Slew in my dark self-righteous pride,
   Art thou return'd to Albion's Land?
And is Jerusalem thy Bride?   68

Come to my arms & never more
Depart, but dwell for ever here:
   Create my Spirit to thy Love:
Subdue my Spectre to thy Fear.   72

Spectre of Albion! warlike Fiend!
In clouds of blood & ruin roll'd,
   I here reclaim thee as my own,
My Selfhood! Satan! arm'd in gold.   76

Is this thy soft Family-Love,
Thy cruel Patriarchal pride,
   Planting thy Family alone,
Destroying all the World beside?   80

A man's worst enemies are those
Of his own house & family;
   And he who makes his law a curse
By his own law shall surely die.   84

In my Exchanges every Land
Shall walk, & mine in every Land,
   Mutual shall build Jerusalem,
Both heart in heart & hand in hand.   88

If Humility is Christianity, you, O Jews, are the true Christians. If your tradition that Man contained in his Limbs all Animals is True, & they were separated from him by cruel Sacrifices, and when compulsory cruel Sacrifices had brought Humanity into a Feminine Tabernacle in the loins of Abraham & David, the Lamb of God, the Saviour became apparent on Earth as the Prophets had foretold, The Return of Israel is a Return to Mental Sacrifice & War. Take up the Cross, O Israel, & follow Jesus.

JERUSALEM

Chap: 2

EVERY ornament of perfection and every labour of love
In all the Garden of Eden & in all the golden mountains
Was become an envied horror and a remembrance of jealousy,
And every Act a Crime, and Albion the punisher & judge.

And Albion spoke from his secret seat and said: 5

" All these ornaments are crimes; they are made by the labours
Of loves, of unnatural consanguinities and friendships
Horrid to think of when enquired deeply into; and all
These hills & valleys are accursed witnesses of Sin.
I therefore condense them into solid rocks, stedfast,   10
A foundation and certainty and demonstrative truth,
That Man be separate from Man, & here I plant my seat."

Cold snows drifted around him: ice cover'd his loins around
He sat by Tyburn's brook, and underneath his heel shot up
A deadly Tree: he nam'd it Moral Virtue and the Law   15
Of God who dwells in Chaos hidden from the human sight,

The Tree spread over him its cold shadows, (Albion groan'd)
They bent down, they felt the earth, and again enrooting
Shot into many a Tree, an endless labyrinth of woe.   19

From willing sacrifice of Self, to sacrifice of (miscall'd) Enemies
For Atonement, Albion began to erect twelve Altars
Of rough unhewn rocks before the Potter's Furnace.
He nam'd them Justice and Truth. And Albion's Sons
Must have become the first Victims, being the first transgressors.
But they fled to the mountains to seek ransom, building A Strong
Fortification against the Divine Humanity and Mercy,
In Shame & Jealousy to annihilate Jerusalem.   27

[29]
Turning his back to the Divine Vision, his Spectrous
Chaos before his face appear'd, an Unformed Memory.

Then spoke the Spectrous Chaos to Albion, dark'ning cold
From the back & loins where dwell the Spectrous Dead:

"I am your Rational Power, O Albion, & that Human Form
You call Divine is but a Worm seventy inches long   6
That creeps forth in a night & is dried in the morning sun,
In fortuitous concourse of memorys accumulated & lost.
It plows the Earth in its own conceit, it overwhelms the Hills
Beneath its winding labyrinths, till a stone of the brook
Stops it in midst of its pride among its hills & rivers.   11
Battersea & Chelsea mourn, London & Canterbury tremble:
Their place shall not be found as the wind passes over:
The ancient Cities of the Earth remove as a traveller,
And shall Albion's Cities remain when I pass over them   15
With my deluge of forgotten remembrances over the tablet?"

So spoke the Spectre to Albion: he is the Great Selfhood,
Satan, Worship'd as God by the Mighty Ones of the Earth,
Having a white Dot call'd a Center, from which branches out
A Circle in continual gyrations: this became a Heart   20
From which sprang numerous branches varying their motions,
Producing many Heads, three or seven or ten, & hands & feet
Innumerable at will of the unfortunate contemplator
Who becomes his food: such is the way of the Devouring Power.

And this is the cause of the appearance in the frowning Chaos:
Albion's Emanation, which he had hidden in Jealousy,   26
Appear'd now in the frowning Chaos, prolific upon the Chaos,
Reflecting back to Albion in Sexual Reasoning Hermaphroditic.

Albion spoke: "Who art thou that appearest in gloomy pomp
Involving the Divine Vision in colours of autumn ripeness?
I never saw thee till this time, nor beheld life abstracted,   31
Nor darkness immingled with light on my furrow'd field.
Whence camest thou? who art thou, O loveliest? the Divine Vision
Is as nothing before thee: faded is all life and joy."

Vala replied in clouds of tears, Albion's garment embracing:

"I was a City & a Temple built by Albion's Children.   36
I was a Garden planted with beauty. I allured on hill & valley
The River of Life to flow against my walls & among my trees.
Vala was Albion's Bride & Wife in great Eternity,
The loveliest of the daughters of Eternity when in day-break
I emanated from Luvah over the Towers of Jerusalem   41
And in her Courts among her little Children, offering up
The Sacrifice of fanatic love! why loved I Jerusalem?
Why was I one with her, embracing in the Vision of Jesus?

Wherefore did I, loving, create love, which never yet   45
Immingled God & Man, when thou & I hid the Divine Vision
In cloud of secret gloom which, behold, involve me round about?
Know me now Albion: look upon me. I alone am Beauty.
The Imaginative Human Form is but a breathing of Vala.
I breathe him forth into the Heaven from my secret Cave,   50
Born of the Woman, to obey the Woman, O Albion the mighty,
For the Divine appearance is Brotherhood, but I am Love
    [30]
'' Elevate into the Region of Brotherhood with my red fires.''

'' Art thou Vala? '' replied Albion, '' image of my repose,
O how I tremble! how my members pour down milky fear!
A dewy garment covers me all over, all manhood is gone!
At thy word & at thy look, death enrobes me about   5
From head to feet, a garment of death & eternal fear.
Is not that Sun thy husband & that Moon thy glimmering Veil?
Are not the Stars of heaven thy Children? Art thou not Babylon?
Art thou Nature, Mother of all? is Jerusalem thy Daughter?
Why have thou elevate inward, O dweller of outward chambers,
From grot & cave beneath the Moon, dim region of death   11
Where I laid my Plow in the hot noon, where my hot team fed,
Where implements of War are forged, the Plow to go over the
    Nations,
In pain girding me round like a rib of iron in heaven. O Vala!
In Eternity they neither marry nor are given in marriage.   15
Albion, the high Cliff of the Atlantic, is become a barren Land.''

Los stood at his Anvil: he heard the contentions of Vala;
He heav'd his thund'ring Bellows upon the valleys of Middlesex,
He open'd his Furnaces before Vala: then Albion frown'd in anger
On his Rock, ere yet the Starry Heavens were fled away   20
From his awful Members; and thus Los cried aloud
To the Sons of Albion & to Hand the eldest Son of Albion:

'' I hear the screech of Childbirth loud pealing, & the groans
Of Death in Albion's clouds dreadful utter'd over all the Earth.
What may Man be? who can tell! but what may Woman be?
To have power over Man from Cradle to corruptible Grave.
There is a Throne in every Man, it is the Throne of God;
This, Woman has claim'd as her own, & Man is no more!
Albion is the Tabernacle of Vala & her Temple,
And not the Tabernacle & Temple of the Most High.   30
O Albion, why wilt thou Create a Female Will?
To hide the most evident God in a hidden covert, even
In the shadows of a Woman & a secluded Holy Place,
That we may prv after him as after a stolen treasure,   34
Hidden among the Dead & mured up from the paths of life.

Hand! art thou not Reuben enrooting thyself into Bashan
Till thou remainest a vaporous Shadow in a Void? O Merlin!
Unknown among the Dead where never before Existence came!
Is this the Female Will, O ye lovely Daughters of Albion? To
Converse concerning Weight & Distance in the Wilds of Newton
    & Locke.''   40

So Los spoke, standing on Mam-Tor, looking over Europe & Asia.
The Graves thunder beneath his feet from Ireland to Japan.

Reuben slept in Bashan like one dead in the valley
Cut off from Albion's mountains & from all the Earth's summits
Between Succoth & Zaretan beside the Stone of Bohan,   45
While the Daughters of Albion divided Luvah into three Bodies.
Los bended his Nostrils down to the Earth, then sent him over
Jordan to the Land of the Hittite; every-one that saw him
Fled! they fled at his horrible Form: they hid in caves
And dens; they looked on one-another & became what they beheld.

Reuben return'd to Bashan; in despair he slept on the Stone.   51
Then Gwendolen divided into Rahab & Tirza in Twelve Portions.
Los rolled his Eyes into two narrow circles, then sent him
Over Jordan; all terrified fled: they became what they beheld.

" If Perceptive Organs vary, Objects of Perception seem to vary:
If the Perceptive Organs close, their Objects seem to close also.
Consider this, O mortal Man, O worm of sixty winters," said Los,
" Consider Sexual Organization & hide thee in the dust."

[31]
Then the Divine hand found the Two Limits, Satan and Adam,
In Albion's bosom, for in every Human bosom those Limits stand;
And the Divine voice came from the Furnaces, as multitudes
    without
Number, the voices of the innumerable multitudes of Eternity.
And the appearance of a Man was seen in the Furnaces   5
Saving those who have sinned from the punishment of the Law
(In pity of the punisher whose state is eternal death)
And keeping them from Sin by the mild counsels of his love.

" Albion goes to Eternal Death. In Me all Eternity   9
Must pass thro' condemnation and awake beyond the Grave.
No individual can keep these Laws, for they are death
To every energy of man and forbid the springs of life.
Albion hath enter'd the State Satan! Be permanent, O State!
And be thou for ever accursed! that Albion may arise again.
And be thou created into a State! I go forth to Create   15
States, to deliver Individuals evermore! Amen."

So spoke the voice from the Furnaces, descending into Non-Entity.

[32]
Reuben return'd to his place; in vain he sought beautiful Tirzah,
For his Eyelids were narrow'd & his Nostrils scented the ground.
And Sixty Winters Los raged in the Divisions of Reuben,
Building the Moon of Ulro plank by plank & rib by rib.   4
Reuben slept in the Cave of Adam, and Los folded his Tongue
Between Lips of mire & clay, then sent him forth over Jordan.
In the love of Tirzah he said: " Doubt is my food day & night."
All that beheld him fled howling and gnawed their tongues
For pain: they became what they beheld. In reasonings Reuben
     returned
To Heshbon: disconsolate he walk'd thro' Moab & he stood
Before the Furnaces of Los in a horrible dreamful slumber   11
On Mount Gilead looking toward Gilgal: and Los bended
His Ear in a spiral circle outward, then sent him over Jordan.

The Seven Nations fled before him: they became what they beheld.
Hand, Hyle & Coban fled: they became what they beheld.
Gwantock & Peachy hid in Damascus beneath Mount Lebanon,
Brereton & Slade in Egypt: Hutton & Skofeld & Kox
Fled over Chaldea in terror, in pains in every nerve.   18
Kotope & Bowen became what they beheld, fleeing over the Earth,
And the Twelve Female Emanations fled with them, agonizing.

Jerusalem trembled, seeing her Children driv'n by Los's Hammer
In the visions of the dreams of Beulah on the edge of Non-Entity.
Hand stood between Reuben & Merlin, as the Reasoning Spectre
Stands between the Vegetative Man & his Immortal Imagination.

And the Four Zoas clouded rage East & West & North & South;
They change their situations in the Universal Man.   26
Albion groans, he sees the Elements divide before his face,
And England, who is Brittannia, divided into Jerusalem & Vala;
And Urizen assumes the East, Luvah assumes the South,
In his dark Spectre ravening from his open Sepulcher.   30

And the Four Zoas, who are the Four Eternal Senses of Man,
Became Four Elements separating from the Limbs of Albion:
These are their names in the Vegetative Generation:
. . . . .¹

And Accident & Chance were found hidden in Length, Bredth &
     Highth,
And they divided into Four ravening deathlike Forms,   35
Faries & Genii & Nymphs & Gnomes of the Elements:
These are States Permanently Fixed by the Divine Power.
The Atlantic Continent sunk round Albion's cliffy shore,

¹ Blake erased the line containing these names.

And the Sea poured in amain upon the Giants of Albion
As Los bended the Senses of Reuben. Reuben is Merlin   40
Exploring the Three States of Ulro: Creation, Redemption &
    Judgment.

And many of the Eternal Ones laughed after their manner:

" Have you known the Judgment that is arisen among the
[1] Zoas of Albion, where a Man dare hardly to embrace
His own Wife for the terrors of Chastity that they call   45
By the name of Morality? their Daughters govern all
In hidden deceit: they are Vegetable, only fit for burning.
Art & Science cannot exist but by Naked Beauty display'd."

Then those in Great Eternity who contemplate on Death
Said thus: " What seems to Be, Is, To those to whom   50
It seems to Be, & is productive of the most dreadful
Consequences to those to whom it seems to Be, even of
Torments, Despair, Eternal Death; but the Divine Mercy
Steps beyond and Redeems Man in the Body of Jesus. Amen.
And Length, Bredth, Highth, again Obey the Divine Vision.
    Hallelujah."

[33]
And One stood forth from the Divine Family & said:
" I feel my Spectre rising upon me! Albion! arouze thyself!
Why dost thou thunder with frozen Spectrous wrath against us?
The Spectre is, in Giant Man, insane and most deform'd.
Thou wilt certainly provoke my Spectre against thine in fury!
He has a Sepulcher hewn out of a Rock ready for thee,   6
And a Death of Eight thousand years, forg'd by thyself, upon
The point of his Spear! if thou persistest to forbid with Laws
Our Emanations and to attack our secret supreme delights."

So Los spoke. But when he saw pale [2] death in Albion's feet
Again he join'd the Divine Body, following merciful,
While Albion fled more indignant, revengeful covering   12
[34]
His face and bosom with petrific hardness, and his hands
And feet, lest any should enter his bosom & embrace
His hidden heart; his Emanation wept & trembled within him,
Uttering not his jealousy but hiding it as with   4
Iron and steel, dark and opake, with clouds & tempests brooding;
His strong limbs shudder'd upon his mountains high and dark.

    [1] " Zoas." In the British Museum copy this word is clearly " Zoas," and
not " Sons."
    [2] " Pale." The original word was " blue," and this remains in some copies.
In the British Museum copy (paper watermarked 1818) the word is altered in
ink to " pale."

Turning from Universal Love, petrific as he went,
His cold against the warmth of Eden rag'd with loud
Thunders of deadly war (the fever of the human soul)   9
Fires and clouds of rolling smoke! but mild, the Saviour follow'd
    him,
Displaying the Eternal Vision, the Divine Similitude,
In loves and tears of brothers, sisters, sons, fathers and friends,
Which if Man ceases to behold, he ceases to exist,

Saying, " Albion! Our wars are wars of life, & wounds of love
With intellectual spears & long winged arrows of thought.
Mutual in one another's love and wrath all renewing   16
We live as One Man; for contracting our infinite senses
We behold multitude, or expanding, we behold as one,
As One Man all the Universal Family, and that One Man
We call Jesus the Christ; and he in us, and we in him
Live in perfect harmony in Eden, the land of life,   21
Giving, recieving, and forgiving each other's trespasses.
He is the Good shepherd, he is the Lord and master,
He is the Shepherd of Albion, he is all in all   24
In Eden, in the garden of God, and in heavenly Jerusalem.
If we have offended, forgive us: take not vengeance against us."

Thus speaking, the Divine Family follow Albion.
I see them in the Vision of God upon my pleasant valleys.

I behold London, a Human awful wonder of God!
He says: " Return, Albion, return! I give myself for thee.   30
My Streets are my Ideas of Imagination.
Awake Albion, awake! and let us awake up together.
My Houses are Thoughts: my Inhabitants, Affections,
The children of my thoughts walking within my blood-vessels,
Shut from my nervous form which sleeps upon the verge of Beulah
In dreams of darkness, while my vegetating blood in veiny pipes
Rolls dreadful thro' the Furnaces of Los and the Mills of Satan.
For Albion's sake and for Jerusalem thy Emanation   38
I give myself, and these my brethren give themselves for Albion."

So spoke London, immortal Guardian! I heard in Lambeth's
    shades.
In Felpham I heard and saw the Visions of Albion.
I write in South Molton Street what I both see and hear
In regions of Humanity, in London's opening streets.

I see thee, awful Parent Land in light, behold I see!
Verulam! Canterbury! venerable parent of men,   45
Generous immortal Guardian, golden clad!—for Cities
Are Men, fathers of multitudes, and Rivers & Mountains

Are also Men; every thing is Human, mighty! sublime!
In every bosom a Universe expands as wings   49
Let down at will around and call'd the Universal Tent—
York, crown'd with loving kindness, Edinburgh, cloth'd
With fortitude as with a garment of immortal texture
Woven in looms of Eden, in spiritual deaths of mighty men
Who give themselves in Golgotha, Victims to Justice, where
There is in Albion a Gate of precious stones and gold   55
Seen only by Emanations, by vegetations viewless:
Bending across the road of Oxford Street, it from Hyde Park
To Tyburn's deathful shades admits the wandering souls
Of multitudes who die from Earth: this Gate cannot be found
[35]
By Satan's Watch-fiends, tho' they search numbering every grain
Of sand on Earth every night, they never find this Gate.
It is the Gate of Los. Withoutside is the Mill, intricate, dreadful
And fill'd with cruel tortures; but no mortal man can find the Mill
Of Satan in his mortal pilgrimage of seventy years,   5
For Human beauty knows it not, nor can Mercy find it! But
In the Fourth region of Humanity, Urthona nam'd,
Mortality begins to roll the billows of Eternal Death
Before the Gate of Los. Urthona here is named Los,   9
And here begins the System of Moral Virtue named Rahab.
Albion fled thro' the Gate of Los and he stood in the Gate.

Los was the friend of Albion who most lov'd him. In Cambridge-
    shire
His eternal station, he is the twenty-eighth & is four-fold.
Seeing Albion had turn'd his back against the Divine Vision,
Los said to Albion: " Whither fleest thou? " Albion reply'd:

" I die! I go to Eternal Death! the shades of death   16
Hover within me & beneath, and spreading themselves outside
Like rocky clouds, build me a gloomy monument of woe.
Will none accompany me in my death, or be a Ransom for me
In that dark Valley? I have girded round my cloke, and on my feet
Bound these black shoes of death, & on my hands, death's iron
    gloves.
God hath forsaken me & my friends are become a burden,
A weariness to me, & the human footstep is a terror to me."

Los answer'd troubled, and his soul was rent in twain: 24
" Must the Wise die for an Atonement? does Mercy endure
    Atonement?
No! It is Moral Severity & destroys Mercy in its Victim."
So speaking, not yet infected with the Error & Illusion,
[36]
Los shudder'd at beholding Albion, for his disease

Arose upon him pale and ghastly, and he call'd around
The Friends of Albion: trembling at the sight of Eternal Death
The four appear'd with their Emanations in fiery   4
Chariots: black their fires roll, beholding Albion's House of
    Eternity:
Damp couch the flames beneath, and silent, sick, stand shuddering
Before the Porch of sixteen pillars; weeping, every one
Descended and fell down upon their knees round Albion's knees,
Swearing the Oath of God with awful voice of thunders round
Upon the hills & valleys, and the cloudy Oath roll'd far and wide.

" Albion is sick! " said every Valley, every mournful Hill   11
And every River: " our brother Albion is sick to death.
He hath leagued himself with robbers! he hath studied the arts
Of unbelief! Envy hovers over him! his Friends are his abhorrence!
Those who give their lives for him are despised!   15
Those who devour his soul are taken into his bosom!
To destroy his Emanation is their intention.
Arise! awake, O Friends of the Giant Albion!
They have perswaded him of horrible falshoods!
They have sown errors over all his fruitful fields! "   20

The Twenty-four heard! they came trembling on wat'ry chariots
Borne by the Living Creatures of the third procession
Of Human Majesty: the Living Creatures wept aloud as they
Went along Albion's roads, till they arriv'd at Albion's House.

O! how the torments of Eternal Death waited on Man,   25
And the loud-rending bars of the Creation ready to burst,
That the wide world might fly from its hinges & the immortal
    mansion
Of Man for ever be possess'd by monsters of the deeps,
And Man himself become a Fiend, wrap'd in an endless curse,
Consuming and consum'd for-ever in flames of Moral Justice.

For had the Body of Albion fall'n down and from its dreadful
    ruins   31
Let loose the enormous Spectre on the darkness of the deep
At enmity with the Merciful & fill'd with devouring fire,
A nether-world must have reciev'd the foul enormous spirit
Under pretence of Moral Virtue, fill'd with Revenge and Law,
There to eternity chain'd down and issuing in red flames   36
And curses, with his mighty arms brandish'd against the heavens,
Breathing cruelty, blood & vengeance, gnashing his teeth with pain,
Torn with black storms & ceaseless torrents of his own consuming
    fire,
Within his breast his mighty Sons chain'd down & fill'd with
    cursings,

And his dark Eon, that once fair crystal form divinely clear,   41
Within his ribs producing serpents whose souls are flames of fire.
But glory to the Merciful-One, for he is of tender mercies!
And the Divine Family wept over him as One Man.

And these the Twenty-four in whom the Divine Family   45
Appear'd; and they were One in Him, A Human Vision!
Human Divine, Jesus the Saviour, blessed for ever and ever.

Selsey, true friend! who afterwards submitted to be devour'd
By the waves of Despair, whose Emanation rose above   49
The flood and was nam'd Chichester, lovely mild & gentle! Lo!
Her lambs bleat to the sea-fowls' cry, lamenting still for Albion.

Submitting to be call'd the son of Los the terrible vision,
Winchester stood devoting himself for Albion, his tents
Outspread with abundant riches, and his Emanations
Submitting to be call'd Enitharmon's daughters and be born   55
In vegetable mould, created by the Hammer and Loom
In Bowlahoola & Allamanda where the Dead wail night & day.

(I call them by their English names: English, the rough basement.
Los built the stubborn structure of the Language, acting against
Albion's melancholy, who must else have been a Dumb despair.)

Gloucester and Exeter and Salisbury and Bristol, and benevolent
[37]
Bath who is Legions; he is the Seventh, the physician and
The poisoner, the best and worst in Heaven and Hell,
Whose Spectre first assimilated with Luvah in Albion's moun-
     tains.
A triple octave he took, to reduce Jerusalem to twelve,
To cast Jerusalem forth upon the wilds to Poplar & Bow,   5
To Malden & Canterbury in the delights of cruelty.
The Shuttles of death sing in the sky to Islington & Pancrass,
Round Marybone to Tyburn's River, weaving black melancholy
     as a net,
And despair as meshes closely wove over the west of London
Where mild Jerusalem sought to repose in death & be no more.
She fled to Lambeth's mild Vale and hid herself beneath   11
The Surrey Hills where Rephaim terminates: her Sons are siez'd
For victims of sacrifice; but Jerusalem cannot be found, Hid
By the Daughters of Beulah, gently snatch'd away and hid in
     Beulah.

There is a Grain of Sand in Lambeth that Satan cannot find,   15
Nor can his Watch Fiends find it; 'tis translucent & has many
     Angles;

But he who finds it will find Oothoon's palace; for within
Opening into Beulah, every angle is a lovely heaven.
But should the Watch Fiends find it, they would call it Sin
And lay its Heavens & their inhabitants in blood of punishment.
Here Jerusalem & Vala were hid in soft slumberous repose,
Hid from the terrible East, shut up in the South & West.   22

The Twenty-eight trembled in Death's dark caves; in cold despair
They kneel'd around the Couch of Death, in deep humiliation
And tortures of self condemnation, while their Spectres rag'd
      within.
The Four Zoas in terrible combustion clouded rage,   26
Drinking the shuddering fears & loves of Albion's Families,
Destroying by selfish affections the things that they most admire,
Drinking & eating, & pitying & weeping, as at a trajic scene
The soul drinks murder & revenge & applauds its own holiness.

They saw Albion endeavouring to destroy their Emanations.[1]

[38]
They saw their Wheels rising up poisonous against Albion:
Urizen cold & scientific, Luvah pitying & weeping,
Tharmas indolent & sullen, Urthona doubting & despairing,
Victims to one another & dreadfully plotting against each other
To prevent Albion walking about in the Four Complexions.   5

They saw America clos'd out by the Oaks of the western shore,
And Tharmas dash'd on the Rocks of the Altars of Victims in
      Mexico.
"If we are wrathful, Albion will destroy Jerusalem with rooty
      Groves:
If we are merciful, ourselves must suffer destruction on his Oaks.
Why should we enter into our Spectres to behold our own corrup-
      tions?   10
O God of Albion, descend! deliver Jerusalem from the Oaken
      Groves!"

Then Los grew furious, raging: "Why stand we here trembling
      around
Calling on God for help, and not ourselves, in whom God dwells,
Stretching a hand to save the falling Man? are we not Four   14
Beholding Albion upon the Precipice ready to fall into Non-Entity?

---

[1] The illustration of Plate 37 is of a giant man, seated and bowed in grief.
At his side is a scroll inscribed in reverse writing:

> "Each Man is in his Spectre's power
> Untill the arrival of that hour
> When his Humanity awake
> And cast his Spectre into the Lake."

Seeing these Heavens & Hells conglobing in the Void, Heavens
    over Hells
Brooding in holy hypocritic lust, drinking the cries of pain
From howling victims of Law, building Heavens Twenty-seven-
    fold,
Swell'd & bloated General Forms repugnant to the Divine-
Humanity who is the Only General and Universal Form,   20
To which all Lineaments tend & seek with love & sympathy.
All broad & general principles belong to benevolence
Who protects minute particulars every one in their own identity;
But here the affectionate touch of the tongue is clos'd in by
    deadly teeth,
And the soft smile of friendship & the open dawn of benevolence
Become a net & a trap, & every energy render'd cruel,   26
Till the existence of friendship & benevolence is denied:
The wine of the Spirit & the vineyards of the Holy-One
Here turn into poisonous stupor & deadly intoxication,
That they may be condemn'd by Law & the Lamb of God be
    slain;
And the two Sources of Life in Eternity, Hunting and War,   31
Are become the Sources of dark & bitter Death & of corroding Hell.
The open heart is shut up in integuments of frozen silence
That the spear that lights it forth may shatter the ribs & bosom.
A pretence of Art to destroy Art; a pretence of Liberty   35
To destroy Liberty; a pretence of Religion to destroy Religion.
Oshea and Caleb fight: they contend in the valleys of Peor,
In the terrible Family Contentions of those who love each other.
The Armies of Balaam weep—no women come to the field:
Dead corses lay before them, & not as in Wars of old;   40
For the Soldier who fights for Truth calls his enemy his brother:
They fight & contend for life & not for eternal death;
But here the Soldier strikes, & a dead corse falls at his feet,
Nor Daughter nor Sister nor Mother come forth to embosom the
    Slain;
But Death, Eternal Death, remains in the Valleys of Peor.   45
The English are scatter'd over the face of the Nations: are these
Jerusalem's children? Hark! hear the Giants of Albion cry at
    night:
' We smell the blood of the English! we delight in their blood on
    our Altars.
The living & the dead shall be ground in our rumbling Mills
For bread of the Sons of Albion, of the Giants Hand & Scofield.'
Scofeld & Kox are let loose upon my Saxons! they accumulate   51
A World in which Man is by his Nature the Enemy of Man,
In pride of Selfhood unwieldy stretching out into Non Entity
Generalizing Art & Science till Art & Science is lost.
Bristol & Bath, listen to my words, & ye Seventeen, give ear!   55
It is easy to acknowledge a man to be great & good while we

Derogate from him in the trifles & small articles of that goodness.
Those alone are his friends who admire his minutest powers.
Instead of Albion's lovely mountains & the curtains of Jerusalem,
I see a Cave, a Rock, a Tree deadly and poisonous, unimaginative.
Instead of the Mutual Forgivenesses, the Minute Particulars, I see
Pits of bitumen ever burning, artificial Riches of the Canaanite
Like Lakes of liquid lead: instead of heavenly Chapels built
By our dear Lord, I see Worlds crusted with snows & ice.
I see a Wicker Idol woven round Jerusalem's children. I see   65
The Canaanite, the Amalekite, the Moabite, the Egyptian,
By Demonstrations the cruel Sons of Quality & Negation,
Driven on the Void in incoherent despair into Non Entity.
I see America clos'd apart, & Jerusalem driven in terror
Away from Albion's mountains, far away from London's spires.
I will not endure this thing! I alone withstand to death
This outrage! Ah me! how sick & pale you all stand round me!
Ah me! pitiable ones! do you also go to death's vale?
All you my Friends & Brothers, all you my beloved Companions,
Have you also caught the infection of Sin & stern Repentance?
I see Disease arise upon you! yet speak to me and give   76
Me some comfort! why do you all stand silent? I alone
Remain in permanent strength. Or is all this goodness & pity only
That you may take the greater vengeance in your Sepulcher? ''

So Los spoke. Pale they stood around the House of Death,   80
In the midst of temptations & despair, among the rooted Oaks,
Among reared Rocks of Albion's Sons: at length they rose
[39]
With one accord in love sublime, &, as on Cherubs' wings,
They Albion surround with kindest violence to bear him back
Against his will thro' Los's Gate to Eden, Four-fold loud
Their Wings waving over the bottomless Immense, to bear
Their awful charge back to his native home; but Albion dark,
Repugnant, roll'd his Wheels backward into Non-Entity.   6
Loud roll the Starry Wheels of Albion into the World of Death,
And all the Gate of Los clouded with clouds redounding from
Albion's dread Wheels, stretching out spaces immense between,
That every little particle of light & air became Opake,
Black & immense, a Rock of difficulty & a Cliff   11
Of black despair, that the immortal Wings labour'd against
Cliff after cliff & over Valleys of despair & death.
The narrow Sea between Albion & the Atlantic Continent,
Its waves of pearl became a boundless Ocean bottomless,   15
Of grey obscurity, fill'd with clouds & rocks & whirling waters,
And Albion's Sons ascending & descending in the horrid Void.

But as the Will must not be bended but in the day of Divine
Power, silent calm & motionless in the mid-air sublime
The Family Divine hover around the darken'd Albion.   20

Such is the nature of the Ulro, that whatever enters
Becomes Sexual & is Created and Vegetated and Born.
From Hyde Park spread their vegetating roots beneath Albion,
In dreadful pain, the Spectrous Uncircumcised Vegetation
Forming a Sexual Machine, an Aged Virgin Form,　　　　25
In Erin's Land toward the north, joint after joint, & burning
In love & jealousy immingled, & calling it Religion.
And feeling the damps of death, they with one accord delegated
　　Los,
Conjuring him by the Highest that he should Watch over them
Till Jesus shall appear; & they gave their power to Los　　30
Naming him the Spirit of Prophecy, calling him Elijah.

Strucken with Albion's disease, they become what they behold.
They assimilate with Albion in pity & compassion:
Their Emanations return not: their Spectres rage in the Deep:
The Slumbers of Death came over them around the Couch of
　　Death,
Before the Gate of Los & in the depths of Non Entity,　　36
Among the Furnaces of Los, among the Oaks of Albion.

Man is adjoin'd to Man by his Emanative portion
Who is Jerusalem in every individual Man, and her
Shadow is Vala, builded by the Reasoning power in Man.　　40
O search & see: turn your eyes inward [1]! open, O thou World
Of Love & Harmony in Man! expand thy ever lovely Gates!

They wept into the deeps a little space: at length was heard
The voice of Bath, faint as the voice of the Dead in the House
　　of Death,
[40]
Bath, healing City! whose wisdom, in midst of Poetic
Fervor, mild spoke thro' the Western Porch in soft gentle tears:

" O Albion, mildest Son of Eden! clos'd is thy Western Gate.
Brothers of Eternity, this Man whose great example
We all admir'd & lov'd, whose all benevolent countenance seen
In Eden, in lovely Jerusalem, drew even from envy　　6
The tear, and the confession of honesty open & undisguis'd
From mistrust and suspition: The Man is himself become
A piteous example of oblivion, To teach the Sons
Of Eden that however great and glorious, however loving　　10
And merciful the Individuality, however high
Our palaces and cities and however fruitful are our fields,
In Selfhood we are nothing, but fade away in morning's breath.
Our mildness is nothing: the greatest mildness we can use
Is incapable and nothing: none but the Lamb of God can heal
This dread disease, none but Jesus. O Lord, descend and save!
____
[1] " Inward ": in some copies " upward " (see plates 5. l. 19 and 71. l. 6.)

Albion's Western Gate is clos'd: his death is coming apace.
Jesus alone can save him; for alas, we none can know   18
How soon his lot may be our own. When Africa in sleep
Rose in the night of Beulah and bound down the Sun & Moon,
His friends cut his strong chains & overwhelm'd his dark
Machines in fury & destruction, and the Man reviving repented:
He wept before his wrathful brethren, thankful & considerate
For their well timed wrath; But Albion's sleep is not
Like Africa's, and his machines are woven with his life.   25
Nothing but mercy can save him! nothing but mercy interposing
Lest he should slay Jerusalem in his fearful jealousy.
O God, descend! gather our brethren: deliver Jerusalem!
But that we may omit no office of the friendly spirit,   29
Oxford, take thou these leaves of the Tree of Life; with eloquence
That thy immortal tongue inspires, present them to Albion:
Perhaps he may recieve them, offer'd from thy loved hands.''

So spoke, unheard by Albion, the merciful Son of Heaven
To those whose Western Gates were open, as they stood weeping
Around Albion; but Albion heard him nqt: obdurate, hard,   35
He frown'd on all his Friends, counting them enemies in his
        sorrow.

And the Seventeen conjoining with Bath, the Seventh
In whom the other Ten shone manifest, a Divine Vision,
Assimilated and embrac'd Eternal Death for Albion's sake.

And these the names of the Eighteen combining with those Ten:
[41]
Bath, mild Physician of Eternity, mysterious power
Whose springs are unsearchable & knowledge infinite:
Hereford, ancient Guardian of Wales, whose hands
Builded the mountain palaces of Eden, stupendous works!
Lincoln, Durham & Carlisle, Councellors of Los,   5
And Ely, Scribe of Los, whose pen no other hand
Dare touch: Oxford, immortal Bard, with eloquence
Divine he wept over Albion speaking the words of God
In mild perswasion, bringing leaves of the Tree of Life:

'' Thou art in Error, Albion, the Land of Ulro.   10
One Error not remov'd will destroy a human Soul.
Repose in Beulah's night till the Error is remov'd.
Reason not on both sides. Repose upon our bosoms
Till the Plow of Jehovah and the Harrow of Shaddai
Have passed over the Dead to awake the Dead to Judgment.''
But Albion turn'd away refusing comfort.   16

Oxford trembled while he spoke, then fainted in the arms
Of Norwich; Peterboro, Rochester, Chester awful, Worcester,

Litchfield, Saint David's, Landaff, Asaph, Bangor, Sodor,
Bowing their heads devoted: and the Furnaces of Los   20
Began to rage; thundering loud the storms began to roar
Upon the Furnaces, and loud the Furnaces rebellow beneath.

And these the Four in whom the twenty-four appear'd four-fold:
Verulam, London, York, Edinburgh, mourning one towards
    another.
Alas!—The time will come when a man's worst enemies   25
Shall be those of his own house and family, in a Religion
Of Generation to destroy, by Sin and Atonement, happy Jeru-
    salem
The Bride and Wife of the Lamb. O God, thou art Not an
    Avenger!

[42]
Thus Albion sat, studious of others in his pale disease,
Brooding on evil; but when Los open'd the Furnaces before him
He saw that the accursed things were his own affections
And his own beloveds; then he turn'd sick: his soul died within
    him;
Also Los, sick & terrified, beheld the Furnaces of Death   5
And must have died, but the Divine Saviour descended
Among the infant loves & affections, and the Divine Vision wept
Like evening dew on every herb upon the breathing ground.

Albion spoke in his dismal dreams: " O thou deceitful friend,
Worshipping mercy & beholding thy friend in such affliction!
Los! thou now discoverest thy turpitude to the heavens.   11
I demand righteousness & justice. O thou ingratitude!
Give me my Emanations back, food for my dying soul.
My daughters are harlots: my sons are accursed before me.
Enitharmon is my daughter, accursed with a father's curse.   15
O! I have utterly been wasted! I have given my daughters to
    devils."

So spoke Albion in gloomy majesty, and deepest night
Of Ulro roll'd round his skirts from Dover to Cornwall.

Los answer'd: " Righteousness & justice I give thee in return
For thy righteousness, but I add mercy also and bind   20
Thee from destroying these little ones: am I to be only
Merciful to thee and cruel to all that thou hatest?
Thou wast the Image of God surrounded by the Four Zoas.
Three thou hast slain. I am the Fourth: thou canst not destroy me.
Thou art in Error: trouble me not with thy righteousness.   25
I have innocence to defend and ignorance to instruct:
I have no time for seeming and little arts of compliment

In morality and virtue, in self-glorying and pride.
There is a limit of Opakeness and a limit of Contraction
In every Individual Man, and the limit of Opakeness   30
Is named Satan, and the limit of Contraction is named Adam.
But when Man sleeps in Beulah, the Saviour in Mercy takes
Contraction's Limit, and of the Limit he forms Woman, That
Himself may in process of time be born Man to redeem.
But there is no Limit of Expansion; there is no Limit of Translu-
          cence
In the bosom of Man for ever from eternity to eternity.   36
Therefore I break thy bonds of righteousness, I crush thy mes-
          sengers,
That they may not crush me and mine: do thou be righteous
And I will return it; otherwise I defy thy worst revenge.
Consider me as thine enemy: on me turn all thy fury;   40
But destroy not these little ones, nor mock the Lord's anointed:
Destroy not by Moral Virtue the little ones whom he hath chosen,
The little ones whom he hath chosen in preference to thee.
He hath cast thee off for ever: the little ones he hath anointed!
They Selfhood is for ever accursed from the Divine presence."

So Los spoke, then turn'd his face & wept for Albion.   46

Albion replied: " Go, Hand & Hyde! sieze the abhorred friend
As you have siez'd the Twenty-four rebellious ingratitudes,
To atone for you, for spiritual death. Man lives by deaths of Men,
Bring him to justice before heaven here upon London stone,
Between Blackheath & Hounslow, between Norwood & Finchley.
All that they have is mine: from my free gen'rous gift   52
They now hold all they have; ingratitude to me,
To me their benefactor, calls aloud for vengeance deep."

Los stood before his Furnaces awaiting the fury of the Dead,
And the Divine hand was upon him, strengthening him mightily

The Spectres of the Dead cry out from the deeps beneath
Upon the hills of Albion: Oxford groans in his iron furnace,
Winchester in his den & cavern: they lament against
Albion: they curse their human kindness & affection: 60
They rage like wild beasts in the forests of affliction:
In the dreams of Ulro they repent of their human kindness.

" Come up, build Babylon. Rahab is ours & all her multitudes
With her in pomp and glory of victory. Depart,
Ye twenty-four, into the deeps; let us depart to glory!"   65

Their Human majestic forms sit up upon their Couches
Of death: they curb their Spectres as with iron curbs:

They enquire after Jerusalem in the regions of the dead
With the voices of dead men, low, scarcely articulate,
And with tears cold on their cheeks they weary repose.   70

" O when shall the morning of the grave appear, and when
Shall our salvation come? we sleep upon our watch,
We cannot awake! and our Spectres rage in the forests.
O God of Albion, where art thou? pity the watchers!"

Thus mourn they. Loud the Furnaces of Los thunder upon   75
The clouds of Europe & Asia among the Serpent Temples.

And Los drew his Seven Furnaces around Albion's Altars;
And as Albion built his frozen Altars, Los built the Mundane Shell
In the Four Regions of Humanity, East & West & North & South,
Till Norwood & Finchley & Blackheath & Hounslow cover'd the
        whole Earth.
This is the Net & Veil of Vala among the Souls of the Dead.   81

[43]
Then the Divine Vision like a silent Sun appear'd above
Albion's dark rocks, setting behind the Gardens of Kensington
On Tyburn's River in clouds of blood, where was mild Zion Hill's
Most ancient promontory; and in the Sun a Human Form appear'd,
And thus the Voice Divine went forth upon the rocks of Albion:

" I elected Albion for my glory: I gave him the Nations   6
Of the whole Earth. He was the Angel of my Presence, and all
The Sons of God were Albion's Sons, and Jerusalem was my joy.
The Reactor hath hid himself thro' envy. I behold him,
But you cannot behold him till he be reveal'd in his System. 10
Albion's Reactor must have a Place prepar'd. Albion must Sleep
The Sleep of Death till the Man of Sin & Repentance be reveal'd.
Hidden in Albion's Forests he lurks: he admits of no Reply
From Albion, but hath founded his Reaction into a Law
Of Action, for Obedience to destroy the Contraries of Man.   15
He hath compell'd Albion to become a Punisher & hath possess'd
Himself of Albion's Forests & Wilds, and Jerusalem is taken,
The City of the Woods in the Forest of Ephratah is taken!
London is a stone of her ruins, Oxford is the dust of her walls, 19
Sussex & Kent are her scatter'd garments, Ireland her holy place,
And the murder'd bodies of her little ones are Scotland and Wales.
The Cities of the Nations are the smoke of her consummation,
The Nations are her dust, ground by the chariot wheels
Of her lordly conquerers, her palaces levell'd with the dust.
I come that I may find a way for my banished ones to return. 25
Fear not, O little Flock, I come! Albion shall rise again."

So saying, the mild Sun inclos'd the Human Family.

Forthwith from Albion's dark'ning locks came two Immortal forms,
Saying: "We alone are escaped. O merciful Lord and Saviour,
We flee from the interiors of Albion's hills and mountains,   30
From his Valleys Eastward, from Amalek Canaan & Moab
Beneath his vast ranges of hills surrounding Jerusalem.

" Albion walk'd on the steps of fire before his Halls,
And Vala walk'd with him in dreams of soft deluding slumber;
He looked up & saw the Prince of Light with splendor faded.   35
Then Albion ascended mourning into the porches of his Palace,
Above him rose a Shadow from his wearied intellect,
Of living gold, pure, perfect, holy; in white linen pure he hover'd,
A sweet entrancing self-delusion, a wat'ry vision of Albion,
Soft exulting in existence, all the Man absorbing.   40

" Albion fell upon his face prostrate before the wat'ry Shadow,
Saying: ' O Lord, whence is this change? thou knowest I am nothing!'
And Vala trembled & cover'd her face, & her locks were spread on the pavement.

" We heard, astonish'd at the Vision, & our hearts trembled within us;
We heard the voice of slumberous Albion, and thus he spake,
Idolatrous to his own Shadow, words of eternity uttering: 46

" ' O I am nothing when I enter into judgment with thee!
If thou withdraw thy breath, I die & vanish into Hades;
If thou dost lay thine hand upon me, behold I am silent;
If thou withhold thine hand, I perish like a fallen leaf.   50
O I am nothing, and to nothing must return again!
If thou withdraw thy breath, Behold, I am oblivion.'

" He ceas'd: the shadowy voice was silent: but the cloud hover'd over their heads
In golden wreathes, the sorrow of Man, & the balmy drops fell down.
And lo! that son of Man, that Shadowy Spirit of mild Albion,
Luvah, descended from the cloud; in terror Albion rose: 56
Indignant rose the awful Man & turn'd his back on Vala.

" We heard the voice of Albion starting from his sleep:

" ' Whence is this voice crying, Enion! that soundeth in my ears?
O cruel pity! O dark deceit! can love seek for dominion? '

" And Luvah strove to gain dominion over Albion: 61
They strove together above the Body where Vala was inclos'd
And the dark Body of Albion left prostrate upon the crystal
    pavement,
Cover'd with boils from head to foot, the terrible smitings of
    Luvah.

" Then frown'd the fallen Man and put forth Luvah from his
    presence,
Saying, ' Go and Die the Death of Man for Vala the sweet wan-
    derer.
I will turn the volutions of your ears outward, and bend your
    nostrils
Downward, and your fluxile eyes englob'd roll round in fear;
Your with'ring lips and tongue shrink up into a narrow circle,
Till into narrow forms you creep: go take your fiery way,   70
And learn what 'tis to absorb the Man, you Spirits of Pity & Love.'

" They heard the voice and fled swift as the winter's setting sun.
And now the human blood foam'd high; the Spirits Luvah & Vala
Went down the Human Heart, where Paradise & its joys abounded,
In jealous fears & fury & rage, & flames roll round their fervid feet,
And the vast form of Nature like a serpent play'd before them. 76
And as they fled in folding fires & thunders of the deep,
Vala shrunk in like the dark sea that leaves its slimy banks,
And from her bosom Luvah fell far as the east and west,
And the vast form of Nature like a serpent roll'd between,   80
Whether of Jerusalem's or Vala's ruins congenerated, we know not:
All is confusion, all is tumult, & we alone are escaped."
So spoke the fugitives; they join'd the Divine Family, trembling.

[44]
And the Two that escaped were the Emanation of Los & his
Spectre; for where ever the Emanation goes, the Spectre
Attends her as her Guard, & Los's Emanation is named
Enitharmon, & his Spectre is named Urthona; they knew
Not where to flee: they had been on a visit to Albion's Children,
And they strove to weave a Shadow of the Emanation   6
To hide themselves, weeping & lamenting for the Vegetation
Of Albion's Children, fleeing thro' Albion's vales in streams of gore.

Being not irritated by insult, bearing insulting benevolences,
They percieved that corporeal friends are spiritual enemies:
They saw the Sexual Religion in its embryon Uncircumcision,
And the Divine hand was upon them, bearing them thro' darkness
Back safe to their Humanity, as doves to their windows.
Therefore the Sons of Eden praise Urthona's Spectre in Songs,
Because he kept the Divine Vision in time of trouble.   15

They wept & trembled, & Los put forth his hand & took them in,
Into his Bosom, from which Albion shrunk in dismal pain,
Bending the fibres of Brotherhood & in Feminine Allegories
Inclosing Los; but the Divine Vision appear'd with Los
Following Albion into his Central Void among his Oaks.   20

And Los prayed and said, " O Divine Saviour, arise
Upon the Mountains of Albion as in ancient time! Behold!
The Cities of Albion seek thy face: London groans in pain
From Hill to Hill, & the Thames laments along the Valleys:
The little Villages of Middlesex & Surrey hunger & thirst: 25
The Twenty-eight Cities of Albion stretch their hands to thee
Because of the Opressors of Albion in every City & Village.
They mock at the Labourer's limbs: they mock at his starv'd
   Children:
They buy his Daughters that they may have power to sell his Sons:
They compell the Poor to live upon a crust of bread by soft mild
   arts:
They reduce the Man to want, then give with pomp & ceremony:
The praise of Jehovah is chaunted from lips of hunger & thirst.
Humanity knows not of Sex: wherefore are Sexes in Beulah?
In Beulah the Female lets down her beautiful Tabernacle   34
Which the Male enters magnificent between her Cherubim
And becomes One with her, mingling, condensing in Self-love
The Rocky Law of Condemnation & double Generation & Death.
Albion hath enter'd the Loins, the place of the Last Judgment,
And Luvah hath drawn the Curtains around Albion in Vala's
   bosom.
The Dead awake to Generation! Arise O Lord, & rend the Veil! "

So Los in lamentations follow'd Albion. Albion cover'd   41
[45]
His western heaven with rocky clouds of death & despair.

Fearing that Albion should turn his back against the Divine
   Vision,
Los took his globe of fire to search the interiors of Albion's
Bosom, in all the terrors of friendship entering the caves   4
Of despair & death to search the tempters out, walking among
Albion's rocks & precipices, caves of solitude & dark despair,
And saw every Minute Particular of Albion degraded & murder'd,
But saw not by whom; they were hidden within in the minute
   particulars
Of which they had possess'd themselves; and there they take up
The articulations of a man's soul and laughing throw it down   10
Into the frame, then knock it out upon the plank, & souls are bak'd
In bricks to build the pyramids of Heber & Terah. But Los
Search'd in vain; clos'd from the minutia, he walk'd difficult.

He came down from Highgate thro' Hackney & Holloway towards
   London
Till he came to old Stratford, & thence to Stepney & the Isle 15
Of Leutha's Dogs, thence thro' the narrows of the River's side—
And saw every minute particular: the jewels of Albion running
   down
The kennels of the streets & lanes as if they were abhorr'd:
Every Universal Form was become barren mountains of Moral
Virtue and every Minute Particular harden'd into grains of sand,
And all the tendernesses of the soul cast forth as filth & mire—
Among the winding places of deep contemplation intricate,
To where the Tower of London frown'd dreadful over Jerusalem,
A building of Luvah, builded in Jerusalem's eastern gate, to be
His secluded Court: thence to Bethlehem, where was builded
Dens of despair in the house of bread; enquiring in vain 26
Of stones and rocks he took his way, for human form was none;
And thus he spoke, looking on Albion's City with many tears:

"What shall I do? what could I do if I could find these Criminals?
I could not dare to take vengeance, for all things are so constructed
And builded by the Divine hand that the sinner shall always
   escape,
And he who takes vengeance alone is the criminal of Providence.
If I should dare to lay my finger on a grain of sand
In way of vengeance, I punish the already punish'd. O whom
Should I pity if I pity not the sinner who is gone astray! 35
O Albion, if thou takest vengeance, if thou revengest thy wrongs,
Thou art for ever lost! What can I do to hinder the Sons
Of Albion from taking vengeance? or how shall I them perswade?"

So spoke Los, travelling thro' darkness & horrid solitude.
And he beheld Jerusalem in Westminster & Marybone 40
Among the ruins of the Temple, and Vala who is her Shadow.
Jerusalem's Shadow bent northward over the Island white.
At length he sat on London Stone & heard Jerusalem's voice:

"Albion, I cannot be thy Wife; thine own Minute Particulars
Belong to God alone, and all thy little ones are holy; 45
They are of Faith & not of Demonstration: wherefore is Vala
Cloth'd in black mourning upon my river's currents? Vala awake!
I hear thy shuttles sing in the sky, and round my limbs
I feel the iron threads of love & jealousy & despair." 49

Vala reply'd: "Albion is mine! Luvah gave me to Albion
And now recieves reproach & hate. Was it not said of old,
'Set your Son before a man & he shall take you & your sons
For slaves; but set your Daughter before a man & She
Shall make him & his sons & daughters your slaves for ever'?

And is this Faith? Behold the strife of Albion & Luvah   55
Is great in the east; their spears of blood rage in the eastern
    heaven.
Urizen is the champion of Albion; they will slay my Luvah,
And thou, O harlot daughter, daughter of despair, art all
This cause of these shakings of my towers on Euphrates.
Here is the House of Albion & here is thy secluded place,   60
And here we have found thy sins; & hence we turn thee forth
For all to avoid thee, to be astonish'd at thee for thy sins,
Because thou art the impurity & the harlot, & thy children
Children of whoredoms, born for Sacrifice, for the meat & drink
Offering, to sustain the glorious combat & the battle & war,
That Man may be purified by the death of thy delusions.''   66

So saying she her dark threads cast over the trembling River
And over the valleys, from the hills of Hertfordshire to the hills
Of Surrey across Middlesex, & across Albion's House
Of Eternity: pale stood Albion at his eastern gate,   70
[46]
Leaning against the pillars, & his disease rose from his skirts:
Upon the Precipice he stood, ready to fall into Non-Entity.

Los was all astonishment & terror, he trembled sitting on the Stone
Of London; but the interiors of Albion's fibres & nerves were
    hidden
From Los, astonish'd he beheld only the petrified surfaces   5
And saw his Furnaces in ruins, for Los is the Demon of the
    Furnaces;
He saw also the Four Points of Albion revers'd inwards.
He siez'd his Hammer & Tongs, his iron Poker & his Bellows,
Upon the valleys of Middlesex, Shouting loud for aid Divine.   9

In stern defiance came from Albion's bosom Hand, Hyle, Koban,
Gwantok, Peachy, Brertun, Slaid, Huttn, Skofeld, Kock, Kotope,
Bowen, Albion's Sons; they bore him a golden couch into the porch
And on the Couch repos'd his limbs trembling from the bloody
    field,
Rearing their Druid Patriarchal rocky Temples around his limbs.
(All things begin & end in Albion's Ancient Druid Rocky Shore.)

[47]
From Camberwell to Highgate where the mighty Thames shudders
    along,
Where Los's Furnaces stand, where Jerusalem & Vala howl,
Luvah tore forth from Albion's Loins in fibrous veins, in rivers
Of blood over Europe: a Vegetating Root, in grinding pain   4
Animating the Dragon Temples, soon to become that Holy Fiend
The Wicker Man of Scandinavia, in which, cruelly consumed,

The Captives rear'd to heaven howl in flames among the stars.
Loud the cries of War on the Rhine & Danube with Albion's Sons:
Away from Beulah's hills & vales break forth the Souls of the
 Dead,
With cymbal, trumpet, clarion & the scythed chariots of Britain.

And the Veil of Vala is composed of the Spectres of the Dead. 11

Hark! the mingling cries of Luvah with the Sons of Albion.
Hark! & Record the terrible wonder! that the Punisher
Mingles with his Victim's Spectre, enslaved & tormented
To him whom he has murder'd, bound in vengeance & enmity.
Shudder not, but Write, & the hand of God will assist you! 16
Therefore I write Albion's last words: "Hope is banish'd from
 me."

[48]
These were his last words; and the merciful Saviour in his arms
Reciev'd him, in the arms of tender mercy, and repos'd
The pale limbs of his Eternal Individuality
Upon the Rock of Ages. Then, surrounded with a Cloud,
In silence the Divine Lord builded with immortal labour, 5
Of gold & jewels, a sublime Ornament, a Couch of repose
With Sixteen pillars, canopied with emblems & written verse,
Spiritual Verse, order'd & measur'd: from whence time shall reveal
The Five books of the Decalogue, the books of Joshua & Judges:
Samuel, a double book, & Kings, a double book, the Psalms &
 Prophets,
The Four-fold Gospel, and the Revelations everlasting. 11
Eternity groan'd & was troubled at the image of Eternal Death!

Beneath the bottoms of the Graves, which is Earth's central joint,
There is a place where Contrarieties are equally true:
(To protect from the Giant blows in the sports of intellect, 15
Thunder in the midst of kindness, & love that kills its beloved;
Because Death is for a period, and they renew tenfold.)
From this sweet Place Maternal Love awoke Jerusalem;
With pangs she forsook Beulah's pleasant lovely shadowy
 Universe
Where no dispute can come, created for those who Sleep. 20

Weeping was in all Beulah, and all the Daughters of Beulah
Wept for their Sister, the Daughter of Albion, Jerusalem,
When out of Beulah the Emanation of the Sleeper descended
With solemn mourning, out of Beulah's moony shades and hills
Within the Human Heart, whose Gates closed with solemn sound.

And this the manner of the terrible Separation. 26

The Emanations of the grievously afflicted Friends of Albion
Concenter in one Female form, an Aged pensive Woman.
Astonish'd! lovely! embracing the sublime shade, the Daughters
   of Beulah
Beheld her with wonder! With awful hands she took   30
A Moment of Time, drawing it out, with many tears & afflictions
And many sorrows, oblique across the Atlantic Vale,
Which is the Vale of Rephaim dreadful from East to West
Where the Human Harvest waves abundant in the beams of Eden,
Into a Rainbow of jewels and gold, a mild Reflection from   35
Albion's dread Tomb: Eight thousand and five hundred years
In its extension. Every two hundred years has a door to Eden.
She also took an Atom of Space, with dire pain opening it a Center
Into Beulah; trembling the Daughters of Beulah dried   39
Her tears; she ardent embrac'd her sorrows, occupied in labours
Of sublime mercy in Rephaim's Vale. Perusing Albion's Tomb
She sat: she walk'd among the ornaments, solemn mourning.
The Daughters attended her shudderings, wiping the death sweat.
Los also saw her in his seventh Furnace; he also, terrified,
Saw the finger of God go forth upon his seventh Furnace   45
Away from the Starry Wheels to prepare Jerusalem a place,
When with a dreadful groan the Emanation mild of Albion
Burst from his bosom in the Tomb like a pale snowy cloud,
Female and lovely, struggling to put off the Human form,
Writhing in pain. The Daughters of Beulah in kind arms reciev'd
Jerusalem, weeping over her among the Spaces of Erin   51
In the Ends of Beulah, where the Dead wail night & day.

And thus Erin spoke to the Daughters of Beulah in soft tears:

" Albion the Vortex of the Dead! Albion the Generous!
Albion the mildest son of Heaven! The Place of Holy Sacrifice
Where Friends Die for each other, will become the Place   56
Of Murder & Unforgiving Never-awaking Sacrifice of Enemies.
The Children must be sacrific'd! (a horror never known
Till now in Beulah) unless a Refuge can be found
To hide them from the wrath of Albion's Law that freezes sore
Upon his Sons & Daughters, self-exiled from his bosom.   61
Draw ye Jerusalem away from Albion's Mountains
To give a Place for Redemption, let Sihon and Og
Remove Eastward to Bashan and Gilead, and leave
[49]
" The secret coverts of Albion & the hidden places of America.
Jerusalem! Jerusalem! why wilt thou turn away?
Come ye, O Daughters of Beulah, lament for Og & Sihon
Upon the Lakes of Ireland from Rathlin to Baltimore.
Stand ye upon the Dargle from Wicklow to Drogheda,   5
Come & mourn over Albion, the White Cliff of the Atlantic.

The Mountain of Giants: all the Giants of Albion are become
Weak, wither'd, darken'd, & Jerusalem is cast forth from Albion.
They deny that they ever knew Jerusalem, or ever dwelt in Shiloh.
The Gigantic roots & twigs of the vegetating Sons of Albion,
Fill'd with the little-ones, are consumed in the Fires of their Altars.
The vegetating Cities are burned & consumed from the Earth,
And the Bodies in which all Animals & Vegetations, the Earth & Heaven
Were contain'd in the All Glorious Imagination, are wither'd & darken'd.
The golden Gate of Havilah and all the Garden of God   15
Was caught up with the Sun in one day of fury and war.
The Lungs, the Heart, the Liver, shrunk away far distant from Man
And left a little slimy substance floating upon the tides.
In one night the Atlantic Continent was caught up with the Moon
And became an Opake Globe far distant, clad with moony beams.
The Visions of Eternity, by reason of narrowed perceptions,   21
Are become weak Visions of Time & Space, fix'd into furrows of death,
Till deep dissimulation is the only defence an honest man has left.
O Polypus of Death! O Spectre over Europe and Asia
Withering the Human Form by Laws of Sacrifice for Sin!   25
By Laws of Chastity & Abhorrence I am wither'd up:
Striving to Create a Heaven in which all shall be pure & holy
In their Own Selfhoods: in Natural Selfish Chastity to banish Pity
And dear Mutual Forgiveness, & to become One Great Satan
Inslav'd to the most powerful Selfhood: to murder the Divine Humanity
In whose sight all are as the dust & who chargeth his Angels with folly.
Ah! weak & wide astray! Ah! shut in narrow doleful form!
Creeping in reptile flesh upon the bosom of the ground!
The Eye of Man, a little narrow orb, clos'd up & dark,   34
Scarcely beholding the Great Light, conversing with the ground:
The Ear, a little shell, in small volutions shutting out
True Harmonies & comprehending great as very small:
The Nostrils, bent down to the earth & clos'd with senseless flesh
That odours cannot them expand, nor joy on them exult:
The Tongue, a little moisture fills, a little food it cloys,   40
A little sound it utters, & its cries are faintly heard.
Therefore they are removed: therefore they have taken root
In Egypt & Philistea, in Moab & Edom & Aram:
In the Erythrean Sea their Uncircumcision in Heart & Loins
Be lost for ever & ever; then they shall arise from Self   45
By Self Annihilation into Jerusalem's Courts & into Shiloh,
Shiloh, the Masculine Emanation among the Flowers of Beulah.
Lo, Shiloh dwells over France, as Jerusalem dwells over Albion.

Build & prepare a Wall & Curtain for America's shore!
Rush on! Rush on! Rush on, ye vegetating Sons of Albion!
The Sun shall go before you in Day, the Moon shall go   51
Before you in Night. Come on! Come on! Come on! The Lord
Jehovah is before, behind, above, beneath, around.
He has builded the arches of Albion's Tomb, binding the Stars
In merciful Order, bending the Laws of Cruelty to Peace.   55
He hath placed Og & Anak, the Giants of Albion, for their Guards,
Building the Body of Moses in the Valley of Peor, the Body
Of Divine Analogy; and Og & Sihon in the tears of Balaam
The Son of Beor, have given their power to Joshua & Caleb.
Remove from Albion, far remove these terrible surfaces: 60
They are beginning to form Heavens & Hells in immense
Circles, the Hells for food to the Heavens, food of torment,
Food of despair: they drink the condemn'd Soul & rejoice
In cruel holiness in their Heavens of Chastity & Uncircumcision;
Yet they are blameless, & Iniquity must be imputed only   65
To the State they are enter'd into, that they may be deliver'd.
Satan is the State of Death & not a Human existence;
But Luvah is named Satan because he has enter'd that State:
A World where Man is by Nature the enemy of Man,
Because the Evil is Created into a State, that Men   70
May be deliver'd time after time, evermore. Amen.
Learn therefore, O Sisters, to distinguish the Eternal Human
That walks about among the stones of fire in bliss & woe
Alternate, from those States or Worlds in which the Spirit travels.
This is the only means to Forgiveness of Enemies.   75
Therefore remove from Albion these terrible Surfaces
And let wild seas & rocks close up Jerusalem away from
[50]
" The Atlantic Mountains where Giants dwelt in Intellect,
Now given to stony Druids and Allegoric Generation,
To the Twelve Gods of Asia, the Spectres of those who Sleep
Sway'd by a Providence oppos'd to the Divine Lord Jesus: 4
A murderous Providence! A Creation that groans, living on
      Death,
Where Fish & Bird & Beast & Man & Tree & Metal & Stone
Live by Devouring, going into Eternal Death continually.
Albion is now possess'd by the War of Blood! the Sacrifice
Of envy Albion is become, and his Emanation cast out.
Come Lord Jesus. Lamb of God descend! for if, O Lord!   10
If thou hadst been here, our brother Albion had not died.
Arise sisters! Go ye & meet the Lord, while I remain.
Behold the foggy mornings of the Dead on Albion's cliffs!
Ye know that if the Emanation remains in them
She will become an Eternal Death, an Avenger of Sin,   15
A Self-righteousness, the proud Virgin-Harlot! Mother of War!
And we also & all Beulah consume beneath Albion's curse.''

So Erin spoke to the Daughters of Beulah. Shuddering
With their wings, they sat in the Furnace, in a night
Of stars, for all the Sons of Albion appear'd distant stars   20
Ascending and descending into Albion's sea of death.
And Erin's lovely Bow enclos'd the Wheels of Albion's Sons.

Expanding on wing, the Daughters of Beulah replied in sweet
    response:

" Come, O thou Lamb of God, and take away the remembrance
    of Sin.
To Sin & to hide the Sin in sweet deceit is lovely!   25
To Sin in the open face of day is cruel & pitiless! But
To record the Sin for a reproach, to let the Sun go down
In a remembrance of the Sin, is a Woe & a Horror,
A brooder of an Evil Day and a Sun rising in blood!
Come then, O Lamb of God, and take away the remembrance
    of Sin." [1]

End of Chap: 2d

---

[1] The full-page illustration which concludes this chapter shows three des-
pairing figures in a dungeon of flames. They are Vala, who is seated on the
left; Hyle, sitting on the ground, his head sunk between his knees; and
Skofeld, a bald man on the right who totters in the flames dragging his
chains.

[52]

| Rahab is an Eternal State. } | To The Deists. | { The Spiritual States of the Soul are all Eternal. Distinguish between the Man & his present State. |

HE never can be a Friend to the Human Race who is the Preacher of Natural Morality or Natural Religion; he is a flatterer who means to betray, to perpetuate Tyrant Pride & the Laws of that Babylon which, he foresees, shall shortly be destroyed, with the Spiritual and not the Natural Sword. He is in the State named Rahab, which State must be put off before he can be the Friend of Man.

You, O Deists, profess yourselves the Enemies of Christianity, and you are so: you are also the Enemies of the Human Race & of Universal Nature. Man is born a Spectre or Satan & is altogether an Evil, & requires a New Selfhood continually, & must continually be changed into his direct Contrary. But your Greek Philosophy (which is a remnant of Druidism) teaches that Man is Righteous in his Vegetated Spectre: an Opinion of fatal & accursed consequence to Man, as the Ancients saw plainly by Revelation, to the intire abrogation of Experimental Theory; and many believed what they saw and Prophecied of Jesus.

Man must & will have Some Religion: if he has not the Religion of Jesus, he will have the Religion of Satan & will erect the Synagogue of Satan, calling the Prince of this World, God, and destroying all who do not worship Satan under the Name of God. Will any one say, ' Where are those who worship Satan under the name of God? ' Where are they? Listen! Every Religion that Preaches Vengeance for Sin is the Religion of the Enemy & Avenger and not of the Forgiver of Sin, and their God is Satan, Named by the Divine Name. Your Religion, O Deists! Deism, is the Worship of the God of this World by the means of what you call Natural Religion and Natural Philosophy, and of Natural Morality or Self-Righteousness, the Selfish Virtues of the Natural Heart. This was the Religion of the Pharisees who murder'd Jesus. Deism is the same & ends in the same.

Voltaire, Rousseau, Gibbon, Hume, charge the Spiritually Religious with Hypocrisy; but how a Monk, or a Methodist either, can be a Hypocrite, I cannot concieve. We are Men of like passions with others & pretend not to be holier than others; therefore, when a Religious Man falls into Sin, he ought not to be call'd a Hypocrite; this title is more properly to be given to a Player who falls into Sin, whose profession is Virtue & Morality & the making Men Self-Righteous. Foote in calling Whitefield Hypocrite, was himself one; for Whitefield pretended not to be holier than others, but confessed his Sins before all the World. Voltaire! Rousseau! You cannot escape my charge that you are

I 792

Pharisees & Hypocrites, for you are constantly talking of the Virtues of the Human Heart and particularly of your own, that you may accuse others, & especially the Religious, whose errors you, by this display of pretended Virtue, chiefly design to expose. Rousseau thought Men Good by Nature: he found them Evil & found no friend. Friendship cannot exist without Forgiveness of Sins continually. The Book written by Rousseau call'd his Confessions, is an apology & cloke for his sin & not a confession.

But you also charge the poor Monks & Religious with being the causes of War, while you acquit & flatter the Alexanders & Caesars, the Lewis's & Fredericks, who alone are its causes & its actors. But the Religion of Jesus, Forgiveness of Sin, can never be the cause of a War, nor of a single Martyrdom.

Those who Martyr others or who cause War are Deists, but never can be Forgivers of Sin. The Glory of Christianity is To Conquer by Forgiveness. All the Destruction, therefore, in Christian Europe has arisen from Deism, which is Natural Religion.

    I saw a Monk of Charlemaine
Arise before my sight:
    I talk'd with the Grey Monk as we stood
In beams of infernal light.   4

    Gibbon arose with a lash of steel,
And Voltaire with a wracking wheel:
    The Schools, in clouds of learning roll'd,
Arose with War in iron & gold.   8

    " Thou lazy Monk," they sound afar,
" In vain condemning glorious War;
    And in your Cell you shall ever dwell:
Rise, War, & bind him in his Cell! "   12

    The blood red ran from the Grey Monk's side,
His hands & feet were wounded wide,
    His body bent; his arms & knees
Like to the roots of ancient trees.   16

    When Satan first the black bow bent
And the Moral Law from the Gospel rent,
    He forg'd the Law into a Sword
And spill'd the blood of mercy's Lord.   20

    Titus! Constantine! Charlemaine!
O Voltaire! Rousseau! Gibbon! Vain
    Your Grecian Mocks and Roman Sword
Against this image of his Lord!   24

    For a Tear is an Intellectual thing,
And a Sigh is the Sword of an Angel King,
    And the bitter groan of a Martyr's woe
Is an Arrow from the Almightie's Bow.   28

JERUSALEM

53

Chap: 3

But Los, who is the Vehicular Form of strong Urthona,
Wept vehemently over Albion where Thames' currents spring
From the rivers of Beulah; pleasant river! soft, mild, parent
    stream.
And the roots of Albion's Tree enter'd the Soul of Los,
As he sat before his Furnaces clothed in sackcloth of hair,   5
In gnawing pain dividing him from his Emanation,
Inclosing all the Children of Los time after time,
Their Giant forms condensing into Nations & Peoples & Tongues.
Translucent the Furnaces, of Beryll & Emerald immortal
And Seven-fold each within other, incomprehensible   10
To the Vegetated Mortal Eye's perverted & single vision.
The Bellows are the Animal Lungs, the Hammers the Animal
    Heart,
The Furnaces the Stomach for Digestion; terrible their fury
Like seven burning heavens rang'd from South to North.

Here, on the banks of the Thames, Los builded Golgonooza,   15
Outside of the Gates of the Human Heart beneath Beulah
In the midst of the rocks of the Altars of Albion. In fears
He builded it, in rage & in fury. It is the Spiritual Fourfold
London, continually building & continually decaying desolate.
In eternal labours, loud the Furnaces & loud the Anvils   20
Of Death thunder incessant around the flaming Couches of
The Twenty-four Friends of Albion, and round the awful Four,
For the protection of the Twelve Emanations of Albion's Sons,
The Mystic Union of the Emanation in the Lord. Because
Man divided from his Emanation is a dark Spectre,   25
His Emanation is an ever-weeping melancholy Shadow;
But she is made receptive of Generation, thro' mercy,
In the Potter's Furnace among the Funeral Urns of Beulah,
From Surrey hills thro' Italy and Greece to Hinnom's vale.

54

In Great Eternity every particular Form gives forth or Emanates
Its own peculiar Light, & the Form is the Divine Vision

And the Light is his Garment. This is Jerusalem in every Man,
A Tent & Tabernacle of Mutual Forgiveness, Male & Female
    Clothings.
And Jerusalem is called Liberty among the Children of Albion. 5

But Albion fell down, a Rocky fragment from Eternity hurl'd
By his own Spectre, who is the Reasoning Power in every Man,
Into his own Chaos, which is the Memory between Man & Man.

The silent broodings of deadly revenge springing from the
All powerful parental affection, fills Albion from head to foot, 10
Seeing his Sons assimilate with Luvah, bound in the bonds
Of spiritual Hate, from which springs Sexual Love as iron chains;
He tosses like a cloud outstretch'd among Jerusalem's Ruins
Which overspread all the Earth; he groans among his ruin'd
    porches.¹

But the Spectre, like a hoar frost & a Mildew, rose over Albion,
Saying, "I am God, O Sons of Men! I am your Rational Power!
Am I not Bacon & Newton & Locke who teach Humility to Man,
Who teach Doubt & Experiment? & my two Wings, Voltaire,
    Rousseau?
Where is that Friend of Sinners? that Rebel against my Laws 19
Who teaches Belief to the Nations & an unknown Eternal Life?
Come hither into the Desart & turn these stones to bread.
Vain foolish Man! wilt thou believe without Experiment?
And build a World of Phantasy upon my Great Abyss?
A World of Shapes in craving lust & devouring appetite." 24

So spoke the hard cold constrictive Spectre: he is named Arthur,
Constricting into Druid Rocks round Canaan, Agag & Aram &
    Pharoh.

Then Albion drew England into his bosom in groans & tears,
But she stretch'd out her starry Night in Spaces against him like
A long Serpent in the Abyss of the Spectre, which augmented
The Night with Dragon wings cover'd with stars, & in the Wings 30
Jerusalem & Vala appear'd; & above, between the Wings magni-
    ficent,
The Divine Vision dimly appear'd in clouds of blood weeping.

[55]
When those who disregard all Mortal Things saw a Mighty-One
Among the Flowers of Beulah still retain his awful strength,

¹ The upper half of Plate 54 contains an illustration of a globe with female
figures ascending on either side. The globe is inscribed "This World": the
word "Reason" is placed in the North, "Desire" in the South, "Wrath"
in the East, and "Pity" in the West. The design shows the displacement of
the Four Zoas.

They wonder'd, checking their wild flames; & Many gathering
Together into an Assembly, they said, "let us go down
And see these changes." Others said, "If you do so, prepare   5
For being driven from our fields: what have we to do with the
  Dead?
To be their inferiors or superiors we equally abhor:
Superior, none we know: inferior, none: all equal share
Divine Benevolence & Joy; for the Eternal Man
Walketh among us, calling us his Brothers & his Friends,   10
Forbidding us that Veil which Satan puts between Eve & Adam,
By which the Princes of the Dead enslave their Votaries
Teaching them to form the Serpent of precious stones & gold,
To sieze the Sons of Jerusalem & plant them in One Man's Loins,
To make One Family of Contraries, that Joseph may be sold   15
Into Egypt for Negation, a Veil the Saviour born & dying rends."

But others said: "Let us to him who only Is, & who
Walketh among us, give decision: bring forth all your fires!"

So saying, an eternal deed was done: in fiery flames   19
The Universal Concave raged such thunderous sounds as never
Were sounded from a mortal cloud, nor on Mount Sinai old,
Nor in Havilah where the Cherub roll'd his redounding flame.

Loud! loud! the Mountains lifted up their voices, loud the Forests:
Rivers thunder'd against their banks, loud Winds furious fought:
Cities & Nations contended in fires & clouds & tempests: 25
The Seas rais'd up their voices & lifted their hands on high:
The Stars in their courses fought, the Sun, Moon, Heaven, Earth,
Contending for Albion & for Jerusalem his Emanation,
And for Shiloh the Emanation of France, & for lovely Vala.

Then far the greatest number were about to make a Separation;
And they Elected Seven, call'd the Seven Eyes of God,   31
Lucifer, Molech, Elohim, Shaddai, Pahad, Jehovah, Jesus.
They nam'd the Eighth: he came not, he hid in Albion's Forests.
But first they said: (& their Words stood in Chariots in array
Curbing their Tygers with golden bits & bridles of silver & ivory)

"Let the Human Organs be kept in their perfect Integrity,
At will Contracting into Worms or Expanding into Gods,
And then, behold! what are these Ulro Visions of Chastity?
Then as the moss upon the tree, or dust upon the plow,   39
Or as the sweat upon the labouring shoulder, or as the chaff
Of the wheat-floor, or as the dregs of the sweet wine-press:
Such are these Ulro Visions; for tho' we sit down within
The plowed furrow, list'ning to the weeping clods till we
Contract or Expand Space at will, or if we raise ourselves   44

Upon the chariots of the morning, Contracting or Expanding Time,
Every one knows we are One Family, One Man blessed for ever.''

Silençe remain'd & every one resum'd his Human Majesty.
And many conversed on these things as they labour'd at the
　　furrow,
Saying: '' It is better to prevent misery than to release from misery:
It is better to prevent error than to forgive the criminal.　　　50
Labour well the Minute Particulars, attend to the Little-ones,
And those who are in misery cannot remain so long
If we do but our duty: labour well the teeming Earth.''

They Plow'd in tears, the trumpets sounded before the golden
　　Plow;
And the voices of the Living Creatures were heard in the clouds
　　of heaven,
Crying: ''Compell the Reasoner to Demonstrate with unhewn
　　Demonstrations.
Let the Indefinite be explored, and let every Man be Judged
By his own Works. Let all Indefinites be thrown into Demonstra-
　　tions,
To be pounded to dust & melted in the Furnaces of Affliction.　59
He who would do good to another must do it in Minute Parti-
　　culars:
General Good is the plea of the scoundrel, hypocrite & flatterer,
For Art & Science cannot exist but in minutely organized Parti-
　　culars
And not in generalizing Demonstrations of the Rational Power.
The Infinite alone resides in Definite & Determinate Identity;
Establishment of Truth depends on destruction of Falshood con-
　　tinually,
On Circumcision, not on Virginity, O Reasoners of Albion! ''　66

So cried they at the Plow. Albion's Rock frowned above,
And the Great Voice of Eternity rolled above terrible in clouds,
Saying, '' Who will go forth for us, & Who shall we send before
　　our face? ''

[56]
Then Los heaved his thund'ring Bellows on the Valley of Middle-
　　sex,
And thus he chaunted his Song: the Daughters of Albion reply:

'' What may Man be? who can tell! But what may Woman be?
To have power over Man from Cradle to corruptible Grave.
He who is an Infant and whose Cradle is a Manger　　　　　5
Knoweth the Infant sorrow, whence it came and where it goeth
And who weave it a Cradle of the grass that withereth away.

This World is all a Cradle for the erred wandering Phantom,
Rock'd by Year, Month, Day & Hour; and every two Moments
Between dwells a Daughter of Beulah, to feed the Human
    Vegetable.
Entune, Daughters of Albion, your hymning Chorus mildly,
Cord of affection thrilling extatic on the iron Reel
To the golden Loom of Love, to the moth-labour'd Woof,
A Garment and Cradle weaving for the infantine Terror,
For fear, at entering the gate into our World of cruel   15
Lamentation, it flee back & hide in Non-Entity's dark wild
Where dwells the Spectre of Albion, destroyer of Definite Form.
The Sun shall be a Scythed Chariot of Britain: the Moon, a Ship
In the British Ocean, Created by Los's Hammer, measured out
Into Days & Nights & Years & Months, to travel with my feet
Over these desolate rocks of Albion. O daughters of despair!
Rock the Cradle, and in mild melodies tell me where found
What you have enwoven with so much tears & care? so much
Tender artifice, to laugh, to weep, to learn, to know:
Remember! recollect! what dark befel in wintry days."   25

" O it was lost for ever! and we found it not: it came
And wept at our wintry Door. Look! look! behold! Gwendolen
Is become a Clod of Clay! Merlin is a Worm of the Valley!"

Then Los uttered with Hammer & Anvil: " Chaunt! revoice!
I mind not your laugh, and your frown I not fear, and   30
You must my dictate obey: from your gold-beam'd Looms trill
Gentle to Albion's Watchman; on Albion's mountains reeccho
And rock the Cradle while.[1] Ah me! Of [2] that Eternal Man
And of the cradled Infancy in his bowels of compassion   34
Who fell beneath his instruments of husbandry & became
Subservient to the clods of the furrow, the cattle and even
The emmet and earth-worm are his superiors & his lords."

Then the response came warbling from trilling Looms in Albion:
" We Women tremble at the light, therefore hiding fearful   39
The Divine Vision with Curtain & Veil & fleshly Tabernacle."
Los utter'd, swift as the rattling thunder upon the mountains:
" Look back into the Church Paul! Look! Three Women around
The Cross! O Albion, why didst thou a Female Will Create?"

[57]
And the voices of Bath & Canterbury & York & Edinburgh Cry
Over the Plow of Nations in the strong hand of Albion, thunder-
    ing along
Among the Fires of the Druid & the deep black rethundering
    Waters

      [1] " while," i.e. the while   [2] " Of," i.e. Concerning.

Of the Atlantic which poured in, impetuous, loud, loud, louder
    & louder.
And the Great Voice of the Atlantic howled over the Druid Altars,
Weeping over his Children in Stone-henge, in Malden & Col-
    chester,
Round the Rocky Peak of Derbyshire, London Stone & Rosa-
    mond's Bower:

"What is a Wife & what is a Harlot? What is a Church & What
Is a Theatre? are they Two & not One? can they Exist Separate? 9
Are not Religion & Politics the Same Thing? Brotherhood is
    Religion,
O Demonstrations of Reason Dividing Families in Cruelty &
    Pride!"

But Albion fled from the Divine Vision; with the Plow of Nations
    enflaming,
The Living Creatures madden'd, and Albion fell into the Furrow;
    and
The Plow went over him & the Living was Plowed in among the
    Dead.
But his Spectre rose over the starry Plow. Albion fled beneath
    the Plow   15
Till he came to the Rock of Ages, & he took his Seat upon the
    Rock.

Wonder siez'd all in Eternity, to behold the Divine Vision open
The Center into an Expanse, & the Center rolled out into an
    Expanse.

[58]
In beauty the Daughters of Albion divide & unite at will.
Naked & drunk with blood, Gwendolen dancing to the timbrel
Of War, reeling up the Street of London, she divides in twain
Among the Inhabitants of Albion: the People fall around.
The Daughters of Albion divide & unite in jealousy & cruelty.   5
The Inhabitants of Albion at the Harvest & the Vintage
Feel their Brain cut round beneath the temples, shrieking,
Bonifying into a Scull, the Marrow exuding in dismal pain.
They flee over the rocks bonifying. Horses, Oxen feel the knife.
And while the Sons of Albion by severe War & Judgment bonify,
The Hermaphroditic Condensations are divided by the Knife,   11
The obdurate Forms are cut asunder by Jealousy & Pity.

Rational Philosophy and Mathematic Demonstration
Is divided in the intoxications of pleasure & affection:
Two Contraries War against each other in fury & blood,   15
And Los fixes them on his Anvil, incessant his blows:

He fixes them with strong blows, placing the stones & timbers
To Create a World of Generation from the World of Death,
Dividing the Masculine & Feminine; for the comingling
Of Albion's & Luvah's Spectres was Hermaphroditic.   20

Urizen wrathful strode above directing the awful Building
As a Mighty Temple, delivering Form out of confusion.
Jordan sprang beneath its threshold, bubbling from beneath
Its pillars: Euphrates ran under its arches: white sails   24
And silver oars reflect on its pillars & sound on its ecchoing
Pavements, where walk the Sons of Jerusalem who remain
     Ungenerate.
But the revolving Sun and Moon pass thro' its porticoes,
Day & night in sublime majesty & silence they revolve
And shine glorious within. Hand & Koban arch'd over the Sun
In the hot noon as he travel'd thro' his journey. Hyle & Skofield
Arch'd over the Moon at midnight, & Los fix'd them there
With his thunderous Hammer: terrified the Spectres rage & flee.
Canaan is his portico. Jordan is a fountain in his porch,
A fountain of milk & wine to relieve the traveller.   34
Egypt is the eight steps within. Ethiopia supports his pillars.
Lybia & the Lands unknown are the ascent without;
Within is Asia & Greece, ornamented with exquisite art.
Persia & Media are his halls: his inmost hall is Great Tartary.
China & India & Siberia are his temples for entertainment.
Poland & Russia & Sweden, his soft retired chambers.   40
France & Spain & Italy & Denmark & Holland & Germany
Are the temples among his pillars. Britain is Los's Forge.
America North & South are his baths of living waters.

Such is the Ancient World of Urizen, in the Satanic Void
Created from the Valley of Middlesex by London's River,   45
From Stone-henge & from London Stone, from Cornwall to
     Cathnes.
The Four Zoas rush around on all sides in dire ruin:
Furious in pride of Selfhood the terrible Spectres of Albion
Rear their dark Rocks among the Stars of God, stupendous
Works! A World of Generation continually Creating out of
The Hermaphroditic Satanic World of rocky destiny,   51
[59]
And formed into Four precious stones for enterance from Beulah.

For the Veil of Vala, which Albion cast into the Atlantic Deep
To catch the Souls of the Dead, began to Vegetate & Petrify
Around the Earth of Albion among the Roots of his Tree.   4
This Los formed into the Gates & mighty Wall between the Oak
Of Weeping & the Palm of Suffering beneath Albion's Tomb.
Thus in process of time it became the beautiful Mundane Shell,

The Habitation of the Spectres of the Dead, & the Place
Of Redemption & of awaking again into Eternity. 9

For Four Universes round the Mundane Egg remain Chaotic:
One to the North, Urthona: One to the South, Urizen:
One to the East, Luvah: One to the West, Tharmas.
They are the Four Zoas that stood around the Throne Divine,
Verulam, London, York & Edinburgh, their English names.
But when Luvah assumed the World of Urizen Southward 15
And Albion was slain upon his Mountains & in his Tent,
All fell towards the Centre, sinking downwards in dire ruin.
In the South remains a burning Fire: in the East, a Void:
In the West, a World of raging Waters: in the North, solid Dark-
ness
Unfathomable without end; but in the midst of these 20
Is Built eternally the sublime Universe of Los & Enitharmon.

And in the North Gate, in the West of the North, toward Beulah,
Cathedron's Looms are builded, and Los's Furnaces in the South.
A wondrous golden Building immense with ornaments sublime
Is bright Cathedron's golden Hall, its Courts, Towers & Pinnacles.

And one Daughter of Los sat at the fiery Reel, & another
Sat at the shining Loom with her Sisters attending round,
Terrible their distress, & their sorrow cannot be utter'd:
And another Daughter of Los sat at the Spinning Wheel,
Endless their labour, with bitter food, void of sleep; 30
Tho' hungry, they labour: they rouze themselves anxious
Hour after hour labouring at the whirling Wheel,
Many Wheels & as many lovely Daughters sit weeping.

Yet the intoxicating delight that they take in their work
Obliterates every other evil; none pities their tears, 35
Yet they regard not pity & they expect no one to pity,
For they labour for life & love regardless of any one
But the poor Spectres that they work for always, incessantly.

They are mock'd by every one that passes by; they regard not,
They labour, & when their Wheels are broken by scorn & malice
They mend them sorrowing with many tears & afflictions. 41

Other Daughters Weave on the Cushion & Pillow Network fine
That Rahab & Tirzah may exist & live & breathe & love.
Ah, that it could be as the Daughters of Beulah wish!

Other Daughters of Los, labouring at Looms less fine, 45
Create the Silk-worm & the Spider & the Catterpiller
To assist in their most grievous work of pity & compassion;

And others Create the wooly Lamb & the downy Fowl
To assist in the work; the Lamb bleats, the Sea-fowl cries:
Men understand not the distress & the labour & sorrow 50
That in the Interior Worlds is carried on in fear & trembling,
Weaving the shudd'ring fears & loves of Albion's Families:
Thunderous rage the Spindles of iron, & the iron Distaff
Maddens in the fury of their hands, weaving in bitter tears
The Veil of Goats-hair & Purple & Scarlet & fine twined Linen.

[60]
The clouds of Albion's Druid Temples rage in the eastern heaven
While Los sat terrified beholding Albion's Spectre, who is Luvah,
Spreading in bloody veins in torments over Europe & Asia,
Not yet formed, but a wretched torment unformed & abyssal.
In flaming fire within the Furnaces the Divine Vision appear'd
On Albion's hills, often walking from the Furnaces in clouds
And flames among the Druid Temples & the Starry Wheels,
Gather'd Jerusalem's Children in his arms & bore them like
A Shepherd in the night of Albion which overspread all the Earth.

" I gave thee liberty and life, O lovely Jerusalem, 10
And thou hast bound me down upon the Stems of Vegetation.
I gave thee Sheep-walks upon the Spanish Mountains, Jerusalem,
I gave thee Priam's City and the Isles of Grecia lovely,
I gave thee Hand & Scofield & the Counties of Albion,
They spread forth like a lovely root into the Garden of God,
They were as Adam before me, united into One Man, 16
They stood in innocence & their skiey tent reach'd over Asia
To Nimrod's Tower, to Ham & Caanan walking with Mizraim
Upon the Egyptian Nile, with solemn songs, to Grecia
And sweet Hesperia, even to Great Chaldea & Tesshina, 20
Following thee as a Shepherd by the Four Rivers of Eden.
Why wilt thou rend thyself apart, Jerusalem,
And build this Babylon, & sacrifice in secret Groves
Among the Gods of Asia, among the fountains of pitch & nitre?
Therefore thy Mountains are become barren, Jerusalem, 25
Thy Valleys, Plains of burning sand; thy Rivers, waters of
    death;
Thy Villages die of the Famine, and thy Cities
Beg bread from house to house, lovely Jerusalem.
Why wilt thou deface thy beauty & the beauty of thy little-ones
To please thy Idols in the pretended chastities of Uncircumcision?
Thy Sons are lovelier than Egypt or Assyria; wherefore 31
Dost thou blacken their beauty by a Secluded place of rest
And a peculiar Tabernacle, to cut the integuments of beauty
Into veils of tears and sorrows, O lovely Jerusalem?
They have perswaded thee to this; therefore their end shall come.

        [1] " Gather'd," i.e. He (the Divine Vision) gather'd.

And I will lead thee thro' the Wilderness in shadow of my cloud,
And in my love I will lead thee, lovely Shadow of Sleeping
　　Albion.''

This is the Song of the Lamb, sung by Slaves in evening time.

But Jerusalem faintly saw him: clos'd in the Dungeons of Babylon
Her Form was held by Beulah's Daughters; but all within unseen
She sat at the Mills, her hair unbound, her feet naked　　　　41
Cut with the flints, her tears run down, her reason grows like
The Wheel of Hand incessant turning day & night without rest,
Insane she raves upon the winds, hoarse, inarticulate.
All night Vala hears, she triumphs in pride of holiness　　　45
To see Jerusalem deface her lineaments with bitter blows
Of despair, while the Satanic Holiness triumph'd in Vala
In a Religion of Chastity & Uncircumcised Selfishness
Both of the Head & Heart & Loins, clos'd up in Moral Pride.

But the Divine Lamb stood beside Jerusalem; oft she saw　　50
The lineaments Divine & oft the Voice heard, & oft she said:

'' O Lord & Saviour, have the Gods of the Heathen pierced thee?
Or hast thou been pierced in the House of thy Friends?
Art thou alive, & livest thou for evermore? or art thou
Not but a delusive shadow, a thought that liveth not?
Babel mocks, saying there is no God nor Son of God,　　　56
That thou, O Human Imagination, O Divine Body, art all
A delusion; but I know thee, O Lord, when thou arisest upon
My weary eyes, even in this dungeon & this iron mill.
The Stars of Albion cruel rise; thou bindest to sweet influences,
For thou also sufferest with me, altho' I behold thee not;　　61
And altho' I sin & blaspheme thy holy name, thou pitiest me
Because thou knowest I am deluded by the turning mills
And by these visions of pity & love because of Albion's death.''

Thus spake Jerusalem, & thus the Divine Voice replied:　　65
'' Mild Shade of Man, pitiest thou these Visions of terror & woe?
Give forth thy pity & love: fear not! lo, I am with thee always.
Only believe in me, that I have power to raise from death
Thy Brother who Sleepeth in Albion: fear not, trembling Shade.[2]

[61]
'' Behold! in the Visions of Elohim Jehovah, behold Joseph & Mary,
And be comforted, O Jerusalem, in the Visions of Jehovah
　　Elohim.''

　　　[1] '' Not.'' Blake possibly intended this to be read as '' Nought.''
　　　[2] This sentence is completed with the first line of Plate 62. Plate 61 is a
particularly obvious example of Blake's habit of inserting an extra plate
whenever he wished to expand a theme.

She looked & saw Joseph, the Carpenter in Nazareth, & Mary
His espoused Wife. And Mary said, " If thou put me away from
    thee
Dost thou not murder me? " Joseph spoke in anger & fury,
    " Should I   5
Marry a Harlot & an Adulteress? " Mary answer'd, " Art thou
    more pure
Than thy Maker who forgiveth Sins & calls again Her that is Lost?
Tho' She hates, he calls her again in love. I love my dear Joseph,
But he driveth me away from his presence; yet I hear the voice
    of God
In the voice of my Husband; tho' he is angry for a moment, he
    will not   10
Utterly cast me away: if I were pure, never could I taste the sweets
Of the Forgiveness of Sins: if I were holy, I never could behold
    the tears
Of love of him who loves me in the midst of his anger in furnace
    of fire."

" Ah my Mary!" said Joseph, weeping over & embracing her
    closely in
His arms, " Doth he forgive Jerusalem, & not exact Purity from
    her who is   15
Polluted? I heard his voice in my sleep & his Angel in my dream,
Saying, ' Doth Jehovah Forgive a Debt only on condition that
    it shall
Be Payed? Doth he Forgive Pollution only on conditions of
    Purity?
That Debt is not Forgiven! That Pollution is not Forgiven!
Such is the Forgiveness of the Gods, the Moral Virtues of the   20
Heathen, whose tender Mercies are Cruelty. But Jehovah's
    Salvation
Is without Money & without Price, in the Continual Forgiveness
    of Sins,
In the Perpetual Mutual Sacrifice in Great Eternity; for behold,
There is none that liveth & Sinneth not! And this is the Covenant
Of Jehovah: If you Forgive one-another, so shall Jehovah
    Forgive You,   25
That He Himself may Dwell among You. Fear not then to take
To thee Mary thy Wife, for she is with Child by the Holy Ghost.' "

Then Mary burst forth into a Song: she flowed like a River of
Many Streams in the arms of Joseph & gave forth her tears of joy
Like many waters, and Emanating into gardens & palaces upon
Euphrates, & to forests & floods & animals wild & tame from
Gihon to Hiddekel, & to corn fields & villages & inhabitants
Upon Pison & Arnon & Jordan. And I heard the voice among

The Reapers, Saying, " Am I Jerusalem the lost Adulteress? or
am I
Babylon come up to Jerusalem? " And another voice answer'd,
Saying,   35

" Does the voice of my Lord call me again? am I pure thro' his
Mercy
And Pity? Am I become lovely as a Virgin in his sight, who am
Indeed a Harlot drunken with the Sacrifice of Idols? does he
Call her pure as he did in the days of her Infancy when She
Was cast out to the loathing of her person? The Chaldean took   40
Me from my Cradle. The Amalekite stole me away upon his
Camels
Before I had ever beheld with love the Face of Jehovah, or known
That there was a God of Mercy. O Mercy, O Divine Humanity!
O Forgiveness & Pity & Compassion! If I were Pure I should never
Have known Thee: If I were Unpolluted I should never have
Glorified thy Holiness or rejoiced in thy great Salvation."   46

Mary leaned her side against Jerusalem. Jerusalem recieved
The Infant into her hands in the Visions of Jehovah. Times
passed on.
Jerusalem fainted over the Cross & Sepulcher. She heard the voice:
" Wilt thou make Rome thy Patriarch Druid & the Kings of
Europe his   50
Horsemen? Man in the Resurrection changes his Sexual Garments
at Will.
Every Harlot was once a Virgin: every Criminal an Infant Love.

[62]
" Repose on me till the morning of the Grave. I am thy life."

Jerusalem replied: " I am an outcast: Albion is dead:
I am left to the trampling foot & the spurning heel:
A Harlot I am call'd: I am sold from street to street:
I am defaced with blows & with the dirt of the Prison,
And wilt thou become my Husband, O my Lord & Saviour?
Shall Vala bring thee forth? shall the Chaste be ashamed also?
I see the Maternal Line, I behold the Seed of the Woman:
Cainah & Ada & Zillah, & Naamah, Wife of Noah,
Shuah's daughter & Tamar & Rahab the Canaanites,   10
Ruth the Moabite, & Bathsheba of the daughters of Heth,
Naamah the Ammonite, Zibeah the Philistine, & Mary:
These are the Daughters of Vala, Mother of the Body of death.
But I, thy Magdalen, behold thy Spiritual Risen Body.
Shall Albion arise? I know he shall arise at the Last Day!   15
I know that in my flesh I shall see God; but Emanations
Are weak, they know not whence they are, nor whither tend."

Jesus replied, '' I am the Resurrection & the Life.
I Die & pass the limits of possibility as it appears
To individual perception. Luvah must be Created   20
And Vala, for I cannot leave them in the gnawing Grave
But will prepare a way for my banished-ones to return.
Come now with me into the villages, walk thro' all the cities;
Tho' thou art taken to prison & judgment, starved in the streets,
I will command the cloud to give thee food & the hard rock   25
To flow with milk & wine: tho' thou seest me not a season,
Even a long season, & a hard journey & a howling wilderness,
Tho' Vala's cloud hide thee & Luvah's fires follow thee,
Only believe & trust in me. Lo, I am always with thee!''   29

So spoke the Lamb of God while Luvah's Cloud reddening above
Burst forth in streams of blood upon the heavens, & dark night
Involv'd Jerusalem, & the Wheels of Albion's Sons turn'd hoarse
Over the Mountains, & the fires blaz'd on Druid Altars,
And the Sun set in Tyburn's Brook where Victims howl & cry. 34

But Los beheld the Divine Vision among the flames of the
    Furnaces.
Therefore he lived & breathed in hope; but his tears fell incessant
Because his Children were clos'd from him apart & Enitharmon
Dividing in fierce pain; also the Vision of God was clos'd in clouds
Of Albion's Spectres, that Los in despair oft sat & often ponder'd
On Death Eternal, in fierce shudders upon the mountains of
    Albion
Walking, & in the vales in howlings fierce: then to his Anvils 41
Turning, anew began his labours, tho' in terrible pains.

[63]
Jehovah stood among the Druids in the Valley of Annandale
When the Four Zoas of Albion, the Four Living Creatures, the
    Cherubim
Of Albion, tremble before the Spectre in the starry Harness of
    the Plow
Of Nations. And their Names are Urizen & Luvah & Tharmas &
    Urthona.

Luvah slew Tharmas, the Angel of the Tongue, & Albion brought
    him   5
To Justice in his own City of Paris, denying the Resurrection.
Then Vala, the Wife of Albion, who is the Daughter of Luvah,
Took vengeance Twelve-fold among the Chaotic Rocks of the
    Druids
Where the Human Victims howl to the Moon & Thor & Friga
Dance the dance of death contending with Jehovah among the
    Cherubim.   10

The Chariot Wheels filled with Eyes rage along the howling Valley
In the Dividing of Reuben & Benjamin bleeding from Chester's
    River.

The Giants & the Witches & the Ghosts of Albion dance with
Thor & Friga, & the Fairies lead the Moon along the Valley of
    Cherubim
Bleeding in torrents from Mountain to Mountain, a lovely Victim.
And Jehovah stood in the Gates of the Victim, & he appeared
A weeping Infant in the Gates of Birth in the midst of Heaven.

The Cities & Villages of Albion became Rock & Sand Unhumanized,
The Druid Sons of Albion; & the Heavens a Void around, un-
    fathomable;
No Human Form but Sexual, & a little weeping Infant pale
    reflected   20
Multitudinous in the Looking Glass of Enitharmon, on all sides
Around in the clouds of the Female, on Albion's Cliffs of the Dead.

Such the appearance in Cheviot, in the Divisions of Reuben,
When the Cherubim hid their heads under their wings in deep
    slumbers,
When the Druids demanded Chastity from Woman & all was lost.

" How can the Female be Chaste, O thou stupid Druid," Cried Los,
" Without the Forgiveness of Sins in the merciful clouds of Jehovah
And without the Baptism of Repentance to wash away Calumnies
    and
The Accusations of Sin, that each may be Pure in their Neigh-
    bours' sight?
O when shall Jehovah give us Victims from his Flocks & Herds 30
Instead of Human Victims by the Daughters of Albion &
    Canaan? "

Then laugh'd Gwendolen, & her laughter shook the Nations &
    Familys of
The Dead beneath Beulah from Tyburn to Golgotha and from
Ireland to Japan: furious her Lions & Tygers & Wolves sport
    before
Los on the Thames & Medway: London & Canterbury groan in
    pain.   35

Los knew not yet what was done: he thought it was all in Vision,
In Visions of the Dreams of Beulah among the Daughters of
    Albion;
Therefore the Murder was put apart in the Looking-Glass of
    Enitharmon.

He saw in Vala's hand the Druid Knife of Revenge & the
    Poison Cup
Of Jealousy, and thought it a Poetic Vision of the Atmospheres, 40
Till Canaan roll'd apart from Albion across the Rhine, along the
    Danube,

And all the Land of Canaan suspended over the Valley of Cheviot,
From Bashan to Tyre & from Troy to Gaza of the Amalekite.
And Reuben fled with his head downwards among the Caverns
[64]
Of the Mundane Shell which froze on all sides round Canaan on
The vast Expanse, where the Daughters of Albion Weave the Web
Of Ages & Generations, folding & unfolding it like a Veil of
    Cherubim;
And sometimes it touches the Earth's summits, & sometimes
    spreads
Abroad into the Indefinite Spectre, who is the Rational Power. 5

Then All the Daughters of Albion became One before Los, even
    Vala;
And she put forth her hand upon the Looms in dreadful howlings
Till she vegetated into a hungry Stomach & a devouring Tongue.
Her Hand is a Court of Justice: her Feet two Armies in Battle: 9
Storms & Pestilence in her Locks, & in her Loins Earthquake
And Fire & the Ruin of Cities & Nations & Families & Tongues.

She cries: " The Human is but a Worm, & thou, O Male! Thou art
Thyself Female, a Male, a breeder of Seed, a Son & Husband: &
    Lo,
The Human Divine is Woman's Shadow, a Vapor in the summer's
    heat.
Go assume Papal dignity, thou Spectre, thou Male Harlot! Arthur,
Divide into the Kings of Europe in times remote, O Woman-born
And Woman-nourish'd & Woman-educated & Woman-scorn'd! "

" Wherefore art thou living? " said Los, " & Man cannot live in
    thy presence.
Art thou Vala the Wife of Albion, O thou lovely Daughter of
    Luvah?
All Quarrels arise from Reasoning: the secret Murder and   20
The violent Man-slaughter, these are the Spectre's double Cave,
The Sexual Death living on accusation of Sin & Judgment,
To freeze Love & Innocence into the gold & silver of the Merchant.
Without Forgiveness of Sin, Love is Itself Eternal Death. "

Then the Spectre drew Vala into his bosom, magnificent, terrific, 25
Glittering with precious stones & gold, with Garments of blood
    & fire.

He wept in deadly wrath of the Spectre, in self-contradicting agony,
Crimson with Wrath & green with Jealousy, dazling with Love
And Jealousy immingled, & the purple of the violet darken'd deep
Over the Plow of Nations thund'ring in the hand of Albion's
    Spectre.   30

A dark Hermaphrodite they stood frowning upon London's River;
And the Distaff & Spindle in the hands of Vala, with the Flax of
Human Miseries, turn'd fierce with the Lives of Men along the
    Valley
As Reuben fled before the Daughters of Albion, Taxing the
    Nations.

Derby Peak yawn'd a horrid Chasm at the Cries of Gwendolen
    & at   35
The stamping feet of Ragan upon the flaming Treddles of her
    Loom
That drop with crimson gore with the Loves of Albion & Canaan,
Opening along the Valley of Rephaim, weaving over the Caves
    of Machpelah;

[65]
To decide Two Worlds with a great decision, a World of Mercy and
A World of Justice, the World of Mercy for Salvation:
To cast Luvah into the Wrath and Albion into the Pity,
In the Two Contraries of Humanity & in the Four Regions.

For in the depths of Albion's bosom in the eastern heaven   5
They sound the clarions strong, they chain the howling Captives,
They cast the lots into the helmet, they give the oath of blood in
    Lambeth,
They vote the death of Luvah & they nail'd him to Albion's Tree
    in Bath,
They stain'd him with poisonous blue, they inwove him in cruel
    roots
To die a death of Six thousand years bound round with vegetation.
The sun was black & the moon roll'd a useless globe thro' Britain.

Then left the Sons of Urizen the plow & harrow, the loom,   12
The hammer & the chisel & the rule & compasses; from London
    fleeing,
They forg'd the sword on Cheviot, the chariot of war & the
    battle-ax,
The trumpet fitted to mortal battle, & the flute of summer in
    Annandale;
And all the Arts of Life they chang'd into the Arts of Death in
    Albion:

The hour-glass contemn'd because its simple workmanship
Was like the workmanship of the plowman, & the water wheel
That raises water into cisterns, broken & burn'd with fire   19
Because its workmanship was like the workmanship of the
    shepherd;
And in their stead, intricate wheels invented, wheel without wheel,
To perplex youth in their outgoings & to bind to labours in Albion
Of day & night the myriads of eternity: that they may grind
And polish brass & iron hour after hour, laborious task,   24
Kept ignorant of its use: that they might spend the days of wisdom
In sorrowful drudgery to obtain a scanty pittance of bread,
In ignorance to view a small portion & think that All,
And call it Demonstration, blind to all the simple rules of life.

" Now, now the battle rages round thy tender limbs, O Vala!
Now smile among thy bitter tears, now put on all thy beauty.   30
Is not the wound of the sword sweet & the broken bone delightful?
Wilt thou now smile among the scythes when the wounded groan
    in the field?
We were carried away in thousands from London & in tens
Of thousands from Westminster & Marybone, in ships clos'd up,
Chain'd hand & foot, compell'd to fight under the iron whips
Of our captains, fearing our officers more than the enemy.   36
Lift up thy blue eyes, Vala, & put on thy sapphire shoes:
O melancholy Magdalen, behold the morning over Malden break!
Gird on thy flaming zone, descend into the sepulcher of Canter-
    bury.
Scatter the blood from thy golden brow, the tears from thy silver
    locks;
Shake off the waters from thy wings & the dust from thy white
    garments.
Remember all thy feigned terrors on the secret couch of Lambeth's
    Vale
When the sun rose in glowing morn with arms of mighty hosts
Marching to battle, who was wont to rise with Urizen's harps
Girt as a sower with his seed to scatter life abroad over Albion.   45
Arise, O Vala! bring the bow of Urizen, bring the swift arrows
    of light.
How rag'd the golden horses of Urizen, compell'd to the chariot
    of love!
Compell'd to leave the plow to the ox, to snuff up the winds of
    desolation,
To trample the corn fields in boastful neighings: this is no gentle
    harp,
This is no warbling brook nor shadow of a mirtle tree,   50
But blood and wounds and dismal cries and shadows of the oak,
And hearts laid open to the light by the broad grizly sword,
And bowels, hid in hammer'd steel, rip'd quivering on the ground.

Call forth thy smiles of soft deceit: call forth thy cloudy tears.
We hear thy sighs in trumpets shrill when morn shall blood
    renew.''   55

So Sang the Spectre Sons of Albion round Luvah's Stone of Trial,
Mocking and deriding at the writhings of their Victim on Salisbury,
Drinking his Emanation in intoxicating bliss, rejoicing in Giant
    dance;
For a Spectre has no Emanation but what he imbibes from
    decieving
A Victim: Then he becomes her Priest & she his Tabernacle   60
And his Oak Grove, till the Victim rend the woven Veil
In the end of his sleep when Jesus calls him from his grave.

Howling, the Victims on the Druid Altars yield their souls
To the stern Warriors; lovely sport the Daughters round their
    Victims,
Drinking their lives in sweet intoxication; hence arose from Bath
Self deluding odours, in spiral volutions intricately winding   66
Over Albion's mountains a feminine indefinite cruel delusion.
Astonish'd, terrified & in pain & torment, Sudden they behold
Their own Parent, the Emanation of their murder'd Enemy
Become their Emanation and their Temple and Tabernacle.   70
They knew not this Vala was their beloved Mother Vala, Albion's
    Wife

Terrified at the sight of the Victim, at his distorted sinews,
The tremblings of Vala vibrate thro' the limbs of Albion's Sons.
While they rejoice over Luvah in mockery & bitter scorn,   74
Sudden they become like what they behold, in howlings & deadly
    pain:
Spasms smite their features, sinews & limbs: pale they look on
    one another;
They turn, contorted: their iron necks bend unwilling towards
Luvah: their lips tremble: their muscular fibres are cramp'd &
    smitten:
They become like what they behold! Yet immense in strength &
    power,
[66]
In awful pomp & gold, in all the precious unhewn stones of Eden
They build a stupendous Building on the Plain of Salisbury, with
    chains
Of rocks round London Stone, of Reasonings, of unhewn Demon-
    strations
In labyrinthine arches (mighty Urizen the Architect) thro' which
The Heavens might revolve & Eternity be bound in their chain.   5
Labour unparallell'd! a wondrous rocky World of cruel destiny,

Rocks piled on rocks reaching the stars, stretching from pole to
    pole.
The Building is Natural Religion & its Altars Natural Morality,
A building of eternal death, whose proportions are eternal despair.
Here Vala stood turning the iron Spindle of destruction   10
From heaven to earth, howling, invisible; but not invisible
Her Two Covering Cherubs, afterwards named Voltaire & Rous-
    seau,
Two frowning Rocks on each side of the Cove & Stone of Torture,
Frozen Sons of the feminine Tabernacle of Bacon, Newton &
    Locke;
For Luvah is France, the Victim of the Spectres of Albion.   15

Los beheld in terror: he pour'd his loud storms on the Furnaces.
The Daughters of Albion, clothed in garments of needle work,
Strip them off from their shoulders and bosoms; they lay aside
Their garments, they sit naked upon the Stone of trial.   19
The Knife of flint passes over the howling Victim: his blood
Gushes & stains the fair side of the fair Daughters of Albion.
They put aside his curls, they divide his seven locks upon
His forehead, they bind his forehead with thorns of iron,
They put into his hand a reed, they mock, Saying: " Behold
The King of Canaan whose are seven hundred chariots of iron! "
They take off his vesture whole with their Knives of flint,
But they cut asunder his inner garments, searching with
Their cruel fingers for his heart, & there they enter in pomp,
In many tears, & there they erect a temple & an altar.
They pour cold water on his brain in front, to cause   30
Lids to grow over his eyes in veils of tears, and caverns
To freeze over his nostrils, while they feed his tongue from cups
And dishes of painted clay. Glowing with beauty & cruelty
They obscure the sun & the moon: no eye can look upon them.

Ah! alas! at the sight of the Victim & at sight of those who are
    smitten,   35
All who see become what they behold; their eyes are cover'd
With veils of tears and their nostrils & tongues shrunk up,
Their ear bent outwards; as their Victim, so are they, in the pangs
Of unconquerable fear, amidst delights of revenge Earth-shaking.
And as their eye & ear shrunk, the heavens shrunk away: 40
The Divine Vision became first a burning flame, then a column
Of fire, then an awful fiery wheel surrounding earth & heaven,
And then a globe of blood wandering distant in an unknown night.
Afar into the unknown night the mountains fled away,   44
Six months of mortality, a summer, & six months of mortality, a
    winter.
The Human form began to be alter'd by the Daughters of Albion
And the perceptions to be dissipated into the Indefinite, Becoming

A mighty Polypus nam'd Albion's Tree: they tie the Veins
And Nerves into two knots & the Seed into a double knot.   49
They look forth: the Sun is shrunk: the Heavens are shrunk
Away into the far remote, and the Trees & Mountains wither'd
Into indefinite cloudy shadows in darkness & separation.
By Invisible Hatreds adjoin'd, they seem remote and separate
From each other, and yet are a Mighty Polypus in the Deep!
As the Mistletoe grows on the Oak, so Albion's Tree on Eternity.
    Lo!
He who will not comingle in Love must be adjoin'd by Hate.   56

They look forth from Stone-henge: from the Cove round London
    Stone
They look on one another: the mountain calls out to the mountain
Plinlimmon shrunk away: Snowdon trembled: the mountains
Of Wales & Scotland beheld the descending War, the routed flying.
Red run the streams of Albion: Thames is drunk with blood   61
As Gwendolen cast the shuttle of war, as Cambel return'd the
    beam,
The Humber & the Severn are drunk with the blood of the slain.
London feels his brain cut round: Edinburgh's heart is circum-
    scribed:
York & Lincoln hide among the flocks because of the griding Knife.
Worcester & Hereford, Oxford & Cambridge reel & stagger   66
Overwearied with howling. Wales & Scotland alone sustain the
    fight!
The inhabitants are sick to death: they labour to divide into
    Days
And Nights the uncertain Periods, and into Weeks & Months. In
    vain
They send the Dove & Raven & in vain the Serpent over the
    mountains
And in vain the Eagle & Lion over the four-fold wilderness: 71
They return not, but generate in rocky places desolate:
They return not, but build a habitation separate from Man.
The Sun forgets his course; like a drunken man he hesitates
Upon the Cheselden hills, thinking to sleep on the Severn.   75
In vain: he is hurried afar into an unknown Night:
He bleeds in torrents of blood as he rolls thro' heaven above.
He chokes up the paths of the sky; the Moon is leprous as snow,
Trembling & descending down, seeking to rest on high Mona,
Scattering her leprous snows in flakes of disease over Albion.   80
The Stars flee remote; the heaven is iron, the earth is sulphur,
And all the mountains & hills shrink up like a withering gourd
As the Senses of Men shrink together under the Knife of flint
In the hands of Albion's Daughters among the Druid Temples,
[67]
By those who drink their blood & the blood of their Covenant.

And the Twelve Daughters of Albion united in Rahab & Tirzah,
A Double Female: and they drew out from the Rocky Stones
Fibres of Life to Weave; for every Female is a Golden Loom,
The Rocks are opake hardnesses covering all Vegetated things;
And as they Wove & Cut from the Looms, in various divisions
Stretching over Europe & Asia from Ireland to Japan,
They divided into many lovely Daughters, to be counterparts
To those they Wove; for when they Wove a Male, they divided
Into a Female to the Woven Male: in opake hardness   10
They cut the Fibres from the Rocks: groaning in pain they Weave,
Calling the Rocks Atomic Origins of Existence, denying Eternity
By the Atheistical Epicurean Philosophy of Albion's Tree.
Such are the Feminine & Masculine when separated from Man.
They call the Rocks Parents of Men, & adore the frowning Chaos,
Dancing around in howling pain, clothed in the bloody Veil,
Hiding Albion's Sons within the Veil, closing Jerusalem's
Sons without, to feed with their Souls the Spectres of Albion,
Ashamed to give Love openly to the piteous & merciful Man,
Counting him an imbecile mockery, but the Warrior   20
They adore & his revenge cherish with the blood of the Innocent.
They drink up Dan & Gad to feed with milk Skofeld & Kotope;
They strip off Joseph's Coat & dip it in the blood of battle.

Tirzah sits weeping to hear the shrieks of the dying: her Knife
Of flint is in her hand: she passes it over the howling Victim.   25
The Daughters Weave their Work in loud cries over the Rock
Of Horeb, still eyeing Albion's Cliffs eagerly siezing & twisting
The threads of Vala & Jerusalem running from mountain to
     mountain
Over the whole Earth: loud the Warriors rage in Beth Peor
Beneath the iron whips of their Captains & consecrated banners.
Loud the Sun & Moon rage in the conflict: loud the Stars   31
Shout in the night of battle, & their spears grow to their hands
With blood, weaving the deaths of the Mighty into a Tabernacle
For Rahab & Tirzah, till the Great Polypus of Generation covered
     the Earth.

In Verulam the Polypus's Head, winding around his bulk   35
Thro' Rochester and Chichester & Exeter & Salisbury
To Bristol, & his Heart beat strong on Salisbury Plain
Shooting out Fibres round the Earth thro' Gaul & Italy
And Greece & along the Sea of Rephaim into Judea
To Sodom & Gomorrha: thence to India, China & Japan.   40

The Twelve Daughters in Rahab & Tirzah have circumscrib'd
     the Brain
Beneath & pierced it thro' the midst with a golden pin.
Blood hath stain'd her fair side beneath her bosom.

" O thou poor Human Form! " said she. " O thou poor child
of woe!
Why wilt thou wander away from Tirzah? why me compel to
bind thee?
If thou dost go away from me I shall consume upon these Rocks.
These fibres of thine eyes that used to beam in distant heavens
Away from me, I have bound down with a hot iron.   48
These nostrils that expanded with delight in morning skies
I have bent downward with lead melted in my roaring furnaces
Of affliction, of love, of sweet despair, of torment unendurable.
My soul is seven furnaces; incessant roars the bellows
Upon my terribly flaming heart, the molten metal runs
In channels thro' my fiery limbs. O love! O pity! O fear!
O pain! O the pangs, the bitter pangs of love forsaken!   55
Ephraim was a wilderness of joy where all my wild beasts ran.
The River Kanah wander'd by my sweet Manasseh's side
To see the boy spring into heavens sounding from my sight!
Go Noah, fetch the girdle of strong brass, heat it red-hot,
Press it around the loins of this ever expanding cruelty.   60
Shriek not so my only love. I refuse thy joys: I drink
Thy shrieks because Hand & Hyle are cruel & obdurate to me.
[68]
" O Skofield, why art thou cruel? Lo, Joseph is thine! to make
You One, to weave you both in the same mantle of skin.
Bind him down, Sisters, bind him down on Ebal, Mount or cursing.
Malah, come forth from Lebanon, & Hoglah, from Mount Sinai:
Come, circumscribe this tongue of sweets, & with a screw of iron
Fasten this ear into the rock, Milcah, the task is thine.   6
Weep not so, Sisters, weep not so: our life depends on this,
Or mercy & truth are fled away from Shechem & Mount Gilead,
Unless my beloved is bound upon the Stems of Vegetation."

And thus the Warriors cry, in the hot day of Victory, in Songs:

" Look! the beautiful Daughter of Albion sits naked upon the
Stone,
Her panting Victim beside her: her heart is drunk with blood
Tho' her brain is not drunk with wine: she goes forth from Albion
In pride of beauty, in cruelty of holiness, in the brightness   14
Of her tabernacle & her ark & secret place: the beautiful Daughter
Of Albion delights the eyes of the Kings: their hearts & the
Hearts of their Warriors glow hot before Thor & Friga. O Molech!
O Chemosh! O Bacchus! O Venus! O Double God of Generation!
The Heavens are cut like a mantle around from the Cliffs of Albion
Across Europe, across Africa: in howlings & deadly War,   20
A sheet & veil & curtain of blood is let down from Heaven
Across the hills of Ephraim & down Mount Olivet to
The Valley of the Jebusite. Molech rejoices in heaven,

He sees the Twelve Daughters naked upon the Twelve Stones
Themselves condensing to rocks & into the Ribs of a Man. 25
Lo, they shoot forth in tender Nerves across Europe & Asia.
Lo, they rest upon the Tribes, where their panting Victims lie.
Molech rushes into the Kings, in love to the beautiful Daughters,
But they frown & delight in cruelty, refusing all other joy. 29
Bring your Offerings, your first begotten, pamper'd with milk &
blood,
Your first born of seven years old, be they Males or Females,
To the beautiful Daughters of Albion! they sport before the Kings
Clothed in the skin of the Victim! blood, human blood is the life
And delightful food of the Warrior; the well fed Warrior's flesh
Of him who is slain in War fills the Valleys of Ephraim with 35
Breeding Women walking in pride & bringing forth under green
trees
With pleasure, without pain, for their food is blood of the Captive.
Molech rejoices thro' the Land from Havilah to Shur: he rejoices
In moral law & its severe penalties: loud Shaddai & Jehovah
Thunder above, when they see the Twelve panting Victims 40
On the Twelve Stones of Power, & the beautiful Daughters of
Albion:
' If you dare rend their Veil with your spear, you are healed of
Love.'
From the Hills of Camberwell & Wimbledon, from the Valleys
Of Walton & Esher, from Stone-henge & from Malden's Cove,
Jerusalem's Pillars fall in the rendings of fierce War 45
Over France & Germany, upon the Rhine & Danube.
Reuben & Benjamin flee: they hide in the Valley of Rephaim.
Why trembles the Warrior's limbs when he beholds thy beauty
Spotted with Victims' blood, by the fires of thy secret tabernacle
And thy ark & holy place? at thy frowns, at thy dire revenge, 50
Smitten as Uzzah of hold, his armour is soften'd, his spear
And sword faint in his hand from Albion across Great Tartary.
O beautiful Daughter of Albion, cruelty is thy delight.
O Virgin of terrible eyes who dwellest by Valleys of springs 54
Beneath the Mountains of Lebanon in the City of Rehob in
Hamath,
Taught to touch the harp, to dance in the Circle of Warriors
Before the Kings of Canaan, to cut the flesh from the Victim,
To roast the flesh in fire, to examine the Infant's limbs
In cruelties of holiness, to refuse the joys of love, to bring 59
The Spies from Egypt, to raise jealousy in the bosoms of the
Twelve
Kings of Canaan, then to let the Spies depart to Meribah Kadesh,
To the place of the Amalekite: I am drunk with unsatiated love,
I must rush again to War, for the Virgin has frown'd & refus'd.
Sometimes I curse & sometimes bless thy fascinating beauty. 64
Once Man was occupied in intellectual pleasures & energies,

But now my Soul is harrow'd with grief & fear & love & desire,
And now I hate & now I love, & Intellect is no more.
There is no time for any thing but the torments of love & desire.
The Feminine & Masculine Shadows, soft, mild & ever varying
In beauty, are Shadows now no more, but Rocks in Horeb.''   70

[69]
Then all the Males conjoined into One Male, & every one
Became a ravening eating Cancer growing in the Female,
A Polypus of Roots of Reasoning, Doubt, Despair & Death,
Going forth & returning from Albion's Rocks to Canaan,
Devouring Jerusalem from every Nation of the Earth.   5

Envying stood the enormous Form, at variance with Itself
In all its Members, in eternal torment of love & jealousy,
Driv'n forth by Los time after time from Albion's cliffy shore,
Drawing the free loves of Jerusalem into infernal bondage
That they might be born in contentions of Chastity & in   10
Deadly Hate between Leah & Rachel, Daughters of Deceit &
     Fraud,
Bearing the Images of various Species of Contention
And Jealousy & Abhorrence & Revenge & deadly Murder,
Till they refuse liberty to the Male, & not like Beulah
Where every Female delights to give her maiden to her husband:
The Female searches sea & land for gratifications to the   16
Male Genius, who in return clothes her in gems & gold
And feeds her with the food of Eden; hence all her beauty beams.
She Creates at her will a little moony night & silence
With Spaces of sweet gardens & a tent of elegant beauty,   20
Closed in by a sandy desart & a night of stars shining
And a little tender moon & hovering angels on the wing.
And the Male gives a Time & Revolution to her Space
Till the time of love is passed in ever varying delights.
For All Things Exist in the Human Imagination,   25
And thence in Beulah they are stolen by secret amorous theft
Till they have had Punishment enough to make them commit
     Crimes.
Hence rose the Tabernacle in the Wilderness & all its Offerings,
From Male & Female Loves in Beulah & their Jealousies;
But no one can consummate Female bliss in Los's World without
Becoming a Generated Mortal, a Vegetating Death.   31

And now the Spectres of the Dead awake in Beulah; all
The Jealousies become Murderous, uniting together in Rahab
A Religion of Chastity, forming a Commerce to sell Loves,
With Moral Law an Equal Balance not going down with decision.
Therefore the Male severe & cruel, fill'd with stern Revenge, 36
Mutual Hate returns & mutual Deceit & mutual Fear.

Hence the Infernal Veil grows in the disobedient Female,
Which Jesus rends & the whole Druid Law removes away
From the Inner Sanctuary, a False Holiness hid within the Center.
For the Sanctuary of Eden is in the Camp, in the Outline,   41
In the Circumference, & every Minute Particular is Holy:
Embraces are Cominglings from the Head even to the Feet,
And not a pompous High Priest entering by a Secret Place.

Jerusalem pined in her inmost soul over Wandering Reuben   45
As she slept in Beulah's Night, hid by the Daughters of Beulah.

[70]
And this the form of mighty Hand sitting on Albion's cliffs
Before the face of Albion, a mighty threat'ning Form:

His bosom wide & shoulders huge, overspreading wondrous,
Bear Three strong sinewy Necks & Three awful & terrible Heads,
Three Brains, in contradictory council brooding incessantly,   5
Neither daring to put in act its councils, fearing each-other,
Therefore rejecting Ideas as nothing & holding all Wisdom
To consist in the agreements & disagreements of Ideas,
Plotting to devour Albion's Body of Humanity & Love.   9

Such Form the aggregate of the Twelve Sons of Albion took, &
    such
Their appearance when combin'd; but often by birth-pangs &
    loud groans
They divide to Twelve; the key-bones & the chest dividing in pain
Disclose a hideous orifice; thence issuing, the Giant-brood
Arise, as the smoke of the furnace, shaking the rocks from sea
    to sea,
And there they combine into Three Forms named Bacon &
    Newton & Locke
In the Oak Groves of Albion which overspread all the Earth.   16

Imputing Sin & Righteousness to Individuals, Rahab
Sat, deep within him hid, his Feminine Power unreveal'd,
Brooding Abstract Philosophy to destroy Imagination, the Divine-
Humanity: A Three-fold Wonder, feminine, most beautiful,
    Three-fold
Each within other. On her white marble & even Neck, her Heart,
Inorb'd and bonified, with locks of shadowing modesty, shining
Over her beautiful Female features soft flourishing in beauty,
Beams mild, all love and all perfection, that when the lips
Recieve a kiss from Gods or Men, a threefold kiss returns   25
From the press'd loveliness; so her whole immortal form three-
    fold,
Three-fold embrace returns, consuming lives of Gods & Men,

In fires of beauty melting them as gold & silver in the furnace.
Her Brain enlabyrinths the whole heaven of her bosom & loins
To put in act what her Heart wills. O who can withstand her
    power!
Her name is Vala in Eternity: in Time her name is Rahab.   31

The Starry Heavens all were fled from the mighty limbs of Albion.
[71]
And above Albion's Land was seen the Heavenly Canaan
As the Substance is to the Shadow, and above Albion's Twelve
    Sons
Were seen Jerusalem's Sons and all the Twelve Tribes spreading
Over Albion. As the Soul is to the Body, so Jerusalem's Sons   4
Are to the Sons of Albion, and Jerusalem is Albion's Emanation.

What is Above is Within, for every-thing in Eternity is trans-
    lucent:
The Circumference is Within, Without is formed the Selfish
    Center,
And the Circumference still expands going forward to Eternity,
And the Center has Eternal States; these States we now explore.

And these the Names of Albion's Twelve Sons & of his Twelve
    Daughters   10
With their Districts: Hand dwelt in Selsey & had Sussex & Surrey
And Kent & Middlesex, all their Rivers & their Hills of flocks &
    herds,
Their Villages, Towns, Cities, Sea-Ports, Temples, sublime
    Cathedrals,
All were his Friends, & their Sons & Daughters intermarry in
    Beulah;
For all are Men in Eternity, Rivers, Mountains, Cities, Villages, 15
All are Human, & when you enter into their Bosoms you walk
In Heavens & Earths, as in your own Bosom you bear your Heaven
And Earth; & all you behold, tho' it appears Without, it is Within,
In your Imagination, of which this World of Mortality is but a
    Shadow.

Hyle dwelt in Winchester, comprehending Hants, Dorset, Devon,
    Cornwall,   20
Their Villages, Cities, Sea Ports, their Corn fields & Gardens
    spacious,
Palaces, Rivers & Mountains; and between Hand & Hyle arose
Gwendolen & Cambel who is Boadicea: they go abroad & return
Like lovely beams of light from the mingled affections of the
    Brothers.
The Inhabitants of the whole Earth rejoice in their beautiful
    light.   25

Coban dwelt in Bath: Somerset, Wiltshire, Gloucestershire
Obey'd his awful voice: Ignoge is his lovely Emanation;
She adjoin'd with Gwantoke's Children; soon lovely Cordella
    arose;
Gwantoke forgave & joy'd over South Wales & all its Mountains.

Peachey had North Wales, Shropshire, Cheshire & the Isle of
    Man;   30
His Emanation is Mehetabel, terrible & lovely upon the Mountains.

Brertun had Yorkshire, Durham, Westmoreland, & his Emanation
Is Ragan; she adjoin'd to Slade, & produced Gonorill far beaming.

Slade had Lincoln, Stafford, Derby, Nottingham, & his lovely
Emanation, Gonorill, rejoices over hills & rocks & woods & rivers.

Huttn had Warwick, Northampton, Bedford, Buckingham,
Leicester & Berkshire, & his Emanation is Gwinefred beautiful.

Skofeld had Ely, Rutland, Cambridge, Huntingdon, Norfolk,
Suffolk, Hartford & Essex, & his Emanation is Gwinevera
Beautiful, she beams towards the east all kinds of precious stones
And pearl, with instruments of music in holy Jerusalem.   41

Kox had Oxford, Warwick, Wilts; his Emanation is Estrild;
Join'd with Cordella she shines southward over the Atlantic.

Kotope had Hereford, Stafford, Worcester, & his Emanation
Is Sabrina; join'd with Mehetabel she shines west over America.

Bowen had all Scotland, the Isles, Northumberland & Cumberland;
His Emanation is Conwenna; she shines a triple form
Over the north with pearly beams gorgeous & terrible.
Jerusalem & Vala rejoice in Bowen & Conwenna.   49

But the Four Sons of Jerusalem that never were Generated
Are Rintrah and Palamabron and Theotormon and Bromion. They
Dwell over the Four Provinces of Ireland in heavenly light,
The Four Universities of Scotland, & in Oxford & Cambridge &
    Winchester.

But now Albion is darkened & Jerusalem lies in ruins
Above the Mountains of Albion, above the head of Los.   55

And Los shouted with ceaseless shoutings, & his tears poured down
His immortal cheeks, rearing his hands to heaven for aid Divine!
But he spoke not to Albion, fearing lest Albion should turn his
    Back

Against the Divine Vision & fall over the Precipice of Eternal
    Death;
But he receded before Albion & before Vala weaving the Veil
With the iron shuttle of War among the rooted Oaks of Albion,
Weeping & shouting to the Lord day & night; and his Children
Wept round him as a flock silent Seven Days of Eternity.   63

[72]
And the Thirty-two Counties of the Four Provinces of Ireland
Are thus divided: The Four Counties are in the Four Camps,
Munster South in Reuben's Gate, Connaut West in Joseph's Gate,
Ulster North in Dan's Gate, Leinster East in Judah's Gate;

For Albion in Eternity has Sixteen Gates among his Pillars,   5
But the Four towards the West were Walled up, & the Twelve
That front the Four other Points were turned Four Square
By Los for Jerusalem's sake & called the Gates of Jerusalem,
Because Twelve Sons of Jerusalem fled successive thro' the Gates.
But the Four Sons of Jerusalem who fled not but remain'd,   10
Are Rintrah & Palamabron & Theotormon & Bromion,
The Four that remain with Los to guard the Western Wall;
And these Four remain to guard the Four Walls of Jerusalem
Whose foundations remain in the Thirty-two Counties of Ireland
And in Twelve Counties of Wales & in the Forty Counties   15
Of England & in the Thirty-six Counties of Scotland.

And the names of the Thirty-two Counties of Ireland are these:
Under Judah & Issachar & Zebulun are Lowth, Longford,
Eastmeath, Westmeath, Dublin, Kildare, King's County,
Queen's County, Wicklow, Catherloh, Wexford, Kilkenny.   20
And those under Reuben & Simeon & Levi are these:
Waterford, Tipperary, Cork, Limerick, Kerry, Clare.
And those under Ephraim, Manasseh & Benjamin are these:
Galway, Roscommon, Mayo, Sligo, Leitrim.
And those under Dan, Asher & Napthali are these: 25
Donnegal, Antrim, Tyrone, Fermanagh, Armagh, Londonderry,
Down, Managhan, Cavan. These are the Land of Erin.

All these Center in London & in Golgonooza, from whence
They are Created continually, East & West & North & South,
And from them are Created all the Nations of the Earth,   30
Europe & Asia & Africa & America, in fury Fourfold.

And Thirty-two the Nations to dwell in Jerusalem's Gates.
O Come ye Nations! Come ye People! Come up to Jerusalem!
Return Jerusalem, & dwell together as of old! Return,
Return, O Albion! let Jerusalem overspread all Nations   35

As in the times of old! O Albion awake! Reuben wanders,
The Nations wait for Jerusalem, they look up for the Bride.

France, Spain, Italy, Germany, Poland, Russia, Sweden, Turkey,
Arabia, Palestine, Persia, Hindostan, China, Tartary, Siberia,
Egypt, Lybia, Ethiopia, Guinea, Caffraria, Negroland, Morocco,
Congo, Zaara, Canada, Greenland, Carolina, Mexico,   41
Peru, Patagonia, Amazonia, Brazil: Thirty-two Nations,
And under these Thirty-two Classes of Islands in the Ocean
All the Nations, Peoples & Tongues throughout all the Earth.

And the Four Gates of Los surround the Universe Within and
Without; & whatever is visible in the Vegetable Earth, the same
Is visible in the Mundane Shell, revers'd in mountain & vale.
And a Son of Eden was set over each Daughter of Beulah to guard
In Albion's Tomb the wondrous Creation, & the Four-fold Gate
Towards Beulah is to the South. Fenelon, Guion, Teresa,   50
Whitefield & Hervey guard that Gate, with all the gentle Souls
Who guide the great Wine-press of Love. Four precious Stones
       that Gate.[1]

[73]
Such are Cathedron's golden Halls in the City of Golgonooza.

And Los's Furnaces howl loud, living, self-moving, lamenting
With fury & despair, & they stretch from South to North
Thro' all the Four Points. Lo! the Labourers at the Furnaces,
Rintrah & Palamabron, Theotormon & Bromion, loud lab'ring
With the innumerable multitudes of Golgonooza round the Anvils
Of Death. But how they came forth from the Furnaces, & how long
Vast & severe the anguish e'er they knew their Father, were
Long to tell; & of the iron rollers, golden axle-trees & yokes
Of brass, iron chains & braces, & the gold, silver & brass,   10
Mingled or separate, for swords, arrows, cannons, mortars,
The terrible ball, the wedge, the loud sounding hammer of
       destruction,
The sounding flail to thresh, the winnow to winnow kingdoms,
The water wheel & mill of many innumerable wheels resistless,
Over the Four fold Monarchy from Earth to the Mundane Shell: 15

Perusing Albion's Tomb in the starry characters of Og & Anak,
To Create the lion & wolf, the bear, the tyger & ounce,

---

[1] In the middle of Plate 72 is an illustration showing two angels weeping
over a world which is inscribed clockwise, " Continually Building, Continu-
ally Decaying because of Love & Jealousy."
    At the foot of the plate, beneath a drawing of a serpent, are the words,
written in reverse writing, " Women, the comforters of Men, become the
Tormenters & Punishers."

To Create the wooly lamb & downy fowl & scaly serpent,
The summer & winter, day & night, the sun & moon & stars,
The tree, the plant, the flower, the rock, the stone, the metal   20
Of Vegetatiye Nature by their hard restricting condensations.

Where Luvah's World of Opakeness grew to a period, It
Became a Limit, a Rocky hardness without form & void,
Accumulating without end: here Los, who is of the Elohim,
Opens the Furnaces of affliction in the Emanation,   25
Fixing the Sexual into an ever-prolific Generation,
Naming the Limit of Opakeness, Satan, & the Limit of Contrac-
        tion,
Adam, who is Peleg & Joktan, & Esau & Jacob, & Saul & David.

Voltaire insinuates that these Limits are the cruel work of God,
Mocking the Remover of Limits & the Resurrection of the Dead,
Setting up Kings in wrath, in holiness of Natural Religion: 31
Which Los with his mighty Hammer demolishes time on time
In miracles & wonders in the Four-fold Desart of Albion:
Permanently Creating, to be in Time Reveal'd & Demolish'd,
Satan, Cain, Tubal, Nimrod, Pharoh, Priam, Bladud, Belin,
Arthur, Alfred, the Norman Conqueror, Richard, John,   36
And all the Kings & Nobles of the Earth & all their Glories:
These are Created by Rahab & Tirzah in Ulro; but around
These, to preserve them from Eternal Death, Los Creates
Adam, Noah, Abraham, Moses, Samuel, David, Ezekiel,   40
Dissipating the rocky forms of Death by his thunderous Hammer.
As the Pilgrim passes, while the Country permanent remains,
So Men pass on, but States remain permanent for ever.

The Spectres of the Dead howl round the porches of Los
In the terrible Family feuds of Albion's cities & villages,   45
To devour the Body of Albion, hung'ring & thirsting & rav'ning.
The Sons of Los clothe them & feed, & provide houses & gardens,
And every Human Vegetated Form in its inward recesses
Is a house of pleasantness & a garden of delight Built by the
Sons & Daughters of Los in Bowlahoola & in Cathedron.   50

From London to York & Edinburgh the Furnaces rage terrible
Primrose Hill is the mouth of the Furnace & the Iron Door.

[74]
The Four Zoas clouded rage. Urizen stood by Albion
With Rintrah and Palamabron and Theotormon and Bromion:
These Four are Verulam & London & York & Edinburgh.
And the Four Zoas are Urizen & Luvah & Tharmas & Urthona,
In opposition deadly, and their Wheels in poisonous   5
And deadly stupor turn'd against each other loud & fierce,

Entering into the Reasoning Power, forsaking Imagination,
They became Spectres, & their Human Bodies were reposed
In Beulah by the Daughters of Beulah with tears & lamentations.

The Spectre is the Reasoning Power in Man, & when separated
From Imagination and closing itself as in steel in a Ratio   11
Of the Things of Memory, It thence frames Laws & Moralities
To destroy Imagination, the Divine Body, by Martyrdoms & Wars.

Teach me, O Holy Spirit, the Testimony of Jesus! let me
Comprehend wonderous things out of the Divine Law.   15
I behold Babylon in the opening Streets of London. I behold
Jerusalem in ruins wandering about from house to house.
This I behold: the shudderings of death attend my steps.
I walk up and down in Six Thousand Years, their Events are
    present before me,
To tell how Los in grief & anger, whirling round his Hammer on
    high,   20
Drave the Sons & Daughters of Albion from their ancient moun-
    tains.
They became the Twelve Gods of Asia Opposing the Divine Vision.

The Sons of Albion are Twelve, the Sons of Jerusalem Sixteen.
I tell how Albion's Sons, by Harmonies of Concords & Discords
Opposed to Melody, and by Lights & Shades opposed to Outline,
And by Abstraction opposed to the Visions of Imagination,   26
By cruel Laws, divided Sixteen into Twelve Divisions:
How Hyle roof'd Los in Albion's Cliffs by the Affections rent
Asunder & opposed to Thought, to draw Jerusalem's Sons
Into the Vortex of his Wheels; therefore Hyle is called Gog,   30
Age after age drawing them away towards Babylon,
Babylon, the Rational Morality, deluding to death the little ones
In strong temptations of stolen beauty. I tell how Reuben slept
On London Stone, & the Daughters of Albion ran around admiring
His awful beauty; with Moral Virtue, the fair deciever, offspring
Of Good & Evil, they divided him in love upon the Thames & sent
Him over Europe, in streams of gore, out of Cathedron's Looms:
How Los drave them from Albion & they became Daughters of
    Canaan;
Hence Albion was call'd the Canaanite & all his Giant Sons.   39
Hence is my Theme. O Lord my Saviour, open thou the Gates
And I will lead forth thy Words, telling how the Daughters
Cut the Fibres of Reuben, how he roll'd apart & took Root
In Bashan: terror-struck Albion's Sons look toward Bashan.
They have divided Simeon: he also roll'd apart in blood   44
Over the Nations till he took Root beneath the shining Looms
Of Albion's Daughters in Philistia by the side of Amalek.
They have divided Levi: he hath shot out into Forty eight Roots

Over the Land of Canaan; they have divided Judah:
He hath took Root in Hebron, in the Land of Hand & Hyle.
Dan, Napthali, Gad, Asher, Issachar, Zebulun roll apart   50
From all the Nations of the Earth to dissipate into Non Entity.

I see a Feminine Form arise from the Four terrible Zoas,
Beautiful but terrible, struggling to take a form of beauty,
Rooted in Shechem: this is Dinah, the youthful form of Erin.
The Wound I see in South Molton Street & Stratford place,   55
Whence Joseph & Benjamin roll'd apart away from the Nations.
In vain they roll'd apart: they are fix'd into the Land of Cabul.
[75]
And Rahab, Babylon the Great, hath destroyed Jerusalem.
Bath stood upon the Severn with Merlin & Bladud & Arthur,
The Cup of Rahab in his hand, her Poisons Twenty-seven-fold.

And all her Twenty-seven Heavens, now hid & now reveal'd,
Appear in strong delusive light of Time & Space, drawn out   5
In shadowy pomp, by the Eternal Prophet created evermore.
For Los in Six Thousand Years walks up & down continually
That not one Moment of Time be lost, & every revolution
Of Space he makes permanent in Bowlahoola & Cathedron.

And these the names of the Twenty-seven Heavens & their
          Churches:
Adam, Seth, Enos, Cainan, Mahalaleel, Jared, Enoch,   11
Methuselah, Lamech: these are the Giants mighty, Hermaphro-
          ditic.
Noah, Shem, Arphaxad, Cainan the Second, Salah, Heber,
Peleg, Reu, Serug, Nahor, Terah: these are the Female Males,
A Male within a Female hid as in an Ark & Curtains.   15
Abraham, Moses, Solomon, Paul, Constantine, Charlemaine,
Luther: these Seven are the Male Females, the Dragon Forms,
The Female hid within a Male; thus Rahab is reveal'd,
Mystery, Babylon the Great, the Abomination of Desolation,
Religion hid in War, a Dragon red & hidden Harlot.   20
But Jesus, breaking thro' the Central Zones of Death & Hell,
Opens Eternity in Time & Space, triumphant in Mercy.

Thus are the Heavens form'd by Los within the Mundane Shell.
And where Luther ends Adam begins again in Eternal Circle
To awake the Prisoners of Death, to bring Albion again   25
With Luvah into light eternal in his eternal day.

But now the Starry Heavens are fled from the mighty limbs of
          Albion.[1]

---

[1] The chapter concludes with a full-page illustration showing Jesus cruci-
fied on the Tree of Mystery. In the dark night, light radiates from the
Saviour: Albion stands beneath with head uplifted and arms outstretched.

[77]   To The Christians

Devils are   I give you the end of a golden string,
False Religions.   Only wind it into a ball,
    " Saul, Saul,   It will lead you in at Heaven's gate
Why persecutest thou me? "   Built in Jerusalem's wall.

WE are told to abstain from fleshly desires that we may lose no
time from the Work of the Lord. Every moment lost is a moment
that cannot be redeemed; every pleasure that intermingles with
the duty of our station is a folly unredeemable, & is planted like
the seed of a wild flower among our wheat. All the tortures of
repentance are tortures of self-reproach on account of our leaving
the Divine Harvest to the Enemy, the struggles of intanglement
with incoherent roots. I know of no other Christianity and of
no other Gospel than the liberty both of body & mind to exercise
the Divine Arts of Imagination, Imagination, the real & eternal
World of which this Vegetable Universe is but a faint shadow,
& in which we shall live in our Eternal or Imaginative Bodies
when these Vegetable Mortal Bodies are no more. The Apostles
knew of no other Gospel. What were all their spiritual gifts?
What is the Divine Spirit? is the Holy Ghost any other than an
Intellectual Fountain? What is the Harvest of the Gospel & its
Labours? What is that Talent which it is a curse to hide? What
are the Treasures of Heaven which we are to lay up for ourselves,
are they any other than Mental Studies & Performances? What
are all the Gifts of the Gospel, are they not all Mental Gifts? Is
God a Spirit who must be worshipped in Spirit & in Truth, and
are not the Gifts of the Spirit Every-thing to Man? O ye Religious,
discountenance every one among you who shall pretend to despise
Art & Science! I call upon you in the Name of Jesus! What is the
Life of Man but Art & Science? is it Meat & Drink? is not the
Body more than Raiment? What is Mortality but the things
relating to the Body which Dies? What is Immortality but the
things relating to the Spirit which Lives Eternally? What is the
Joy of Heaven but Improvement in the things of the Spirit?
What are the Pains of Hell but Ignorance, Bodily Lust, Idleness
& devastation of the things of the Spirit? Answer this to your-
selves, & expel from among you those who pretend to despise
the labours of Art & Science, which alone are the labours of the

Gospel. Is not this plain & manifest to the thought? Can you
think at all & not pronounce heartily That to Labour in Know-
ledge is to Build up Jerusalem, and to Despise Knowledge is to
Despise Jerusalem & her Builders. And remember: He who
despises & mocks a Mental Gift in another, calling it pride &
selfishness & sin, mocks Jesus the giver of every Mental Gift,
which always appear to the ignorance-loving Hypocrite as Sins;
but that which is a Sin in the sight of cruel Man is not so in the
sight of our kind God. Let every Christian, as much as in him
lies, engage himself openly & publicly before all the World in
some Mental pursuit for the Building up of Jerusalem.

<pre>
            I stood among my valleys of the south
            And saw a flame of fire, even as a Wheel
            Of fire surrounding all the heavens: it went
            From west to east, against the current of
            Creation, and devour'd all things in its loud   5
            Fury & thundering course round heaven & earth.
            By it the Sun was roll'd into an orb,
            By it the Moon faded into a globe
            Travelling thro' the night; for, from its dire
            And restless fury, Man himself shrunk up   10
            Into a little root a fathom long.
            And I asked a Watcher & a Holy-One
            Its Name; he answer'd: " It is the Wheel of Religion."
            I wept & said: " Is this the law of Jesus,
            This terrible devouring sword turning every way? "   15
            He answer'd: " Jesus died because he strove
            Against the current of this Wheel; its Name
            Is Caiaphas, the dark Preacher of Death,
            Of sin, of sorrow & of punishment:
            Opposing Nature! It is Natural Religion;   20
            But Jesus is the bright Preacher of Life
            Creating Nature from this fiery Law
            By self-denial & forgiveness of Sin.
            Go therefore, cast out devils in Christ's name,
            Heal thou the sick of spiritual disease,   25
            Pity the evil, for thou art not sent
            To smite with terror & with punishments
            Those that are sick, like to the Pharisees
            Crucifying & encompassing sea & land
            For proselytes to tyranny & wrath;   30
            But to the Publicans & Harlots go,
            Teach them True Happiness, but let no curse
            Go forth out of thy mouth to blight their peace;
            For Hell is open'd to Heaven: thine eyes beheld
            The dungeons burst & the Prisoners set free."   35
</pre>

England! awake! awake! awake!
   Jerusalem thy Sister calls!
Why wilt thou sleep the sleep of death?
   And close her from thy ancient walls.

Thy hills & valleys felt her feet
   Gently upon their bosoms move:
Thy gates beheld sweet Zion's ways:
   Then was a time of joy and love.

And now the time returns again:
   Our souls exult, & London's towers
Recieve the Lamb of God to dwell
   In England's green & pleasant bowers.

JERUSALEM, C. 4

THE Spectres of Albion's Twelve Sons revolve mightily
Over the Tomb & over the Body, rav'ning to devour
The Sleeping Humanity. Los with his mace of iron
Walks round; loud his threats, loud his blows fall
On the rocky Spectres, as the Potter breaks the potsherds,   5
Dashing in pieces Self-righteousnesses, driving them from Albion's
Cliffs, dividing them into Male & Female forms in the Furnaces
And on his Anvils; lest they destroy the Feminine Affections
They are broken. Loud howl the Spectres in his iron Furnace.

While Los laments at his dire labours, viewing Jerusalem   10
Sitting before his Furnaces clothed in sackcloth of hair,
Albion's Twelve Sons surround the Forty-two Gates of Erin
In terrible armour, raging against the Lamb & against Jerusalem,
Surrounding them with armies to destroy the Lamb of God.
They took their Mother Vala and they crown'd her with gold;
They nam'd her Rahab & gave her power over the Earth,   16
The Concave Earth round Golgonooza in Entuthon Benython,
Even to the stars exalting her Throne, to build beyond the Throne
Of God and the Lamb, to destroy the Lamb & usurp the Throne
     of God,
Drawing their Ulro Voidness round the Four-fold Humanity.

Naked Jerusalem lay before the Gates upon Mount Zion   21
The Hill of Giants, all her foundations levell'd with the dust,

Her Twelve Gates thrown down, her children carried into capti-
     vity,
Herself in chains; this from within was seen in a dismal night
Outside, unknown before in Beulah; & the twelve gates were fill'd
With blood, from Japan eastward to the Giants causway west 26
In Erin's Continent; and Jerusalem wept upon Euphrates' banks,
Disorganiz'd, an evanescent shade, scarce seen or heard among
Her children's Druid Temples, dropping with blood, wander'd
     weeping!
And thus her voice went forth in the darkness of Philisthea: 30

" My brother & my father are no more! God hath forsaken me.
The arrows of the Almighty pour upon me & my children.
I have sinned and am an outcast from the Divine Presence!

[79]
" My tents are fall'n! my pillars are in ruins! my children dash'd
Upon Egypt's iron floors & the marble pavements of Assyria.
I melt my soul in reasonings among the towers of Heshbon.
Mount Zion is become a cruel rock, & no more dew
Nor rain, no more the spring of the rock appears, but cold   5
Hard & obdurate are the furrows of the mountain of wine & oil:
The mountain of blessing is itself a curse & an astonishment.
The hills of Judea are fallen with me into the deepest hell.
Away from the Nations of the Earth & from the Cities of the
        Nations
I walk to Ephraim. I seek for Shiloh. I walk like a lost sheep
Among precipices of despair: in Goshen I seek for light   11
In vain, and in Gilead for a physician and a comforter.
Goshen hath follow'd Philistea. Gilead hath join'd with Og.
They are become narrow places in a little and dark land,
How distant far from Albion! his hills & his valleys no more   15
Recieve the feet of Jerusalem: they have cast me quite away,
And Albion is himself shrunk to a narrow rock in the midst of
        the sea!
The plains of Sussex & Surrey, their hills of flocks & herds
No more seek to Jerusalem nor to the sound of my Holy-ones.
The Fifty-two Counties of England are harden'd against me   20
As if I was not their Mother; they despise me & cast me out.
London cover'd the whole Earth: England encompass'd the
        Nations,
And all the Nations of the Earth were seen in the Cities of Albion.
My pillars reach'd from sea to sea. London beheld me come
From my east & from my west; he blessed me and gave   25
His children to my breasts, his sons & daughters to my knees.
His aged parents sought me out in every city & village;
They discern'd my countenance with joy, they shew'd me to their
        sons,
Saying, ' Lo Jerusalem is here! she sitteth in our secret chambers.
Levi and Judah & Issachar, Ephram, Manasseh, Gad and Dan
Are seen in our hills & valleys: they keep our flocks & herds: 31
They watch them in the night, and the Lamb of God appears
        among us.'
The river Severn stay'd his course at my command:
Thames poured his waters into my basons and baths:
Medway mingled with Kishon: Thames reciev'd the heavenly
        Jordan.
Albion gave me to the whole Earth to walk up & down, to pour 36
Joy upon every mountain, to teach songs to the shepherd &
        plowman:
I taught the ships of the sea to sing the songs of Zion.
Italy saw me in sublime astonishment: France was wholly mine
As my garden & as my secret bath: Spain was my heavenly couch,

I slept in his golden hills; the Lamb of God met me there,   41
There we walked as in our secret chamber among our little ones,
They looked upon our loves with joy, they beheld our secret joys
With holy raptures of adoration, rap'd sublime in the Visions of
      God.
Germany, Poland & the North wooed my footsteps, they found 45
My gates in all their mountains & my curtains in all their vales;
The furniture of their houses was the furniture of my chamber.
Turkey & Grecia saw my instruments of music; they arose,
They siez'd the harp, the flute, the mellow horn of Jerusalem's joy;
They sounded thanksgivings in my courts. Egypt & Lybia heard,
The swarthy sons of Ethiopia stood round the Lamb of God   51
Enquiring for Jerusalem: he led them up my steps to my altar.
And thou, America! I once beheld thee, but now behold no more
Thy golden mountains where my Cherubim & Seraphim rejoic'd
Together among my little-ones. But now my Altars run with blood,
My fires are corrupt, my incense is a cloudy pestilence   56
Of seven diseases! Once a continual cloud of salvation rose
From all my myriads, once the Four-fold World rejoic'd among
The pillars of Jerusalem between my winged Cherubim;
But now I am clos'd out from them in the narrow passages   60
Of the valleys of destruction into a dark land of pitch & bitumen,
From Albion's Tomb afar and from the four-fold wonders of God
Shrunk to a narrow doleful form in the dark land of Cabul.
There is Reuben & Gad & Joseph & Judah & Levi, clos'd up
In narrow vales. I walk & count the bones of my beloveds   65
Along the Valley of Destruction, among these Druid Temples
Which overspread all the Earth in patriarchal pomp & cruel pride.
Tell me, O Vala, thy purposes; tell me wherefore thy shuttles
Drop with the gore of the slain, why Euphrates is red with blood,
Wherefore in dreadful majesty & beauty outside appears   70
Thy Masculine from thy Feminine, hardening against the heavens
To devour the Human! Why dost thou weep upon the wind among
These cruel Druid Temples? O Vala! Humanity is far above
Sexual organization & the Visions of the Night of Beulah   74
Where Sexes wander in dreams of bliss among the Emanations,
Where the Masculine & Feminine are nurs'd into Youth & Maiden
By the tears & smiles of Beulah's Daughters till the time of Sleep
      is past.
Wherefore then do you realize these nets of beauty & delusion
In open day to draw the souls of the Dead into the light,
Till Albion is shut out from every Nation under Heaven?   80
[80]
" Encompass'd by the frozen Net and by the rooted Tree
I walk weeping in pangs of a Mother's torment for her Children.
I walk in affliction! I am a worm and no living soul!
A worm going to eternal torment, rais'd up in a night
To an eternal night of pain, lost! lost! lost! for ever!"   5

Beside her Vala howl'd upon the winds in pride of beauty,
Lamenting among the timbrels of the Warriors, among the
    Captives
In cruel holiness, and her lamenting songs were from Arnon
And Jordan to Euphrates. Jerusalem follow'd, trembling,
Her children in captivity, listening to Vala's lamentation   10
In the thick cloud & darkness; & the voice went forth from
The cloud: " O rent in sunder from Jerusalem the Harlot daughter!
In an eternal condemnation, in fierce burning flames
Of torment unendurable! and if once a Delusion be found
Woman must perish & the Heavens of Heavens remain no more.

" My Father gave to me command to murder Albion   16
In unreviving Death: my Love, my Luvah, order'd me in night
To murder Albion, the King of Men; he fought in battles fierce,
He conquer'd Luvah, my beloved, he took me and my Father,
He slew them. I revived them to life in my warm bosom.   20
He saw them issue from my bosom: dark in Jealousy
He burn'd before me. Luvah fram'd the Knife & Luvah gave
The Knife into his daughter's hand; such thing was never known
Before in Albion's land, that one should die a death never to be
    reviv'd!
For, in our battles, we the Slain men view with pity and love,   25
We soon revive them in the secret of our tabernacles;
But I, Vala, Luvah's daughter, keep his body embalm'd in moral
    laws
With spices of sweet odours of lovely jealous stupefaction
Within my bosom, lest he arise to life & slay my Luvah.
Pity me then, O Lamb of God! O Jesus pity me!   30
Come into Luvah's Tents and seek not to revive the Dead! "

So sang she, and the Spindle turn'd furious as she sang.
The Children of Jerusalem, the Souls of those who sleep,
Were caught into the flax of her Distaff & in her Cloud
To weave Jerusalem a body according to her will,   35
A Dragon form on Zion Hill's most ancient promontory.

The Spindle turn'd in blood & fire: loud sound the trumpets
Of war: the cymbals play loud before the Captains
With Cambel & Gwendolen in dance and solemn song.
The Cloud of Rahab vibrating with the Daughters of Albion   40
Los saw terrified, melted with pity & divided in wrath
He sent them over the narrow seas in pity and love
Among the Four Forests of Albion which overspread all the Earth.
They go forth & return, swift as a flash of lightning,
Among the tribes of warriors, among the Stones of power;   45
Against Jerusalem they rage thro' all the Nations of Europe,
Thro' Italy & Grecia to Lebanon & Persia & India.

The Serpent Temples thro' the Earth, from the wide Plain of
  Salisbury
Resound with cries of Victims, shouts & songs & dying groans
And flames of dusky fire, to Amalek, Canaan and Moab.   50
And Rahab, like a dismal and indefinite hovering Cloud,
Refus'd to take a definite form; she hover'd over all the Earth
Calling the definite, sin, defacing every definite form
Invisible or Visible, stretch'd out in length or spread in breadth
Over the Temples, drinking groans of victims, weeping in pity
And joying in the pity, howling over Jerusalem's walls.   56

Hand slept on Skiddaw's top, drawn by the love of beautiful
Cambel, his bright beaming Counterpart, divided from him;
And her delusive light beam'd fierce above the Mountain,
Soft, invisible, drinking his sighs in sweet intoxication,   60
Drawing out fibre by fibre, returning to Albion's Tree
At night and in the morning to Skiddaw: she sent him over
Mountainous Wales into the Loom of Cathedron fibre by fibre.
He ran in tender nerves across Europe to Jerusalem's Shade
To weave Jerusalem a Body repugnant to the Lamb.   65

Hyle on East Moor in rocky Derbyshire rav'd to the Moon
For Gwendolen: she took up in bitter tears his anguish'd heart
That, apparent to all in Eternity, glows like the Sun in the breast:
She hid it in his ribs & back; she hid his tongue with teeth,
In terrible convulsions, pitying & gratified, drunk with pity,   70
Glowing with loveliness before him, becoming apparent
According to his changes; she roll'd his kidneys round
Into two irregular forms, and looking on Albion's dread Tree,
She wove two vessels of seed, beautiful as Skiddaw's snow,
Giving them bends of self interest & selfish natural virtue.   75
She hid them in his loins; raving he ran among the rocks,
Compell'd into a shape of Moral Virtue against the Lamb,
The invisible lovely one giving him a form according to
His Law, a form against the Lamb of God, oppos'd to Mercy,
And playing in the thunderous Loom in sweet intoxication,   80
Filling cups of silver & crystal with shrieks & cries, with groans
And dolorous sobs, the wine of lovers in the Wine-press of Luvah.

"O sister Cambel," said Gwendolen, as their long beaming light
Mingled above the Mountain, "what shall we do to keep   84
These awful forms in our soft bands distracted with trembling?
[81]
"I have mock'd those who refused cruelty, & I have admired
The cruel Warrior. I have refused to give love to Merlin the piteous.
He brings to me the Images of his Love & I reject in chastity
And turn them out into the streets for Harlots, to be food

To the stern Warrior. I am become perfect in beauty over my
    Warrior;
For Men are caught by Love, Woman is caught by Pride,   6
That Love may only be obtain'd in the passages of Death.
Let us look: let us examine: is the Cruel become an Infant,
Or is he still a cruel Warrior? look Sisters, look! O piteous!
I have destroy'd Wand'ring Reuben who strove to bind my Will.
I have strip'd off Joseph's beautiful integument for my Beloved,
The Cruel-one of Albion, to clothe him in gems of my Zone.
I have named him Jehovah of Hosts. Humanity is become
A weeping Infant in ruin'd lovely Jerusalem's folding Cloud.[1]   14
[82]
" I have heard Jerusalem's groans; from Vala's cries & lamenta-
    tions
I gather our eternal fate. Outcasts from life and love,
Unless we find a way to bind these awful Forms to our
Embrace, we shall perish annihilate, discover'd our Delusions.
Look! I have wrought without delusion. Look! I have wept,
And given soft milk mingled together with the spirits of flocks
Of lambs and doves, mingled together in cups and dishes   7
Of painted clay; the mighty Hyle is become a weeping infant;
Soon shall the Spectres of the Dead follow my weaving threads."

The Twelve Daughters of Albion attentive listen in secret shades,
On Cambridge and Oxford beaming soft, uniting with Rahab's
    cloud,
While Gwendolen spoke to Cambel, turning soft the spinning reel,
Or throwing the wing'd shuttle, or drawing the cords with softest
    songs.
The golden cords of the Looms animate beneath their touches soft
Along the Island white, among the Druid Temples, while Gwen-
    dolen
Spoke to the Daughters of Albion standing on Skiddaw's top.   16

[1] Three-quarters of Plate 81 is taken up with an elaborate drawing of
Albion's Twelve Daughters. Two of them, Gwendolen and Cambel, are con-
versing. Cambel faces outwards: Gwendolen, enclosed in a cloud that divides
the design, turns inwards, standing with her left foot crossing the right, her
left hand behind her back ("upon her back behind her loins"), while with her
right hand she points to the words written in reverse script upon the clouds:
            " In Heaven the only Art of Living
              Is Forgetting & Forgiving.
              Especially to the Female."
In the darkness behind the cloud, again in reverse writing, are the words:
            " But if you on Earth forgive
              You shall not find where to live."
Below the drawing, but included in the design, are the words (this time not
reversed):
    " In Heaven, Love begets Love; but Fear is the Parent of Earthly Love,
      And he who will not bend to Love must be subdu'd by Fear."

So saying she took a Falshood & hid it in her left hand
To entice her Sisters away to Babylon on Euphrates.
And thus she closed her left hand and utter'd her Falshood,
Forgetting that Falshood is prophetic: she hid her hand behind her,
Upon her back behind her loins, & thus utter'd her Deceit:

" I heard Enitharmon say to Los: ' Let the Daughters of Albion
Be scatter'd abroad and let the name of Albion be forgotten.
Divide them into three; name them Amalek, Canaan & Moab.
Let Albion remain a desolation without an inhabitant,   25
And let the Looms of Enitharmon & the Furnaces of Los
Create Jerusalem & Babylon & Egypt & Moab & Amalek
And Helle & Hesperia & Hindostan & China & Japan;
But hide America, for a Curse, an Altar of Victims & a Holy
    Place.'
See Sisters, Canaan is pleasant, Egypt is as the Garden of Eden,
Babylon is our chief desire, Moab our bath in summer.   31
Let us lead the stems of this Tree, let us plant it before Jerusalem,
To judge the Friend of Sinners to death without the Veil,
To cut her off from America, to close up her secret Ark
And the fury of Man exhaust in War, Woman permanent remain.
See how the fires of our loins point eastward to Babylon!   36
Look, Hyle is become an infant Love! look! behold! see him lie
Upon my bosom; look! here is the lovely wayward form
That gave me sweet delight by his torments beneath my Veil!
By the fruit of Albion's Tree I have fed him with sweet milk:
By contentions of the mighty for Sacrifice of Captives,   41
Humanity, the Great Delusion, is chang'd to War & Sacrifice:
I have nail'd his hands on Beth Rabbim & his hands on Hesh-
    bon's Wall.
O that I could live in his sight! O that I could bind him to my
    arm! "

So saying, She drew aside her Veil, from Mam-Tor to Dovedale,
Discovering her own perfect beauty to the Daughters of Albion
And Hyle a winding Worm beneath
.   .   .   .   .   .   & not a weeping Infant
Trembling & pitying she scream'd & fled upon the wind.
Hyle was a winding Worm and herself perfect in beauty.
The desarts tremble at his wrath, they shrink themselves in fear.

Cambel trembled with jealousy: she trembled! she envied!   51
The envy ran thro' Cathedron's Looms into the Heart
Of mild Jerusalem to destroy the Lamb of God. Jerusalem
Languish'd upon Mount Olivet, East of mild Zion's Hill.

Los saw the envious blight above his Seventh Furnace   55
On London's Tower on the Thames; he drew Cambel in wrath

Into his thundering Bellows, heaving it for a loud blast,
And with the blast of his Furnace upon fishy Billingsgate,
Beneath Albion's fatal Tree before the Gate of Los,
Shew'd her the fibres of her beloved to ameliorate   60
The envy; loud she labour'd in the Furnace of fire
To form the mighty form of Hand according to her will
In the Furnaces of Los & in the Wine-press, treading day & night
Naked among the human clusters, bringing wine of anguish
To feed the afflicted in the Furnaces; she minded not   65
The raging flames, tho' she return'd   .   .
    .   .   .   .   .   instead of beauty
Deformity; she gave her beauty to another, bearing abroad
Her struggling torment in her iron arms, and like a chain
Binding his wrists & ankles with the iron arms of love.

Gwendolen saw the Infant in her sister's arms; she howl'd
Over the forests with bitter tears and over the winding Worm
Repentant, and she also in the eddying wind of Los's Bellows
Began her dolorous task of love in the Wine-press of Luvah
To form the Worm into a form of love by tears & pain.   74
The Sisters saw: trembling ran thro' their Looms, softening mild
Towards London: then they saw the Furnaces open'd & in tears
Began to give their souls away in the Furnaces of affliction.

Los saw & was comforted at his Furnaces, uttering thus his voice:
" I know I am Urthona, keeper of the Gates of Heaven,
And that I can at will expatiate in the Gardens of bliss;   80
But pangs of love draw me down to my loins, which are
Become a fountain of veiny pipes. O Albion! my brother!
[83]
" Corruptibility appears upon thy limbs, and never more
Can I arise and leave thy side, but labour here incessant
Till thy awaking: yet alas, I shall forget Eternity!
Against the Patriarchal pomp and cruelty labouring incessant
I shall become an Infant horror. Enion! Tharmas! friends,   5
Absorb me not in such dire grief. O Albion, my brother!
Jerusalem hungers in the desart: affection to her children!
The scorn'd and contemn'd youthful girl, where shall she fly?
Sussex shuts up her Villages: Hants, Devon & Wilts,
Surrounded with masses of stone in order'd forms: determine then
A form for Vala and a form for Luvah, here on the Thames   11
Where the Victim nightly howls beneath the Druid's knife,
A form of Vegetation; nail them down on the stems of Mystery.
O when shall the Saxon return with the English, his redeemed
        brother?
O when shall the Lamb of God descend among the Reprobate?
I woo to Amalek to protect my fugitives: Amalek trembles.   16
I call to Canaan & Moab in my night watches: they mourn,

They listen not to my cry, they rejoice among their warriors.
Woden and Thor and Friga wholly consume my Saxons
On their enormous Altars built in the terrible north   20
From Ireland's rocks to Scandinavia, Persia and Tartary,
From the Atlantic Sea to the universal Erythrean.
Found ye London! enormous City! weeps thy River?
Upon his parent bosom lay thy little ones, O Land
Forsaken! Surrey and Sussex are Enitharmon's Chamber   25
Where I will build her a Couch of repose, & my pillars
Shall surround her in beautiful labyrinths. Oothoon!
Where hides my child? in Oxford hidest thou with Antamon?
In graceful hidings of error, in merciful deceit   29
Lest Hand the terrible destroy his Affection, thou hidest her;
In chaste appearances for sweet deceits of love & modesty
Immingled, interwoven, glistening to the sickening sight.
Let Cambel and her Sisters sit within the Mundane Shell
Forming the fluctuating Globe according to their will: 34
According as they weave the little embryon nerves & veins,
The Eye, the little Nostrils & the delicate Tongue, & Ears
Of labyrinthine intricacy, so shall they fold the World,
That whatever is seen upon the Mundane Shell, the same
Be seen upon the Fluctuating Earth woven by the Sisters.   39
And sometimes the Earth shall roll in the Abyss & sometimes
Stand in the Center & sometimes stretch flat in the Expanse,
According to the will of the lovely Daughters of Albion;
Sometimes it shall assimilate with mighty Golgonooza,
Touching its summits, & sometimes divided roll apart.   44
As a beautiful Veil, so these Females shall fold & unfold,
According to their will the outside surface of the Earth,
An outside shadowy Surface superadded to the real Surface
Which is unchangeable for ever & ever. Amen: so be it!
Separate Albion's Sons gently from their Emanations,   49
Weaving bowers of delight on the current of infant Thames,
Where the old Parent still retains his youth, as I alas!
Retain my youth eight thousand and five hundred years,
The labourer of ages in the Valleys of Despair!
The land is mark'd for desolation, & unless we plant
The seeds of Cities & of Villages in the Human bosom   55
Albion must be a rock of blood: mark ye the points
Where Cities shall remain & where Villages; for the rest,
It must lie in confusion till Albion's time of awaking.
Place the Tribes of Llewellyn in America for a hiding place
Till sweet Jerusalem emanates again into Eternity.   60
The night falls thick: I go upon my watch: be attentive.
The Sons of Albion go forth; I follow from my Furnaces
That they return no more, that a place be prepar'd on Euphrates.
Listen to your Watchman's voice: sleep not before the Furnaces,
Eternal Death stands at the door. O God, pity our labours."   65

So Los spoke to the Daughters of Beulah while his Emanation
Like a faint rainbow waved before him in the awful gloom
Of London City on the Thames from Surrey Hills to Highgate.
Swift turn the silver spindles & the golden weights play soft
And lulling harmonies beneath the Looms from Caithness in the
    north
To Lizard-point & Dover in the south: his Emanation   71
Joy'd in the many weaving threads in bright Cathedron's Dome,
Weaving the Web of life for Jerusalem; the Web of life,
Down flowing into Entuthon's Vales, glistens with soft affections.

While Los arose upon his Watch and down from Golgonooza,   75
Putting on his golden sandals to walk from mountain to mountain,
He takes his way, girding himself with gold & in his hand
Holding his iron mace, The Spectre remains attentive.
Alternate they watch in night, alternate labour in day,
Before the Furnaces labouring, while Los all night watches   80
The stars rising & setting & the meteors & terrors of night.
With him went down the Dogs of Leutha; at his feet
They lap the water of the trembling Thames, then follow swift;
And thus he heard the voice of Albion's daughters on Euphrates:

"Our Father Albion's land, O it was a lovely land! & the
    Daughters of Beulah   85
Walked up and down in its green mountains; but Hand is fled
Away & mighty Hyle, & after them Jerusalem is gone. Awake

[84]
"Highgate's heights & Hampstead's, to Poplar, Hackney & Bow,
To Islington & Paddington & the Brook of Albion's River.
We builded Jerusalem as a City & a Temple; from Lambeth
We began our Foundations, lovely Lambeth. O lovely Hills   4
Of Camberwell, we shall behold you no more in glory & pride,
For Jerusalem lies in ruins & the Furnaces of Los are builded there.
You are now shrunk up to a narrow Rock in the midst of the Sea;
But here we build Babylon on Euphrates, compell'd to build
And to inhabit, our Little-ones to clothe in armour of the gold
Of Jerusalem's Cherubims & to forge them swords of her Altars.
I see London, blind & age bent, begging thro' the Streets   11
Of Babylon, led by a child; his tears run down his beard.
The voice of Wandering Reuben ecchoes from street to street
In all the Cities of the Nations, Paris, Madrid, Amsterdam.
The Corner of Broad Street weeps; Poland Street languishes   15
To Great Queen Street & Lincoln's Inn; all is distress & woe.

"The night falls thick. Hand comes from Albion in his strength:
He combines into a Mighty-one, the Double Molech & Chemosh,
Marching thro' Egypt in his fury: the East is pale at his course.

The Nations of India, the Wild Tartar that never knew Man   20
Starts from his lofty places & casts down his tents & flees away;
But we woo him all the night in songs. O Los come forth, O Los
Divide us from these terrors & give us power them to subdue.
Arise upon thy Watches; let us see the Globe of fire   24
On Albion's Rocks, & let thy voice be heard upon Euphrates.''

Thus sang the Daughters in lamentation, uniting into One
With Rahab as she turn'd the iron Spindle of destruction.

Terrified at the Sons of Albion they took the Falshood which
Gwendolen hid in her left hand: it grew & grew till it   29
[85]
Became a Space & an Allegory around the Winding Worm.
They nam'd it Canaan & built for it a tender Moon.
Los smil'd with joy, thinking on Enitharmon; & he brought
Reuben from his twelvefold wand'rings & led him into it,
Planting the Seeds of the Twelve Tribes & Moses & David,   5
And gave a Time & Revolution to the Space, Six Thousand Years.
He call'd it Divine Analogy, for in Beulah the Feminine
Emanations Create Space, the Masculine Create Time & plant
The Seeds of beauty in the Space: list'ning to their lamentation
Los walks upon his ancient Mountains in the deadly darkness,   10
Among his Furnaces directing his laborious Myriads, watchful
Looking to the East, & his voice is heard over the whole Earth
As he watches the Furnaces by night & directs the labourers.

And thus Los replies upon his Watch: the Valleys listen silent,
The Stars stand still to hear: Jerusalem & Vala cease to mourn:
His voice is heard from Albion: the Alps & Appenines   16
Listen: Hermon & Lebanon bow their crowned heads:
Babel & Shinar look toward the Western Gate, they sit down
Silent at his voice; they view the red Globe of fire in Los's hand
As he walks from Furnace to Furnace directing the Labourers.
And this is the Song of Los, the Song that he sings on his Watch:

" O lovely mild Jerusalem; O Shiloh of Mount Ephraim!
I see thy Gates of precious stones, thy Walls of gold & silver.
Thou art the soft reflected Image of the Sleeping Man   24
Who, stretch'd on Albion's rocks, reposes amidst his Twenty-eight
Cities, where Beulah lovely terminates in the hills & valleys of
     Albion,
Cities not yet embodied in Time and Space: plant ye
The Seeds, O Sisters, in the bosom of Time & Space's womb,
To spring up for Jerusalem, lovely Shadow of Sleeping Albion.
Why wilt thou rend thyself apart & build an Earthly Kingdom
To reign in pride & to opress & to mix the Cup of Delusion?   31
O thou that dwellest with Babylon! Come forth, O lovely-one!

[86]
" I see thy Form, O lovely mild Jerusalem, Wing'd with Six Wings
In the opacous Bosom of the Sleeper, lovely, Three-fold
In Head & Heart & Reins, three Universes of love & beauty.
Thy forehead bright, Holiness to the Lord, with Gates of pearl
Reflects Eternity; beneath, thy azure wings of feathery down   5
Ribb'd delicate & cloth'd with feather'd gold & azure & purple,
From thy white shoulders shadowing purity in holiness!
Thence, feather'd with soft crimson of the ruby, bright as fire,
Spreading into the azure, Wings which like a canopy
Bends over thy immortal Head in which Eternity dwells.   10
Albion, beloved Land! I see thy mountains & thy hills
And valleys & thy pleasant Cities, Holiness to the Lord.
I see the Spectres of thy Dead, O Emanation of Albion.

" Thy Bosom white, translucent, cover'd with immortal gems,
A sublime ornament not obscuring the outlines of beauty,   15
Terrible to behold for thy extreme beauty & perfection;
Twelve-fold here all the Tribes of Israel I behold
Upon the Holy Land. I see the River of Life & Tree of Life,
I see the New Jerusalem descending out of Heaven,
Between thy Wings of gold & silver, feather'd, immortal,   20
Clear as the rainbow, as the cloud of the Sun's tabernacle.

" Thy Reins, cover'd with Wings translucent, sometimes covering
And sometimes spread abroad, reveal the flames of holiness
Which like a robe covers & like a Veil of Seraphim
In flaming fire unceasing burns from Eternity to Eternity.   25
Twelvefold I there behold Israel in her Tents;
A Pillar of Cloud by day, a Pillar of fire by night
Guides them; there I behold Moab & Ammon & Amalek.
There, Bells of silver round thy knees living articulate
Comforting sounds of love & harmony, & on thy feet   30
Sandals of gold & pearl, & Egypt & Assyria before me,
The Isles of Javan, Philistea, Tyre and Lebanon."

Thus Los sings upon his Watch, walking from Furnace to Furnace.
He siezes his Hammer every hour; flames surround him as
He beats, seas roll beneath his feet, tempests muster   35
Around his head, the thick hail stones stand ready to obey
His voice in the black cloud, his Sons labour in thunders
At his Furnaces, his Daughters at their Looms sing woes,
His Emanation separates in milky fibres agonizing   39
Among the golden Looms of Cathedron, sending fibres of love
From Golgonooza with sweet visions for Jerusalem, wanderer.

Nor can any consummate bliss without being Generated
On Earth, of those whose Emanations weave the loves

Of Beulah for Jerusalem & Shiloh in immortal Golgonooza,
Concentering in the majestic form of Erin in eternal tears,   45
Viewing the Winding Worm on the Desarts of Great Tartary,
Viewing Los in his shudderings, pouring balm on his sorrows:
So dread is Los's fury that none dare him to approach
Without becoming his Children in the Furnaces of affliction.

And Enitharmon like a faint rainbow waved before him   50
Filling with Fibres from his loins which redden'd with desire
Into a Globe of blood beneath his bosom trembling in darkness
Of Albion's clouds; he fed it with his tears & bitter groans,
Hiding his Spectre in invisibility from the timorous Shade,
Till it became a separated cloud of beauty, grace & love   55
Among the darkness of his Furnaces, dividing asunder till
She separated stood before him, a lovely Female weeping,
Even Enitharmon separated outside; & his Loins closed
And heal'd after the separation; his pains he soon forgot,
Lured by her beauty outside of himself in shadowy grief.   60
Two Wills they had, Two Intellects, & not as in times of old.

Silent they wander'd hand in hand, like two Infants, wand'ring
From Enion in the desarts, terrified at each other's beauty,
Envying each other, yet desiring in all devouring Love,
[87]
Repelling weeping Enion, blind & age-bent, into the fourfold
Desarts. Los first broke silence & began to utter his love:

"O lovely Enitharmon! I behold thy graceful forms
Moving beside me till, intoxicated with the woven labyrinth
Of beauty & perfection, my wild fibres shoot in veins   5
Of blood thro' all my nervous limbs; soon overgrown in roots
I shall be closed from thy sight: sieze therefore in thy hand
The small fibres as they shoot around me, draw out in pity
And let them run on the winds of thy bosom: I will fix them
With pulsations; we will divide them into Sons & Daughters   10
To live in thy Bosom's translucence as in an eternal morning."

Enitharmon answer'd: "No! I will sieze thy Fibres & weave
Them, not as thou wilt, but as I will; for I will Create
A round Womb beneath my bosom, lest I also be overwoven
With Love: be thou assured I never will be thy slave.   15
Let Man's delight be Love, but Woman's delight be Pride.
In Eden our Loves were the same; here they are opposite.
I have Loves of my own; I will weave them in Albion's Spectre.
Cast thou in Jerusalem's shadows thy Loves, silk of liquid
Rubies, Jacinths, Crysolites, issuing from thy Furnaces. While
Jerusalem divides thy care, while thou carest for Jerusalem,
Know that I never will be thine; also thou hidest Vala: 22

From her these fibres shoot to shut me in a Grave.
You are Albion's Victim; he has set his Daughter in your path."

[88]
Los answer'd, sighing like the Bellows of his Furnaces:

" I care not! the swing of my Hammer shall measure the starry
   round.
When in Eternity Man converses with Man, they enter
Into each other's Bosom (which are Universes of delight)
In mutual interchange; and first their Emanations meet   5
Surrounded by their Children; if they embrace & comingle,
The Human Four-fold Forms mingle also in thunders of Intellect;
But if the Emanations mingle not, with storms & agitations
Of earthquakes & consuming fires they roll apart in fear;
For Man cannot unite with Man but by their Emanations   10
Which stand both Male & Female at the Gates of each Humanity.
How then can I ever again be united as Man with Man
While thou, my Emanation, refusest my Fibres of dominion?
When Souls mingle & join thro' all the Fibres of Brotherhood
Can there be any secret joy on Earth greater than this? "   15

Enitharmon answer'd: " This is Woman's World, nor need she any
Spectre to defend her from Man. I will Create secret places,
And the masculine names of the places, Merlin & Arthur.
A triple Female Tabernacle for Moral Law I weave,
That he who loves Jesus may loathe, terrified, Female love,   20
Till God himself become a Male subservient to the Female."

She spoke in scorn & jealousy, alternate torments; and
So speaking she sat down on Sussex shore, singing lulling
Cadences & playing in sweet intoxication among the glistening
Fibres of Los, sending them over the Ocean eastward into   25
The realms of dark death. O perverse to thyself, contrarious
To thy own purposes! for when she began to weave,
Shooting out in sweet pleasure, her bosom in milky Love
Flow'd into the aching fibres of Los, yet contending against him
In pride, sending his Fibres over to his objects of jealousy   30
In the little lovely Allegoric Night of Albion's Daughters
Which stretch'd abroad, expanding east & west & north & south
Thro' all the World of Erin & of Los & all their Children.

A sullen smile broke from the Spectre in mockery & scorn
Knowing himself the author of their divisions & shrinkings,
   gratified
At their contentions, he wiped his tears, he wash'd his visage. 36

" The Man who respects Woman shall be despised by Woman,
And deadly cunning & mean abjectness only shall enjoy them.

For I will make their places of joy & love excrementitious.
Continually building, continually destroying in Family feuds,
While you are under the dominion of a jealous Female,   41
Unpermanent for ever because of love & jealousy,
You shall want all the Minute Particulars of Life."

Thus joy'd the Spectre in the dusky fires of Los's Forge, eyeing
Enitharmon who at her shining Looms sings lulling cadences
While Los stood at his Anvil in wrath, the victim of their love
And hate, dividing the Space of Love with brazen Compasses
In Golgonooza & in Udan-Adan & in Entuthon of Urizen.

The blow of his Hammer is Justice, the swing of his Hammer
        Mercy,
The force of Los's Hammer is eternal Forgiveness; but   50
His rage or his mildness were vain, she scatter'd his love on the
        wind
Eastward into her own Center, creating the Female Womb
In mild Jerusalem around the Lamb of God. Loud howl
The Furnaces of Los! loud roll the Wheels of Enitharmon!
The Four Zoas in all their faded majesty burst out in fury   55
And fire. Jerusalem took the Cup which foam'd in Vala's hand
Like the red Sun upon the mountains in the bloody day
Upon the Hermaphroditic Wine-presses of Love & Wrath.

[89]
Tho' divided by the Cross & Nails & Thorns & Spear
In cruelties of Rahab & Tirzah, permanent endure
A terrible indefinite Hermaphroditic form,
A Wine-press of Love & Wrath, double, Hermaphroditic,
Twelvefold in Allegoric pomp, in selfish holiness:
The Pharisaion, the Grammateis, the Presbuterion,
The Archiereus, the Iereus, the Saddusaion, double
Each withoutside of the other, covering eastern heaven.

Thus was the Covering Cherub reveal'd, majestic image
Of Selfhood, Body put off, the Antichrist accursed,   10
Cover'd with precious stones: a Human Dragon terrible
And bright stretch'd over Europe & Asia gorgeous.
In three nights he devour'd the rejected corse of death.

His Head, dark, deadly, in its Brain incloses a reflexion
Of Eden all perverted: Egypt on the Gihon, many tongued   15
And many mouth'd, Ethiopia, Lybia, the Sea of Rephaim.
Minute Particulars in slavery I behold among the brick-kilns
Disorganiz'd; & there is Pharoh in his iron Court
And the Dragon of the River & the Furnaces of iron.

Outwoven from Thames & Tweed & Severn, awful streams,   20
Twelve ridges of Stone frown over all the Earth in tyrant pride,
Frown over each River, stupendous Works of Albion's Druid Sons,
And Albion's Forests of Oaks cover'd the Earth from Pole to Pole.

His Bosom wide reflects Moab & Ammon on the River
Pison, since call'd Arnon: there is Heshbon beautiful,   25
The Rocks of Rabbath on the Arnon & the Fish-pools of Heshbon
Whose currents flow into the Dead Sea by Sodom & Gomorra.
Above his Head high arching Wings, black, fill'd with Eyes,
Spring upon iron sinews from the Scapulæ & Os Humeri:
There Israel in bondage to his Generalizing Gods,   30
Molech & Chemosh; & in his left breast is Philistea,
In Druid Temples over the whole Earth with Victim's Sacrifice
From Gaza to Damascus, Tyre & Sidon, & the Gods
Of Javan thro' the Isles of Grecia & all Europe's Kings,
Where Hiddekel pursues his course among the rocks.   35
Two Wings spring from his ribs of brass, starry, black as night,
But translucent their blackness as the dazling of gems.

His Loins inclose Babylon on Euphrates beautiful
And Rome in sweet Hesperia: there Israel scatter'd abroad
In martyrdoms & slavery I behold, ah vision of sorrow!   40
Inclosed by eyeless Wings, glowing with fire as the iron
Heated in the Smith's forge, but cold the wind of their dread fury.

But in the midst of a devouring Stomach, Jerusalem
Hidden within the Covering Cherub, as in a Tabernacle
Of threefold workmanship, in allegoric delusion & woe: 45
There the Seven Kings of Canaan & Five Baalim of Philistea,
Sihon & Og, the Anakim & Emim, Nephilim & Gibborim,
From Babylon to Rome; & the Wings spread from Japan,
Where the Red Sea terminates the World of Generation & Death,
To Ireland's farthest rocks, where Giants builded their Causeway,
Into the Sea of Rephaim, but the Sea o'erwhelm'd them all.   51

A Double Female now appear'd within the Tabernacle,
Religion hid in War, a Dragon red & hidden Harlot
Each within other, but without, a Warlike Mighty-one
Of dreadful power sitting upon Horeb, pondering dire   55
And mighty preparations, mustering multitudes innumerable
Of warlike sons among the sands of Midian & Aram.
For multitudes of those who sleep in Alla descend,
Lured by his warlike symphonies of tabret, pipe & harp,
Burst the bottoms of the Graves & Funeral Arks of Beulah.   60
Wandering in that unknown Night beyond the silent Grave
They become One with the Antichrist & are absorbed in him.

[90]
The Feminine separates from the Masculine & both from Man,
Ceasing to be His Emanations, Life to Themselves assuming:
And while they circumscribe his Brain & while they circumscribe
His Heart & while they circumscribe his Loins, a Veil & Net
Of Veins of red Blood grows around them like a scarlet robe   5
Covering them from the sight of Man, like the woven Veil of Sleep
Such as the Flowers of Beulah weave to be their Funeral Mantles;
But dark, opake, tender to touch, & painful & agonizing
To the embrace of love & to the mingling of soft fibres
Of tender affection, that no more the Masculine mingles   10
With the Feminine, but the Sublime is shut out from the Pathos
In howling torment, to build stone walls of separation, compelling
The Pathos to weave curtains of hiding secresy from the torment.

Bowen & Conwenna stood on Skiddaw cutting the Fibres   14
Of Benjamin from Chester's River: loud the River, loud the
        Mersey
And the Ribble thunder into the Irish sea as the Twelve Sons
Of Albion drank & imbibed the Life & eternal Form of Luvah;
Cheshire & Lancashire & Westmoreland groan in anguish
As they cut the fibres from the Rivers; he sears them with hot
Iron of his Forge & fixes them into Bones of chalk & Rock.   20
Conwenna sat above; with solemn cadences she drew
Fibres of life out from the Bones into her golden Loom.
Hand had his Furnace on Highgate's heights & it reach'd
To Brockley Hills across the Thames; he with double Boadicea
In cruel pride cut Reuben apart from the Hills of Surrey,   25
Comingling with Luvah & with the Sepulcher of Luvah.
For the Male is a Furnace of beryll, the Female is a golden Loom.

Los cries: " No Individual ought to appropriate to Himself
Or to his Emanation any of the Universal Characteristics
Of David or of Eve, of the Woman or of the Lord,   30
Of Reuben or of Benjamin, of Joseph or Judah or Levi.
Those who dare appropriate to themselves Universal Attributes
Are the Blasphemous Selfhoods, & must be broken asunder.
A Vegetated Christ & a Virgin Eve are the Hermaphroditic
Blasphemy; by his Maternal Birth he is that Evil-One   35
And his Maternal Humanity must be put off Eternally,
Lest the Sexual Generation swallow up Regeneration.
Come Lord Jesus, take on thee the Satanic Body of Holiness!''

So Los cried in the Valleys of Middlesex in the Spirit of Prophecy,
While in Selfhood Hand & Hyle & Bowen & Skofeld appropriate
The Divine Names, seeking to Vegetate the Divine Vision   41
In a corporeal & ever dying Vegetation & Corruption;
Mingling with Luvah in One, they become One Great Satan.

Loud scream the Daughters of Albion beneath the Tongs &
    Hammer,
Dolorous are their lamentations in the burning Forge.   45
They drink Reuben & Benjamin as the iron drinks the fire:
They are red hot with cruelty, raving along the Banks of Thames
And on Tyburn's Brook among the howling Victims in loveliness,
While Hand & Hyle condense the Little-ones & erect them into
A mighty Temple even to the stars; but they Vegetate   50
Beneath Los's Hammer, that Life may not be blotted out.

For Los said: " When the Individual appropriates Universality
He divides into Male & Female, & when the Male & Female
Appropriate Individuality they become an Eternal Death.
Hermaphroditic worshippers of a God of cruelty & law!   55
Your Slaves & Captives you compell to worship a God of Mercy.
These are the Demonstrations of Los & the blows of my mighty
    Hammer."

So Los spoke. And the Giants of Albion, terrified & ashamed
With Los's thunderous Words, began to build trembling rocking
    Stones—
For his Words roll in thunders & lightnings among the Temples
Terrified rocking to & fro upon the earth, & sometimes   61
Resting in a Circle in Malden or in Strathness or Dura—
Plotting to devour Albion & Los the friend of Albion,
Denying in private, mocking God & Eternal Life, & in Public
Collusion calling themselves Deists, Worshipping the Maternal
Humanity, calling it Nature and Natural Religion.   66

But still the thunder of Los peals loud, & thus the thunders cry:
" These beautiful Witchcrafts of Albion are gratifyd by Cruelty.
[91]
" It is easier to forgive an Enemy than to forgive a Friend.
The man who permits you to injure him deserves your vengeance:
He also will recieve it: go Spectre! obey my most secret desire
Which thou knowest without my speaking. Go to these Fiends of
    Righteousness,
Tell them to obey their Humanities & not pretend Holiness   5
When they are murderers, as far as my Hammer & Anvil permit.
Go, tell them that the Worship of God is honouring his gifts
In other men & loving the greatest men best, each according
To his Genius which is the Holy Ghost in Man; there is no other
God than that God who is the intellectual fountain of Humanity.
He who envies or calumniates, which is murder & cruelty,   11
Murders the Holy-one. Go, tell them this, & overthrow their cup,
Their bread, their altar-table, their incense & their oath,
Their marriage & their baptism, their burial & consecration.
I have tried to make friends by corporeal gifts but have only   15

Made enemies. I never made friends but by spiritual gifts,
By severe contentions of friendship & the burning fire of thought.
He who would see the Divinity must see him in his Children,
One first, in friendship & love, then a Divine Family, & in the
    midst
Jesus will appear; so he who wishes to see a Vision, a perfect
    Whole,
Must see it in its Minute Particulars, Organized, & not as thou, 21
O Fiend of Righteousness, pretendest; thine is a Disorganized
And snowy cloud, brooder of tempests & destructive War.
You smile with pomp & rigor, you talk of benevolence & virtue;
I act with benevolence & Virtue & get murder'd time after time. 25
You accumulate Particulars & murder by analyzing, that you
May take the aggregate, & you call the aggregate Moral Law,
And you call that swell'd & bloated Form a Minute Particular,
But General Forms have their vitality in Particulars, & every
Particular is a Man, a Divine Member of the Divine Jesus." 30

So Los cried at his Anvil in the horrible darkness weeping.

The Spectre builded stupendous Works, taking the Starry Heavens
Like to a curtain & folding them according to his will,
Repeating the Smaragdine Table of Hermes to draw Los down
Into the Indefinite, refusing to believe without demonstration. 35
Los reads the Stars of Albion, the Spectre reads the Voids
Between the Stars among the arches of Albion's Tomb sublime,
Rolling the Sea in rocky paths, forming Leviathan
And Behemoth, the War by Sea enormous & the War
By Land astounding, erecting pillars in the deepest Hell 40
To reach the heavenly arches. Los beheld undaunted; furious
His heav'd Hammer; he swung it round & at one blow
In unpitying ruin driving down the pyramids of pride,
Smiting the Spectre on his Anvil & the integuments of his Eye
And Ear unbinding in dire pain, with many blows 45
Of strict severity self-subduing, & with many tears labouring.

Then he sent forth the Spectre: all his pyramids were grains
Of sand, & his pillars dust on the fly's wing, & his starry
Heavens a moth of gold & silver, mocking his anxious grasp.
Thus Los alter'd his Spectre, & every Ratio of his Reason 50
He alter'd time after time with dire pain & many tears
Till he had completely divided him into a separate space.

Terrified Los sat to behold, trembling & weeping & howling.
" I care not whether a Man is Good or Evil; all that I care 54
Is whether he is a Wise Man or a Fool. Go, put off Holiness
And put on Intellect, or my thund'rous Hammer shall drive thee
To wrath which thou condemnest, till thou obey my voice."

So Los terrified cries, trembling & weeping & howling: " Be-
     holding,
[92]
" What do I see! The Briton, Saxon, Roman, Norman amalgama-
     ting
In my Furnaces into One Nation, the English, & taking refuge
In the Loins of Albion: The Canaanite united with the fugitive
Hebrew, whom she divided into Twelve & sold into Egypt,
Then scatter'd the Egyptian & Hebrew to the four Winds,   5
This sinful Nation Created in our Furnaces & Looms is Albion.''

So Los spoke. Enitharmon answer'd in great terror in Lambeth's
     Vale:

" The Poet's Song draws to its period, & Enitharmon is no more.
For if he be that Albion, I can never weave him in my Looms,
But when he touches the first fibrous thread, like filmy dew   10
My Looms will be no more & I annihilate vanish for ever.
Then thou wilt Create another Female according to thy Will.''

Los answer'd swift as the shuttle of gold: " Sexes must vanish &
     cease
To be when Albion arises from his dread repose, O lovely Enith-
     armon:
When all their Crimes, their Punishments, their Accusations of Sin,
All their Jealousies, Revenges, Murders, hidings of Cruelty in
     Deceit   16
Appear only in the Outward Spheres of Visionary Space and Time,
In the shadows of Possibility, by Mutual Forgiveness for evermore,
And in the Vision & in the Prophecy, that we may Foresee & Avoid
The terrors of Creation & Redemption & Judgment: Beholding
     them
Display'd in the Emanative Visions of Canaan, in Jerusalem & in
     Shiloh
And in the Shadows of Remembrance & in the Chaos of the Spectre,
Amalek, Edom, Egypt, Moab, Ammon, Ashur, Philistea, around
     Jerusalem   23
Where the Druids rear'd their Rocky Circles to make permanent
     Remembrance
Of Sin, & the Tree of Good & Evil sprang from the Rocky Circle
     & Snake
Of the Druid, along the Valley of Rephaim from Camberwell to
     Golgotha,
And framed the Mundane Shell Cavernous in Length, Bredth &
     Highth.''

[93]
Enitharmon heard. She rais'd her head like the mild Moon:

" O Rintrah! O Palamabron! What are your dire & awful pur-
     poses?

Enitharmon's name is nothing before you; you forget all my Love.
The Mother's love of obedience is forgotten, & you seek a Love
Of the pride of dominion that will Divorce Ocalythron & Elynittria
Upon East Moor in Derbyshire & along the Valleys of Cheviot.
Could you Love me Rintrah, if you Pride not in my Love,   7
As Reuben found Mandrakes in the field & gave them to his
    Mother?
Pride meets with Pride upon the Mountains in the stormy day,
In that terrible Day of Rintrah's Plow & of Satan's driving the
    Team.
Ah! then I heard my little ones weeping along the Valley,   11
Ah! then I saw my beloved ones fleeing from my Tent.
Merlin was like thee, Rintrah, among the Giants of Albion,
Judah was like Palamabron. O Simeon! O Levi! ye fled away.
How can I hear my little ones weeping along the Valley,   15
Or how upon the distant Hills see my beloveds' Tents? ''

Then Los again took up his speech as Enitharmon ceast:

'' Fear not, my Sons, this Waking Death; he is become One with
    me.
Behold him here! We shall not Die! we shall be united in Jesus. 19
Will you suffer this Satan, this Body of Doubt that Seems but
    Is Not,
To occupy the very threshold of Eternal Life? if Bacon, Newton,
    Locke
Deny a Conscience in Man & the Communion of Saints & Angels,
Contemning the Divine Vision & Fruition, Worshiping the Deus
Of the Heathen, The God of This World, & the Goddess Nature,
Mystery, Babylon the Great, The Druid Dragon & hidden Harlot,
Is it not that Signal of the Morning which was told us in the
    Beginning? ''

Thus they converse upon Mam-Tor; the Graves thunder under
    their feet.

[94]
Albion cold lays on his Rock: storms & snows beat round him,
Beneath the Furnaces & the starry Wheels & the Immortal Tomb:
Howling winds cover him: roaring seas dash furious against him:
In the deep darkness broad lightnings glare, long thunders roll.

The weeds of Death inwrap his hands & feet, blown incessant   5
And wash'd incessant by the for-ever restless sea-waves foaming
    abroad

At the head of Plate 93 Blake engraved the figures of three kneeling men
pointing right in unison. On their backs and loins are the words:
    '' Anytus, Melitus & Lycon thought Socrates a
    Very Pernicious Man. So Caiphas thought Jesus.''

Upon the white Rock, England, a Female Shadow, as deadly damps
Of the Mines of Cornwall & Derbyshire, lays upon his bosom heavy,
Moved by the wind in volumes of thick cloud, returning, folding round
His loins & bosom, unremovable by swelling storms & loud rending 10
Of enraged thunders. Around them the Starry Wheels of their Giant Sons
Revolve, & over them the Furnaces of Los, & the Immortal Tomb around,
Erin sitting in the Tomb to watch them unceasing night and day:
And the Body of Albion was closed apart from all Nations.

Over them the famish'd Eagle screams on boney Wings, and around 15
Them howls the Wölf of famine; deep heaves the Ocean black, thundering
Around the wormy Garments of Albion, then pausing in deathlike silence.

Time was Finished! The Breath Divine Breathed over Albion
Beneath the Furnaces & starry Wheels and in the Immortal Tomb;
And England, who is Brittannia, awoke from Death on Albion's bosom: 20
She awoke pale & cold; she fainted seven times on the Body of Albion.

" O pitious Sleep, O pitious Dream! O God, O God awake! I have slain
In Dreams of Chastity & Moral Law: I have Murdered Albion! Ah!
In Stone-henge & on London Stone & in the Oak Groves of Malden
I have Slain him in my Sleep with the Knife of the Druid. O England, 25
O all ye Nations of the Earth, behold ye the Jealous Wife!
The Eagle & the Wolf & Monkey & Owl & the King & Priest were there."

[95]
Her voice pierc'd Albion's clay cold ear: he moved upon the Rock.
The Breath Divine went forth upon the morning hills. Albion mov'd
Upon the Rock; he open'd his eyelids in pain, in pain he mov'd
His stony members; he saw England. Ah! shall the Dead live again? 4

The Breath Divine went forth over the morning hills. Albion rose
In anger, the wrath of God, breaking bright, flaming on all sides around

His awful limbs: into the Heavens he walked, clothed in flames,
Loud thund'ring, with broad flashes of flaming lightning & pillars
Of fire, speaking the Words of Eternity in Human Forms, in direful
Revolutions of Action & Passion, thro' the Four Elements on
    all sides   10
Surrounding his awful Members. Thou seest the Sun in heavy
    clouds
Struggling to rise above the Mountains, in his burning hand
He takes his Bow, then chooses out his arrows of flaming gold;
Murmuring the Bowstring breathes with ardor! clouds roll round
    the
Horns of the wide Bow, loud sounding winds sport on the moun-
    tain brows: 15
Compelling Urizen to his Furrow & Tharmas to his Sheepfold
And Luvah to his Loom, Urthona he beheld, mighty labouring at
His Anvil in the Great Spectre Los, unwearied labouring &
    weeping.
Therefore the Sons of Eden praise Urthona's Spectre in songs,
Because he kept the Divine Vision in time of trouble.   20

As the Sun & Moon lead forward the Visions of Heaven & Earth,
England, who is Brittannia, enter'd Albion's bosom rejoicing,
Rejoicing in his indignation, adoring his wrathful rebuke.
She who adores not your frowns will only loathe your smiles.   24

[96]
As the Sun & Moon lead forward the Visions of Heaven & Earth,
England, who is Brittannia, entered Albion's bosom rejoicing.

Then Jesus appeared standing by Albion as the Good Shepherd
By the lost Sheep that he hath found, & Albion knew that it
Was the Lord, the Universal Humanity; & Albion saw his Form   5
A Man, & they conversed as Man with Man in Ages of Eternity.
And the Divine Appearance was the likeness & similitude of Los.

Albion said: "O Lord, what can I do? my Selfhood cruel
Marches against thee, deceitful, from Sinai & from Edom
Into the Wilderness of Judah, to meet thee in his pride.   10
I behold the Visions of my deadly Sleep of Six Thousand Years
Dazling around thy skirts like a Serpent of precious stones & gold.
I know it is my Self, O my Divine Creator & Redeemer."

Jesus replied: "Fear not Albion; unless I die thou canst not live,
But if I die I shall arise again & thou with me.   15
This is Friendship & Brotherhood: without it Man Is Not."

So Jesus spoke: the Covering Cherub coming on in darkness
Overshadow'd them, & Jesus said: "Thus do Men in Eternity
One for another, to put off, by forgiveness, every sin."

Albion reply'd: " Cannot Man exist without Mysterious   20
Offering of Self for Another? is this Friendship & Brotherhood?
I see thee in the likeness & similitude of Los my Friend."

Jesus said: " Wouldest thou love one who never died
For thee, or ever die for one who had not died for thee?
And if God dieth not for Man & giveth not himself   25
Eternally for Man, Man could not exist; for Man is Love
As God is Love: every kindness to another is a little Death
In the Divine Image, nor can Man exist but by Brotherhood."

So saying the Cloud overshadowing divided them asunder.
Albion stood in terror, not for himself but for his Friend   30
Divine; & Self was lost in the contemplation of faith
And wonder at the Divine Mercy & at Los's sublime honour.

" Do I sleep amidst danger to Friends? O my Cities & Counties,
Do you sleep? rouze up, rouze up! Eternal Death is abroad!"

So Albion spoke & threw himself into the Furnaces of affliction.
All was a Vision, all a Dream: the Furnaces became   36
Fountains of Living Waters flowing from the Humanity Divine.
And all the Cities of Albion rose from their Slumbers, and All
The Sons & Daughters of Albion on soft clouds, Waking from Sleep.
Soon all around remote the Heavens burnt with flaming fires, 40
And Urizen & Luvah & Tharmas & Urthona arose into
Albion's Bosom. Then Albion stood before Jesus in the Clouds
Of Heaven, Fourfold among the Visions of God in Eternity.

[97]
" Awake, Awake, Jerusalem! O lovely Emanation of Albion,
Awake and overspread all Nations as in Ancient Time;
For lo! the Night of Death is past and the Eternal Day
Appears upon our Hills. Awake, Jerusalem, and come away!"

So spake the Vision of Albion, & in him so spake in my hearing
The Universal Father. Then Albion stretch'd his hand into
    Infinitude   6
And took his Bow. Fourfold the Vision; for bright beaming Urizen
Lay'd his hand on the South & took a breathing Bow of carved
    Gold:
Luvah his hand stretch'd to the East & bore a Silver Bow, bright
    shining:
Tharmas Westward a Bow of Brass, pure flaming, richly wrought:
Urthona Northward in thick storms a Bow of Iron, terrible
    thundering.   11

And the Bow is a Male & Female, & the Quiver of the Arrows
  of Love
Are the Children of his Bow, a Bow of Mercy & Loving-kindness
  laying
Open the hidden Heart in Wars of mutual Benevolence, Wars of
  Love:
And the Hand of Man grasps firm between the Male & Female
  Loves.   15
And he Clothed himself in Bow & Arrows, in awful state, Fourfold,
In the midst of his Twenty-eight Cities, each with his Bow breathing.

[98]
Then each an Arrow flaming from his Quiver fitted carefully;
They drew fourfold the unreprovable String, bending thro' the
  wide Heavens
The horned Bow Fourfold; loud sounding flew the flaming Arrow
  fourfold.

Murmuring the Bowstring breathes with ardor. Clouds roll round
  the horns
Of the wide Bow; loud sounding Winds sport on the Mountains'
  brows.   5
The Druid Spectre was Annihilate, loud thund'ring, rejoicing
  terrific, vanishing,
Fourfold Annihilation; & at the clangor of the Arrows of Intellect
The innumerable Chariots of the Almighty appear'd in Heaven,
And Bacon & Newton & Locke, & Milton & Shakspear & Chaucer,
A Sun of blood red wrath surrounding heaven, on all sides around,
Glorious, incomprehensible by Mortal Man, & each Chariot was
  Sexual Threefold.[1]   11

And every Man stood Fourfold; each Four Faces had: One to the
  West,
One toward the East, One to the South, One to the North, the
  Horses Fourfold.
And the dim Chaos brighten'd beneath, above, around: Eyed as
  the Peacock,
According to the Human Nerves of Sensation, the Four Rivers of
  the Water of Life.   15

South stood the Nerves of the Eye; East, in Rivers of bliss, the
  Nerves of the
Expansive Nostrils; West flow'd the Parent Sense, the Tongue;
  North stood

[1] " Threefold." In some lithographic ' facsimiles ' of " Jerusalem " the
word " Twofold " is here substituted. In the British Museum copy the word
is discernibly " Threefold," though a little broken; but in the only copy of
" Jerusalem " Blake finished with colouring, the word is restored and reads
" Threefold " clearly.

The labyrinthine Ear: Circumscribing & Circumcising the excre-
    mentitious
Husk & Covering, into Vacuum evaporating, revealing the
    lineaments of Man,
Driving outward the Body of Death in an Eternal Death &
    Resurrection, 20
Awaking it to Life among the Flowers of Beulah, rejoicing in Unity
In the Four Senses, in the Outline, the Circumference & Form, for
    ever
In Forgiveness of Sins which is Self Annihilation; it is the Cove-
    nant of Jehovah.

The Four Living Creatures, Chariots of Humanity, Divine, In-
    comprehensible,
In beautiful Paradises expand. These are the Four Rivers of
    Paradise 25
And the Four Faces of Humanity, fronting the Four Cardinal
    Points
Of Heaven, going forward, forward irresistible from Eternity to
    Eternity.

And they conversed together in Visionary forms dramatic which
    bright
Redounded from their Tongues in thunderous majesty, in Visions
In new Expanses, creating exemplars of Memory and of Intellect,
Creating Space, Creating Time, according to the wonders Divine
Of Human Imagination throughout all the Three Regions immense
Of Childhood, Manhood & Old Age; & the all tremendous
    unfathomable Non Ens
Of Death was seen in regenerations terrific or complacent, varying
According to the subject of discourse; & every Word & every
    Character 35
Was Human according to the Expansion or Contraction, the
    Translucence or
Opakeness of Nervous fibres: such was the variation of Time &
    Space
Which vary according as the Organs of Perception vary; & they
    walked
To & fro in Eternity as One Man, reflecting each in each &
    clearly seen
And seeing, according to fitness & order. And I heard Jehovah
    speak 40
Terrific from his Holy Place, & saw the Words of the Mutual
    Covenant Divine
On Chariots of gold & jewels, with Living Creatures, starry &
    flaming
With every Colour, Lion, Tyger, Horse, Elephant, Eagle, Dove,
    Fly, Worm

And the all wondrous Serpent clothed in gems & rich array,
    Humanize
In the Forgiveness of Sins according to thy Covenant, Jehovah.
    They Cry: 45

"Where is the Covenant of Priam, the Moral Virtues of the
    Heathen?
Where is the Tree of Good & Evil that rooted beneath the cruel
    heel
Of Albion's Spectre, the Patriarch Druid? where are all his
    Human Sacrifices
For Sin in War & in the Druid Temples of the Accuser of Sin,
    beneath
The Oak Groves of Albion that cover'd the whole Earth beneath
    his Spectre?   50
Where are the Kingdoms of the World & all their glory that grew
    on Desolation,
The Fruit of Albion's Poverty Tree, when the Triple Headed
    Gog-Magog Giant
Of Albion Taxed the Nations into Desolation & then gave the
    Spectrous Oath? ''

Such is the Cry from all the Earth, from the Living Creatures
    of the Earth
And from the great City of Golgonooza in the Shadowy Genera-
    tion,   55
And from the Thirty-two Nations of the Earth among the Living
    Creatures.

[99]
All Human Forms identified, even Tree, Metal, Earth & Stone: all
Human Forms identified, living, going forth & returning wearied
Into the Planetary lives of Years, Months, Days & Hours;
    reposing,
And then Awaking into his Bosom in the Life of Immortality.

And I heard the Name of their Emanations: they are named
    Jerusalem.

The End of The Song
of Jerusalem.

¹ The fourth and final full-page illustration to " Jerusalem " shows the
giant forms of Los, with hammer and tongs, and Vala with her distaff, to-
gether with another (? Luvah) who bears the sun on his shoulder. They
stand before the Serpent Temple.

ON HOMER'S POETRY

(About 1818)

EVERY Poem must necessarily be a perfect Unity, but why Homer's is peculiarly so, I cannot tell: he has told the story of Bellerophon & omitted the Judgment of Paris, which is not only a part, but a principal part of Homer's subject.

But when a Work has Unity, it is as much in a Part as in the Whole: the Torso is as much a Unity as the Laocoön.

As Unity is the cloke of folly, so Goodness is the cloke of knavery. Those who will have Unity exclusively in Homer come out with a Moral like a sting in the tail. Aristotle says Characters are either Good or Bad: now Goodness or Badness has nothing to do with Character: an Apple tree, a Pear tree, a Horse, a Lion, are Characters; but a Good Apple tree or a Bad is an Apple tree still: a Horse is not more a Lion for being a Bad Horse; that is its Character: its Goodness or Badness is another consideration.

It is the same with the Moral of a whole Poem as with the Moral Goodness of its parts. Unity & Morality are secondary considerations, & belong to Philosophy & not to Poetry, to Exception & not to Rule, to Accident & not to Substance: the Ancients call'd it eating of the tree of good & evil.

The Classics: it is the Classics & not Goths nor Monks that Desolate Europe with Wars.

On Virgil

SACRED Truth has pronounced that Greece & Rome, as Babylon & Egypt, so far from being parents of Arts & Sciences, as they pretend, were destroyers of all Art. Homer, Virgil & Ovid confirm this opinion & make us

L 792

reverence The Word of God, the only light of antiquity that remains unperverted by War. Virgil in the Eneid, Book vi. line 848,[1] says, " Let others study Art: Rome has somewhat better to do, namely War & Dominion."

Rome & Greece swept Art into their maw & destroyed it: a Warlike State never can produce Art. It will Rob & Plunder & accumulate into one place, & Translate & Copy & Buy & Sell & Criticise, but not Make. Grecian is Mathematic Form: Gothic is Living Form. Mathematic Form is Eternal in the Reasoning Memory. Living Form is Eternal Existence.

[1] See note, p. 289.

יה & HIS TWO SONS, SATAN & ADAM

[*The Laocoön Plate*]

(*About* 1820)

In the year 1815, *Blake, in pursuit of his occupation as an engraver, made a number of engravings for "Rees' Encyclopedia." Among these was one of the "Laocoön" Group, an engraving derived from a drawing Blake had previously made of the cast at the Royal Academy Antique School. Having used the plate, Blake subsequently added to it inscriptions which converted the "Laocoön" into an emblem and made it a vehicle for his own religious and artistic ideas. When he had given the figures his own symbolic significance, he added to the plate, probably from time to time, aphorisms on spiritual and corporeal warfare and upon art and money in relation to Christianity. The plate itself has not survived, indeed only one print from it is now known to exist; but it is of great interest in view of the reflected light it casts upon "Jerusalem," "The Ghost of Abel" and other of Blake's later works.*

The Group is entitled

¹ יה & his two Sons, Satan & Adam, as they were copied from the Cherubim of Solomon's Temple by three Rhodians & applied to Natural Fact, or History of Ilium.

Above the head of the principal figure is written

The Angel of the Divine Presence, ²מלאך יהוה

and again

ὀφιοῦχος,³

¹יה = Jah: shortened form of Jehovah.

² מלאך יהוה = Angel of Jehovah.

³ The Serpent-bearer: "Ophiuchus" (cf. "Milton," plate 41, line 50).

287

Around his right arm is written

The Gods of Priam are the Cherubim of Moses & Solomon:
The Hosts of Heaven.

The Serpent on the right, biting one of the sons, is called
Evil.
The Serpent on the left, biting the father, is called
Good.

and again

לילית ¹

The aphorisms written about the plate:

He repented that he had made Adam (of the Female, the Adamah) & it grieved him at his heart.

What can be Created Can be Destroyed. Adam is only The Natural Man & not the Soul or Imagination.

The Eternal Body of Man is The Imagination: that is
God himself }
The Divine Body } ישע, ² Jesus: we are his Members.
It manifests itself in his Works of Art (In Eternity All is Vision).

All that we See is Vision: from Generated Organs gone as soon as come: Permanent in The Imagination: Consider'd as Nothing by the Natural Man.

Satan's Wife, The Goddess Nature, is War & Misery & Heroism a Miser.³

Good & Evil are Riches & Poverty, a Tree of Misery propagating Generation & Death.

If Morality was Christianity, Socrates was the Saviour.

Art Degraded, Imagination Denied, War Governed the Nations.

---

¹ לילית = Lilith.   ² Probably should be ישוע " Jeshua," i.e. Jesus.
³ cf. " Everlasting Gospel," p. 347, ll. 35, 36.

Where any view of Money exists, Art cannot be carried on, but War only by pretences to the Two Impossibilities, Chastity & Abstinence, Gods of the Heathen.
                                    [1] *Read Matthew C. x. 9 & 10 v.*

Spiritual War. Israel deliver'd from Egypt is Art deliver'd from Nature & Imitation.

Divine Union Deriding, And Denying Immediate Communion with God, The Spoilers say: "Where are his Works That he did in the Wilderness? Lo, what are these? Whence came they? These are not the Works of Egypt nor Babylon "—Whose Gods are the Powers Of this World, Goddess Nature: Who first spoil & then destroy Imaginative Art, For their Glory is War and Dominion.

Empire against Art.   [2] *See Virgil's Eneid. Lib. VI. v.* 848.

There are States in which all Visionary Men are accounted Mad Men: such are Greece & Rome: Such is Empire or Tax.
                                    [3] *See Luke. Ch.* 2. *v.* 1.

The Old & New Testaments are the Great Code of Art. The whole Business of Man Is The Arts & All Things Common. No Secresy in Art.

Art is the Tree of Life.
Science is the Tree of Death.
God is Jesus.

Jesus & his Apostles & Disciples were all Artists. Their Works were destroy'd by the Seven Angels of the Seven Churches in Asia, Antichrist Science.

[1] "Provide neither gold, nor silver, nor brass in your purses,
    Nor script for your journey, neither two coats, neither shoes, nor yet staves: for the workman is worthy of his meat."

[2] "Excudent alii spirantia mollius æra." Translated by Mackail, " Others shall beat out the breathing bronze to softer lines."; and by Page, " Others shall more softly fashion the breathing brass."; (with a note in explanation, " i.e. Statues which seem alive."). (Ref. should be to l. 847.)
[3] " And it came to pass in those days, that there went out a decree from Cæsar Augustus, that all the world should be taxed " (taxed= registered).

The unproductive Man is not a Christian, much less the Destroyer.

A Poet, a Painter, a Musician, an Architect: the Man Or Woman who is not one of these is not a Christian.

You must leave Fathers & Mothers & Houses & Lands if they stand in the way of Art.

Prayer is the Study of Art.
Praise is the Practise of Art.
Fasting &⁰ all relate to Art.
The outward Ceremony is Antichrist.

Without Unceasing Practise, nothing can be done. Practise is Art. If you leave off you are Lost.

Art can never exist without Naked Beauty displayed.[1]
The Gods of Greece & Egypt were Mathematical Diagrams.
See Plato's Works.

Hebrew Art is called Sin by the Deist Science.

What we call Antique Gems are the Gems of Aaron's Breast Plate.

Is not every Vice possible to Man described in the Bible openly?
All is not Sin that Satan calls so—all the Loves & Graces of Eternity.

The True Christian Charity: not dependent on Money (the life's blood of Poor Families), that is, on Caesar or Empire or Natural Religion—Money which is The Great Satan, or Reason, the Root of Good & Evil In The Accusation of Sin.

Christianity is Art & not Money. Money is its Curse.

For every Pleasure Money Is Useless.

[1] i.e. Beauty freed from mortal disguise.

For the Sexes

The Gates of Paradise

Mutual Forgiveness of each Vice
Such are the Gates of Paradise
Against the Accusers chief desire
Who walked among the Stones of Fire
Jehovahs Finger Wrote the Law
Then Wept: then rose in Zeal & Awe
And the Dead Corpse from Sinais heat
Buried beneath his Mercy-Seat,
O Christians Christians tell me Why
You rear it on your Altars high

291

What is Man
The Suns Light when he unfolds it
Depends on the Organ that beholds it
Publishd by W Blake 17 May 1793

I found him beneath a Tree ~

Publishd 17 May 1793 by W Blake

Water

Thou Waterest him with Tears

Published by WBlake 17 May 1793

2

294

3   Earth
He struggles into Life
Publishd by WBlake 17 May 1793

Air.

4 On Cloudy Doubts & Reasoning Cares.

Feblishd 17 May 1793 by W.Blakr. Liambeth.

5   Fire *That end in endless Strife*
P: 6: by W Blake 9 May 1793

At length for hatching ripe
      he breaks the shell
6
    Publishd by WBlake 17 May 1793

7 What are these 'Alas!' the Female Martyr
Is She also the Divine Image
Published 17 May 1793 by WBlake Lambeth

8   My Son! my Son!

Publishd by WBlake 17 May 1793 Lambeth

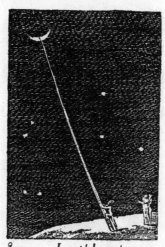

9   *I want! I want!*

Pub^d by WBlake 17 May 1793

301

10   Help! Help!

Publish'd by W Blake 17 May 1793

Aged Ignorance
"Perceptive Organs closed their Objects close
Published 17 May 1793 by W Blake Lambeth.

303

12   Does thy God O Priest take such vengeance
             as this?
      Publishd 17 May 1793 by W Blake Lambeth

13 Fear & Hope are — Vision

The Traveller hasteth in the
Evening

14

Publ, hd 17 May 1793 by W Blake Lambeth

15   Death's Door

Publish'd 1 May 1793 by W Blake Lambeth

16 I have said to the Worm: Thou
    art my mother & my sister
    Publishd by WBlake~1 May 1793

The Keys

The Catterpiller on the Leaf
Reminds thee of thy Mothers Grief

of the Gates

1 My Eternal Man set in Repose
The Female from his darkness rose
And She found me beneath a Tree
A Mandrake & in her Veil hid me
Serpent Reasonings us entice
Of Good & Evil. Virtue & Vice
2 Doubt Self Jealous Watry folly
3 Struggling thro Earths Melancholy
4 Naked in Air in Shame & Fear
5 Blind in Fire with shield & spear
Two Horn'd Reasoning Cloven Fiction
In Doubt which is Self contradiction
A dark Hermaphrodite We stood
Rational Truth Root of Evil & Good
Round me flew the Flaming Sword
Round her snowy Whirlwinds roard
Freezing her Veil the Mundane Shell
6 I rent the Veil where the Dead dwell
When weary Man enters his Cave

17

309

He meets his Saviour in the Grave.
Some find a Female Garment there
And some a Male. woven with care
Lest the Sexual Garments sweet
Should grow a devouring Winding sheet
7 One Dies! Alas! the Living & Dead
One is slain & One is fled
8 In Vain-glory hatcht & nurst
By double Spectres Self Accurst
My Son! my Son! thou treatest me
But as I have instructed thee
9 On the shadows of the Moon
Climbing thro Nights highest noon
10 In Times Ocean falling drownd
In Aged Ignorance profound.
11 Holy & cold I clipd the Wings
Of all Sublunary Things
12 And in depths of my Dungeons
Closed the Father & the Sons
13 But when once I did descry
The Immortal Man that cannot Die
14 Thro evening shades I haste away
To close the Labours of my Day
15 The Door of Death I open found
And the Worm Weaving in the Ground
16 Thou'rt my Mother from the Womb
Wife. Sister. Daughter to the Tomb
Weaving to Dreams the Sexual strife
And weeping over the Web of Life

To The Accuser who is

The God of This World

Truly My Satan thou art but a Dunce
And dost not know the Garment from the Man
Every Harlot was a Virgin once
Nor canst thou ever change Kate into Nan

Tho thou art Worshipd by the Names Divine
Of Jesus & Jehovah: thou art still
The Son of Morn in weary Nights decline
The lost Travellers Dream under the Hill

19.

The GHOST of ABEL

A Revelation In the Visions of Jehovah
Seen by William Blake

(1822)

To LORD BYRON in the Wilderness:

What doest thou here, Elijah?
Can a Poet doubt the Visions of Jehovah? Nature has no
Outline, but Imagination has. Nature has no Tune, but
Imagination has. Nature has no Supernatural, & dissolves;
Imagination is Eternity.

SCENE.—*A rocky Country*. Eve, *fainted over the dead body*
    of Abel *which lays near a Grave*. Adam *kneels by her*.
    Jehovah *stands above*.

Jehovah. Adam!

Adam.   I will not hear thee more, thou Spiritual Voice.
    Is this Death?

Jehovah.   Adam!

Adam.   It is in vain: I will not hear thee
    Henceforth! Is this thy Promise, that the Woman's
        Seed
    Should bruise the Serpent's head? Is this the
        Serpent? Ah!
    Seven times, O Eve, thou hast fainted over the
        Dead. Ah! Ah!

                Eve *revives*.

Eve. Is this the Promise of Jehovah? O it is all a vain
        delusion,
    This Death & this Life & this Jehovah!

Jehovah.   Woman, lift thine eyes.

A Voice is heard coming on.

Voice. O Earth, cover not thou my Blood! cover not thou
    my Blood!

Enter the Ghost of Abel

Eve. Thou Visionary Phantasm, thou art not the real Abel.

Abel. Among the Elohim, a Human Victim I wander. I am
    their House,
        Prince of the Air, & our dimensions compass Zenith
        and Nadir.
        Vain is thy Covenant, O Jehovah. I am the Accuser
        & Avenger
        Of Blood. O Earth, Cover not thou the Blood of Abel.

Jehovah. What Vengeance dost thou require?

Abel.   Life for Life! Life for Life!

Jehovah. He who shall take Cain's life must also Die, O Abel.
        And who is he? Adam, wilt thou, or Eve, thou do
        this?

Adam. It is all a Vain delusion of the all creative Imagina-
    tion.
        Eve, come away, & let us not believe these vain
        delusions.
        Abel is dead, & Cain slew him. We shall also Die a
        Death,
        And then? what then? be as poor Abel, a Thought;
        or as
        This! O what shall I call thee Form Divine! Father
        of Mercies
        That appearest to my Spiritual Vision? Eve, seest
        thou also?

Eve. I see him plainly with my Mind's Eye. I see also Abel
    living,
        Tho' terribly afflicted, as We also are; yet Jehovah
        sees him
        Alive & not Dead: were it not better to believe
        Vision
        With all our might & strength, tho' we are fallen &
        lost?

Adam. Eve, thou hast spoken truly: let us kneel before his
          feet.

They Kneel before Jehovah

Abel. Are these the Sacrifices of Eternity, O Jehovah: a
          Broken Spirit
          And a Contrite Heart? O I cannot Forgive! the
          Accuser hath
          Enter'd into Me as into his House & I loathe thy
          Tabernacles.
          As thou hast said, so is it come to pass: My desire
          is unto Cain
          And He doth rule over Me; therefore My Soul in
          fumes of Blood
          Cries for Vengeance, Sacrifice on Sacrifice, Blood on
          Blood.

Jehovah. Lo, I have given you a Lamb for an Atonement
          instead
          Of the Transgressor, or no Flesh or Spirit could ever
          Live.

Abel. Compelled I cry, "O Earth, cover not the Blood of
          Abel."

Abel *sinks down into the Grave, from which arises* Satan
Armed in glittering scales, with a Crown & a Spear.

Satan. I will have Human Blood & not the blood of Bulls or
          Goats,
          And no Atonement, O Jehovah: the Elohim live on
          Sacrifice
          Of Men: hence I am God of Men: Thou Human, O
          Jehovah.
          By the Rock & Oak of the Druid, creeping Mistletoe
          & Thorn,
          Cain's City built with Human Blood, not Blood of
          Bulls & Goats,
          Thou shalt Thyself be Sacrificed to Me, thy God, on
          Calvary.

Jehovah. Such is My Will   *Thunders*
               that Thou Thyself go to Eternal Death

In Self Annihilation, even till Satan Self-subdu'd
    Put off Satan
Into the Bottomless Abyss, whose torment arises
    for ever & ever.

On each side a Chorus of Angels *entering Sing the following:*

The Elohim of the Heathen Swore Vengeance for Sin! Then
    Thou stood'st
Forth, O Elohim Jehovah! in the midst of the darkness of
    the Oath, All Clothed
In Thy Covenant of the Forgiveness of Sins: Death. O
    Holy Is this Brotherhood!
The Elohim saw their Oath, Eternal Fire: they rolled apart
    trembling over The
Mercy Seat, each in his station fixt in the Firmament by
    Peace, Brotherhood and Love.

The Curtain falls.

NOTE.—The colophon illustration shows Adam lying prostrate over
Eve: in the background are the head and shoulders of a man crying on
the wind; with arms crossed, he points with his left hand to the words,
" The Voice of Abel's Blood." In the right-hand corner of the plate are
the words, " 1822. W. Blake's Original Stereotype was 1788."

II

FRAGMENTS FROM BLAKE'S MSS.

TWO POEMS
from
Blake's letters to Thomas Butts
(1800 & 1802)

I

To my Friend Butts I write
My first Vision of Light,
On the yellow sands sitting.
The Sun was Emitting
His Glorious beams   5
From Heaven's high Streams.
Over Sea, over Land
My Eyes did Expand
Into regions of air
Away from all Care,   10
Into regions of fire
Remote from Desire.
The Light of the Morning
Heaven's Mountains adorning,
In particles bright   15
The jewels of Light
Distinct shone & clear.
Amaz'd & in fear
I each particle gazed,
Astonish'd, amazed;   20
For each was a Man
Human form'd. Swift I ran,
For they beckon'd to me
Remote by the Sea,
Saying: " Each grain of Sand,   25
Every stone on the Land,

Each rock & each hill,
Each fountain & rill,
Each herb & each tree,
Mountain, hill, earth & sea,   30
Cloud, Meteor & Star,
Are Men Seen Afar.''
I stood in the Streams
Of Heaven's bright beams
And Saw Felpham sweet   35
Beneath my bright feet
In soft Female charms,
And in her fair arms
My Shadow I knew,
And my wife's shadow too,   40
And My Sister, & Friend.
We like Infants descend
In our Shadows on Earth,
Like a weak mortal birth.
My Eyes, more & more,   45
Like a Sea without Shore,
Continue expanding,
The Heavens commanding,
Till the Jewels of Light,
Heavenly Men beaming bright,   50
Appear'd as One Man
Who Complacent began
My limbs to infold
In his beams of bright gold.
Like dross purg'd away   55
All my mire & my clay:
Soft consum'd in delight,
In his bosom Sun bright
I remain'd. Soft he smil'd,
And I heard his voice Mild   60
Saying: '' This is My Fold,
O thou Ram horn'd with gold,
Who awakest from Sleep
On the Sides of the Deep.
On the Mountains around   65
The roarings resound
Of the lion & wolf,

The loud sea & deep gulf:
These are guards of My Fold,
O thou Ram horn'd with gold."   70
And the voice faded mild,
I remain'd as a Child,
All I ever had known
Before me bright shone,
I saw you & your wife   75
By the fountains of life.
Such the Vision to me
Appear'd on the Sea.

Felpham,
Octr 24 1800.

II

WITH happiness stretch'd across the hills
In a cloud that dewy sweetness distills,
With a blue sky spread over with wings,
And a mild sun that mounts & sings,
With trees & fields full of Fairy elves,   5
And little devils who fight for themselves.
Rememb'ring the Verses that Hayley sung
When my heart knock'd against the root of my tongue,
With Angels planted in Hawthorn bowers,
And God himself in the passing hours,   10
With Silver Angels across my way
And Golden Demons that none can stay,
With my Father hovering upon the wind
And my Brother Robert just behind,
And my Brother John, the evil one,   15
In a black cloud making his mone—
Tho' dead, they appear upon my path,
Notwithstanding my terrible wrath
They beg, they intreat, they drop their tears,
Fill'd full of hopes, fill'd full of fears—   20
With a thousand Angels upon the Wind,
Pouring disconsolate from behind
To drive them off, & before my way
A frowning Thistle implores my stay.

What to others a trifle appears 25
Fills me full of smiles or tears;
For double the vision my Eyes do see,
And a double vision is always with me.
With my inward Eye, 'tis an old Man grey,
With my outward, a Thistle across my way. 30

" If thou goest back," the thistle said,
" Thou art to endless woe betray'd;
For here does Theotormon lower,
And here is Enitharmon's bower,
And Los the terrible thus hath sworn, 35
Because thou backward dost return,
Poverty, Envy, old age & fear
Shall bring thy Wife upon a bier,
And Butts shall give what Fuseli gave,
A dark black Rock & a gloomy Cave." 40

I struck the Thistle with my foot
And broke him up from his delving root.
" Must the duties of life each other cross?
Must every joy be dung & dross?
Must my dear Butts feel cold neglect 45
Because I give Hayley his due respect?
Must Flaxman look upon me as wild
And all my friends be with doubts beguil'd?
Must my Wife live in my Sister's bane,
Or my Sister survive on my Love's pain? 50
The curses of Los, the terrible shade,
And his dismal terrors make me afraid."

So I spoke, & struck in my wrath
The old man weltering upon my path.
Then Los appear'd in all his power: 55
In the Sun he appear'd, descending before
My face in fierce flames; in my double sight
'Twas outward a Sun, inward Los in his might.

" My hands are labour'd day & night,
And Ease comes never in my sight. 60

My Wife has no indulgence given
Except what comes to her from heaven.
We eat little, we drink less,
This Earth breeds not our happiness.
Another Sun feeds our life's streams, 65
We are not warmed with thy beams;
Thou measurest not the Time to me,
Nor yet the Space that I do see;
My Mind is not with thy light array'd,
Thy Terrors shall not make me afraid.'' 70

When I had my Defiance given,
The Sun stood trembling in heaven,
The Moon, that glow'd remote below,
Became leprous & white as snow,
And every soul of men on the Earth 75
Felt affliction & sorrow & sickness & dearth.
Los flam'd in my path, & the Sun was hot
With the bows of my Mind & the arrows of Thought.
My bowstring fierce with ardour breathes,
My arrows glow in their golden sheaves, 80
My brothers & father march before,
The heavens drop with human gore.

Now I a fourfold vision see,
And a fourfold vision is given to me;
'Tis fourfold in my supreme delight 85
And threefold in soft Beulah's night
And twofold Always. May God us keep
From single vision & Newton's sleep.

Felpham,
Nov.? 22: 1802.

THE "PICKERING" MS.

(About 1803)

The Smile

THERE is a Smile of Love,
And there is a Smile of Deceit,
And there is a Smile of Smiles
In which these two Smiles meet.   4

And there is a Frown of Hate,
And there is a Frown of Disdain,
And there is a Frown of Frowns
Which you strive to forget in vain;   8

For it sticks in the Heart's deep Core
And it sticks in the deep Back bone,
And no Smile that ever was smil'd,
But only one Smile alone,   12

That betwixt the Cradle & Grave
It only once Smil'd can be;
But, when it once is Smil'd,
There's an end to all Misery.   16

The Golden Net

THREE Virgins at the break of day:
" Whither, young Man, whither away?
Alas for woe! alas for woe!"
They cry, & tears for ever flow.

The one was Cloth'd in flames of fire,   5
The other Cloth'd in iron wire,
The other Cloth'd in tears & sighs.
Dazling bright before my Eyes
They bore a Net of golden twine
To hang upon the Branches fine.   10
Pitying I wept to see the woe
That Love & Beauty undergo,
To be consum'd in burning Fires
And in ungratified Desires,
And in tears cloth'd night & day   15
Melted all my Soul away.
When they saw my Tears, a Smile
That did Heaven itself beguile,
Bore the Golden Net aloft
As on downy Pinions soft   20
Over the Morning of my Day.
Underneath the Net I stray,
Now intreating Burning Fire,
Now intreating Iron Wire,
Now intreating Tears & Sighs,   25
O when will the morning rise?

The Mental Traveller

I TRAVEL'D thro' a Land of Men,
A Land of Men & Women too,
And heard & saw such dreadful things
As cold Earth wanderers never knew.   4

For there the Babe is born in joy
That was begotten in dire woe,
Just as we Reap in joy the fruit
Which we in bitter tears did sow.   8

And if the Babe is born a Boy
He's given to a Woman Old
Who nails him down upon a rock,
Catches his shrieks in cups of gold.   12

She binds iron thorns around his head,
She pierces both his hands & feet,
She cuts his heart out at his side
To make it feel both cold & heat.   16

Her fingers number every Nerve,
Just as a Miser counts his gold;
She lives upon his shrieks & cries,
And She grows young as he grows old.   20

Till he becomes a bleeding youth
And She becomes a Virgin bright;
Then he rends up his Manacles
And binds her down for his delight.   24

He plants himself in all her Nerves,
Just as a Husbandman his mould;
And She becomes his dwelling place
And Garden fruitful seventy fold.   28

An Aged Shadow, soon he fades,
Wand'ring round an Earthly Cot,
Full filled all with gems & gold
Which he by industry had got.   32

And these are the gems of the Human Soul,
The rubies & pearls of a lovesick eye,
The countless gold of the akeing heart,
The martyr's groan & the lover's sigh.   36

They are his meat, they are his drink;
He feeds the Beggar & the Poor
And the wayfaring Traveller:
For ever open is his door.   40

His grief is their eternal joy;
They make the roofs & walls to ring;
Till from the fire on the hearth
A little Female Babe does spring.   44

And She is all of solid fire
And gems & gold, that none his hand
Dares stretch to touch her Baby form,
Or wrap her in his swaddling-band.   48

But She comes to the Man she loves,
If young or old, or rich or poor;
They soon drive out the aged Host,
A Beggar at another's door,   52

He wanders weeping far away,
Untill some other take him in;
Oft blind & age-bent, sore distrest,
Untill he can a Maiden win.   56

And to allay his freezing Age,
The Poor Man takes her in his arms;
The Cottage fades before his sight,
The Garden & its lovely Charms.   60

The Guests are scatter'd thro' the land,
For the Eye altering alters all;
The Senses roll themselves in fear
And the flat Earth becomes a Ball;   64

The Stars, Sun, Moon, all shrink away,
A desart vast without a bound,
And nothing left to eat or drink,
And a dark desart all around.   68

The honey of her Infant lips,
The bread & wine of her sweet smile,
The wild game of her roving eye,
Does him to Infancy beguile;   72

For as he eats & drinks he grows
Younger & younger every day;
And on the desart wild they both
Wander in terror & dismay.   76

Like the wild Stag she flees away,
Her fear plants many a thicket wild;
While he pursues her night & day,
By various arts of Love beguil'd;   80

By various arts of Love & Hate,
Till the wide desart planted o'er
With Labyrinths of wayward Love,
Where roams the Lion, Wolf & Boar;   84

Till he becomes a wayward Babe,
And she a weeping Woman Old;
Then many a Lover wanders here,
The Sun & Stars are nearer roll'd,   88

The trees bring forth sweet Extacy
To all who in the desert roam,
Till many a City there is Built
And many a pleasant Shepherd's home.   92

But when they find the frowning Babe,
Terror strikes thro' the region wide:
They cry, " the Babe! the Babe is Born! "
And flee away on every side.   96

For who dare touch the frowning form,
His arm is wither'd to its root;
Lions, Boars, Wolves, all howling flee,
And every Tree does shed its fruit.   100

And none can touch that frowning form,
Except it be a Woman Old;
She nails him down upon the Rock,
And all is done as I have told.   104

The Land of Dreams

" AWAKE, awake, my little Boy!
Thou wast thy Mother's only joy;
Why dost thou weep in thy gentle sleep?
Awake! thy Father does thee keep."   4

" O what Land is the Land of Dreams?
What are its Mountains, & what are its Streams?
O Father! I saw my Mother there,
Among the Lillies by waters fair.   8

" Among the Lambs, clothed in white,
She walk'd with her Thomas in sweet delight.
I wept for joy, like a dove I mourn;
O when shall I again return? "   12

" Dear Child, I also by pleasant Streams
Have wander'd all Night in the Land of Dreams;
But tho' calm & warm the waters wide,
I could not get to the other side."   16

" Father, O father! what do we here
In this Land of unbelief & fear?
The Land of Dreams is better far,
Above the light of the Morning Star."   20

Mary

SWEET Mary, the first time she ever was there,
Came into the Ball room among the Fair;
The young Men & Maidens around her throng,
And these are the words upon every tongue: 4

" An Angel is here from the heavenly climes,
Or again does return the golden times;
Her eyes outshine every brilliant ray,
She opens her lips—'tis the Month of May."   8

Mary moves in soft beauty & conscious delight,
To augment with sweet smiles all the joys of the Night,
Nor once blushes to own to the rest of the Fair
That sweet Love & Beauty are worthy our care.   12

In the Morning the Villagers rose with delight,
And repeated with pleasure the joys of the night,

And Mary arose among Friends to be free,
But no Friend from henceforward thou, Mary, shalt see. 16

Some said she was proud, some call'd her a whore,
And some, when she passed by, shut to the door;
A damp cold came o'er her, her blushes all fled;
Her lillies & roses are blighted & shed. 20

" O why was I born with a different Face?
Why was I not born like this Envious Race?
Why did Heaven adorn me with bountiful hand,
And then set me down in an envious Land? 24

" To be weak as a Lamb & smooth as a Dove,
And not to raise Envy, is call'd Christian Love;
But if you raise Envy your Merit's to blame
For planting such spite in the weak & the tame. 28

" I will humble my Beauty, I will not dress fine,
I will keep from the Ball, & my Eyes shall not shine;
And if any Girl's Lover forsakes her for me
I'll refuse him my hand, & from Envy be free." 32

She went out in Morning, attir'd plain & neat;
" Proud Mary's gone Mad," said the Child in the Street;
She went out in Morning in plain neat attire,
And came home in Evening bespatter'd with mire. 36

She trembled & wept, sitting on the Bed side,
She forgot it was Night, & she trembled & cried;
She forgot it was Night, she forgot it was Morn,
Her soft Memory imprinted with Faces of Scorn; 40

With Faces of Scorn & with Eyes of Disdain
Life foul Fiends inhabiting Mary's mild Brain,
She remembers no Face like the Human Divine;
All Faces have Envy, sweet Mary, but thine; 44

And thine is a Face of sweet Love in despair,
And thine is a Face of mild sorrow & care,
And thine is a Face of wild terror & fear
That shall never be quiet till laid on its bier. 48

The Crystal Cabinet

THE Maiden caught me in the Wild,
Where I was dancing merrily;
She put me into her Cabinet,
And Lock'd me up with a golden Key.   4

This Cabinet is form'd of Gold
And Pearl & Crystal shining bright,
And within it opens into a World
And a little lovely Moony Night.   8

Another England there I saw,
Another London with its Tower,
Another Thames & other Hills,
And another pleasant Surrey Bower,   12

Another Maiden like herself,
Translucent, lovely, shining clear,
Threefold each in the other clos'd—
O what a pleasant trembling fear!   16

O what a smile! a threefold Smile
Fill'd me, that like a flame I burn'd;
I bent to Kiss the lovely Maid,
And found a Threefold Kiss return'd.   20

I strove to sieze the inmost Form
With ardor fierce & hands of flame,
But burst the Crystal Cabinet
And like a Weeping Babe became: 24

A weeping Babe upon the wild,
And weeping Woman pale reclin'd,
And in the outward air again
I fill'd with woes the passing Wind.   28

The Grey Monk

" I DIE, I die!'' the Mother said,
" My Children die for lack of Bread.
What more has the merciless Tyrant said?"
The Monk sat down on the Stony Bed.   4

The blood red ran from the Grey Monk's side,
His hands & feet were wounded wide,
His Body bent, his arms & knees
Like to the roots of ancient trees.   8

His eye was dry; no tear could flow:
A hollow groan first spoke his woe.
He trembled & shudder'd upon the Bed;
At length with a feeble cry he said: 12

" When God commanded this hand to write
In the studious hours of deep midnight,
He told me the writing I wrote should prove
The Bane of all that on Earth I lov'd.   16

" My Brother starv'd between two Walls,
His Children's Cry my Soul appalls;
I mock'd at the wrack & griding chain,
My bent body mocks their torturing pain.   20

" Thy Father drew his Sword in the North,
With his thousands strong he marched forth,
Thy Brother has arm'd himself in Steel,
To avenge the wrongs thy Children feel.   24

" But vain the Sword & vain the Bow,
They never can work War's overthrow.
The Hermit's Prayer & the Widow's tear
Alone can free the World from fear.   28

" For a Tear is an Intellectual Thing,
And a Sigh is the Sword of an Angel King,

And the bitter groan of the Martyr's woe
Is an arrow from the Almightie's Bow.   32

" The hand of Vengeance found the Bed
To which the Purple Tyrant fled;
The iron hand crush'd the Tyrant's head,
And became a Tyrant in his stead."   36

Auguries of Innocence

To see a World in a Grain of Sand
And a Heaven in a Wild Flower,
Hold Infinity in the palm of your hand
And Eternity in an hour.

A Robin Red breast in a Cage   5
Puts all Heaven in a Rage.

A Dove house fill'd with Doves & Pigeons
Shudders Hell thro' all its regions.

A Dog starv'd at his Master's Gate
Predicts the ruin of the State.   10

A Horse misus'd upon the Road
Calls to Heaven for Human blood.

Each outcry of the hunted Hare
A fibre from the Brain does tear.

A Skylark wounded in the wing,   15
A Cherubim does cease to sing.

The Game Cock clip'd & arm'd for fight
Does the Rising Sun affright.

Every Wolf's & Lion's howl
Raises from Hell a Human Soul.   20

The wild Deer wand'ring here & there
Keeps the Human Soul from Care.

The Lamb misus'd breeds Public strife
And yet forgives the Butcher's Knife.

The Bat that flits at close of Eve   25
Has left the Brain that won't Believe.
The Owl that calls upon the Night
Speaks the Unbeliever's fright.

He who shall hurt the little Wren
Shall never be belov'd by Men.   30

He who the Ox to wrath has mov'd
Shall never be by Woman lov'd.

The wanton Boy that kills the Fly
Shall feel the Spider's enmity.

He who torments the Chafer's sprite   35
Weaves a Bower in endless Night.

The Catterpiller on the Leaf
Repeats to thee thy Mother's grief.

Kill not the Moth nor Butterfly
For the Last Judgment draweth nigh.   40

He who shall train the Horse to war
Shall never pass the Polar Bar.

The Beggar's Dog & Widow's Cat,
Feed them, & thou wilt grow fat.

The Gnat that sings his Summer's song   45
Poison gets from Slander's tongue.
The poison of the Snake & Newt
Is the sweat of Envy's Foot.
The Poison of the Honey Bee
Is the Artist's Jealousy.   50

The Prince's Robes & Beggar's Rags
Are Toadstools on the Miser's Bags.

A truth that's told with bad intent
Beats all the Lies you can invent.
It is right it should be so; 55
Man was made for Joy & Woe,
And when this we rightly know,
Thro' the World we safely go.

Joy & Woe are woven fine,
A Clothing for the Soul divine; 60
Under every grief & pine
Runs a joy with silken twine.

The Babe is more than Swadling Bands,
Throughout all these Human Lands;
Tools were made, & Born were hands, 65
Every Farmer Understands.

Every Tear from Every Eye
Becomes a Babe in Eternity;
This is caught by Females bright
And return'd to its own delight. 70

The Bleat, the Bark, Bellow & Roar
Are Waves that Beat on Heaven's Shore.

The Babe that weeps the Rod beneath
Writes Revenge in realms of Death.

The Beggar's Rags fluttering in Air 75
Does to Rags the Heavens tear.

The Soldier arm'd with Sword & Gun
Palsied strikes the Summer's Sun.

The poor Man's Farthing is worth more
Than all the Gold on Afric's Shore. 80

One Mite wrung from the Lab'rer's hands
Shall buy & sell the Miser's Lands
Or if protected from on high
Does that whole Nation sell & buy.

He who mocks the Infant's Faith　　　85
Shall be mock'd in Age & Death.
He who shall teach the Child to Doubt
The rotting Grave shall ne'er get out.
He who respects the Infant's faith
Triumphs over Hell & Death.　　　90

The Child's Toys & the Old Man's Reasons
Are the Fruits of the Two seasons.

The Questioner who sits so sly
Shall never know how to Reply.
He who replies to words of Doubt　　　95
Doth put the Light of Knowledge out.

The Strongest Poison ever known
Came from Cæsar's Laurel Crown.

Nought can deform the Human Race
Like to the Armour's iron brace.　　　100

When Gold & Gems adorn the Plow
To peaceful Arts shall Envy Bow.

A Riddle or the Cricket's Cry
Is to Doubt a fit Reply.

The Emmet's Inch & Eagle's Mile　　　105
Make Lame Philosophy to smile.

He who Doubts from what he sees
Will ne'er Believe, do what you Please.
If the Sun & Moon should doubt,
They'd immediately Go out.　　　110

To be in a Passion you Good may do,
But no Good if a Passion is in you.

The Whore & Gambler, by the State
Licenc'd, build that Nation's Fate.
The Harlot's cry from Street to Street　　　115
Shall weave Old England's winding Sheet.

The Winner's Shout, the Loser's Curse,
Dance before dead England's Hearse.

Every Night & every Morn
Some to Misery are Born.   120
Every Morn & every Night
Some are Born to sweet delight.
Some are Born to sweet delight,
Some are Born to Endless Night.

We are led to Believe a Lie   125
When we see not Thro' the Eye
Which was Born in a Night, to perish in a Night,
When the Soul Slept in Beams of Light.

God Appears, & God is Light
To those poor Souls who dwell in Night,   130
But does a Human Form Display
To those who Dwell in Realms of Day.

Long John Brown & Little Mary Bell

LITTLE Mary Bell had a Fairy in a Nut,
Long John Brown had the Devil in his Gut;
Long John Brown lov'd Little Mary Bell,
And the Fairy drew the Devil into the Nut-shell.   4

Her Fairy Skip'd out & her Fairy Skip'd in;
He laugh'd at the Devil saying " Love is a Sin."
The Devil he raged & the Devil he was wroth,
And the Devil enter'd into the Young Man's broth.   8

He was soon in the Gut of the loving Young Swain,
For John eat & drank to drive away Love's pain;
But all he could do he grew thinner & thinner,
Tho' he eat & drank as much as ten Men for his dinner. 12

Some said he had a Wolf in his stomach day & night,
Some said he had the Devil, & they guess'd right;

The fairy skip'd about in his Glory, Joy & Pride,
And he laugh'd at the Devil till poor John Brown died. 16

Then the Fairy skip'd out of the old Nut-shell,
And woe & alack for Pretty Mary Bell!
For the Devil crept in where the Fairy skip'd out,
And there goes Miss Bell with her fusty old Nut. 20

William Bond

I WONDER whether the Girls are mad,
And I wonder whether they mean to kill,
And I wonder if William Bond will die,
For assuredly he is very ill. 4

He went to Church in a May morning,
Attended by Fairies, one, two, & three;
But the Angels of Providence drove them away,
And he return'd home in Misery. 8

He went not out to the Field nor Fold,
He went not out to the Village nor Town,
But he came home in a black black cloud,
And he took to his Bed, & there lay down. 12

And an Angel of Providence at his Feet,
And an Angel of Providence at his Head,
And in the midst a Black Black Cloud,
And in the midst the Sick Man on his Bed. 16

And on his Right hand was Mary Green,
And on his Left hand was his Sister Jane,
And their tears fell thro' the black black Cloud
To drive away the sick man's pain. 20

" O William, if thou dost another Love,
Dost another Love better than poor Mary,
Go & take that other to be thy Wife,
And Mary Green shall her Servant be." 24

" Yes, Mary, I do another Love,
Another I Love far better than thee,
And Another I will have for my Wife;
Then what have I to do with thee?   28

" For thou art Melancholy Pale,
And on thy Head is the cold Moon's Shine,
But she is ruddy & bright as day,
And the sun beams dazzle from her eyne."   32

Mary trembled & Mary chill'd,
And Mary fell down on the right hand floor.
That William Bond & his Sister Jane
Scarce could recover Mary more.   36

When Mary woke & found her Laid
On the Right hand of her William dear,
On the Right hand of his loved Bed,
And saw her William Bond so near,   40

The Fairies that fled from William Bond
Danced around her Shining Head;
They danced over the Pillow white,
And the Angels of Providence left the Bed. 44

I thought Love liv'd in the hot sun shine,
But O he lives in the Moony light!
I thought to find Love in the heat of day,
But sweet Love is the Comforter of Night. 48

Seek Love in the Pity of others' Woe,
In the gentle relief of another's care,
In the darkness of night & the winter's snow,
In the naked & outcast, Seek Love there.   52

POEMS FROM BLAKE'S MS. BOOK

(Commonly known as The " Rossetti " MS.)

(About 1800–1803*)*

(The following verses exist only in MS., and were written,
probably about the year 1800, *in the early pages of what*
had been a sketch-book containing some seventy small
drawings, similar in size and character to those of
" The Gates of Paradise," and about a dozen full-page
illustrations. Blake had already used the other end of
this book for the early versions of the " Songs of Experi-
ence " (see p. 373), *and a little later he crowded the*
pages with prose comments, tags and quips on paint-
ing, which comprise the so-called " Public Address,"
the more carefully written and more important para-
graphs concerning his picture, " The Last Judgment "
(see p. 357), *the couplets of " The Everlasting Gospel "*
(see p. 346), *and a number of hastily-written epigrams*
on friends and acquaintances.)

I

My Spectre around me night & day
Like a Wild beast guards my way;
My Emanation, far within,
Weeps incessantly for my Sin.

2

A Fathomless & boundless Deep
There we wander, there we weep;
On the hungry craving wind
My Spectre follows thee behind.

3

He scents thy footsteps in the snow
Wheresoever thou dost go
Thro' the wintry hail & rain:
When wilt thou return again?

4

Dost thou not in Pride & scorn
Fill with tempests all my morn?
And with jealousies & fears
Fill my pleasant nights with tears?

5

Seven of my sweet loves thy knife
Has bereaved of their life;
Their marble tombs I built with tears
And with cold & shuddering fears.

6

Seven more loves weep night & day
Round the tombs where my loves lay,
And seven more loves attend each night
Around my couch with torches bright.

7

And Seven more Loves in my bed
Crown with wine my mournful head,
Pitying & forgiving all
Thy transgressions great & small.

8

When wilt thou return & view
My loves, & them to life renew?
When wilt thou return & live?
When wilt thou pity, as I forgive?

9

" Never, Never I return!
Still for Victory I burn:
Living, thee alone I'll have,
And when dead I'll be thy Grave.

10

" Thro' the Heav'n & Earth & Hell
Thou shalt never, never quell;
I will fly & thou pursue,
Night & Morn the flight renew."

11

Till I turn from Female Love
And root up the Infernal Grove,
I shall never worthy be
To Step into Eternity.

12

And to end thy cruel mocks
Annihilate thee on the rocks,
And another form create
To be subservient to my Fate.

13

Let us agree to give up Love
And root up the infernal grove;
Then we shall return & see
The worlds of happy Eternity.

14

& Throughout all Eternity
I forgive you, you forgive me;
As our dear Redeemer said,
' This the Wine & this the Bread.'

———

Mock on, Mock on! Voltaire, Rousseau,
Mock on, Mock on! 'tis all in vain!
You throw the sand against the wind,
And the wind blows it back again.

And every sand becomes a Gem
Reflected in the beams divine;
Blown back they blind the mocking Eye,
But still in Israel's paths they shine.

The Atoms of Democritus
And Newton's Particles of Light
Are sands upon the Red sea shore
Where Israel's tents do shine so bright.

Morning

To find the Western path
Right thro' the Gates of Wrath
I urge my way.
Sweet Mercy leads me on,
With soft repentant moan
I see the break of day.

The war of swords & spears
Melted by dewy tears
Exhales on high.
The Sun is freed from fears
And with soft grateful tears
Ascends the sky.

The Birds

He. WHERE thou dwellest, in what grove,
Tell me, Fair one, tell me love
Where thou thy charming Nest doth build,
O thou pride of every field!

She. Yonder stands a lonely tree,
There I live & mourn for thee:
Morning drinks my silent tear,
And evening winds my sorrows bear.

He. O thou Summer's harmony,
I have liv'd & mourn'd for thee:
Each day I mourn along the wood,
And night hath heard my sorrows loud.

She. Dost thou truly long for me?
And am I thus sweet to thee?
Sorrow now is at an End,
O My Lover & my Friend!

He. Come, on wings of joy we'll fly
To where my Bower hangs on high;
Come & make thy calm retreat
Among green leaves & blossoms sweet.

[1] WHY was Cupid a Boy
And why a boy was he?
He should have been a Girl
For ought that I can see;

For he shoots with his bow,
And the Girl shoots with her Eye;
And they both are merry & glad,
And laugh when we do cry.

And to make Cupid a Boy
Was the Cupid Girl's mocking plan;
For a boy can't interpret the thing
Till he is become a man;

And then he's so pierc'd with cares
And wounded with arrowy smarts
That the whole business of his life
Is to pick out the heads of the darts.

'Twas the Greeks' love of war
Turn'd Love into a Boy
And Woman into a Statue of Stone,
And away fled every Joy.

———

I ROSE up at the dawn of day:
" Get thee away, get thee away!
Pray'st thou for Riches? away, away!
This is the Throne of Mammon grey."

Said I: " this sure is very odd,
I took it to be the Throne of God,
For every Thing besides I have,
It is only for Riches that I can crave.

[1] This poem and the two following are certainly of later date, having
been written after Blake returned to London from Felpham in 1803.

" I have Mental Joy & Mental Health.
And Mental Friends & Mental wealth;
I've a Wife I love & that loves me;
I've all But Riches Bodily.

[1] " I am in God's presence night & day,
And he never turns his face away.
The accuser of sins by my side does stand,
And he holds my money bag in his hand.

" For my worldly things God makes him pay,
And he'd pay for more if to him I would pray,
And so you may do the worst you can do,
Be assur'd Mr. Devil, I won't pray to you.

" Then If for Riches I must not Pray,
God knows I little of Prayers need say;
So, as a Church is known by its Steeple,
If I pray it must be for other People.

" He says if I do not worship him for a God
I shall eat coarser food & go worse shod;
So, as I don't value such things as these,
You must do, Mr. Devil, just as God please." [2]

[1] This verse and the next were an afterthought marked for insertion here.

[2] At another time, and upon another page of the MS. Book, Blake wrote:

Since all the Riches of this World
May be gifts from the Devil & Earthly Kings,
I should suspect that I worship'd the Devil
If I thank'd my God for Worldly things.

THE EVERLASTING GOSPEL

Passages collected chiefly from the MS. Book.

(About 1818*)*

¹ I<small>F</small> Moral Virtue was Christianity
Christ's Pretensions were all Vanity,
And Caiaphas & Pilate, Men
Praise Worthy, & the Lion's Den
And not the Sheepfold, Allegories   5
Of God & Heaven & their Glories.
The Moral Christian is the Cause
Of the Unbeliever & his Laws.
² *The Roman Virtues, Warlike Fame,*
Take Jesus' & Jehovah's Name: 10
For what is Antichrist but those
Who against Sinners Heaven close
With Iron bars, in Virtuous State,
And Rhadamanthus at the Gate?

---

¹ The following prose lines preceded this passage in Blake's manuscript:

There is not one Moral Virtue that Jesus Inculcated but
Plato & Cicero did Inculcate before him: what then did
Christ Inculcate? Forgiveness of Sins. This alone is the
Gospel, and this is the Life & Immortality brought to light
by Jesus, Even the Covenant of Jehovah, which is This:
If you forgive one another your Trespasses, so shall
Jehovah forgive you, That he himself may dwell among
you; but if you Avenge, you Murder the Divine Image,
& he cannot dwell among you because you Murder him:
he arises again & you deny that he is Arisen & are blind
to Spirit.

² Blake's additions are usually afterthoughts made without much re-
gard to form or context. Inserted lines are therefore printed in italic.

What can this Gospel of Jesus be?
What Life & Immortality,
What was it that he brought to Light
That Plato & Cicero did not write?
The Heathen Deities wrote them all,   5
These Moral Virtues, great & small.
What is the Accusation of Sin
But Moral Virtue's deadly Gin?
The Moral Virtues in their Pride
Did o'er the World triumphant ride   10
In Wars & Sacrifice for Sin,
And Souls to Hell ran trooping in.
The Accuser, Holy God of All
This Pharisaic Worldly Ball,
Amidst them in his Glory Beams   15
Upon the Rivers & the Streams.
Then Jesus rose & said to Me,
' Thy Sins are all forgiven thee.'
Loud Pilate Howl'd, loud Caiaphas yell'd
When they the Gospel Light beheld.   20
It was when Jesus said to Me
' Thy Sins are all forgiven thee '
The Christian trumpets loud proclaim
Thro' all the World in Jesus' name
Mutual forgiveness of each Vice   25
And oped the Gates of Paradise.
The Moral Virtues in Great fear
Formed the Cross & Nails & Spear,
And the Accuser standing by
Cried out, " Crucify! Crucify!   30
Our Moral Virtues ne'er can be,
Nor Warlike pomp & Majesty,
For Moral Virtues all begin
In the Accusations of Sin,
And all the Heroic Virtues End   35
In destroying the Sinners' Friend.
Am I not Lucifer the Great,
And you, my daughters in Great State,

The fruit of my Mysterious Tree
Of Good & Evil, & Misery
And Death & Hell which now begin
On everyone who Forgives Sin?''

———

Was Jesus Humble, or did he
Give any Proofs of Humility?
Boast of high Things with Humble tone,
And give with Charity a Stone?
When but a Child he ran away,
And left his Parents in dismay.
When they had wander'd three days long
These were the words upon his tongue:
'' No Earthly Parents I confess:
I am doing my Father's business.''
When the rich learned Pharisee
Came to consult him secretly,
Upon his heart with Iron pen
He wrote, '' Ye must be born again.''
He was too proud to take a bribe;
He spoke with authority, not like a Scribe.
He says, with most consummate Art,
'' Follow me, I am meek & lowly of heart,''
As that is the only way to escape
The Miser's net & the Glutton's trap.
He who loves his Enemies betrays his Friends: [1]
This surely is not what Jesus intends,
But the sneaking Pride of Heroic Schools,
And the Scribes' & Pharisees' Virtuous Rules;
For he acts with honest, triumphant Pride,
And this is the cause that Jesus died.
He did not die with Christian Ease,
Asking pardon of his Enemies:
If he had, Caiaphas would forgive:
Sneaking submission can always live.

40

5

10

15

20

25

30

[1] By the side of this line Blake wrote:

What can be done with such desperate Fools
Who follow after the Heathen Schools?
I was standing by when Jesus died;
What I call'd Humility, they call'd Pride.

He had only to say that God was the devil,
And the devil was God, like a Christian Civil,
Mild Christian regrets to the devil confess
For affronting him thrice in the Wilderness,
He had soon been bloody Cæsar's Elf, 35
And at last he would have been Cæsar himself,
Like Dr. Priestly & Bacon & Newton—
Poor Spiritual Knowledge is not worth a button—
For thus the Gospel Sir Isaac confutes:
" God can only be known by his Attributes, 40
And as to the Indwelling of the Holy Ghost
Or of Christ & his Father, it's all a boast
And Pride & Vanity of the imagination
That disdains to follow this World's Fashion."
To teach Doubt & Experiment 45
Certainly was not what Christ meant.
What was he doing all that time,
From twelve years old to manly prime?
Was he then Idle, or the Less
About his Father's business? 50
Or was his wisdom held in scorn
Before his wrath began to burn
In Miracles throughout the Land,
That quite unnerv'd the [1] haughty hand?
If he had been Antichrist, Creeping Jesus, 55
He'd have done any thing to please us:
Gone sneaking into Synagogues,
And not us'd the Elders & Priests like dogs,
But Humble as a Lamb or Ass
Obey'd himself to Caiaphas. 60
God wants not Man to Humble himself:
This is the trick of the ancient Elf.
This is the Race that Jesus ran:
Humble to God, Haughty to Man,
Cursing the Rulers before the People 65
Even to the temple's highest Steeple,
And when he Humbled himself to God
Then descended the Cruel Rod.
" If thou humblest thyself, thou humblest me:
Thou also dwell'st in Eternity. 70

[1] This word is doubtful.

Thou art a Man, God is no more;
Thy own humanity learn to adore,
For that is my Spirit of Life.
Awake, arise to Spiritual Strife,
And thy Revenge abroad display   75
In terrors at the Last Judgment day.
God's Mercy & Long Suffering
Is but the Sinner to Judgment to bring.
Thou on the Cross for them shalt pray,
And take Revenge at the Last Day."   80
[1] *Jesus replied, & thunders hurl'd:*
    " I never will Pray for the World.
    Once I did so when I pray'd in the Garden:
    I wish'd to take with me a Bodily Pardon."
Can that which was of woman born,   85
In the absence of the Morn,
When the Soul fell into Sleep,
And Archangels round it weep,
Shooting out against the Light
Fibres of a deadly night,   90
Reasoning upon its own dark Fiction,
In Doubt which is Self Contradiction?
Humility is only doubt,
And does the Sun & Moon blot out,
Rooting over with thorns & stems   95
The buried Soul & all its gems.
This Life's five [2] Windows of the Soul
Distorts the Heavens from Pole to Pole
And leads you to Believe a Lie
When you see with, not thro' the Eye   100
That was born in a night, to perish in a night,
When the Soul slept in the beams of Light.[3]

---

[1] ll. 81-84. Originally the couplet:
                 " This Corporeal life's a fiction
                 And is made up of contradiction,"
which shows connection with what follows better than the emendation.
[2] Mr. Keynes reads this word as " dim."
[3] Against the end of this line Blake wrote the couplet:
                 I'm sure This Jesus will not do
                 Either for Englishman or Jew.

Was Jesus Chaste, or did he
Give any Lessons of Chastity?
The morning blush'd fiery red: 105
Mary was found in Adulterous bed;
Earth groan'd beneath, & Heaven above
Trembled at discovery of Love.
Jesus was sitting in Moses' Chair,
They brought the trembling Woman There.[1]   110
Moses commands she be ston'd to death:
What was the sound of Jesus' breath?
He laid His hand on Moses' Law;
The Ancient Heavens, in Silent Awe,
Writ with Curses from Pole to Pole,   115
All away began to roll.
The Earth, trembling & Naked lay
In secret bed of Mortal Clay,
On Sinai felt the hand divine
Putting back the bloody shrine,   120
And She heard the breath of God
As She heard by Eden's flood,
" Good & Evil are no more!
Sinai's trumpets, cease to roar!
Cease, finger of God, to write!   125
The Heavens are not clean in thy Sight.
Thou art Good, & thou Alone;
Nor may the sinner cast one stone.
To be Good only is to be
A God or else a Pharisee.   130
Thou Angel of the Presence Divine,
That didst create this Body of Mine,
Wherefore hast thou writ these Laws
And Created Hell's dark jaws?
My Presence I will take from thee: 135

[1] On the right of this passage, written sideways in pencil, are the lines:

> Did Jesus teach Doubt? or did he
> Give any lessons of Philosophy,
> Charge Visionaries with Deceiving,
> Or call Men wise for not Believing?

and to this, apparently at another time, Blake added:

This was spoke by My Spectre to Voltaire, Bacon, &c.

A Cold Leper thou shalt be.
Tho' thou wast so pure & bright
That Heaven was Impure in thy Sight,
Tho' thy Oath turn'd Heaven Pale,
Tho' thy Covenant built Hell's Jail,   140
Tho' thou didst all to Chaos roll
With the Serpent for its soul,
Still the breath Divine does move,
And the breath Divine is Love.
Mary, Fear Not. Let me see   145
The Seven Devils that torment thee:
Hide not from my Sight thy Sin,
That forgiveness thou maist win.
Has no Man Condemned thee? ''
'' No Man, Lord.'' '' then what is he   150
Who shall Accuse thee? Come Ye forth,
Fallen fiends of Heav'nly birth
That have forgot your Ancient love
And driven away my trembling Dove.
You shall bow before her feet;   155
You shall lick the dust for Meat;
And tho' you cannot Love, but Hate,
Shall be beggars at Love's Gate.
What was thy love? let me see it;
Was it love or dark deceit?''   160
'' Love too long from Me has fled;
'Twas dark deceit, to Earn my bread;
'Twas Covet, or 'twas Custom, or
Some trifle not worth caring for;
That they may call a shame & Sin   165
Love's temple that God dwelleth in,
And hide in secret hidden shrine
The Naked Human form divine,
And render that a Lawless thing
On which the Soul Expands its wing,   170
But this, O Lord, this was my Sin
When first I let these devils in:
In dark pretence to Chastity
Blaspheming Love, blaspheming thee.
Thence Rose Secret Adulteries,   175
And thence did Covet also rise.

My Sin thou hast forgiven me,
Canst thou forgive my Blasphemy?
Canst thou return to this dark Hell,
And in my burning bosom dwell? 180
And canst thou die that I may live?
And canst thou Pity & forgive? ''
Then Roll'd the Shadowy Man away
From the Limbs of Jesus, to make them his prey,
An Ever devouring appetite, 185
Glittering with festering venoms bright;
Crying " Crucify this cause of distress,
Who don't keep the secrets of holiness!
All Mental Powers by Diseases we bind,
But he heals the deaf & the dumb & the Blind. 190
Whom God has afflicted for Secret Ends,
He Comforts & Heals & calls them Friends.''
But when Jesus was Crucified,
Then was perfected his glitt'ring pride.
In three Nights he devour'd his prey, 195
And still he devours the Body of Clay;
For Dust & Clay is the Serpent's meat,
Which never was made for Man to Eat.
Seeing this False Christ, In Fury & Passion
I made my Voice heard all over the Nation. 200
What are those, &c.[1]

Was Jesus gentle, or did he
Give any marks of Gentility?
When twelve years old he ran away
And left his Parents in dismay.
When after three days' sorrow found, 5
Loud as Sinai's trumpet sound:
" No Earthly Parents I confess
My Heavenly Father's business.
Ye understand not what I say,
And angry, force me to obey.'' 10
Obedience is a duty then,

[1] The remainder of this passage cannot be identified and is probably lost.

And favour gains with God & Men.
John from the Wilderness loud cried;
Satan gloried in his Pride.
" Come," said Satan, " come away,   15
I'll soon see if you'll obey!
John for disobedience bled,
But you can turn the stones to bread.
God's high king & God's high Priest
Shall Plant their Glories in your breast   20
If Caiaphas you will obey,
If Herod you with bloody Prey
Feed with the Sacrifice, & be
Obedient, fall down, worship me."
Thunders & lightnings broke around,   25
And Jesus' voice in thunders' sound:
" Thus I sieze the Spiritual Prey:
Ye smiters with disease, make way!
I come Your King & God to sieze,
Is God a Smiter with disease? "   30
The God of this World rag'd in vain.
He bound Old Satan in his Chain,
And bursting forth, his furious ire
Became a Chariot of fire:
Throughout the land he took his course,   35
And traced diseases to their Source:
He curs'd the Scribe and Pharisee,
Trampling down Hipocrisy:
Where'er his Chariot took its way
There Gates of death let in the day,   40
Broke down from every Chain & Bar,
And Satan in his Spiritual War
Drag'd at his Chariot wheels: loud howl'd
The God of this World: louder roll'd
The Chariot Wheels, & louder still   45
His voice was heard from Zion's hill,
And in his hand the Scourge shone bright;
He scourg'd the Merchant Canaanite
From out the Temple of his Mind,
And in his Body tight does bind   50
Satan & all his Hellish Crew;
And thus with wrath he did subdue

The Serpent Bulk of Nature's dross,
Till he had nail'd it to the Cross.
He took on Sin in the Virgin's Womb   55
And put it off on the Cross & Tomb
To be Worship'd by the Church of Rome.

Was Jesus Born of a Virgin Pure
With narrow Soul & looks demure?
If he intended to take on Sin
The Mother should an Harlot been,
Just such a one as Magdalen   5
With seven devils in her Pen:
Or were Jew Virgins still more Curst,
And more sucking devils nurst?
Or what was it which he took on
That he might bring Salvation?   10
A Body subject to be Tempted,
From neither pain nor grief exempted;
Or such a body as might not feel
The passions that with Sinners deal?
Yes, but they say he never fell.   15
Ask Caiaphas, for he can tell.
" He mock'd the Sabbath, & he mock'd
The Sabbath's God, & he unlock'd
The Evil spirits from their Shrines,
And turn'd Fishermen to Divines;   20
O'erturn'd the Tent of Secret Sins,
& its Golden cords & Pins:
'Tis the Bloody Shrine of War
Pinn'd around from Star to Star:
Halls of justice, hating Vice,   25
Where the devil Combs his lice:
He turn'd the devils into Swine
That he might tempt the Jews to dine;
Since which, a Pig has got a look
That for a Jew may be mistook.   30
' Obey your parents.'—what says he?
' Woman, what have I to do with thee?
No Earthly Parents I confess:
I am doing my Father's Business.'

He scorn'd Earth's Parents, scorn'd Earth's God,   35
And mock'd the one & the other's Rod;
His Seventy Disciples sent
Against Religion & Government:
They by the Sword of Justice fell,
And him their Cruel Murderer tell.   40
He left his Father's trade to roam,
A wand'ring Vagrant without Home;
And thus he other's labour stole,
That he might live above Controll.
The Publicans & Harlots he   45
Selected for his Company,
And from the Adulteress turn'd away
God's righteous Law, that lost its Prey."

---

[1] The Vision of Christ that thou dost see
Is my Vision's Greatest Enemy:
Thine has a great hook nose like thine,
Mine has a snub nose like to mine:
Thine is the friend of All Mankind,
Mine speaks in parables to the Blind.   5
Thine loves the same world that mine hates,
Thy Heaven doors are my Hell Gates.
Socrates taught what Meletus
Loath'd as a Nation's bitterest Curse,
And Caiaphas was in his own Mind   10
A benefactor to Mankind.
Both read the Bible day & night,
But thou read'st black where I read white.

[1] These fourteen lines were written sideways on p. 33 of the MS. Book, and are probably later than most of the foregoing.

¹THE LAST JUDGMENT

Paragraphs from Blake's MS. Book concerning his picture of The Last Judgment, a picture now lost

(*About* 1818)

§ I. (pp. 68–78)

THE Last Judgment is not Fable or Allegory, but Vision. Fable or Allegory are a totally distinct & inferior kind of Poetry. Vision or Imagination is a Representation of what Eternally Exists, Really & Unchangeably. Fable or Allegory is Form'd by the daughters of Memory. Imagination is Surrounded by the daughters of Inspiration, who in the aggregate are call'd Jerusalem.² *Fable is Allegory, but what Critics call The Fable, is Vision itself.* The Hebrew Bible & the Gospel of Jesus are not Allegory, but Eternal Vision, or Imagination of All that Exists.ᵃ

Note here that Fable or Allegory is seldom without some Vision. Pilgrim's Progress is full of it, the Greek Poets the same; but Allegory & Vision ought to be known as Two Distinct Things, & so call'd for the Sake of Eternal Life.

Plato has made Socrates say that Poets & Prophets do not Know or Understand what they write or Utter; this is a most Pernicious Falshood. If they do not, pray is an inferior kind to be call'd Knowing? Plato confutes himself. ᵝ

The Last Judgment is one of these Stupendous Visions. I have represented it as I saw it; to different People it appears differently as every thing else does; for tho' on Earth things seem Permanent, they are less permanent than a Shadow, as we all know too well.

The Nature of Visionary Fancy, or Imagination, is very little Known, & the Eternal nature & permanence of its ever Existent Images is consider'd as less permanent than

---

¹ This title, adopted for convenience, is not Blake's.
² Inserted passages are printed in italics.
ᵃ, ᵝ. See additional paragraphs on p. 370.

the things of Vegetative & Generative Nature; yet the Oak dies as well as the Lettuce, but Its Eternal Image & Individuality never dies, but renews by its seed; just so the Imaginative Image returns by the seed of Contemplative Thought; the Writings of the Prophets illustrate these conceptions of the Visionary Fancy by their various sublime & Divine Images as seen in the Worlds of Vision.

This world of Imagination is the world of Eternity; it is the divine bosom into which we shall all go after the death of the Vegetated body. This World of Imagination is Infinite & Eternal, whereas the world of Generation, or Vegetation, is Finite & Temporal. There Exist in that Eternal World the Permanent Realities of Every Thing which we see reflected in this Vegetable Glass of Nature. All Things are comprehended in their Eternal Forms in the divine body of the Saviour, the True Vine of Eternity, The Human Imagination, who appear'd to Me as Coming to Judgment among his Saints & throwing off the Temporal that the Eternal might be Establish'd; around him were seen the Images of Existences according to a certain order Suited to my Imaginative Eye as follows [1] :

Jesus seated between the Two Pillars, Jachin & Boaz, with the Word of *divine* Revelation on his knees, *& on each side the four & twenty Elders sitting in judgment;* the Heavens opening around him by unfolding the clouds around his throne. *The Old H. & O. Earth are passing away & the N. H. & N. Earth descending.* The Just arise on his right & the wicked on his Left hand. *A sea of fire issues from before the throne.* Adam & Eve appear first, before the Judgment seat in humiliation. Abel surrounded by Innocents, & Cain, *with the flint in his hand with which he slew his brother,* falling with the head downward. From the Cloud on which Eve stands, Satan is seen falling headlong, wound round by the tail of the serpent whose bulk, nail'd to the Cross round which he wreathes, is falling into the Abyss. Sin is also represented as a female bound in one of the Serpent's folds, surrounded by her fiends. Death is

[1] Blake evidently intended to arrange the foregoing so that comments on the nature of the Last Judgment should follow a description of his picture, for he has two notes here: " Here follows the description of the Picture," and then, probably later: " Query, the above ought to follow the description."

Chain'd to the Cross, & Time falls together with Death, dragged down by a demon crown'd with Laurel; another demon with a Key has the charge of Sin & is dragging her down by the hair; beside them a figure is seen, scaled with iron scales from head to feet precipitating himself into the Abyss with the Sword & Balances: he is Og, King of Bashan.

On the Right, Beneath the Cloud on which Abel Kneels, is Abraham with Sarah & Isaac, also Hagar & Ishmael.

Abel kneels on a bloody cloud, descriptive of those Churches before the flood, that they were fill'd with blood & fire & vapour of smoke: even till Abraham's time the vapor & heat was not extinguish'd: these States Exist now. Man Passes on, but States remain for Ever: he passes thro' them like a traveller who may as well suppose that the places he has passed thro' exist no more as a Man may suppose that the States he has pass'd thro' Exist no more. Every Thing is Eternal. γ

Ishmael is Mahomed, & on the left, beneath the falling figure of Cain, is Moses casting his tables of stone into the deeps. It ought to be understood that the Persons, Moses & Abraham, are not here meant, but the States Signified by those Names, the Individuals being representatives, or Visions, of those States as they were reveal'd to Mortal Man in the Series of Divine Revelations as they are written in the Bible; these various States I have seen in my Imagination; when distant they appear as One Man, but as you approach they appear Multitudes of Nations. Abraham hovers above his posterity, which appear as Multitudes of Children ascending from the Earth, surrounded by Stars, as it was said: ' As the Stars of Heaven for Multitude.' Jacob & his Twelve Sons hover beneath the feet of Abraham & recieve their children from the Earth. *I have seen, when at a distance, Multitudes of Men in Harmony appear like a Single Infant, sometimes in the Arms of a Female which represented the Church.*

But to proceed with the description of those on the Left hand:—beneath the Cloud on which Moses kneels is two figures, a Male & Female, chain'd together by the feet; they represent those who perish'd by the flood; beneath them a multitude of their associates are seen falling head-

γ See additional paragraphs on p. 371.

long; by the side of them is a Mighty fiend with a Book in his hand, which is Shut; he represents the person nam'd in Isaiah, xxii c. & 20 v., Eliakim, the Son of Hilkiah: he drags Satan down headlong: he is crown'd with oak; by the side of the Scaled figure representing Og, King of Bashan, is a Figure with a Basket, emptying out the vanities of Riches & Worldly Honours: *he is Araunah, the Jebusite, master of the threshing floor*; above him are two figures, *elevated on a Cloud,* representing the Pharisees who plead their own Righteousness before the throne; they are weighed down by two fiends. Beneath the Man with the Basket are three fiery fiends with grey beards & scourges of fire: they represent Cruel Laws; they scourge a groupe of figures down into the deeps; beneath them are various figures in attitudes of contention representing various States of Misery, which, alas, every one on Earth is liable to enter into, & against which we should all watch.

The Ladies will be pleas'd to see that I have represented the Furies by Three Men & not by three Women. It is not because I think the Ancients wrong, but they will be pleas'd to remember that mine is Vision & not Fable.

The Spectator may suppose them Clergymen in the Pulpit, scourging Sin instead of Forgiving it.

The Earth beneath these falling Groupes of figures is rocky & burning, and seems as if convuls'd by Earthquakes; a Great City *on fire* is seen in the distance; *the armies are fleeing upon the Mountains.* On the foreground, hell is opened & many figures are descending into it down stone steps & beside a Gate beneath a rock *where sin & death are to be closed Eternally by that Fiend who carries the key in one hand & drags them down with the other.* On the rock & above the Gate, a fiend with wings urges the wicked onwards with fiery darts; he is Hazael, the Syrian, who drives abroad all those who rebell against their Saviour; beneath the steps Babylon, represented by a King crowned, grasping his Sword & his Sceptre: he is just awaken'd out of his Grave; around him are other Kingdoms arising to Judgment, represented in this Picture as Single Personages according to the descriptions in the Prophets. *The Figure dragging up a Woman by her hair represents the Inquisition, as do those contending on the sides of the Pit, & in Particular, the Man strangling two women represents a Cruel Church.*

Two persons, one in Purple, the other in Scarlet, are descending down the Steps into the Pit; these are Caiaphas & Pilate—Two States where all those reside who Calumniate & Murder *under Pretence of Holiness & Justice.* Caiaphas has a Blue Flame like a Miter on his head: Pilate had bloody hands that never can be cleansed; the Females behind them represent the Females belonging to such States, who are under perpetual terrors & vain dreams, plots & secret deceit. Those figures that descend into the Flames before Caiaphas & Pilate are Judas & those of his Class. Achitophel is also here with the cord in his hand.

§ II. (pp. 80–85)

Between the Figures of Adam & Eve appears a fiery Gulph descending from the sea of fire. Before the throne in this Cataract Four Angels descend headlong with four trumpets to awake the dead; beneath these is the Seat of the Harlot, *nam'd* Mystery in the Revelations. She is siezed by Two Beings each with three heads; they Represent Vegetative Existence; as it is written in Revelations, they strip her naked & burn her with fire; *it represents the Eternal Consummation of Vegetable Life & Death with its Lusts. The wreathed Torches in their hands represents Eternal Fire which is the fire of Generation or Vegetation; it is an Eternal Consummation. Those who are blessed with Imaginative Vision see This Eternal Female & tremble at what others fear not, while they despise & laugh at what others fear.*

Her Kings & Councillors & Warriors descend in Flames, Lamenting & looking upon her in astonishment & Terror, & Hell is open'd beneath her Seat on the Left hand: beneath her feet is a flaming Cavern in which is seen the Great Red Dragon with seven heads & ten Horns; *he has Satan's book of Accusations lying on the Rock open before him;* he is bound in chains by Two Strong Demons; they are Gog & Magog, *who have been compell'd to subdue their Master (Ezekiel, xxxviii c, 8 v.) with their Hammer & Tongs, about to new*

Create the Seven Headed Kingdoms. The Graves beneath are open'd, & the dead awake & obey the call of the Trumpet; those on the Right hand awake in joy, those on the Left in Horror; beneath the Dragon's Cavern a Skeleton begins to Animate, starting into life at the Trumpet's sound, while the Wicked contend with each other on the brink of perdition. *On the Right,* a Youthful couple are awaked by their Children; an Aged patriarch is awaked by his aged wife—*He is Albion, our Ancestor, patriarch of the Atlantic Continent, whose History Preceded that of the Hebrews & in whose Sleep, or Chaos, Creation began; at their head the Aged Woman is Britannica, the Wife of Albion: Jerusalem is their daughter*—little Infants creep out of the flowery mould into the Green fields of the blessed, who in various joyful companies embrace & ascend to meet Eternity.

The Persons who ascend to Meet the Lord coming in the Clouds with power & great Glory, are representations of those States described in the Bible under the Names of the Fathers before & after the Flood. Noah is seen in the Midst of these, canopied by a Rainbow, on his right hand Shem & on his Left Japhet; these three Persons represent Poetry, Painting & Music, the three Powers *in Man* of conversing with Paradise, which the flood did not Sweep away.

Above Noah is the Church Universal, represented by a Woman Surrounded by Infants. There is such a State in Eternity: it is composed of the Innocent *civilized* Heathen & the Uncivilized Savage, who, having not the Law, do by Nature the things contain'd in the Law. This State appears like a Female crown'd with Stars, driven into the Wilderness; she has the Moon under her feet.

The Aged Figure with Wings, having a writing tablet & taking account of the numbers who arise, is That Angel of the Divine Presence mention'd in Exodus, xiv c., 19 v. & in other Places; this Angel is frequently call'd by the Name of Jehovah Elohim, The ' I am ' of the Oaks of Albion.

Around Noah & beneath him are various figures Risen into the Air; among these are Three Females, representing those who are not of the dead but of those found alive at the Last Judgment; they appear to be innocently gay &

thoughtless, not being among the condemn'd because ignorant of crime in the midst of a corrupted Age; *the Virgin Mary was of this Class.* A Mother Meets her numerous Family in the Arms of their Father; these are representations of the Greek Learned & Wise, as also of those of other Nations, such as Egypt & Babylon, in which were multitudes who shall meet the Lord coming in the Clouds.

The Children of Abraham, or Hebrew Church, are represented as a Stream of Figures,[1] on which are seen Stars somewhat like the Milky way; they ascend from the Earth where Figures kneel Embracing above the Graves, & Represent Religion, or Civilised Life such as it is in the Christian Church, who are the Offspring of the Hebrew.

Just above the graves & above the spot where the Infants creep out of the Ground stand two, a Man & Woman; these are the Primitive Christians. The two Figures in *purifying* flames by the side of the dragon's cavern represents the Latter state of the Church when on the verge of Perdition, yet protect'd by a Flaming Sword. Multitudes are seen ascending from the Green fields of the blessed in which a Gothic Church is representative of true Art, Call'd Gothic in All Ages by those who follow'd *the* Fashion, *as that is call'd which is without Shape or Fashion. On the right hand of Noah a Woman with Children Represents the State Call'd Laban the Syrian: it is the Remains of Civilization in the State from whence Abraham was taken. Also* On the right hand of Noah A Female descends to meet her Lover or Husband, representative of that Love, call'd Friendship, which Looks for no other heaven than their Beloved & in him sees all reflected as in a Glass of Eternal Diamond.

On the right hand of these rise the diffident & Humble, & on their left a *solitary* Woman with her infant: these are caught up by three aged Men who appear as suddenly emerging from the blue sky for their help. These three Aged Men represent divine Providence as oppos'd to, & distinct from, divine vengeance, represented by three Aged men on the side of the Picture among the Wicked, with scourges of fire.

If the Spectator could Enter into these Images in his

---

[1] The original word was "Light."

Imagination, approaching them on the Fiery Chariot of his Contemplative Thought, if he could Enter into Noah's Rainbow, or into his bosom, or could make a Friend & Companion of one of these Images of wonder, which always intreats him to leave mortal things (as he must know), then would he arise from his Grave, then would he meet the Lord in the Air, & then he would be happy. General Knowledge is Remote Knowledge; it is in Particulars that Wisdom consists & Happiness too. Both in Art & in Life, General Masses are as Much Art as a Pasteboard Man is Human. Every Man has Eyes, Nose & Mouth; this Every Idiot knows, but he who enters into & discriminates most minutely the Manners & Intentions, the Characters in all their branches, is the alone Wise or Sensible Man, & on this discrimination All Art is founded. I intreat, then, that the Spectator will attend to the Hands & Feet, to the Lineaments of the Countenances; they are all descriptive of Character, & not a line is drawn without intention, & that most discriminate & particular. *As Poetry admits not a Letter that is Insignificant, so Painting admits not a Grain of Sand or a Blade of Grass Insignificant—much less an Insignificant Blur or Mark.*

Above the Head of Noah is Seth; this State call'd Seth is Male & Female in a higher state of Happiness & wisdom than Noah, being nearer the State of Innocence; beneath the feet of Seth two figures represent the two Seasons of Spring & Autumn, while beneath the feet of Noah, Four Seasons represent the Changed State made by the flood.

By the side of Seth is Elijah; he comprehends all the Prophetic Characters; he is seen on his fiery Chariot, bowing before the throne of the Saviour; in like manner The figures of Seth & his wife comprehends the Fathers before the flood & their Generations; when seen remote they appear as One Man; a little below Seth on his right are Two Figures, a Male & Female, with numerous Children; these represent those who were not in the Line of the Church & yet were Saved from among the Antediluvians who Perished; between Seth & these a female figure represents the Solitary State of those who, previous to the Flood, walked with God.

All these arise toward the opening Cloud before the

Throne, led onward by triumphant Groupes of Infants, *& the Morning Stars sing together*. Between Seth & Elijah three Female Figures crown'd with Garlands Represent Learning & Science, which accompanied Adam out of Eden.

The Cloud that opens, rolling apart before the throne & before the New Heaven & the New Earth, is Composed of Various Groupes of Figures, particularly the Four Living Creatures mention'd in Revelations as Surrounding the Throne; these I suppose to have the chief agency in removing the old heavens & the old Earth to make way for the New Heaven & the New Earth, to descend from the throne of God & of the Lamb; that Living Creature on the Left of the Throne Gives to the Seven Angels the Seven Vials of the wrath of God, with which they, hovering over the deeps beneath, pour out upon the wicked their Plagues; the Other Living Creatures are descending with a Shout & with the Sound of the Trumpet [1] directing the Combats in the upper Elements; in the two Corners of the Picture on the Left hand Apollyon is foiled before the Sword of Michael, & on the Right the Two Witnesses are subduing their Enemies.

On the Cloud are open'd the Books of Remembrance of Life & of Death: before that of Life, *on the Right,* some figures bow in humiliation; before that of Death, *on the Left,* the Pharisees are pleading their own Righteousness; the one shines with beams of Light, the other utters Lightnings & tempests.

A Last Judgment is Necessary because Fools flourish. Nations Flourish under Wise Rulers & are depress'd under foolish Rulers: it is the same with Individuals as Nations: works of Art can only be produc'd in Perfection where the Man is either in Affluence or is Above the Care of it. Poverty is the Fool's Rod, which at last is turn'd on his own back: this is A Last Judgment—when Men of Real Art Govern & Pretenders Fall. [8]

Some People, & not a few Artists, have asserted that the Painter of this Picture would not have done so well if he had been properly Encourag'd. Let those who think so, reflect on the State of Nations under Poverty & their incapability

[1] In the MS. the words " & with " are repeated here, presumably in error.
[8] See additional paragraphs on p. 371.

of Art: tho' Art is Above Either, the Argument is better for Affluence than Poverty: & tho' he would not have been a greater Artist, yet he would have produc'd Greater works of Art in proportion to his means. A Last Judgment is not for the purpose of making Bad Men better, but for the Purpose of hindering them from opressing the Good with Poverty & Pain by means of Such Vile Arguments & Insinuations.

Around the Throne, Heaven is open'd & the Nature of Eternal Things Display'd, All Springing from the Divine Humanity. All beams from him. He is the Bread & the Wine; he is the Water of Life; accordingly, on Each Side of the opening Heaven appears an Apostle; that on the Right Represents Baptism, that on the Left Represents the Lord's Supper. All Life consists of these Two, Throwing off Error *& Knaves from our company* continually, & Recieving Truth, *or Wise Men into our Company* Continually. He who is out of the Church & opposes it is no less an Agent of Religion than he who is in it; to be an Error & to be Cast out is a part of God's design. No man can Embrace True Art till he has explor'd & Cast out False Art (*such is the Nature of Mortal Things*), or he will be himself Cast out by those who have Already Embraced True Art. Thus My Picture is a History of Art & Science, *the Foundation of Society*, Which is Humanity itself. What are All the Gifts of the Spirit but Mental Gifts? Whenever any Individual Rejects Error & Embraces Truth, a Last Judgment passes upon that Individual.

Over the Head of the Saviour & Redeemer The Holy Spirit, like a Dove, is surrounded by a blue Heaven in which are the two Cherubim that bow'd over the Ark, for here the temple is open'd in Heaven & the Ark of the Covenant is as a Dove of Peace. The Curtains are drawn apart, Christ having rent the Veil. The Candlestick & the Table of Shewbread appear on Each side; a Glorification of Angels with Harps surround the Dove.

The Temple stands on the Mount of God; from it flows on each side the River of Life, on whose banks Grows the tree of Life, among whose branches, temples & Pinnacles, tents & pavilions, Gardens & Groves, display Paradise with its Inhabitants walking up & down in Conversations concerning Mental Delights.

*Here they are no longer talking of what is Good & Evil,
or of what is Right or Wrong, & puzzling themselves in
Satan's Labyrinth, But are Conversing with Eternal Reali-
ties as they Exist in the Human Imagination. We are in a
World of Generation & death, & this world we must cast off
if we would be Painters, such as Rafael, Mich. Angelo & the
Ancient Sculptors: if we do not cast off this world we shall be
only Venetian Painters, who will be cast off & Lost from Art.*

Jesus is surrounded by Beams of Glory in which are seen
all around him Infants emanating from him; these represent
the Eternal Births of Intellect from the Divine Humanity.
A Rainbow surrounds the throne & the Glory, in which
youthful Nuptials recieve the infants in their hands.

*In Eternity Woman is the Emanation of Man: she has No
Will of her own. There is no such thing in Eternity as a
Female Will, & Queens.*

On the Side next Baptism are seen those call'd in the
Bible Nursing Fathers & Nursing Mothers; they represent
Education. On the Side next the Lord's Supper The Holy
Family, consisting of Mary, Joseph, John the Baptist,
Zacharias & Elizabeth, recieving the Bread & Wine, among
other Spirits of the Just made perfect: beneath these a
Cloud of Women & Children are taken up, fleeing from the
rolling Cloud which separates the Wicked from the Seats
of Bliss. These represent those who, tho' willing, were
too weak to Reject Error without the Assistance &
Countenance of those Already in the Truth; for a Man
Can only Reject Error by the Advice of a Friend or by the
Immediate Inspiration of God; it is for this Reason, among
many others, that I have put the Lord's Supper on the
Left hand of the Throne, for it appears so at the Last
Judgment, for a Protection.

§ III. (pp. 91–95)

Many suppose that before the Creation All was Solitude
& Chaos. This is the most pernicious Idea that can enter
the Mind, as it takes away all sublimity from the Bible &
Limits All Existence to Creation & to Chaos, To the Time ᶜ
& Space fixed by the Corporeal Vegetative Eye, & leaves

ᶜ See additional paragraphs on p. 371.

the Man who entertains such an Idea the habitation of Unbelieving Demons. Eternity Exists, and All things in Eternity, Independent of Creation which was an act of Mercy. I have represented those who are in Eternity by some in a Cloud within the Rainbow that Surrounds the Throne; they merely appear as in a Cloud when any thing of Creation, Redemption or Judgment are the Subjects of Contemplation, tho' their Whole Contemplation is Concerning these things; the Reason they so appear is The Humiliation of *the Reasoning & doubting* Selfhood, & the Giving all up to Inspiration. By this it will be seen that I do not consider either the Just or the Wicked to be in a Supreme State, but to be every one of them States of the Sleep which the Soul may fall into in its deadly dreams of Good & Evil when it leaves Paradise following the Serpent.

Many Persons, such as Paine & Voltaire, *with some of the Ancient Greeks,* say: ' we will not converse concerning Good & Evil; we will live in Paradise & Liberty.' You may do so in Spirit, but not in the *Mortal* Body as you pretend, till after the Last Judgment; for in Paradise they have no Corporeal *& Mortal* Body—that originated with the Fall & was call'd Death & cannot be removed but by a Last Judgment: while we are in the world of Mortality we Must Suffer. The Whole Creation Groans to be deliver'd; there will always be as many Hypocrites born as Honest Men, & they will always have superior Power in Mortal Things. You cannot have Liberty in this World without *what you call* Moral Virtue, & you cannot have Moral Virtue without the Slavery of that half of the Human Race who hate *what you call* Moral Virtue.

The Nature of Hatred & Envy & of All the Mischiefs in the World are here depicted. No one Envies or Hates one of his Own Party; even the devils love one another in their way; they torment one another for other reasons than Hate or Envy; these are only employ'd against the Just. Neither can Seth Envy Noah, or Elijah Envy Abraham, but they may both of them Envy the Success of Satan or of Og or Molech. The Horse never Envies the Peacock, nor the Sheep the Goat, but they Envy a Rival in Life & Existence whose ways & means exceed their own, let him be of what Class of Animals he will; a dog will envy a Cat who is pamper'd at the expense of his comfort, as I have often seen. The Bible never tells us that Devils torment one another thro' Envy; it is thro' this that they torment the Just—but for what do they torment one another? I answer: For the Coercive Laws of Hell, Moral Hypocrisy. They torment a Hypocrite when he is discover'd; they punish a Failure in the tormentor who has suffer'd the Subject of his torture to Escape. In Hell all is Self Righteousness; there is no such thing there as Forgiveness of Sin; he who does Forgive Sin is Crucified as an Abettor of Criminals, & he who performs Works of Mercy in Any shape whatever is punish'd &, if possible, destroy'd, not thro' envy or Hatred or Malice, but thro' Self Righteousness that thinks its does God service, which God is Satan. *They do not Envy one another: They contemn & despise one another*: Forgiveness of Sin is only at the Judgment Seat of Jesus the Saviour, where the Accuser is cast out, not because he Sins, but because he torments the Just & makes them do what he condemns as Sin & what he knows is opposite to their own Identity.ᶜ

It is not because Angels are Holier than Men or Devils that makes them Angels, but because they do not Expect Holiness from one another, but from God only.ⁿ

The Player is a liar when he says: ' Angels are happier than Men because they are better.' Angels are happier than Men & *Devils* because they are not always Prying after Good & Evil in one another & eating the Tree of Knowledge for Satan's Gratification.

The Last Judgment is an Overwhelming of Bad Art & Science. Mental Things are alone Real; what is call'd Corporeal, Nobody Knows of its Dwelling Place: it is in Fallacy, & its Existence an Imposture. Where is the Existence Out of Mind or Thought? Where is it but in the Mind of a Fool? Some People flatter themselves that there will be No Last Judgment & that Bad Art will be adopted & mixed with Good Art. That Error or Experiment will make a Part of Truth, & they Boast that it is its Foundation; these People flatter themselves: I will not Flatter them. Error is Created. Truth is Eternal. Error, or Creation,

will be Burned up, & then, & not till Then, Truth or
Eternity will appear. It is Burnt up the Moment Men cease
to behold it. I assert for My Self that I do not behold the
outward Creation & that to me it is hindrance & not
Action; it is as the dirt upon my feet, No part of Me.
' What,' it will be Question'd, ' When the Sun rises, do
you not see a round disk of fire somewhat like a Guinea? '
O no, no, I see an Innumerable company of the Heavenly
host crying, "Holy, Holy, Holy is the Lord God Almighty."
I question not my Corporeal or Vegetative Eye any more
than I would Question a Window concerning a Sight.
I look thro' it & not with it.

*(The following paragraphs were not assigned places in the
essay: their context, therefore, can only be guessed. The
references given are to similar comments in the preceding
pages.)*

ᵃ (written sideways on p. 91):

Allegories are things that Relate to Moral Virtues.
Moral Virtues do not Exist; they are Allegories & dis-
simulations. But Time & Space are Real Beings, a Male &
a Female. Time is a Man, Space is a Woman, & her Mas-
culine Portion is Death.

β (This passage is incomplete, the corner of p. 71 in the MS. Book
having been cut off, thus destroying the first eight lines):

. . . . The . . . .
when they Assert that Jupiter usurped the Throne of his
Father, Saturn, & brought on an Iron Age & Begat on
Mnemosyne, or Memory, The Greek Muses, which are not
Inspiration as the Bible is. Reality was Forgot, & the
Vanities of Time & Space only Remember'd & call'd
Reality. Such is the Mighty difference between Allegoric
Fable & Spiritual Mystery. Let it here be Noted that the
Greek Fables originated in Spiritual Mystery and Real
Visions which are lost & clouded in Fable & Allegory,
while the Hebrew Bible & the Greek Gospel are Genuine,
Perserv'd by the Saviour's Mercy. The Nature of my
Work is Visionary or Imaginative; it is an Endeavour to
Restore *what the Ancients call'd* the Golden Age.

γ (p. 79):

In Eternity one Thing never Changes into another Thing. Each Identity is Eternal: consequently Apuleius's Golden Ass & Ovid's Metamorphosis & others of the like kind are Fable; yet they contain Vision in a sublime degree, being derived from real Vision in More Ancient Writings. Lot's Wife being Changed into a Pillar of Salt alludes to the Mortal Body being render'd a Permanent Statue,[1] but not Changed or Transformed into Another Identity while it retains its own Individuality. A Man can never become Ass nor Horse; some are born with shapes of Men, who may be both, but Eternal Identity is one thing & Corporeal Vegetation is another thing. Changing Water into Wine by Jesus & into Blood by Moses relates to Vegetable Nature also.

(written sideways on p. 70):

The Last Judgment—when all those are Cast away who trouble Religion with Questions concerning Good & Evil or Eating of the Tree of those Knowledges or Reasonings which hinder the Vision of God, turning all into a Consuming fire. When Imagination, Art & Science & all Intellectual Gifts, all the Gifts of the Holy Ghost, are look'd upon as of no use & only Contention remains to Man, then the Last Judgment begins, & its Vision is seen by Every one according to the situation he holds.

ε (written sideways on p. 91):

The Greeks represent Chronos, or Time, as a very Aged Man; this is Fable, but the Real Vision of Time is in Eternal Youth. I have, *however,* somewhat accomodated my Figure of Time to the common opinion, as I myself am also infected with it & my Vision is also infected, & I see Time Aged, alas, too much so.

ζ (This paragraph, from pp. 86 and 90, and this alone of all in this series, has a thick vertical line drawn through it. Perhaps Blake intended that it should be deleted. The original gives that impression):

The Combats of Good & Evil is Eating of the Tree of Knowledge. The Combats of Truth & Error is Eating of the Tree of Life; these are not only Universal, but Particular. Each are Personified. There is not an Error but it has a Man for its Agent, that is, it is a Man. There is not a Truth

[1] Query a miswriting of "State."

but it has also a Man. *Good & Evil are Qualities in Every Man, whether a Good or Evil Man.* These are Enemies & destroy one another by every Means in their power, both of deceit & of open Violence. The Deist & the Christian are but the Results of these Opposing Natures. Many are Deists who would in certain Circumstances have been Christians in outward appearance. Voltaire was one of this number; he was as intolerant as an Inquisitor. Manners make the Man, not Habits. It is the same in Art: by their Works ye shall know them; the Knave who is Converted to Deism & the Knave who is Converted to Christianity is still a Knave, but he himself will not know it, tho' Every body else does. Christ comes, as he came at first, to deliver those who were bound under the Knave, not to deliver the Knave. He Comes to deliver Man, the Accused, & not Satan, the Accuser. We do not find any where that Satan is Accused of Sin; he is only accused of Unbelief & thereby drawing Man into Sin that he may accuse him. Such is the Last Judgment: a deliverance from Satan's Accusation. Satan thinks that Sin is displeasing to God; he ought to know that Nothing is displeasing to God but Unbelief & Eating of the Tree of Knowledge of Good & Evil.

η (written sideways on p. 87):

Men are admitted into Heaven not because they have *curbed &* govern'd their Passions or have No Passions, but because they have Cultivated their Understandings. The Treasures of Heaven are not Negations of Passion, but Realities of Intellect, from which All the Passions Emanate *Uncurbed* in their Eternal Glory. The Fool shall not enter into Heaven, let him be ever so Holy. Holiness is not The Price of Enterance into Heaven.

Those who are cast out are All Those who, having no Passions of their own, because No Intellect, Have spent their lives in Curbing & Governing other People's by the Various arts of Poverty & Cruelty of all kinds. Wo, Wo, Wo to you Hypocrites. Even Murder, the Courts of Justice, *more merciful than the Church,* are compell'd to allow, is not done in Passion, but in Cool Blooded Design & Intention.

The Modern Church Crucifies Christ with the Head Downward.

POEMS FROM BLAKE'S MS. BOOK

(*About* 1793)

*(When Blake was writing the " Songs of Experience " he
turned his sketch-book upside down and copied the
poems neatly on to its last pages. When he came to print
the " Songs of Experience " he appears to have made a
very careful selection from these poems, choosing from
variants upon a theme, and rejecting when the meaning
was indeterminate. We may therefore safely assume
that the poems of this period which are not included in
the " Songs of Experience " were, in many cases, de-
finitely rejected and are therefore of lesser importance
than some other works existing only in manuscript—
such as the Pickering MS.—which Blake might have
committed to type had occasion offered. The following
are the poems referred to, viz., those which remain
after the drafts of the " Songs of Experience " have
been omitted.)*

I TOLD my love, I told my love,
I told her all my heart;
Trembling cold, in ghastly fears,
Ah! she doth depart.

Soon as she was gone from me
A traveller came by;
Silently, invisibly,
O! was no deny.

———

I LAID me down upon a bank
Where love lay sleeping;
I heard among the rushes dank
Weeping, Weeping.

Then I went to the heath & the wild,
To the thistles & thorns of the waste,
And they told me how they were beguil'd,
Driven out & compel'd to be chaste.

———

I SAW a chapel all of gold
That none did dare to enter in,
And many weeping stood without,
Weeping, mourning, worshipping.

I saw a serpent rise between
The white pillars of the door,
And he forc'd & forc'd & forc'd—
Down the golden hinges tore,

And along the pavement sweet,
Set with pearls & rubies bright,
All his slimy length he drew,
Till upon the altar white

Vomiting his poison out
On the bread & on the wine:
So I turn'd into a sty
And laid me down among the swine.

———

I ASKED a thief to steal me a peach,
He turned up his eyes:
I asked a lithe lady to lie her down,
Holy & meek, she cries.

As soon as I went, an angel came,
He wink'd at the thief
And smil'd at the dame,
And without one word said
Had a peach from the tree,
And still as a maid
Enjoy'd the Lady.

———

[1] I HEARD an Angel singing
When the day was springing,
" Mercy, Pity, Peace
Is the world's release."

[1] Obviously an attempt at a contrasted version of " The Divine Image," see p. 14; and first version of " The Human Abstract," p. 31.

Thus he sung all day
Over the new mown hay
Till the sun went down
And haycocks looked brown.

I heard a Devil curse
Over the heath & the furze,
" Mercy could be no more
If there was nobody poor;

" And pity no more could be
If all were as happy as we."
At his curse the sun went down,
And the heavens gave a frown.

And Miserie's increase
Is Mercy, Pity, Peace.

[1] A Cradle Song

SLEEP, Sleep! beauty bright
Dreaming o'er the joys of night.
Sleep, Sleep! in thy sleep
Little sorrows sit & weep.

Sweet Babe, in thy face
Soft desires I can trace,
Secret joys & secret smiles,
Little pretty infant wiles.

As thy softest limbs I feel,
Smiles as of the morning steal
O'er thy cheek, & o'er thy breast
Where thy little heart does rest.

---

[1] An unapproved contrast with the "Cradle Song" of *Songs of Innocence*, p. 13.

O! the cunning wiles that creep
In thy little heart asleep;
When thy little heart does wake
Then the dreadful lightnings break.

From thy cheek & from thy eye,
O'er the youthful harvests nigh,
Infant wiles & infant smiles
Heaven & Earth of peace beguiles.

———

[1] I FEAR'D the fury of my wind
Would blight all blossoms fair & true,
And my sun it shin'd & shin'd,
And my wind it never blew.

But a blossom fair or true
Was not found on any tree,
For all blossoms grew & grew
Fruitless false, tho' fair to see.

———

[2] WHY should I care for the men of thames,
Or the cheating waves of charter'd streams?
Or shrink at the little blasts of fear
That the hireling blows into my ear?

Tho' born on the cheating banks of Thames,
Tho' his waters bathed my infant limbs
[3] The Ohio shall wash his stains from me.
I was born a slave, but I go to be free.

[1] Probably a rejected version of "The Sick Rose," p. 27.
[2] Probably the first version of "London," p. 31.
[3] Originally: "I spurn'd his waters away from me."

Infant Sorrow

MY mother groan'd, my father wept,
Into the dangerous world I leapt,
Helpless, naked, piping loud,
Like a fiend hid in a cloud.

Struggling in my father's hands,
Striving against my swaddling bands,
Bound & weary, I thought best
To sulk upon my mother's breast.

When I saw that rage was vain
And to sulk would nothing gain,
Turning many a trick & wile
I began to soothe & smile.

And I sooth'd day after day,
Till upon the ground I stray;
And I smil'd night after night,
Seeking only for delight.

And I saw before me shine
Clusters of the wand'ring vine,
And many a lovely flower & tree
Stretch'd their blossoms out to me.

My father then with holy look,
In his hands a holy book,
Pronounc'd curses on my head,
¹ And bound me in a mirtle shade.

" Why should I be bound to thee
O my lovely mirtle tree?
Love, free love, cannot be bound
To any tree that grows on ground."

¹ This poem, of which only the first two verses were retained for the
" Songs of Experience," obviously stretched itself out far beyond its
first intention. Hitherto the last four stanzas have been printed as
though they were a separate poem under the title " In a Myrtle Shade ";
but the words " in a mirtle shade," are clearly not a title, but merely
catch-words connecting verses 6 and 7. The necessity for these catch-
words arose because, when Blake desired to add stanzas 7, 8 and 9, the

O, how sick & weary I
Underneath my mirtle lie!
Like to dung upon the ground
Underneath my mirtle bound.

Oft my mirtle sigh'd in vain
To behold my heavy chain;
Oft my father saw us sigh
And laugh'd at our simplicity.

So I smote him, & his gore
Stain'd the roots my mirtle bore;
But the time of youth is fled,
And grey hairs are on my head.

———

[1] SILENT, Silent Night
Quench the holy light
Of thy torches bright;

---

page on which he was writing was full, he was obliged to turn over (the
page opposite being occupied by an important drawing), and on the
original page he had already written verse 10. The last line of stanza 6
originally read: "Who the fruit or blossoms shed," and the substituted
line gains its significance by its connection with the stanzas that imme-
diately follow. A little later, Blake evidently intended to compress
verses 7 and 8; for, under the title "To my Mirtle," he wrote the
following, which, it will be noticed, contains no new matter at all, the
lines marked "1" and "2" being cancelled versions from stanza 8:

5 " Why should I be bound to thee
6   O my lovely mirtle tree
     (Love free love cannot be bound
     To any tree that grows on ground *del.*).

1   To a lovely mirtle bound
2   Blossoms show'ring all around
     (Like to dung upon the ground
     Underneath my mirtle bound *del.*)
3   O how sick & weary I
4   Underneath my mirtle lie."

[1] Possibly begun as a contrasted version of "Night," *Songs of Inno-
cence*, p. 15.

For possess'd of Day
Thousand spirits stray
That sweet joys betray.

Why should joys be sweet
Used with deceit,
Nor with sorrows meet?

But an honest joy
Does itself destroy
For a harlot coy.

———

O LAPWING, thou fliest around the heath
Nor seest the net that is spread beneath,
Why dost thou not fly among the corn fields?
They cannot spread nets where a harvest yields.

———

THOU hast a lap full of seed
And this is a fine country:
Why dost thou not cast thy seed
And live in it merrily?

Shall I cast it on the sand
And turn it into fruitful land?
For on no other ground
Can I sow my seed
Without tearing up
Some stinking weed.

The Wild Flower's Song

As I wander'd the forest
The green leaves among,
I heard a wild flower
Singing a song:

" I slept in the Earth
In the silent night;
I murmur'd my fears
And I felt delight.

" In the morning I went
As rosy as morn
To seek for new Joy,
But O! met with scorn."

To Nobodaddy

WHY art thou silent & invisible,
Father of Jealousy?
Why dost thou hide thyself in clouds
From every searching Eye?

Why darkness & obscurity
In all thy words & laws,
That none dare eat the fruit but from
The wily serpent's jaws?
Or is it because Secresy gains females' loud applause? [1]

ARE not the joys of morning sweeter
Than the joys of night?
And are the vig'rous joys of youth
Ashamed of the light?

Let age & sickness silent rob
The vineyards in the night,
But those who burn with vig'rous youth
Pluck fruits before the light.

THEY said this mystery never shall cease:
The priest promotes war & the soldier peace.

[1] It is evident from the script that this line was an afterthought.

Love to faults is always blind,
Always is to joy inclin'd,
Lawless, wing'd & unconfin'd,
And breaks all chains from every mind.

———————

Deceit to secresy confin'd,
Lawful, cautious & refin'd,
To every thing but interest blind,
And forges fetters for the mind.

———————

[1] There souls of men are bought & sold,
And milkfed infancy for gold,
And youth to slaughter houses led,
And beauty for a bit of bread.

Soft Snow

I walked abroad in a snowy day,
I ask'd the soft snow with me to play;
She play'd & she melted in all her prime,
And the winter call'd it a dreadful crime.

An ancient Proverb

Remove away that black'ning church,
Remove away that marriage hearse,
Remove away that man of blood,
You'll quite remove the ancient curse.

Merlin's prophecy

The harvest shall flourish in wintry weather
When two virginities meet together.

The King & the Priest must be tied in a tether
Before two virgins can meet together.

---

[1] This quatrain was very possibly the concluding stanza of "A Little BOY Lost" (p. 33), but more probably he excluded the verse because he had already more clearly defined in "London," vv. 3 and 4, these three social enormities, against Man, Woman, and Child.

Day

THE Sun arises in the East,
Cloth'd in robes of blood & gold;
Swords & spears, & wrath increast,
All around his bosom roll'd,
Crown'd with warlike fires & raging desires.

[1] The Marriage Ring

" COME hither, my sparrows,
My little arrows.
If a tear or a smile
Will a man beguile,
If an amorous delay
Clouds a sunshiny day,
If the step of a foot
Smites the heart to its root—
'Tis the marriage ring
Makes each fairy a king."

So a fairy sung.
From the leaves I sprung.
He leap'd from the spray
To flee away,
But in my hat caught
He soon shall be taught,
Let him laugh, let him cry,
He's my butterfly,
For I've pull'd out the sting
Of the marriage ring.

[1] Dr. Sampson entitles this poem "The Fairy," but from the photo-
graph of the original page I cannot find any sign of a deletion of the
original title. The vertical line which Blake drew through the preceding
poem (his common practice) was certainly not intended to cancel the
words, "The Marriage Ring"; while the words "The Fairy" appear to
be in the same hand, and to have been written at the same time, as the
adjacent quatrain, "He who binds to himself a joy," etc., to which
Blake added, obviously later, the title, "Eternity." It seems possible,
therefore, that "The Fairy" was the original title of the quatrain. In
this there is no inherent improbability, for to Blake a joy was a fairy,
and a fairy a joy. (cf. "Gates of Paradise," plate 7.)

IF you trap the moment before it's ripe,
The tears of repentance you'll certainly wipe;
But if once you let the ripe moment go
You can never wipe off the tears of woe.

Eternity

HE who binds to himself a joy [1]
Does the winged life destroy;
But he who kisses the joy as it flies
Lives in eternity's sun rise.

———

THE sword sung on the barren heath,
The sickle in the fruitful field;
The sword he sung a song of death,
But could not make the sickle yield.

———

ABSTINENCE sows sand over all
The ruddy limbs & flowing [2] hair;
But Desire Gratified
Plants fruits of life & beauty there.

———

IN a wife I would desire
What in whores is always found,
The lineaments of Gratified desire.

The Question Answer'd

WHAT is it men in women do require?
The lineaments of Gratified Desire.
What is it women do in men require?
The lineaments of Gratified Desire.

[1] Originally, " He who binds himself to a joy."
[2] The word is indistinct, but looks more like " flowing " than " flaming." Swinburne notes " flaming hair " as probable, because it is a phrase used in " A Song of Liberty " (see p. 54, § 10). Wicksteed reads " flow'ring."

Lacedemonian Instruction

" Come hither, my boy, tell me what thou seest there."
" A fool tangled in a religious snare."

Riches

The countless gold of a merry heart,
The rubies & pearls of a loving eye,
The indolent never can bring to the mart,
Nor the secret hoard up in his treasury.

An answer to the parson

" Why of the sheep do you not learn peace? "
" Because I don't want you to shear my fleece."

———

The look of love alarms
Because 'tis fill'd with fire;
But the look of soft deceit
Shall win the lover's hire.

Soft deceit & idleness,
[1] These are beauty's sweetest dress.

Motto to the Songs of Innocence & of Experience

The Good are attracted by Men's perceptions
And think not for themselves,
Till Experience teaches them to catch
And to Cage the Fairies & Elves.

And then the Knave begins to snarl,
And the Hypocrite to howl,
And all his good Friends show their private ends,
And the Eagle is known from the Owl.

———

[1] This line, deleted on p. 103 of the MS. Book, stands on p. 99.

HER whole Life is an Epigram, smart, smooth, & neatly
pen'd,
Platted quite neat to catch applause, with a sliding noose at
the end.

AN old maid early, e'er I knew
Ought but the love that on me grew;
And now I'm cover'd o'er & o'er,
And wish that I had been a whore.

O, I cannot cannot find
The undaunted courage of a Virgin Mind;
For Early I in love was crost
Before my flower of love was lost.

THE Angel that presided o'er my birth
Said, " Little creature, form'd of Joy & Mirth,
Go love, without the help of any Thing on Earth."

III
POETICAL SKETCHES
(1783)

POETICAL SKETCHES
(1783)

[1] ADVERTISMENT

THE following Sketches were the production of untutored youth, commenced in his twelfth, and occasionally resumed by the author till his twentieth year; since which time, his talents having been wholly directed to the attainment of excellence in his profession, he has been deprived of the leisure requisite to such a revisal of these sheets, as might have rendered them less unfit to meet the public eye.

Conscious of the irregularities and defects to be found in almost every page, his friends have still believed that they possessed a poetical originality, which merited some respite from oblivion. These their opinions remain, however, to be now reproved or confirmed by a less partial public.

MISCELLANEOUS POEMS

TO SPRING

O THOU, with dewy locks, who lookest down
Thro' the clear windows of the morning, turn
Thine angel eyes upon our western isle,
Which in full choir hails thy approach, O Spring!   4

The hills tell each other, and the list'ning
Vallies hear; all our longing eyes are turned
Up to thy bright pavilions: issue forth,
And let thy holy feet visit our clime.   8

---

[1] Dr. Sampson credits the Rev. Henry Matthews with this preface.

Come o'er the eastern hills, and let our winds
Kiss thy perfumed garments; let us taste
Thy morn and evening breath; scatter thy pearls
Upon our love-sick land that mourns for thee.   12

O deck her forth with thy fair fingers; pour
Thy soft kisses on her bosom; and put
Thy golden crown upon her languish'd head,
Whose modest tresses were bound up for thee!   16

TO SUMMER

O THOU who passest thro' our vallies in
Thy strength, curb thy fierce steeds, allay the heat
That flames from their large nostrils! thou, O Summer,
Oft pitched'st here thy golden tent, and oft
Beneath our oaks hast slept, while we beheld   5
With joy thy ruddy limbs and flourishing hair.

Beneath our thickest shades we oft have heard
Thy voice, when noon upon his fervid car
Rode o'er the deep of heaven; beside our springs
Sit down, and in our mossy valleys, on   10
Some bank beside a river clear, throw thy
Silk draperies off, and rush into the stream:
Our vallies love the Summer in his pride.

Our bards are fam'd who strike the silver wire:
Our youth are bolder than the southern swains: 15
Our maidens fairer in the sprightly dance:
We lack not songs, nor instruments of joy,
Nor echoes sweet, nor waters clear as heaven,
Nor laurel wreaths against the sultry heat.

TO AUTUMN

O AUTUMN, laden with fruit, and stained
With the blood of the grape, pass not, but sit
Beneath my shady roof; there thou may'st rest,
And tune thy jolly voice to my fresh pipe,

And all the daughters of the year shall dance!   5
Sing now the lusty song of fruits and flowers.

" The narrow bud opens her beauties to
The sun, and love runs in her thrilling veins;
Blossoms hang round the brows of morning, and
Flourish down the bright cheek of modest eve,   10
Till clust'ring Summer breaks forth into singing,
And feather'd clouds strew flowers round her head.

" The spirits of the air live on the smells
Of fruit; and joy, with pinions light, roves round
The gardens, or sits singing in the trees."   15
Thus sang the jolly Autumn as he sat;
Then rose, girded himself, and o'er the bleak
Hills fled from our sight; but left his golden load.

TO WINTER

" O WINTER! bar thine adamantine doors:
The north is thine; there hast thou built thy dark
Deep-founded habitation. Shake not thy roofs,
Nor bend thy pillars with thine iron car."   4

He hears me not, but o'er the yawning deep
Rides heavy; his storms are unchain'd, sheathed
In ribbed steel; I dare not lift mine eyes,
For he hath rear'd his sceptre o'er the world.   8

Lo! now the direful monster, whose skin clings
To his strong bones, strides o'er the groaning rocks:
He withers all in silence, and his hand
Unclothes the earth, and freezes up frail life.   12

He takes his seat upon the cliffs; the mariner
Cries in vain. Poor little wretch! that deal'st
With storms; till heaven smiles, and the monster
Is driv'n yelling to his caves beneath mount Hecla.   16

TO THE
EVENING STAR

Thou fair-hair'd angel of the evening,
Now, whilst the sun rests on the mountains, light
Thy bright torch of love; thy radiant crown
Put on, and smile upon our evening bed!
Smile on our loves, and while thou drawest the   5
Blue curtains of the sky, scatter thy silver dew
On every flower that shuts its sweet eyes
In timely sleep. Let thy west wind sleep on
The lake; speak silence with thy glimmering eyes,
And wash the dusk with silver. Soon, full soon,   10
Dost thou withdraw; then the wolf rages wide,
And the lion glares thro' the dun forest:
The fleeces of our flocks are cover'd with
Thy sacred dew: protect them with thine influence.

TO MORNING

O holy virgin! clad in purest white,
Unlock heav'n's golden gates, and issue forth;
Awake the dawn that sleeps in heaven; let light
Rise from the chambers of the east, and bring
The honied dew that cometh on waking day.   5
O radiant morning, salute the sun
Rous'd like a huntsman to the chace, and with
Thy buskin'd feet appear upon our hills.

FAIR ELENOR

The bell struck one, and shook the silent tower;
The graves give up their dead: fair Elenor
Walk'd by the castle gate, and looked in.
A hollow groan ran thro' the dreary vaults.   4

She shriek'd aloud, and sunk upon the steps
On the cold stone her pale cheeks. Sickly smells

Of death issue as from a sepulchre,
And all is silent but the sighing vaults.   8

Chill death withdraws his hand, and she revives;
Amaz'd she finds herself upon her feet,
And, like a ghost, thro' narrow passages
Walking, feeling the cold walls with her hands.   12

Fancy returns, and now she thinks of bones
And grinning skulls, and corruptible death
Wrap'd in his shroud; and now fancies she hears
Deep sighs, and sees pale sickly ghosts gliding.   16

At length, no fancy but reality
Distracts her. A rushing sound, and the feet
Of one that fled, approaches.—Ellen stood
Like a dumb statue, froze to stone with fear.   20

The wretch approaches, crying: " The deed is done;
Take this, and send it by whom thou wilt send;
It is my life—send it to Elenor:—
He's dead, and howling after me for blood!   24

" Take this," he cry'd; and thrust into her arms
A wet napkin, wrap'd about; then rush'd
Past, howling: she receiv'd into her arms
Pale death, and follow'd on the wings of fear.   28

They pass'd swift thro' the outer gate; the wretch,
Howling, leap'd o'er the wall into the moat,
Stifling in mud. Fair Ellen pass'd the bridge,
And heard a gloomy voice cry " Is it done? "   32

As the deer wounded, Ellen flew over
The pathless plain; as the arrows that fly
By night, destruction flies, and strikes in darkness.
She fled from fear, till at her house arriv'd.   36

Her maids await her; on her bed she falls,
That bed of joy, where erst her lord hath press'd:
" Ah, woman's fear! " she cry'd; " Ah, cursed duke!
Ah, my dear lord! ah, wretched Elenor!   40

" My lord was like a flower upon the brows
Of lusty May! Ah, life as frail as flower!
O ghastly death! withdraw thy cruel hand,
Seek'st thou that flow'r to deck thy horrid temples? 44

" My lord was like a star in highest heav'n
Drawn down to earth by spells and wickedness;
My lord was like the opening eyes of day
When western winds creep softly o'er the flowers; 48

" But he is darken'd; like the summer's noon
Clouded; fall'n like the stately tree cut down;
The breath of heaven dwelt among his leaves.
O Elenor, weak woman, fill'd with woe! " 52

Thus having spoke, she raised up her head,
And saw the bloody napkin by her side,
Which in her arms she brought; and now, tenfold
More terrified, saw it unfold itself. 56

Her eyes were fix'd; the bloody cloth unfolds,
Disclosing to her sight the murder'd head
Of her dear lord, all ghastly pale, clotted
With gory blood; it groan'd, and thus it spake: 60

" O Elenor, I am thy husband's head,
Who, sleeping on the stones of yonder tower,
Was 'reft of life by the accursed duke!
A hired villain turn'd my sleep to death! 64

" O Elenor, beware the cursed duke;
O give not him thy hand now I am dead;
He seeks thy love, who, coward, in the night,
Hired a villain to bereave my life." 68

She sat with dead cold limbs, stiffen'd to stone;
She took the gory head up in her arms;
She kiss'd the pale lips; she had no tears to shed;
She hugg'd it to her breast, and groan'd her last. 72

SONG

How sweet I roam'd from field to field
   And tasted all the summer's pride,
Till I the prince of love beheld
   Who in the sunny beams did glide!   4

He shew'd me lilies for my hair,
   And blushing roses for my brow;
He led me through his gardens fair
   Where all his golden pleasures grow.   8

With sweet May dews my wings were wet,
   And Phœbus fir'd my vocal rage;
He caught me in his silken net,
   And shut me in his golden cage.   12

He loves to sit and hear me sing,
   Then, laughing, sports and plays with me;
Then stretches out my golden wing,
   And mocks my loss of liberty.   16

SONG

My silks and fine array,
   My smiles and languish'd air,
By love are driv'n away;
   And mournful lean Despair
Brings me yew to deck my grave;   5
Such end true lovers have.

His face is fair as heav'n
   When springing buds unfold;
O why to him was't giv'n
   Whose heart is wintry cold?   10
His breast is love's all worship'd tomb,
Where all love's pilgrims come.

Bring me an axe and spade,
  Bring me a winding sheet;
When I my grave have made   15
  Let winds and tempests beat:
Then down I'll lie, as cold as clay.
True love doth pass away!

SONG

Love and harmony combine,
And around our souls intwine
While thy branches mix with mine,
And our roots together join.   4

Joys upon our branches sit,
Chirping loud and singing sweet;
Like gentle streams beneath our feet
Innocence and virtue meet.   8

Thou the golden fruit dost bear,
I am clad in flowers fair,
Thy sweet boughs perfume the air,
And the turtle buildeth there.   12

There she sits and feeds her young,
Sweet I hear her mournful song;
And thy lovely leaves among,
There is love: I hear his tongue.   16

There his charming nest doth lay,
There he sleeps the night away;
There he sports along the day,
And doth among our branches play.   20

SONG

I love the jocund dance,
  The softly-breathing song,
Where innocent eyes do glance,
  And where lisps the maiden's tongue.   4

I love the laughing vale,
   I love the echoing hill,
Where mirth does never fail,
   And the jolly swain laughs his fill.   8

I love the pleasant cot,
   I love the innocent bow'r,
Where white and brown is our lot,
   Or fruit in the mid-day hour.   12

I love the oaken seat,
   Beneath the oaken tree,
Where all the old villagers meet,
   And laugh our sports to see.   16

I love our neighbours all,
   But, Kitty, I better love thee;
And love them I ever shall;
   But thou art all to me.   20

SONG

MEMORY, hither come,
   And tune your merry notes;
And, while upon the wind
   Your music floats,
I'll pore upon the stream   5
Where sighing lovers dream,
And fish for fancies as they pass
Within the watery glass.

I'll drink of the clear stream,
   And hear the linnet's song;   10
And there I'll lie and dream
   The day along:
And when night comes, I'll go
   To places fit for woe,
Walking along the darken'd valley   15
   With silent Melancholy.

MAD SONG

THE wild winds weep,
　　And the night is a-cold;
Come hither, Sleep,
　　And my griefs unfold:
But lo! the morning peeps　　　　　　　5
　　Over the eastern steeps,
And the rustling [1] birds of dawn
The earth do scorn.

Lo! to the vault
　　Of paved heaven,　　　　　　　　10
With sorrow fraught
　　My notes are driven:
They strike the ear of night,
　　Make weep the eyes of day;
They make mad the roaring winds,　　15
　　And with tempests play.

Like a fiend in a cloud
　　With howling woe,
After night I do croud,
　　And with night will go;　　　　　20
I turn my back to the east
From whence comforts have increas'd;
For light doth seize my brain
With frantic pain.

SONG

FRESH from the dewy hill, the merry year
Smiles on my head and mounts his flaming car;
Round my young brows the laurel wreathes a shade,
And rising glories beam around my head.　　　4

[1] " Birds " in the original edition is misprinted " beds." Mr. Keynes
showed some time ago that in a number of copies the correction to
" birds " had been made in Blake's own hand.

My feet are wing'd, while o'er the dewy lawn,
I meet my maiden risen like the morn:
O bless those holy feet, like angels' feet;
O bless those limbs, beaming with heav'nly light!   8

Like as an angel glitt'ring in the sky
In times of innocence and holy joy;
The joyful shepherd stops his grateful song
To hear the music of an angel's tongue.   12

So when she speaks, the voice of Heaven I hear;
So when we walk, nothing impure comes near;
Each field seems Eden, and each calm retreat;
Each village seems the haunt of holy feet.   16

But that sweet village where my black-ey'd maid
Closes her eyes in sleep beneath night's shade,
Whene'er I enter, more than mortal fire
Burns in my soul, and does my song inspire.   20

SONG

WHEN early morn walks forth in sober grey,
Then to my black ey'd maid I haste away;
When evening sits beneath her dusky bow'r,
And gently sighs away the silent hour,
The village bell alarms, away I go,   5
And the vale darkens at my pensive woe.

To that sweet village, where my black ey'd maid
Doth drop a tear beneath the silent shade,
I turn my eyes; and, pensive as I go,
Curse my black stars and bless my pleasing woe.   10

Oft when the summer sleeps among the trees,
Whisp'ring faint murmurs to the scanty breeze,
I walk the village round; if at her side
A youth doth walk in stolen joy and pride,
I curse my stars in bitter grief and woe,   15
That made my love so high, and me so low.

O should she e'er prove false, his limbs I'd tear,
And throw all pity on the burning air;
I'd curse bright fortune for my mixed lot,
And then I'd die in peace, and be forgot.   20

TO THE MUSES

WHETHER on Ida's shady brow,
 Or in the chambers of the East,
The chambers of the sun, that now
From antient melody have ceas'd;   4

Whether in Heav'n ye wander fair,
Or the green corners of the earth,
Or the blue regions of the air
Where the melodious winds have birth;   8

Whether on chrystal rocks ye rove,
Beneath the bosom of the sea
Wand'ring in many a coral grove,
Fair Nine, forsaking Poetry!   12

How have you left the antient love
That bards of old enjoy'd in you!
The languid strings do scarcely move!
The sound is forc'd, the notes are few!   16

GWIN, KING OF NORWAY

COME, Kings, and listen to my song:
 When Gwin, the son of Nore,
Over the nations of the North
 His cruel sceptre bore: 4

The nobles of the land did feed
 Upon the hungry Poor;
They tear the poor man's lamb, and drive
 The needy from their door!   8

The land is desolate; our wives
  And children cry for bread;
Arise, and pull the tyrant down;
  Let Gwin be humbled. 12

Gordred the giant rous'd himself
  From sleeping in his cave;
He shook the hills, and in the clouds
  The troubl'd banners wave. 16

Beneath them roll'd, like tempests black,
  The num'rous sons of blood;
Like lions' whelps, roaring abroad,
  Seeking their nightly food. 20

Down Bleron's hills they dreadful rush,
  Their cry ascends the clouds;
The trampling horse and clanging arms
  Like rushing mighty floods! 24

Their wives and children, weeping loud,
  Follow in wild array,
Howling like ghosts, furious as wolves
  In the bleak wintry day. 28

" Pull down the tyrant to the dust,
  Let Gwin be humbled,"
They cry, " and let ten thousand lives
  Pay for the tyrant's head." 32

From tow'r to tow'r the watchmen cry,
  " O Gwin, the son of Nore,
Arouse thyself! the nations, black
  Like clouds, come rolling o'er! 36

Gwin rear'd his shield, his palace shakes,
  His chiefs come rushing round;
Each, like an awful thunder cloud,
  With voice of solemn sound: 40

Like reared stones around a grave
  They stand around the King;
Then suddenly each seiz'd his spear,
  And clashing steel does ring.   44

The husbandman does leave his plow,
  To wade thro' fields of gore;
The merchant binds his brows in steel,
  And leaves the trading shore;   48

The shepherd leaves his mellow pipe,
  And sounds the trumpet shrill;
The workman throws his hammer down
  To heave the bloody bill.   52

Like the tall ghost of Barraton
  Who sports in stormy sky,
Gwin leads his host, as black as night
  When pestilence does fly.   56

With horses and with chariots—
  And all his spearmen bold
March to the sound of mournful song,
  Like clouds around him roll'd.   60

Gwin lifts his hand—the nations halt;
" Prepare for war! " he cries—
Gordred appears!—his frowning brow
  Troubles our northern skies.   64

The armies stand, like balances
  Held in th' Almighty's hand;
" Gwin, thou hast fill'd thy measure up:
  Thou'rt swept from out the land."   68

And now the raging armies rush'd
  Like warring mighty seas;
The Heav'ns are shook with roaring war,
  The dust ascends the skies!   72

Earth smokes with blood, and groans and shakes
  To drink her children's gore,
A sea of blood; nor can the eye
  See to the trembling shore!   76

And on the verge of this wild sea
  Famine and death doth cry;
The cries of women and of babes
  Over the field doth fly.   80

The King is seen raging afar,
  With all his men of might,
Like blazing comets scattering death
  Thro' the red fev'rous night.   84

Beneath his arm like sheep they die,
  And groan upon the plain;
The battle faints, and bloody men
  Fight upon hills of slain.   88

Now death is sick, and riven men
  Labour and toil for life;
Steed rolls on steed, and shield on shield,
  Sunk in this sea of strife!   92

The god of war is drunk with blood;
  The earth does faint and fail;
The stench of blood makes sick the heav'ns;
  Ghosts glut the throat of hell!   96

O what have Kings to answer for
  Before that awful throne!
When thousand deaths for vengeance cry,
  And ghosts accusing groan!   100

Like blazing comets in the sky,
  That shake the stars of light,
Which drop like fruit unto the earth
  Thro' the fierce burning night;   104

Like these did Gwin and Gordred meet,
  And the first blow decides;
Down from the brow unto the breast
  Gordred his head divides!   108

Gwin fell: the Sons of Norway fled,
  All that remain'd alive;
The rest did fill the vale of death,
  For them the eagles strive.   112

The river Dorman roll'd their blood
  Into the northern sea;
Who mourn'd his sons, and overwhelm'd
  The pleasant south country.   116

AN

IMITATION OF SPENCER

GOLDEN Apollo, that thro' heaven wide
  Scatter'st the rays of light, and truth's beams!
In lucent words my darkling verses dight,
  And wash my earthly mind in thy clear streams,
  That wisdom may descend in fairy dreams,
All while the jocund hours in thy train
  Scatter their fancies at thy poet's feet;
And when thou yields to night thy wide domain,
Let rays of truth enlight his sleeping brain.

For brutish Pan in vain might thee assay   10
  With tinkling sounds to dash thy nervous verse
Sound without sense; yet in his rude affray,
  (For ignorance is Folly's leasing nurse
  And love of Folly needs none other's curse)
Midas the praise hath gain'd of lengthen'd ears,[1]   15
  For which himself might deem him ne'er the worse
To sit in council with his modern peers,
  And judge of tinkling rhimes and elegances terse.

  [1] Misprinted; in the original (1783) edition, "cares."

And thou, Mercurius, that with winged brow
  Dost mount aloft into the yielding sky,   20
And thro' Heav'n's halls thy airy flight dost throw,
   Entering with holy feet to where on high
   Jove weighs the counsel of futurity;
Then, laden with eternal fate, dost go
  Down, like a falling star, from autumn sky,   25
And o'er the surface of the silent deep dost fly:

If thou arrivest at the sandy shore
  Where nought but envious hissing adders dwell,
Thy golden rod, thrown on the dusty floor,
   Can charm to harmony with potent spell.   30
   Such is sweet Eloquence, that does dispel
Envy and Hate, that thirst for human gore;
   And cause in sweet society to dwell
Vile savage minds that lurk in lonely cell.

O Mercury, assist my lab'ring sense   35
  That round the circle of the world would fly!
As the wing'd eagle scorns the tow'ry fence
   Of Alpine hills round his high aery,
   And searches thro' the corners of the sky,
Sports in the clouds to hear the thunder's sound,   40
   And see the winged lightnings as they fly;
Then, bosom'd in an amber cloud, around
Plumes his wide wings, and seeks Sol's palace high.

And thou, O warrior maid invincible,
  Arm'd with the terrors of Almighty Jove!   45
Pallas, Minerva, maiden terrible,
   Lov'st thou to walk the peaceful solemn grove,
   In solemn gloom of branches interwove?
Or bear'st thy Egis o'er the burning field,
   Where, like the sea, the waves of battle move?   50
Or have thy soft piteous eyes beheld
   The weary wanderer thro' the desert rove?
Or does th' afflicted man thy heav'nly bosom move?

BLIND-MAN'S BUFF

WHEN silver Snow decks Susan's cloaths,
And jewel hangs at th' shepherd's nose,
The blushing bank is all my care,
With hearth so red, and walls so fair;
" Heap the sea-coal, come, heap it higher,　5
The oaken log lay on the fire."
The well-wash'd stools, a circling row,
With lad and lass, how fair the show!
The merry can of nut-brown ale,
The laughing jest, the love-sick tale,　10
Till, tir'd of chat, the game begins.
The lasses prick the lads with pins;
Roger from Dolly twitch'd the stool,
She, falling, kiss'd the ground, poor fool!
She blush'd so red, with side-long glance　15
At hob-nail Dick, who griev'd the chance.
But now for Blind-man's Buff they call;
Of each incumbrance clear the hall—
Jenny her silken 'kerchief folds,
And blear-ey'd Will the black lot holds.　20
Now laughing stops, with " Silence! hush! "
And Peggy Pout gives Sam a push.
The Blind-man's arms, extended wide,
Sam slips between:—" O woe betide
Thee, clumsy Will! "—but titt'ring Kate　25
Is pen'd up in the corner strait!
And now Will's eyes beheld the play;
He thought his face was t'other way.
" Now, Kitty, now! what chance hast thou,
Roger so near thee!—Trips, I vow!"　30
She catches him—then Roger ties
His own head up—but not his eyes;
For thro' the slender cloth he sees,
And runs at Sam, who slips with ease
His clumsy hold, and, dodging round,　35
Sukey is tumbled on the ground!—
" See what it is to play unfair!
Where cheating is, there's mischief there."

But Roger still pursues the chace,—
" He sees! he sees! " cries, softly, Grace;   40
" O Roger, thou, unskill'd in art,
Must, surer bound, go thro' thy part!"
Now Kitty, pert, repeats the rhymes,
And Roger turns him round three times,
Then pauses ere he starts—but Dick   45
Was mischief bent upon a trick;
Down on his hands and knees he lay
Directly in the Blind-man's way,
Then cries out " Hem!" Hodge heard, and ran
With hood-wink'd chance—sure of his man;   50
But down he came.—Alas, how frail
Our best of hopes, how soon they fail!
With crimson drops he stains the ground;
Confusion startles all around!
Poor piteous Dick supports his head,   55
And fain would cure the hurt he made;
But Kitty hasted with a key,
And down his back they straight convey
The cold relief; the blood is stay'd,
And Hodge again holds up his head.   60
Such are the fortunes of the game,
And those who play should stop the same
By wholesome laws, such as, all those
Who on the blinded man impose
Stand in his stead; as, long agone,   65
When men were first a nation grown,
Lawless they liv'd, till wantonness
And liberty began t' increase,
And one man lay in another's way;
Then laws were made to keep fair play.   70

KING EDWARD THE THIRD

PERSONS

KING EDWARD.
THE BLACK PRINCE.
QUEEN PHILIPPA.
DUKE OF CLARENCE.
SIR JOHN CHANDOS.
SIR THOMAS DAGWORTH.
SIR WALTER MANNY.

LORD AUDLEY.
LORD PERCY.
BISHOP.
WILLIAM, *Dagworth's Man*.
PETER BLUNT, *a common Soldier*.

SCENE

The Coast of France. KING EDWARD *and Nobles before it.*
The Army.

KING. O thou, to whose fury the nations are
But as dust! maintain thy servant's right.
Without thine aid, the twisted mail, and spear,
And forged helm, and shield of seven times beaten brass,
Are idle trophies of the vanquisher.   5
When confusion rages, when the field is in a flame,
When the cries of blood tear horror from heav'n,
And yelling death runs up and down the ranks,
Let Liberty, the charter'd right of Englishmen,
Won by our fathers in many a glorious field,   10
Enerve my soldiers; let Liberty
Blaze in each countenance, and fire the battle.
The enemy fight in chains, invisible chains, but heavy;
Their minds are fetter'd, then how can they be free?
While, like the mounting flame,   15
We spring to battle o'er the floods of death,
And these fair youths, the flow'r of England,
Vent'ring their lives in my most righteous cause,
O sheathe their hearts with triple steel, that they
May emulate their fathers' virtues!   20
And thou, my son, be strong; thou fightest for a crown
That death can never ravish from thy brow,
A crown of glory: but from thy very dust
Shall beam a radiance, to fire the breasts

POETICAL SKETCHES

Of youth unborn! Our names are written equal 25
In fame's wide trophied hall; 'tis ours to gild
The letters, and to make them shine with gold
That never tarnishes: whether Third Edward,
Or the Prince of Wales, or Montacute, or Mortimer,
Or ev'n the least by birth, shall gain the brightest fame, 30
Is in his hand to whom all men are equal.
The world of men are like the num'rous stars
That beam and twinkle in the depth of night,
Each clad in glory according to his sphere;
But we, that wander from our native seats 35
And beam forth lustre on a darkling world,
Grow larger as we advance! and some perhaps
The most obscure at home, that scarce were seen
To twinkle in their sphere, may so advance
That the astonish'd world, with up-turn'd eyes, 40
Regardless of the moon, and those that once were bright,
Stand only for to gaze upon their splendour!
      [*He here knights the Prince, and other young Nobles.*]
Now let us take a just revenge for those
Brave Lords, who fell beneath the bloody axe
At Paris, Thanks, noble Harcourt, for 'twas
By your advice we landed here in Brittany, 45
A country not yet sown with destruction,
And where the fiery whirlwind of swift war
Has not yet swept its desolating wing.—
Into three parties we divide by day,
And separate march, but join again at night; 50
Each knows his rank, and Heav'n marshal all.
                                        [*Exeunt.*

SCENE. *English Court*. LIONEL, DUKE OF CLARENCE;
      QUEEN PHILIPPA; LORDS, BISHOP, &c.

CLARENCE. My Lords, I have by the advice of her
Whom I am doubly bound to obey, my Parent
And my Sovereign, call'd you together.
My task is great, my burden heavier than
My unfledg'd years; 5
Yet, with your kind assistance, Lords, I hope
England shall dwell in peace; that, while my father
Toils in his wars, and turns his eyes on this
His native shore, and sees commerce fly round
With his white wings, and sees his golden London 10
And her silver Thames, throng'd with shining spires
And corded ships, her merchants buzzing round
Like summer bees, and all the golden cities
In his land overflowing with honey,
Glory may not be dimm'd with clouds of care. 15

Say, Lords, should not our thoughts be first to commerce?
My Lord Bishop, you would recommend us agriculture?
   BISHOP. Sweet Prince! the arts of peace are great,
And no less glorious than those of war,
Perhaps more glorious in the philosophic mind.   **20**
When I sit at my home, a private man,
My thoughts are on my gardens and my fields,
How to employ the hand that lacketh bread.
If Industry is in my diocese,
Religion will flourish; each man's heart   **25**
Is cultivated and will bring forth fruit:
This is my private duty and my pleasure.
But, as I sit in council with my prince,
My thoughts take in the gen'ral good of the whole,
And England is the land favour'd by Commerce;   **30**
For Commerce, tho' the child of Agriculture,
Fosters his parent, who else must sweat and toil,
And gain but scanty fare. Then, my dear Lord,
Be England's trade our care; and we, as tradesmen,
Looking to the gain of this our native land.   **35**
   CLARENCE. O my good Lord, true wisdom drops like honey
From your tongue, as from a worship'd oak!
Forgive, my Lords, my talkative youth, that speaks
Not merely what my narrow observation has
Pick'd up, but what I have concluded from your lessons.   **40**
Now, by the Queen's advice, I ask your leave
To dine to-morrow with the Mayor of London:
If I obtain your leave, I have another boon
To ask, which is, the favour of your company.
I fear Lord Percy will not give me leave.   **45**
   PERCY. Dear Sir, a prince should always keep his state,
And grant his favours with a sparing hand,
Or they are never rightly valued.
These are my thoughts, yet it were best to go;
But keep a proper dignity, for now   **50**
You represent the sacred person of
Your father; 'tis with princes as 'tis with the sun,
If not sometimes o'er-clouded, we grow weary
Of his officious glory.
   CLARENCE. Then you will give me leave to shine sometimes, **55**
My Lord?
   LORD. Thou hast a gallant spirit, which I fear
Will be imposed on by the closer sort!   *[Aside.*
   CLARENCE. Well, I'll endeavour to take
Lord Percy's advice; I have been used so much   **60**
To dignity that I'm sick on't.
   QUEEN PHILIPPA. Fie, fie, Lord Clarence! you proceed not to
    business,

But speak of your own pleasures.
I hope their Lordships will excuse your giddiness.
   CLARENCE. My Lords, the French have fitted out many   65
Small ships of war, that, like to ravening wolves,
Infest our English seas, devouring all
Our burden'd vessels, spoiling our naval flocks.
The merchants do complain and beg our aid.
   PERCY. The merchants are rich enough;   70
Can they not help themselves?
   BISHOP. They can, and may; but how to gain their will
Requires our countenance and help.
   PERCY. When that they find they must, my Lord, they will:
Let them but suffer awhile, and you shall see   75
They will bestir themselves.
   BISHOP. Lord Percy cannot mean that we should suffer
This disgrace: if so, we are not sovereigns
Of the sea, our right, that Heaven gave
To England; when at the birth of nature   80
She was seated in the deep, the Ocean ceas'd
His mighty roar, and fawning play'd around
Her snowy feet, and own'd his awful Queen.
Lord Percy, if the heart is sick, the head
Must be aggriev'd; if but one member suffer,   85
The heart doth fail. You say, my Lord, the merchants
Can, if they will, defend themselves against
These rovers: this is a noble scheme,
Worthy the brave Lord Percy, and as worthy
His generous aid to put it into practice.   90
   PERCY. Lord Bishop, what was rash in me is wise
In you: I dare not own the plan. 'Tis not
Mine. Yet will I, if you please,
Quickly to the Lord Mayor, and work him onward
To this most glorious voyage; on which cast   95
I'll set my whole estate,
But we will bring these Gallic rovers under.
   QUEEN PHILIPPA. Thanks, brave Lord Percy! you have the
    thanks
Of England's Queen, and will, ere long, of England.   [*Exeunt.*

SCENE. *At Cressy.* SIR THOMAS DAGWORTH *and*
LORD AUDLEY *meeting.*

   AUDLEY. Good morrow, brave Sir Thomas; the bright morn
Smiles on our army, and the gallant sun
Springs from the hills like a young hero
Into the battle, shaking his golden locks
Exultingly: this is a promising day.   5

DAGWORTH. Why, my Lord Audley, I don't know.
Give me your hand, and now I'll tell you what
I think you do not know. Edward's afraid of Philip.
    AUDLEY. Ha, Ha, Sir Thomas! you but joke;
Did you ere see him fear? At Blanchetaque,   10
When almost singly he drove six thousand
French from the ford, did he fear then?
    DAGWORTH. Yes, fear; that made him fight so.
    AUDLEY. By the same reason I might say, tis fear
That makes you fight.   15
    DAGWORTH. Mayhap you may: look upon Edward's face,
No one can say he fears. But when he turns
His back, then I will say it to his face,
He is afraid: he makes us all afraid.
I cannot bear the enemy at my back.   20
Now here we are at Cressy; where to-morrow,
To-morrow we shall know. I say, Lord Audley,
That Edward runs away from Philip.
    AUDLEY. Perhaps you think the Prince too is afraid?
    DAGWORTH. No; God forbid! I'm sure he is not.   25
He is a young lion. O I have seen him fight,
And give command, and lightning has flashed
From his eyes across the field: I have seen him
Shake hands with death, and strike a bargain for
The enemy; he has danc'd in the field   30
Of battle, like the youth at morrice play.
I'm sure he's not afraid, nor Warwick, nor none,
None of us but me; and I am very much afraid.
    AUDLEY. Are you afraid too, Sir Thomas?
I believe that as much as I believe   35
The King's afraid: but what are you afraid of?
    DAGWORTH. Of having my back laid open; we turn
Our backs to the fire till we shall burn our skirts.
    AUDLEY. And this, Sir Thomas, you call fear? Your fear
Is of a different kind then from the King's;   40
He fears to turn his face, and you to turn your back.
I do not think, Sir Thomas, you know what fear is.

Enter SIR JOHN CHANDOS.

CHANDOS. Good morrow, Generals; I give you joy:
Welcome to the fields of Cressy. Here we stop,
And wait for Philip.   45
    DAGWORTH. I hope so.
    AUDLEY. There, Sir Thomas, do you call that fear?
    DAGWORTH. I don't know; perhaps he takes it by fits.
Why, noble Chandos, look you here—
One rotten sheep spoils the whole flock;   50
And if the bell-weather is tainted, I wish

The Prince may not catch the distemper too.
  CHANDOS. Distemper, Sir Thomas! what distemper?
I have not heard.
  DAGWORTH. Why, Chandos, you are a wise man,   55
I know you understand me; a distemper
The King caught here in France of running away.
  AUDLEY. Sir Thomas, you say you have caught it too.
  DAGWORTH. And so will the whole army; 'tis very catching,
For when the coward runs, the brave man totters.   60
Perhaps the air of the country is the cause.
I feel it coming upon me, so I strive against it;
You yet are whole, but after a few more
Retreats, we all shall know how to retreat
Better than fight.—To be plain, I think retreating   65
Too often, takes away a soldier's courage.
  CHANDOS. Here comes the King himself: tell him your thoughts
Plainly, Sir Thomas.
  DAGWORTH. I've told him before, but his disorder
Makes him deaf.   70

     Enter KING EDWARD *and* BLACK PRINCE.

  KING. Good morrow, Generals; when English courage fails,
Down goes our right to France.
But we are conquerors every where; nothing
Can stand our soldiers; each man is worthy
Of a triumph. Such an army of heroes   75
Ne'er shouted to the Heav'ns, nor shook the field.
Edward, my son, thou art
Most happy, having such command: the man
Were base who were not fir'd to deeds
Above heroic, having such examples.   80
  PRINCE. Sire! with respect and deference I look
Upon such noble souls, and wish myself
Worthy the high command that Heaven and you
Have given me. When I have seen the field glow,
And in each countenance the soul of war   85
Curb'd by the manliest reason, I have been wing'd
With certain victory; and 'tis my boast,
And shall be still my glory, I was inspir'd
By these brave troops.
  DAGWORTH. Your Grace had better make   90
Them all Generals.
  KING. Sir Thomas Dagworth, you must have your joke,
And shall, while you can fight as you did at
The Ford.
  DAGWORTH. I have a small petition to your Majesty.   95
  KING. What can Sir Thomas Dagworth ask, that Edward
Can refuse?
    P 792

DAGWORTH. I hope your Majesty cannot refuse so great
A trifle; I've gilt your cause with my best blood,
And would again, were I not forbid　　　　　　　　　100
By him whom I am bound to obey: my hands
Are tied up, my courage shrunk and wither'd,
My sinews slacken'd, and my voice scarce heard;
Therefore I beg I may return to England.
　　　KING. I know not what you could have ask'd, Sir Thomas, 105
That I would not have sooner parted with
Than such a soldier as you have been, and such a friend.
Nay, I will know the most remote particulars
Of this your strange petition; that, if I can,
I still may keep you here.　　　　　　　　　　　110
　　　DAGWORTH. Here on the fields of Cressy we are settled
Till Philip springs the tim'rous covey again.
The Wolf is hunted down by causeless fear;
The Lion flees, and fear usurps his heart,
Startled, astonish'd at the clam'rous Cock;　　　　115
The Eagle, that doth gaze upon the sun,
Fears the small fire that plays about the fen.
If, at this moment of their idle fear,
The Dog doth seize the Wolf, the Forester the Lion,
The Negro in the crevice of the rock　　　　　　120
Doth seize the soaring Eagle; undone by flight,
They tame submit: such the effect flight has
On noble souls. Now hear its opposite:
The tim'rous Stag starts from the thicket wild,
The fearful Crane springs from the splashy fen,　　125
The shining Snake glides o'er the bending grass;
The Stag turns head and bays the crying Hounds,
The Crane o'ertaken fighteth with the Hawk,
The Snake doth turn and bite the padding foot;
And, if your Majesty's afraid of Philip,　　　　　130
You are more like a Lion than a Crane:
Therefore I beg I may return to England.
　　　KING. Sir Thomas, now I understand your mirth,
Which often plays with Wisdom for its pastime,
And brings good counsel from the breast of laughter.　135
I hope you'll stay, and see us fight this battle,
And reap rich harvest in the fields of Cressy;
Then go to England, tell them how we fight,
And set all hearts on fire to be with us.
Philip is plum'd, and thinks we flee from him,　　140
Else he would never dare to attack us. Now,
Now the quarry's set! and Death doth sport
In the bright sunshine of this fatal day.
　　　DAGWORTH. Now my heart dances, and I am as light
As the young bridegroom going to be married.　　145

Now must I to my soldiers, get them ready,
Furbish our armours bright, new plume our helms;
And we will sing like the young housewives busied
In the dairy: my feet are wing'd, but not
For flight, an please your grace.   150
    KING. If all my soldiers are as pleas'd as you,
'Twill be a gallant thing to fight or die;
Then I can never be afraid of Philip.
    DAGWORTH. A raw-bon'd fellow t'other day pass'd by me;
I told him to put off his hungry looks—   155
He answer'd me, "I hunger for another battle."
I saw a little Welshman with a fiery face;
I told him he look'd like a candle half
Burn'd out; he answer'd, he was " pig enough
To light another pattle." Last night, beneath   160
The moon I walk'd abroad; when all had pitch'd
Their tents, and all were still,
I heard a blooming youth singing a song
He had compos'd, and at each pause he wip'd
His dropping eyes. The ditty was, " if he   165
Return'd victorious, he should wed a maiden
Fairer than snow, and rich as midsummer."
Another wept, and wish'd health to his father.
I chid them both, but gave them noble hopes.
These are the minds that glory in the battle,   170
And leap and dance to hear the trumpet sound.
    KING. Sir Thomas Dagworth, be thou near our person;
Thy heart is richer than the vales of France:
I will not part with such a man as thee.
If Philip came arm'd in the ribs of death,   175
And shook his mortal dart against my head,
Thou'dst laugh his fury into nerveless shame!
Go now, for thou art suited to the work,
Throughout the camp; enflame the timorous,
Blow up the sluggish into ardour, and   180
Confirm the strong with strength, the weak inspire,
And wing their brows with hope and expectation:
Then to our tent return, and meet to council.   [Exit DAGWORTH.
    CHANDOS. That man's a hero in his closet, and more
A hero to the servants of his house   185
Than to the gaping world; he carries windows
In that enlarged breast of his, that all
May see what's done within.
    PRINCE. He is a genuine Englishman, my Chandos,
And hath the spirit of Liberty within him.   190
Forgive my prejudice, Sir John; I think
My Englishmen the bravest people on
The face of the earth.

CHANDOS. Courage, my Lord, proceeds from self-dependence.
Teach man to think he's a free agent,   195
Give but a slave his liberty, he'll shake
Off sloth, and build himself a hut, and hedge
A spot of ground; this he'll defend; 'tis his
By right of nature: thus set in action,
He will still move onward to plan conveniences,   200
Till glory fires his breast to enlarge his castle,
While the poor slave drudges all day, in hope
To rest at night.
    KING. O Liberty, how glorious art thou!
I see thee hov'ring o'er my army, with   205
Thy wide-stretch'd plumes; I see thee
Lead them on to battle;
I see thee blow thy golden trumpet, while
Thy sons shout the strong shout of victory!
O noble Chandos! think thyself a gardener,   210
My son a vine, which I commit unto
Thy care; prune all extravagant shoots, and guide
Th' ambitious tendrils in the paths of wisdom;
Water him with thy advice; and Heav'n
Rain fresh'ning dew upon his branches. And,   215
O Edward, my dear son! learn to think lowly of
Thyself, as we may all each prefer other—
'Tis the best policy, and 'tis our duty.   [*Exit* KING EDWARD.
    PRINCE. And may our duty, Chandos, be our pleasure.
Now we are alone, Sir John, I will unburden,   220
And breathe my hopes into the burning air
Where thousand deaths are posting up and down,
Commission'd to this fatal field of Cressy.
Methinks I see them arm my gallant soldiers,
And gird the sword upon each thigh, and fit   225
Each shining helm, and string each stubborn bow,
And dance to the neighing of our steeds.
Methinks the shout begins, the battle burns;
Methinks I see them perch on English crests,
And roar the wild flame of fierce war upon   230
The thronged enemy! In truth I am too full;
It is my sin to love the noise of war.
Chandos, thou seest my weakness; strong nature
Will bend or break us; my blood, like a springtide,
Does rise so high to overflow all bounds   235
Of moderation; while Reason, in her
Frail bark, can see no shore or bound for vast
Ambition. Come, take the helm, my Chandos,
That my full-blown sails overset me not
In the wild tempest; condemn my 'ventrous youth,   240
That plays with danger, as the innocent child

Unthinking plays upon the viper's den:
I am a coward in my reason, Chandos.
    CHANDOS. You are a man, my prince, and a brave man,
If I can judge of actions; but your heat   245
Is the effect of youth, and want of use;
Use makes the armed field and noisy war
Pass over as a summer cloud, unregarded,
Or but expected as a thing of course.
Age is contemplative; each rolling year   250
Brings forth fruit to the mind's treasure-house:
While vacant youth doth crave and seek about
Within itself, and findeth discontent,
Then, tir'd of thought, impatient takes the wing,
Seizes the fruits of time, attacks experience,   255
Roams round vast Nature's forest, where no bounds
Are set, the swiftest may have room, the strongest
Find prey; till tired at length, sated and tired
With the changing sameness, old variety,
We sit us down, and view our former joys   260
With distaste and dislike.
    PRINCE. Then if we must tug for experience,
Let us not fear to beat round Nature's wilds,
And rouze the strongest prey; then, if we fall,
We fall with glory. I know the wolf   265
Is dangerous to fight, not good for food,
Nor is the hide a comely vestment; so
We have our battle for our pains. I know
That youth has need of age to point fit prey,
And oft the stander-by shall steal the fruit   270
Of th'other's labour. This is philosophy;
These are the tricks of the world; but the pure soul
Shall mount on native wings, disdaining
Little sport, and cut a path into the heaven of glory,
Leaving a track of light for men to wonder at.   275
I'm glad my father does not hear me talk;
You can find friendly excuses for me, Chandos.
But do you not think, Sir John, that if it please
Th' Almighty to stretch out my span of life,
I shall with pleasure view a glorious action   280
Which my youth master'd?
    CHANDOS. Considerate age, my Lord, views motives,
And not acts; when neither warbling voice
Nor trilling pipe is heard, nor pleasure sits
With trembling age, the voice of Conscience then,   285
Sweeter than music in a summer's eve,
Shall warble round the snowy head, and keep
Sweet symphony to feather'd angels, sitting
As guardians round your chair; then shall the pulse

Beat slow, and taste and touch and sight and sound and smell, 290
That sing and dance round Reason's fine-wrought throne,
Shall flee away, and leave them all forlorn;
Yet not forlorn if Conscience is his friend.   [*Exeunt.*

SCENE. *In Sir Thomas Dagworth's Tent.* DAGWORTH, *and*
WILLIAM *his Man.*

DAGWORTH. Bring hither my armour, William.
Ambition is the growth of ev'ry clime.
    WILLIAM. Does it grow in England, Sir?
    DAGWORTH. Aye, it grows most in lands most cultivated.
    WILLIAM. Then it grows most in France; the vines here
Are finer than any we have in England.
    DAGWORTH. Aye, but the oaks are not.
    WILLIAM. What is the tree you mentioned? I don't think
I ever saw it.
    DAGWORTH. Ambition.
    WILLIAM. Is it a little creeping root that grows in ditches?
    DAGWORTH. Thou dost not understand me, William.
It is a root that grows in every breast;
Ambition is the desire or passion that one man
Has to get before another, in any pursuit after glory;
But I don't think you have any of it.
    WILLIAM. Yes, I have; I have a great ambition to know every
thing, Sir.
    DAGWORTH. But when our first ideas are wrong, what follows
must all be wrong of course; 'tis best to know a little, and to
know that little aright.
    WILLIAM. Then, Sir, I should be glad to know if it was not
ambition that brought over our King to France to fight for
his right?
    DAGWORTH. Tho' the knowledge of that will not profit thee
much, yet I will tell you that it was ambition.
    WILLIAM. Then if ambition is a sin, we are all guilty in coming
with him, and in fighting for him.
    DAGWORTH. Now, William, thou dost thrust the question
home; but I must tell you, that guilt being an act of the mind,
none are guilty but those whose minds are prompted by that
same ambition.
    WILLIAM. Now I always thought that a man might be guilty
of doing wrong without knowing it was wrong.
    DAGWORTH. Thou art a natural philosopher, and knowest
truth by instinct, while reason runs aground, as we have run
our argument. Only remember, William, all have it in their power
to know the motives of their own actions, and 'tis a sin to act
without some reason.

WILLIAM. And whoever acts without reason may do a great deal of harm without knowing it.

DAGWORTH. Thou art an endless moralist.

WILLIAM. Now there's a story come into my head, that I will tell your honour, if you'll give me leave.

DAGWORTH. No, William, save it till another time; this is no time for story-telling; but here comes one who is as entertaining as a good story.

Enter PETER BLUNT.

PETER. Yonder's a musician going to play before the King; it's a new song about the French and English, and the Prince has made the minstrel a 'squire, and given him I don't know what, and I can't tell whether he don't mention us all one by one; and he is to write another about all us that are to die, that we may be remembered in Old England, for all our blood and bones are in France; and a great deal more that we shall all hear by and by; and I came to tell your honour, because you love to hear war-songs.

DAGWORTH. And who is this minstrel, Peter, dost know?

PETER. O aye, I forgot to tell that; he has got the same name as Sir John Chandos, that the Prince is always with—the wise man, that knows us all as well as your honour, only e'nt so good natur'd.

DAGWORTH. I thank you, Peter, for your information, but not for your compliment, which is not true; there's as much difference between him and me as between glittering sand and fruitful mold; or shining glass and a wrought diamond, set in rich gold, and fitted to the finger of an emperor: such is that worthy Chandos.

PETER. I know your honour does not think any thing of yourself, but every body else does.

DAGWORTH. Go, Peter, get you gone; flattery is delicious, even from the lips of a babbler.   [*Exit Peter.*

WILLIAM. I never flatter your honour.

DAGWORTH. I don't know that.

WILLIAM. Why you know, Sir, when we were in England, at the tournament at Windsor, and the Earl of Warwick was tumbled over, you ask'd me if he did not look well when he fell? and I said, No, he look'd very foolish; and you was very angry with me for not flattering you.

DAGWORTH. You mean that I was angry with you for not flattering the Earl of Warwick.   [*Exeunt.*

SCENE. *Sir Thomas Dagworth's Tent*. SIR THOMAS DAGWORTH—*to him*
Enter SIR WALTER MANNY.

SIR WALTER. Sir Thomas Dagworth, I have been weeping Over the men that are to die to-day.

DAGWORTH. Why, brave Sir Walter, you or I may fall.
SIR WALTER. I know this breathing flesh must lie and rot,
Cover'd with silence and forgetfulness.— 5
Death wons in cities' smoke, and in still night,
When men sleep in their beds, walketh about!
How many in walled cities lie and groan,
Turning themselves upon their beds,
Talking with death, answering his hard demands! 10
How many walk in darkness, terrors are round
The curtains of their beds, destruction is
Ready at the door! How many sleep
In earth, cover'd with stones and deathly dust,
Resting in quietness, whose spirits walk 15
Upon the clouds of heaven, to die no more!
Yet death is terrible, tho' borne on angels' wings!
How terrible then is the field of death,
Where he doth rend the vault of heaven,
And shake the gates of hell! 20
O Dagworth, France is sick! the very sky,
Tho' sunshine light it, seems to me as pale
As the pale fainting man on his death-bed,
Whose face is shewn by light of sickly taper!
It makes me sad and sick at very heart, 25
Thousands must fall to-day!
DAGWORTH. Thousands of souls must leave this prison-house,
To be exalted to those heavenly fields,[1]
Where songs of triumph, palms of victory,
Where peace and joy and love and calm content 30
Sit singing in the azure clouds, and strew
Flowers of heaven's growth over the banquet-table:
Bind ardent Hope upon your feet like shoes,
Put on the robe of preparation,
The table is prepar'd in shining heaven, 35
The flowers of immortality are blown;
Let those that fight fight in good steadfastness,
And those that fall shall ise in victory.
SIR WALTER. I've often seen the burning field of war,
And often heard the dismal clang of arms; 40
But never, till this fatal day of Cressy,
Has my soul fainted with these views of death!
I seem to be in one great charnel-house,
And seem to scent the rotten carcases!
I seem to hear the dismal yells of death, 45
While the black gore drops from his horrid jaws;
Yet I not fear the monster in his pride—
But O the souls that are to die to-day!

[1] Cf. " A War Song," p. 424, which seems to have been prompted by this scene.

DAGWORTH. Stop, brave Sir Walter; let me drop a tear,
Then let the clarion of war begin;   50
I'll fight and weep, 'tis in my country's cause;
I'll weep ánd shout for glorious liberty.
Grim war shall laugh and shout, decked in tears,
And blood shall flow like streams across the meadows,
That murmur down their pebbly channels, and   55
Spend their sweet lives to do their country service:
Then shall England's verdure shoot, her fields shall smile,
Her ships shall sing across the foaming sea,
Her mariners shall use the flute and viol,
And rattling guns, and black and dreary war,   60
Shall be no more.
  SIR WALTER. Well, let the trumpet sound, and the drum beat;
Let war stain the blue heavens with bloody banners;
I'll draw my sword, nor ever sheathe it up
Till England blow the trump of victory,   65
Or I lay stretch'd upon the field of death!   [*Exeunt.*

SCENE. *In the Camp. Several of the Warriors met at the King's
    Tent with a Minstrel, who sings the following Song:*

O Sons of Trojan Brutus, cloath'd in war,
Whose voices are the thunder of the field,
Rolling dark clouds o'er France, muffling the sun
In sickly darkness like a dim eclipse,
Threatening as the red brow of storms, as fire   5
Burning up nations in your wrath and fury!

Your ancestors came from the fires of Troy,
(Like lions rouz'd by light'ning from their dens,
Whose eyes do glare against the stormy fires)
Heated with war, fill'd with the blood of Greeks,   10
With helmets hewn, and shields covered with gore,
In navies black, broken with wind and tide!

They landed in firm array upon the rocks
Of Albion; they kiss'd the rocky shore;
" Be thou our mother and our nurse," they said;   15
" Our children's mother, and thou shalt be our grave,
The sepulchre of ancient Troy, from whence
Shall rise cities, and thrones, and arms, and awful pow'rs."

Our fathers swarm from the ships. Giant voices
Are heard from the hills, the enormous sons   20
Of Ocean run from rocks and caves: wild men,
Naked and roaring like lions, hurling rocks.
*p 792

And wielding knotty clubs, like oaks entangled
Thick as a forest, ready for the axe.

Our fathers move in firm array to battle;   25
The savage monsters rush like roaring fire;
Like as a forest roars with crackling flames,
When the red lightning, borne by furious storms,
Lights on some woody shore; the parched heavens
Rain fire into the molten raging sea!   30

The smoking trees are strewn upon the shore,
Spoil'd of their verdure! O how oft have they
Defy'd the storm that howled o'er their heads!
Our fathers, sweating, lean on their spears, and view
The mighty dead: giant bodies streaming blood,   35
Dread visages frowning in silent death!

Then Brutus spoke, inspir'd; our fathers sit
Attentive on the melancholy shore:
Hear ye the voice of Brutus—'' The flowing waves
Of time come rolling o'er my breast,'' he said;   40
'' And my heart labours with futurity:
Our sons shall rule the empire of the sea.

'' Their mighty wings shall stretch from east to west.
Their nest is in the sea, but they shall roam
Like eagles for the prey; nor shall the young   45
Crave or be heard; for plenty shall bring forth,
Cities shall sing, and vales in rich array
Shall laugh, whose fruitful laps bend down with fulness.

'' Our sons shall rise from thrones in joy,
Each one buckling on his armour; Morning   50
Shall be prevented by their swords gleaming,
And Evening hear their song of victory!
Their towers shall be built upon the rocks,
Their daughters shall sing, surrounded with shining spears!

'' Liberty shall stand upon the cliffs of Albion,   55
Casting her blue eyes over the green ocean;
Or, tow'ring, stand upon the roaring waves,
Stretching her mighty spear o'er distant lands;
While, with her eagle wings, she covereth
Fair Albion's shore, and all her families.''   60

PROLOGUE

INTENDED FOR A DRAMATIC PIECE OF

KING EDWARD THE FOURTH

O FOR a voice like thunder, and a tongue
To drown the throat of war! When the senses
Are shaken, and the soul is driven to madness,
Who can stand? When the souls of the oppressed
Fight in the troubled air that rages, who can stand?   5
When the whirlwind of fury comes from the
Throne of God, when the frowns of his countenance
Drive the nations together, who can stand?
When Sin claps his broad wings over the battle,
And sails rejoicing in the flood of Death;   10
When souls are torn to everlasting fire,
And fiends of Hell rejoice upon the slain,
O who can stand? O who hath caused this?
O who can answer at the throne of God?
The Kings and Nobles of the Land have done it!   15
Hear it not, Heaven, thy Ministers have done it!

PROLOGUE TO KING JOHN

JUSTICE hath heaved a sword to plunge in Albion's breast; for
Albion's sins are crimson dy'd, and the red scourge follows her
desolate sons! Then Patriot rose; full oft did Patriot rise, when
Tyranny hath stain'd fair Albion's breast with her own children's
gore. Round his majestic feet deep thunders roll; each heart
does tremble, and each knee grows slack. The stars of heaven
tremble; the roaring voice of war, the trumpet, calls to battle!
Brother in brother's blood must bathe, rivers of death! O land,
most hapless! O beauteous island, how forsaken! Weep from thy
silver fountains; weep from thy gentle rivers! The angel of the
island weeps! Thy widowed virgins weep beneath thy shades!
Thy aged fathers gird themselves for war! The sucking infant
lives to die in battle; the weeping mother feeds him for the
slaughter! The husbandman doth leave his bending harvest!
Blood cries afar! The land doth sow itself! The glittering youth

of courts must gleam in arms! The aged senators their ancient
swords assume! The trembling sinews of old age must work
the work of death against their progeny; for Tyranny hath
stretch'd his purple arm, and "blood," he cries; "the chariots
and the horses, the noise of shout, and dreadful thunder of the
battle heard afar!" Beware, O Proud! thou shalt be humbled;
thy cruel brow, thine iron heart, is smitten, though lingering
Fate is slow. O yet may Albion smile again, and stretch her
peaceful arms, and raise her golden head exultingly! Her citizens
shall throng about her gates, her mariners shall sing upon the
sea, and myriads shall to her temples crowd! Her sons shall
joy as in the morning! Her daughters sing as to the rising year!

A WAR SONG
TO ENGLISHMEN

Prepare, prepare the iron helm of war,
Bring forth the lots, cast in the spacious orb;
Th' Angel of Fate turns them with mighty hands
And casts them out upon the darken'd earth!
              Prepare, prepare.   5

Prepare your hearts for Death's cold hand! prepare
Your souls for flight, your bodies for the earth!
Prepare your arms for glorious victory!
Prepare your eyes to meet a holy God!
              Prepare, prepare.   10

Whose fatal scroll is that? Methinks 'tis mine!
Why sinks my heart, why faultereth my tongue?
Had I three lives, I'd die in such a cause,
And rise, with ghosts, over the well-fought field.
              Prepare, prepare.   15

The arrows of Almighty God are drawn!
Angels of Death stand in the low'ring heavens!
Thousands of souls must seek the realms of light,
And walk together on the clouds of heaven!
              Prepare, prepare.   20

Soldiers, prepare! Our cause is Heaven's cause;
Soldiers, prepare! Be worthy of our cause:
Prepare to meet our fathers in the sky:
Prepare, O troops, that are to fall to-day!
              Prepare, prepare.   25

Alfred shall smile, and make his harp rejoice;
The Norman William, and the learned Clerk,
And Lion Heart, and black-brow'd Edward, with
His loyal queen, shall rise, and welcome us!

                    Prepare, prepare.   30

THE

COUCH OF DEATH

THE veiled Evening walked solitary down the western hills, and
Silence reposed in the valley; the birds of day were heard in
their nests, rustling in brakes and thickets; and the owl and bat
flew round the darkening trees: all is silent when Nature takes her
repose.—In former times, on such an evening, when the cold clay
breathed with life, and our ancestors, who now sleep in their
graves, walked on the stedfast globe, the remains of a family of
the tribes of Earth, a mother and a sister, were gathered to the
sick bed of a youth. Sorrow linked them together, leaning on one
another's necks alternately—like lilies, dropping tears in each
other's bosom, they stood by the bed like reeds bending over a
lake, when the evening drops trickle down. His voice was low as
the whisperings of the woods when the wind is asleep, and the
visions of Heaven unfold their visitation. " Parting is hard and
death is terrible; I seem to walk through a deep valley, far from
the light of day, alone and comfortless! The damps of death fall
thick upon me! Horrors stare me in the face! I look behind, there
is no returning; Death follows after me; I walk in regions of Death,
where no tree is, without a lantern to direct my steps, without a
staff to support me.'' Thus he laments through the still evening,
till the curtains of darkness were drawn. Like the sound of a
broken pipe, the aged woman raised her voice. "O my son, my
son, I know but little of the path thou goest! But lo! there is a
God, who made the world; stretch out thy hand to Him.'' The
youth replied, like a voice heard from a sepulchre, " My hand is
feeble, how should I stretch it out? My ways are sinful, how
should I raise mine eyes? My voice hath used deceit, how should
I call on Him who is Truth? My breath is loathsome, how should
he not be offended? If I lay my face in the dust, the grave opens
its mouth for me; if I lift up my head, sin covers me as a cloak!
O my dear friends, pray ye for me! Stretch forth your hands
that my helper may come! Through the void space I walk,
between the sinful world and eternity! Beneath me burns eternal
fire! O for a hand to pluck me forth!'' As the voice of an omen
heard in the silent valley, when the few inhabitants cling trem-
bling together; as the voice of the Angel of Death, when the

thin beams of the moon give a faint light, such was this young man's voice to his friends! Like the bubbling waters of the brook in the dead of night, the aged woman raised her cry, and said, "O Voice, that dwellest in my breast, can I not cry, and lift my eyes to Heaven? Thinking of this, my spirit is turned within me into confusion! O my child, my child! is thy breath infected? So is mine. As the deer, wounded by the brooks of water, so the arrows of sin stick in my flesh; the poison hath entered into my marrow." Like rolling waves upon a desert shore, sighs succeeded sighs; they covered their faces and wept! The youth lay silent, his mother's arm was under his head; he was like a cloud tossed by the winds, till the sun shine, and the drops of rain glisten, the yellow harvest breathes, and the thankful eyes of the villagers are turned up in smiles. The traveller that hath taken shelter under an oak, eyes the distant country with joy! Such smiles were seen upon the face of the youth! a visionary hand wiped away his tears, and a ray of light beamed around his head! All was still. The moon hung not out her lamp, and the stars faintly glimmered in the summer sky; the breath of night slept among the leaves of the forest; the bosom of the lofty hill drank in the silent dew, while on his majestic brow the voice of Angels is heard, and stringed sounds ride upon the wings of night. The sorrowful pair lift up their heads, hovering Angels are around them, voices of comfort are heard over the Couch of Death, and the youth breathes out his soul with joy into eternity.

CONTEMPLATION

WHO is this, that with unerring step dares tempt the wilds, were only Nature's foot hath trod? 'Tis Contemplation, daughter of the grey Morning! Majestical she steppeth, and with her pure quill on every flower writeth Wisdom's name. Now lowly bending, whispers in mine ear, "O man, how great, how little thou! O man, slave of each moment, lord of eternity! seest thou where Mirth sits on the painted cheek? doth it not seem ashamed of such a place, and grow immoderate to brave it out? O what an humble garb true Joy puts on! Those who want Happiness must stoop to find it; it is a flower that grows in every vale. Vain foolish man, that roams on lofty rocks! where, 'cause his garments are swoln with wind, he fancies he is grown into a giant! Lo, then, Humility, take it, and wear it in thine heart; lord of thyself, thou then art lord of all. Clamour brawls along the streets, and destruction hovers in the city's smoak; but on these plains, and in these silent woods, true joys descend: here build thy nest; here fix thy staff; delights blossom around;

numberless beauties blow; the green grass springs in joy, and the nimble air kisses the leaves; the brook stretches its arms along the velvet meadow, its silver inhabitants sport and play; the youthful sun joys like a hunter rouzed to the chace: he rushes up the sky, and lays hold on the immortal coursers of day; the sky glitters with the jingling trappings! Like a triumph, season follows season, while the airy music fills the world with joyful sounds." I answered, " Heavenly goddess! I am wrapped in mortality, my flesh is a prison, my bones the bars of death, Misery builds over our cottage roofs, and Discontent runs like a brook. Even in childhood, Sorrow slept with me in my cradle; he followed me up and down in the house when I grew up; he was my school-fellow: thus he was in my steps and in my play, till he became to me as my brother. I walked through dreary places with him, and in church-yards; and I oft found myself sitting by Sorrow on a tomb-stone! "

SAMSON

SAMSON, the strongest of the children of men, I sing; how he was foiled by woman's arts, by a false wife brought to the gates of death! O Truth! that shinest with propitious beams, turning our earthly night to heavenly day, from presence of the Almighty Father! thou visitest our darkling world with blessed feet, bringing good news of Sin and Death destroyed! O white-robed Angel, guide my timorous hand to write as on a lofty rock with iron pens the words of truth, that all who pass may read.—Now Night, noon-tide of damned spirits, over the silent earth spreads her pavilion, while in dark council sat Philista's lords; and where strength failed, black thoughts in ambush lay. Their helmed youth and aged warriors in dust together ly, and Desolation spreads his wings over the land of Palestine; from side to side the land groans, her prowess lost, and seeks to hide her bruised head under the mists of night, breeding dark plots. For Dalila's fair arts have long been tried in vain; in vain she wept in many a treacherous tear. " Go on, fair traitress; do thy guileful work; ere once again the changing moon her circuit hath performed, thou shalt overcome, and conquer him, by force unconquerable, and wrest his secret from him. Call thine alluring arts and honest-seeming brow, the holy kiss of love, and the transparent tear; put on fair linen that with the lily vies, purple and silver; neglect thy hair, to seem more lovely in thy loose attire; put on thy country's pride, deceit, and eyes of love decked in mild sorrow, and sell thy Lord for gold." For now, upon her sumptuous couch reclined, in gorgeous pride, she still intreats, and still she grasps

his vigorous knees with her fair arms. "Thou lov'st me not!
thou'rt war, thou art not love! O foolish Dalila! O weak woman!
it is death cloathed in flesh thou lovest, and thou hast been
incircled in his arms! Alas, my Lord, what am I calling thee?
Thou art my God! To thee I pour my tears for sacrifice morning
and evening. My days are covered with sorrow! Shut up; dar-
kened. By night I am deceived! Who says that thou wast born
of mortal kind? Destruction was thy father, a lioness suckled
thee, thy young hands tore human limbs, and gorged human
flesh! Come hither, Death; art thou not Samson's servant? 'Tis
Dalila that calls, thy master's wife; no, stay, and let thy master
do the deed: one blow of that strong arm would ease my pain;
then should I lay at quiet and have rest. Pity forsook thee at
thy birth! O Dagon furious, and all ye gods of Palestine, with-
draw your hand! I am but a weak woman. Alas, I am wedded to
your enemy! I will go mad, and tear my crisped hair; I'll run
about, and pierce the ears o' th' gods! O Samson, hold me not;
thou lovest me not! Look not upon me with those deathful eyes!
Thou wouldst my death, and death approaches fast." Thus, in
false tears, she bath'd his feet, and thus she day by day oppressed
his soul: he seemed a mountain, his brow among the clouds; she
seemed a silver stream, his feet embracing. Dark thoughts rolled
to and fro in his mind, like thunder clouds troubling the sky; his
visage was troubled; his soul was distressed. "Though I should
tell her all my heart, what can I fear? Though I should tell this
secret of my birth, the utmost may be warded off as well when
told as now." She saw him moved, and thus resumes her wiles.
"Samson, I'm thine; do with me what thou wilt; my friends are
enemies; my life is death; I am a traitor to my nation, and de-
spised; my joy is given into the hands of him who hates me,
using deceit to the wife of his bosom. Thrice hast thou mocked
me, and grieved my soul. Didst thou not tell me with green withs
to bind thy nervous arms, and, after that, when I had found
thy falsehood, with new ropes to bind thee fast? I knew thou
didst but mock me. Alas, when in thy sleep I bound thee with
them to try thy truth, I cried, 'The Philistines be upon thee,
Samson!'Then did suspicion wake thee; how didst thou rend
the feeble ties! Thou fearest nought, what shouldst thou fear?
Thy power is more than mortal, none can hurt thee; thy bones
are brass, thy sinews are iron! Ten thousand spears are like the
summer grass; an army of mighty men are as flocks in the vallies;
what canst thou fear? I drink my tears like water; I live upon
sorrow! O worse than wolves and tygers, what canst thou give
when such a trifle is denied me? But O at last thou mockest me
to shame my over-fond inquiry! Thou toldest me to weave thee
to the beam by thy strong hair; I did even that to try thy truth;
but, when I cried 'The Philistines be upon thee,' then didst
thou leave me to bewail that Samson loved me not." He sat,

and inward griev'd; he saw and lov'd the beauteous suppliant, nor could conceal aught that might appease her; then, leaning on her bosom, thus he spoke: "Hear, O Dalila! doubt no more of Samson's love; for that fair breast was made the ivory palace of my inmost heart, where it shall lie at rest; for sorrow is the lot of all of woman born; for care was I brought forth, and labour is my lot: nor matchless might, nor wisdom, nor every gift enjoyed, can from the heart of man hide sorrow. Twice was my birth foretold from heaven, and twice a sacred vow enjoined me that I should drink no wine, nor eat of any unclean thing; for holy unto Israel's God I am, a Nazarite even from my mother's womb. Twice was it told, that it might not be broken, 'Grant me a son, kind Heaven,' Manoa cried; but Heaven refused! Childless he mourned, but thought his God knew best. In solitude, though not obscure, in Israel he lived, till venerable age came on: his flocks increased, and plenty crowned his board: beloved, revered of man! But God hath other joys in store. Is burdened Israel his grief? The son of his old age shall set it free! The venerable sweetner of his life receives the promise first from Heaven. She saw the maidens play, and blessed their innocent mirth; she blessed each new-joined pair; but from her the long-wished deliverer shall spring. Pensive, alone she sat within the house, when busy day was fading, and calm evening, time for contemplation, rose from the forsaken east, and drew the curtains of heaven: pensive she sat, and thought on Israel's grief, and silent prayed to Israel's God; when lo, an angel from the fields of light entered the house! His form was manhood in the prime, and from his spacious brow shot terrors through the evening shade! But mild he hailed her, 'Hail, highly favoured!' said he; 'for lo, thou shalt conceive, and bear a son, and Israel's strength shall be upon his shoulders, and he shall be called Israel's Deliverer! Now therefore drink no wine, and eat not any unclean thing, for he shall be a Nazarite to God.' Then, as a neighbour when his evening tale is told, departs, his blessing leaving, so seemed he to depart: she wondered with exceeding joy, nor knew he was an angel. Manoa left his fields to sit in the house, and take his evening's rest from labour—the sweetest time that God has allotted mortal man. He sat, and heard with joy, and praised God who Israel still doth keep. The time rolled on, and Israel groaned oppressed. The sword was bright, while the plow-share rusted, till hope grew feeble, and was ready to give place to doubting: then prayed Manoa: 'O Lord, thy flock is scattered on the hills! The wolf teareth them, Oppression stretches his rod over our land, our country is plowed with swords, and reaped in blood! The echoes of slaughter reach from hill to hill! Instead of peaceful pipe, the shepherd bears a sword; the ox goad is turned into a spear! O when shall our Deliverer come? The Philistine riots on our flocks, our vintage is gathered by bands of enemies!

Stretch forth thy hand, and save.' Thus prayed Manoa. The aged woman walked into the field, and lo, again the angel came! Clad as a traveller fresh risen on his journey, she ran and called her husband, who came and talked with him. ' O man of God,' said he, ' thou comest from far! Let us detain thee while I make ready a kid, that thou mayest sit and eat, and tell us of thy name and warfare; that when thy sayings come to pass, we may honour thee.' The Angel answered, 'My name is wonderful; enquire not after it, seeing it is a secret: but, if thou wilt, offer an offering unto the Lord.' ''

ADDITIONS IN MS. TO THE POETICAL SKETCHES

Song by a Shepherd

WELCOME, stranger, to this place,
Where joy doth sit on every bough,
Paleness flies from every face;
We reap not what we do not sow.　　　　4

Innocence doth like a rose
Bloom on every maiden's cheek;
Honour twines around her brows,
The jewel health adorns her neck.　　　　8

Song by an Old Shepherd

WHEN silver snow decks Sylvio's clothes,
And jewel hangs at shepherd's nose,
We can abide life's pelting storm
That makes our limbs quake, if our hearts be warm.　4

Whilst Virtue is our walking-staff,
And Truth a lantern to our path,
We can abide life's pelting storm
That makes our limbs quake, if our hearts be warm.　8

Blow, boisterous wind, stern winter frown,
Innocence is a winter's gown.
So clad, we'll abide life's pelting storm
That makes our limbs quake, if our hearts be warm.　12

These two songs, together with an earlier version of the "Laughing Song" of the *Songs of Innocence*, were found in Mrs. Flaxman's copy of the *Poetical Sketches*. They have been received as Blake's though the handwriting is not his.

NOTES

NOTES

Revised 1959

Page 3. *There is No Natural Religion.* The tiny plates on which Blake wrote and illustrated these postulates probably represent his earliest experiments in relief-etched printing. The plates served a double purpose, enabling him to test this new method of printing while he crystallised his ideas on a subject which was engaging the thoughts of French and English philosophers at the time. He seems, however, to have taken little trouble to preserve the plates, for a complete set of them has not survived. Indeed it is by no means certain that he intended to make more than one series under this title, or that he ever completed it, or finally determined the order in which the propositions should be placed. According to Keynes's *Bibliography* the plates were first reproduced in facsimile by William Muir in 1886, and this facsimile is now the most easily available authority for seven of the plates, six of which are to be found only in the Pierpont Morgan Library, New York; the seventh is in private possession.

Despite their bare survival, these postulates are of great importance. Written years after the *Poetical Sketches*, they mark the beginning of Blake's distinctively original work. The *Poetical Sketches* were the imitative efforts of a youth of genius who had not discovered what he wanted to say; but in these postulates Blake is thinking deeply for himself. Here he lays his foundations and states his faith. From the conclusions here reached, he never departed.

Page 5. *All Religions are One.* The plates on which these "principles" are engraved are similar in size and appearance to those of *There is No Natural Religion*, and are therefore believed to have been made about the same time. Two impressions of the title-page are now known in England (one at the Victoria and Albert Museum). Of the remainder of the plates only one set, now in the Huntington Library, California, has survived.

Page 7. *Songs of Innocence and Songs of Experience.* Four years separated the issue of these two books and it seems unlikely that Blake had any thought of the second book when he began writing the first. When, however, he had completed the *Songs of Experience*, in 1793, he printed the two books together under the additional composite title. The text given here is taken from a copy in the British Museum. The order of the poems differs from that of previous transcripts, but is the one (of many (as most valuably shown by Dr. Sampson in his authoritative edition of 1905) which Blake most often adopted, and was possibly his favourite order. Concerning the date of the *Songs of Experience* (1794) it is noteworthy that his catalogue of books dated October 1793 includes the *Songs of Experience*, and there can be little doubt that most of its poems were written before *The Marriage of Heaven and Hell*. It is unthinkable that Blake should have gone back to the portrayal of "contraries" as fundamentally enigmatic, after he had joyously accepted them as essential to existence.

When Blake made a list of the *Songs of Innocence & of Experience* he did not give a separate title to *The Little Girl Found* (p. 25), thereby showing that he regarded the poem as a continuation of *The Little Girl Lost*. His first title for *A Poison Tree* (p. 32) was *Christian Forbearance*.

435

The capital letters used in some of the titles do not denote a printer's holiday: on the contrary, they show an effort to follow Blake's indicative variations in the original books.

Page 38. *The Book of Thel.* The text is taken from a copy at the British Museum. Chronologically this book comes between *Songs of Innocence* and *Songs of Experience*. It describes the soul on the threshold of Experience. The illustrations to the book have all the delicate grace and beauty which characterise the verse.

Page 42. *The Marriage of Heaven and Hell.* The text is taken from a copy at the Fitzwilliam Museum, Cambridge. The approximate date of this work is usually given as 1790, but there are good reasons, notably those advanced by Mr. Foster Damon, for thinking it was written later. The intellectual conundrum of the *Songs of Experience* is here solved. The mood is one of triumph, resolution and buoyant humour. It may be the plates were not all written at the same time, and most probably the work as a whole was not completed before 1793. The form of this book is discussed in the Introduction, to which the reader is also referred for the editor's reasons for believing *A Song of Liberty* to be an integral part of *The Marriage of Heaven and Hell*.

Page 56. *Visions of the Daughters of Albion.* The text is taken from the British Museum copy. The Daughters of Albion (roughly Blake's symbol for Woman) are the object of the poet's visions—i.e. the visions are his, not theirs. With the exception of *The Ghost of Abel* this is the most dramatic of the so-called prophetic works. It is really another Song of Experience, and was possibly written before *The Marriage of Heaven and Hell* was finished.

Page 63. *America.* The text is from an uncoloured copy in the British Museum. The designs and lettering of this "prophecy" are exceptionally fine. *America* is really an expanded form of *A Song of Liberty*, and actually contains most of its lines.

Page 70. *Europe.* The text is from the British Museum copy.

Page 78. *The Book of Urizen.* The text is taken from the Dimsdale copy (copy A in the *Census*, 1953), although a more readable order of the plates has been preferred. This copy is one of three that contain plate 4 (omitted from Muir's facsimile, 1888, and from the Ellis and Yeats edition, 1893). There is no second Book of Urizen and the word "First" occurs in some copies in the title and colophon and is deleted in others. Blake seems to have allowed his interest in the illustrations to this work to detract from his interest in the text; indeed he appears to have regarded the book as a series of emblematic pictures and the text as a more or less needful commentary. Hence there is confusion over the omission of plate 4 (beginning "Muster around the bleak desarts" (Chap. II. l. 10, p. 79), and ending "All the seven deadly sins of the soul" (Chap. III. l. 9, p. 81)), and over the beginning of Chap. IV., of which there are two versions. Moreover, the order in which the plates were arranged, varying with almost every copy, points to Blake's indifference to strict logical sequence in the text. The order here followed was first given by Dr. Sampson; it is that of the Ellis and Yeats edition, with plate 4 added, and is the most readable.

Page 93. *The Song of Los.* The text is taken from the copy in the British Museum. As the books *America* and *Europe* are prophetic, *Asia* and *Africa* are retrospective.

Page 97. *The Book of Ahania.* Only one copy of this book is known. It was formerly in the possession of W. A. White of New York, and is now in the Lessing Rosenwald Collection, Library of Congress, Washington, D.C. *Ahania* is a companion work to *The Book of Los,* both being etched in the ordinary way so that the words and designs were burnt into the copper plate instead of being brought into relief by corrosion of the ground, after Blake's usual method.

Page 104. *The Book of Los.* The text is taken from the only known copy, now in the British Museum.

Page 109. *Milton.* Only four copies of this "poem" are known: at the present time there is one in the British Museum; the other three are in America. Of these four, only two retain the Preface, and with it what has become Blake's best known poem—the four stanzas set to music and entitled "Jerusalem" by the late Sir Hubert Parry. Again, of the four, only one has the plate here numbered "5," and this copy is undoubtedly the latest of the four, the "extra" plates of earlier versions being incorporated by Blake in the work. The present transcript follows this copy both as regards text and order of the plates, saving only that the Preface is reluctantly restored. The text of the extra plate (no. 5) is taken, with permission, from the Nonesuch Blake, 1925. It has also been reproduced in facsimile for the Club of Odd Volumes, Boston, 1925. The text of all the available plates has been carefully collated with the copy in the British Museum which, incidentally, has the Preface. It is evident from at least one of the title-pages to this work that Blake at first intended to compose twelve books, but he must early have abandoned this intention, for the epic is complete as it stands.

Page 162. *Jerusalem.* The text, which in different copies varies slightly, is taken from an uncoloured copy in the British Museum. The order of the plates in Chapter II. is different from that adopted in previous transcripts, but is here given because it is the order adopted in the British Museum copy, and is probably Blake's later re-arrangement. He only coloured one complete copy of *Jerusalem,* which is now in the University Library at Yale. The facsimile issued by the Wm. Blake Trust in 1952 can be seen in many libraries in Great Britain. It is one of the most beautiful books in the world, and to see it is to receive the most effective answer to doubts about the quality or integrity of Blake's mind.

Page 285. *On Homer's Poetry: On Virgil.* This is a single engraved plate of which very few impressions have survived. From its appearance and content it is judged to be contemporaneous with *The Laocoön* and the latter part of *Jerusalem.*

Page 287. הי *& his two Sons, Satan & Adam.* Only two impressions of this plate have survived, one being in the possession of Sir Geoffrey Keynes.

Page 291. *The Gates of Paradise.* The reproductions are from a copy of this booklet re-issued about the year 1820. The plates which compose this series of emblematic pictures are here given in facsimile because without the engravings the letterpress is nearly meaningless. There are two distinct issues of this little work: the first, published in 1793, bears the words "For Children," instead of "For the Sexes," on the title-page, which in the earlier edition has fewer angels and no prefatory couplets. In the later issue Blake added to the inscriptions beneath the designs the following words: (Frontispiece) "The Sun's Light when he unfolds it Depends on the Organ that beholds it." (2) "Thou Waterest him with Tears." (3) "He struggles into Life." (4) "On Cloudy Doubts & Reasoning Cares." (5) "That end in endless Strife." (7) "What are these? the Female Martyr. Is She also the Divine Image?" (11) "Perceptive Organs closed, their Objects close." Plates 17, 18 and 19 also did not, of course, appear in the earlier version.

438 WILLIAM BLAKE

The first version of the second printing (as reproduced in facsimile by Mr. F. Hollyer) shows differences in the design on plate 13, and instead of lines 7 and 8 of the Prologue as given here, the earlier forms:

> "And in the midst of Sinai's heat
> Hid it beneath his Mercy Seat."

—alterations which should be compared with *The Everlasting Gospel*, p. 351, ll. 113 et seq.

In connection with these designs it is noteworthy that Blake made over seventy drawings in his MS. book similar in every way to those used in *The Gates of Paradise*. Each of these drawings bore a quotation from some classic—Job, Shakespeare, Milton, Donne, Dryden and others—although many of these quotations are now illegible. From this it is evident that Blake's first intention was something very different from a book of seventeen designs. A study of the original drawings might throw welcome light on this enigmatic little work; for Blake must have meant much by a book he took the trouble to issue a second time after an interval of about twenty-five years. Possibly some of the drawings were intended for a companion booklet to be entitled *For Children: The Gates of Hell*. A drawing for the title-page of such a work is in the possession of Sir Geoffrey Keynes.

Page 312. *The Ghost of Abel.* This work, etched on two plates and uncoloured, has survived in only four copies, of which three are in America; the fourth belongs to Sir Geoffrey Keynes. Blake was doubtless prompted to write this, his only drama since the days of the *Poetical Sketches*, by the issue of Byron's *Cain* in 1821.

Page 319. *Two Poems from Letters.* Posterity will never be tired of paying its debt of gratitude to Thomas Butts, paragon of patrons, who retained his faith in Blake's genius and filled his house to overflowing with Blake's pictures, at a time when they were unsaleable elsewhere. During Blake's stay at Felpham a delightful correspondence passed between them, and Butts was made a close confidant. Blake sent him these two poems as expressions of intimacy and affection. Apart from intrinsic interest, they are valuable because of the light they throw upon Blake's development at the time.

Page 324. *The "Pickering" MS.* (so called since it was acquired by B. M. Pickering in 1866) consists of eleven sheets carefully written out by Blake. The poems are obviously transcripts, but for whom or for what purpose is not known. The text is taken from photographs of the original pages, which are now in a private collection in America. Dr. Sampson (1905) first dated the MS. about 1800–1803, and this date seems fairly certain, both from the style and subject matter of the poems. The MS. differs greatly from *The "Rossetti" MS.* in being remarkably legible and free from corrections; in fact the only alterations that occur in the whole of *The "Pickering" MS.* are on pp. 18 and 19, and these are trifling: "Little" for "Pretty" Mary Bell, "Long" for "Young" John Brown, and the deletion of the word "with" from the line in the *Auguries*, "When we see with, not thro' the Eye." In the MS. the couplets of the *Auguries* are written without breaks, which are here made to facilitate reading. Whether the order in which the couplets stand was designed, or whether they were collected haphazard, is a matter for conjecture. On the assumption that the order was not designed, Dr. Sampson made an interesting re-arrangement.

Page 340. *The "Rossetti" MS.* (so called because it was acquired and first edited by Dante Gabriel Rossetti, who bought it from a brother of Samuel Palmer in 1847) is more accurately described as "Blake's Notebook." The book is roughly the size of a small exercise book, and contains about

fifty leaves. Blake first used it as a sketch-book, and the centre of almost
every page has a small drawing similar in size and character to those of
The Gates of Paradise: all the designs for *The Gates of Paradise* are here,
and without exception the original drawings are to be preferred to the
engraved copies. About 1793 Blake began to use the far end of the book
for the MS. of the *Songs of Experience*. Later, about 1800, he started
filling up the vacant space at the other end of the book with more poems,
some of which appear in *The "Pickering" MS*. Then he crowded the pages
with notes for a *Public Address* on painting—an essay punctuated with
quips and epigrams concerning his friends and enemies. Still later he added
another essay (possibly an extension of the so-called *Public Address*)
describing his picture of *The Last Judgment*, and finally he added here
and there the sections of *The Everlasting Gospel*. The text is taken from
photographs of the original MS., which was given to the British Museum
by the late Mrs. William Emerson of Cambridge, Massachusetts, in 1957.

Page 346. *The Everlasting Gospel.* All the passages from this un-
finished poem are taken from Blake's Notebook, with the exception of those
here printed on pp. 346, 347. The line numbers (which have been added)
may be taken to indicate all the continuity authorised by Blake. The
poem only exists in rough draft on about a dozen different pages of the
Notebook, and is here and there so crowded and illegibly written as to
offer scope for editorial scrutiny and preference, words occasionally re-
maining doubtful. It is impossible to say with certainty in what order
the passages were written, nor does this greatly matter seeing that the
poem divides itself by its different inquiries: "Was Jesus Humble?"
"Was Jesus Chaste?" "Was Jesus gentle?" "Was Jesus Born of a Virgin
Pure?" The two important passages on pp. 346, 347 were first printed
in their entirety in the Nonesuch Edition of Blake's Writings, 1925,
and are here reprinted by permission of editor and publisher. They are
described as being written on "a small folded leaf which may have been at
one time inserted with the other small leaf at the end of *The 'Rossetti' MS*."

Page 357. *The Last Judgment.* Rossetti first gave the name "A Vision
of the Last Judgment" to the series of detached passages in the MS. book,
first collected by him and printed in Vol. II. of Gilchrist's *Life of Blake*,
1863. Rossetti treated the passages without much editorial respect.
Examination of the MS. shows that they may be found to sort themselves
roughly into three principal, and more or less continuous, passages (here
numbered I., II. and III.) and a few additional passages which Blake seems
to have jotted down whenever a relevant idea occurred. He did not write
an extended essay on the subject of the Last Judgment: what we have
here are notes on a picture which extended themselves to the proportions
of an essay. Similar notes from the same source have made up what has
been called the *Public Address*, omitted from the present volume partly
owing to lack of space, but chiefly because they are considered to be of
lesser interest.

Page 387. *Poetical Sketches.* This is Blake's earliest book of poems,
and the only example of his verse printed in ordinary type and published
during his lifetime. The absence of symbolism puts these early poems
into a different category from the main body of Blake's work. They are
neither so deeply intentioned nor profoundly felt as the poems and
prophecies Blake engraved and illuminated with his own hand. His known
indifference to their fate, attested by the fact that he makes no mention
of them in any of the lists of his books, goes to show that Blake regarded
them as immature work.